Praise for *AI at the Edge*

AI at the Edge introduces the new and fast-growing field of edge AI in a practical, easy-to-follow way. It demystifies jargon and highlights real challenges that you are likely to encounter when building edge AI applications. The book offers an essential guide to going from concept to deployment—a must-read for getting started in the field.

—*Wiebke Hutiri, Delft University of Technology*

I really love the writing style which makes complex technical topics approachable and digestible. I can imagine it being used as a reference book, returning to it time and time again—which I will certainly be doing!

—*Fran Baker, Director of Sustainability and Social Impact, Arm*

What a wonderfully accessible and thorough introduction to the emerging field of edge AI! It covers an impressive breadth of topics, from the core concepts to the latest hardware and software tools, it's full of actionable advice, and includes several end-to-end examples. Anyone joining this exciting new field will benefit from the deep insights and clarity of thought this book provides.

—*Aurélien Geron, former lead of YouTube's automatic video classification team and best-selling author*

This is the guide to creating smarter devices: *AI at the Edge* provides an excellent introduction on combining modern AI techniques and embedded systems.

—*Elecia White, author of* Making Embedded Systems *and host of the* Embedded *podcast*

AI at the Edge
Solving Real-World Problems with Embedded Machine Learning

Daniel Situnayake and Jenny Plunkett

Beijing · Boston · Farnham · Sebastopol · Tokyo

AI at the Edge

by Daniel Situnayake and Jenny Plunkett

Copyright © 2023 Daniel Situnayake and Jenny Plunkett. All rights reserved.

Published by O'Reilly Media, Inc., 1005 Gravenstein Highway North, Sebastopol, CA 95472.

O'Reilly books may be purchased for educational, business, or sales promotional use. Online editions are also available for most titles (*http://oreilly.com*). For more information, contact our corporate/institutional sales department: 800-998-9938 or *corporate@oreilly.com*.

Acquisitions Editor: Nicole Butterfield	**Indexer:** WordCo Indexing Services, Inc.
Development Editor: Angela Rufino	**Interior Designer:** David Futato
Production Editor: Elizabeth Faerm	**Cover Designer:** Karen Montgomery
Copyeditor: nSight, Inc.	**Illustrator:** Kate Dullea
Proofreader: Charles Roumeliotis	

January 2023:   First Edition

Revision History for the First Edition

2023-01-10:   First Release

See *http://oreilly.com/catalog/errata.csp?isbn=9781098120207* for release details.

The O'Reilly logo is a registered trademark of O'Reilly Media, Inc. *AI at the Edge*, the cover image, and related trade dress are trademarks of O'Reilly Media, Inc.

The views expressed in this work are those of the authors, and do not represent the publisher's views. While the publisher and the authors have used good faith efforts to ensure that the information and instructions contained in this work are accurate, the publisher and the authors disclaim all responsibility for errors or omissions, including without limitation responsibility for damages resulting from the use of or reliance on this work. Use of the information and instructions contained in this work is at your own risk. If any code samples or other technology this work contains or describes is subject to open source licenses or the intellectual property rights of others, it is your responsibility to ensure that your use thereof complies with such licenses and/or rights.

978-1-098-12020-7

[LSI]

Jenny would like to dedicate this book to every woman who is currently pursuing, or is interested in pursuing, an engineering degree—you can do anything you put your mind to.

Dan would like to dedicate this book to the Situnayake family. It's been a tough few years, but we always make it through as a team.

Table of Contents

Foreword

In 2022, GitHub CEO Thomas Dohmke said, "I think the shift to the cloud will happen at such a rapid rate, that in just a few years I predict there will be no more code on your local computer."[1] This book does a great job of explaining why I and a lot of other people in the emerging field of edge ML think he's dead wrong.

We're starting to see the emergence of many practical applications like high-quality voice recognition, forest fire prevention, and smart home controls that are only possible because local devices are now capable of running advanced machine learning algorithms. Jenny and Dan have put together a wonderful book that not only explains why adding intelligence to edge applications is so crucial to solving important problems, but also walks the reader through the steps required to design, implement, and test these kinds of applications.

It can feel pretty intimidating when you first start looking at a machine learning project on the edge. The field involves a lot of jargon, is changing rapidly, and requires knowledge from domains like embedded systems and artificial intelligence that have traditionally not been well integrated. What the authors have achieved is a gentle but thorough introduction to everything you need to know to work effectively on an application. They've also managed to make it accessible to a wide range of readers thanks to their emphasis on examples from the real world and use of plain English instead of math or code to explain even complex topics. This makes the book easy to recommend to product managers, executives, and designers, as well as engineers.

They've managed to take a lot of hard-won knowledge gained from experience and distill it down to lessons that will give any team working on these kinds of applications a big head start.

---

1 From GitHub's Twitter account (*https://oreil.iy/WgTQu*).

They also manage to explore beyond the practical concerns of how to build an edge ML application, and will help you understand how to avoid causing harm with your work. The ethical concerns around AI can seem overwhelming, but the authors manage to break them down into questions you can apply in a straightforward way as part of the project planning and testing process. This will help all the stakeholders on your project collaborate, and hopefully avoid a lot of the potential dangers involved in giving computers more decision-making power over our lives.

I've been working on edge ML applications for over ten years now, first at a startup, then as a tech lead at Google—and now as the founder of another startup, and I will be asking everyone who joins our team to read this book. If you have any interest at all in this area, whether as a coder, designer, manager, or just someone who cares about this new technology that's emerging in our world, I can't recommend this book highly enough. I guarantee that reading it will introduce you to a lot of fascinating ideas, as well as help you build the next generation of smart devices.

— Pete Warden, CEO at Useful Sensors Inc.,
creator of TensorFlow Lite for Microcontrollers

Preface

Over the past few years, a growing community of engineers and researchers have quietly rewritten the rules for how computers interact with the physical world. The result, a technology known as "edge artificial intelligence," promises to upend a century of computer history and touch the lives of every human being.

With a tiny software update, edge AI technology can grant cheap, energy-efficient processors—already inside everything from dishwashers to thermostats—the ability to perceive and understand the world. We can empower everyday objects with their own intelligence, no longer dependent on data-hungry centralized servers. And next-generation tools put this magic in reach of everyone, from high school students to conservation researchers.

There are already many edge AI products out there in the world. Here are some that we'll meet in the pages of this book:

- Smart devices that help prevent forest fires caused by electricity transmission, by mounting to electricity pylons and predicting when a fault may occur
- Wearable bands that keep firefighters safe by warning when they're at risk from heat strain and overexertion
- Voice user interfaces that provide hands-free control of technology, no internet connection required
- Smart collars that monitor the movements of wild elephants, helping researchers understand their behavior and protect them from conflict
- Wildlife cameras that identify specific animal species and help scientists understand their behavior

The technology of edge AI is still fresh and new, and these existing applications are just a glimpse of what is possible. As more people learn how to work with edge AI, they'll create applications that solve problems across every avenue of human activity.

The goal of this book is to empower you to be one of them. We want to help you create successful edge AI products based on your own unique perspectives.

About This Book

This book is designed for the engineers, scientists, product managers, and decision makers who will drive this revolution. It's a high-level guide to the entire space, providing a workflow and a framework for solving real-world problems using edge AI.

Among other things, we hope to teach you:

- The opportunities, limitations, and risks inherent to various edge AI technologies
- A framework for analyzing problems and designing solutions using AI and embedded machine learning
- An end-to-end practical workflow for successfully developing edge AI applications

In the first part of the book, the initial chapters will introduce and discuss the key concepts, helping you understand the lay of the land. The next few will take you through the practical processes that will help you design and implement your own applications.

In the second part of the book, starting in Chapter 11, we'll use three end-to-end walkthroughs to demonstrate how to apply your knowledge to solve real problems in scientific, industrial, and consumer projects.

By the end of the book, you'll feel confident in viewing the world through the lens of edge AI, and you'll have a solid set of tools you can use to help build effective solutions.

 This book covers a lot of topics! For an overview of everything we've included, take a quick look at the table of contents.

What to Expect

This isn't a programming book or a tutorial for a particular set of tools, so don't expect a ton of line-by-line code explanations or step-by-step guides to using specific software. Instead, you'll learn how to apply general frameworks to solve problems using whichever tools are best suited to the job.

That said, this is a topic that benefits greatly from tangible, interactive examples that can be explored, customized, and built upon. In the course of the book, we'll provide all sorts of artifacts you can explore—from Git repositories to free online datasets and example training pipelines.

Many of these will be hosted in Edge Impulse (*https://edgeimpulse.com*), which is an engineering tool for building edge AI applications.[1] It's built on open source technologies and standard best practices, so you'll be able to understand the principles even if you do your own work on a different platform. The book's authors are both big fans of Edge Impulse—but they may be biased, since they are part of the team that built it!

> To guarantee portability, all the artifacts of the machine learning pipeline can be exported from Edge Impulse in open formats, including the datasets, machine learning models, and C++ implementations of any signal processing code.

What You Need to Know Already

This book is about building software that runs on edge devices, so some familiarity with the high-level concepts of embedded development will be helpful. This could be on either resource-constrained devices such as microcontrollers or digital signal processors (DSPs), or on general-purpose devices such as embedded Linux computers.

That said, if you're just getting started with embedded software, you should have no trouble keeping up! We'll keep things simple and introduce new topics as they come up.

Beyond that, no particular knowledge is assumed. Since the goal of this book is to provide a practical road map for an entire field of engineering, we'll cover a lot of topics at a high level. If you're interested in digging deeper into anything we mention—from the fundamentals of machine learning to the essentials of ML application design—we'll provide lots of resources that we've found useful in our own learning.

Responsible, Ethical, and Effective AI

The most important part of building any kind of application is ensuring that it works correctly in the real world. Unfortunately, AI applications are especially vulnerable to a class of issues that make them *appear* to work well when in reality they are failing—often in very harmful ways.

---

1 Edge Impulse is described in the academic paper "Edge Impulse: An MLOps Platform for Tiny Machine Learning" (*https://oreil.ly/Dyd-Z*) (S. Hymel et. al, 2022).

Avoiding this class of problems will be a core theme—if not *the* core theme—of this book. Because modern AI development is an iterative process, it isn't enough to test your system at the end of the workflow to see whether it works. Instead, you need to be thinking about the potential pitfalls at every step along the way. You'll have to understand where the risks lie, critically review your intermediate results, and make informed decisions that take the needs of your stakeholders into account.

Over the course of the book, we'll introduce a strong framework that will help you understand, reason, measure performance, and make decisions based on an awareness of the things that can go wrong when building AI applications. It will be the foundation for our entire development process and will shape the way we design our applications.

This process begins at the very inception of a project. To build effective applications, it's critical to understand that there are certain use cases for which our current approach to artificial intelligence is simply not an appropriate tool. In many situations, the risk of causing harm—physical, financial, or societal—outweighs the potential benefit of deploying AI. This book will teach you how to identify these risks and take them into account when exploring the feasibility of a project.

As domain experts, we have the responsibility to make sure the technology we create is used appropriately. Nobody else is better positioned to do this work, so it falls on us to do it well. This book will help you make the right decisions and create applications that perform well, avoid harm, and benefit the wider world.

Further Resources

A book that covered all of embedded AI, from low-level implementation to high-level design patterns, would be the size of an entire bookshelf! Instead of trying to squeeze everything into one volume, the book you're reading will provide a detailed but high-level road map of the whole space.

To zoom in on the minutiae that are relevant for your particular project, "Learning Edge AI Skills" on page 134 recommends plenty of further resources.

Reaching Out

The authors would love to hear from you; get in touch at *hello@edgeaibook.com*.

Conventions Used in This Book

The following typographical conventions are used in this book:

Italic

    Indicates new terms, URLs, email addresses, filenames, and file extensions.

`Constant width`

    Used for program listings, as well as within paragraphs to refer to program elements such as variable or function names, databases, data types, environment variables, statements, and keywords.

`Constant width bold`

    Shows commands or other text that should be typed literally by the user.

`Constant width italic`

    Shows text that should be replaced with user-supplied values or by values determined by context.

 This element signifies a tip or suggestion.

 This element signifies a general note.

 This element indicates a warning or caution.

Using Code Examples

Supplemental material (code examples, exercises, etc.) is available for download at *https://github.com/ai-at-the-edge*.

If you have a technical question or a problem using the code examples, please send email to *bookquestions@oreilly.com*.

This book is here to help you get your job done. In general, if example code is offered with this book, you may use it in your programs and documentation. You do not need to contact us for permission unless you're reproducing a significant portion of the code. For example, writing a program that uses several chunks of code from this book does not require permission. Selling or distributing examples from O'Reilly books does require permission. Answering a question by citing this book and quoting example code does not require permission. Incorporating a significant amount of example code from this book into your product's documentation does require permission.

We appreciate, but generally do not require, attribution. An attribution usually includes the title, author, publisher, and ISBN. For example: "*AI at the Edge* by Daniel Situnayake and Jenny Plunkett (O'Reilly). Copyright 2023 Daniel Situnayake and Jenny Plunkett, 978-1-098-12020-7."

If you feel your use of code examples falls outside fair use or the permission given above, feel free to contact us at *permissions@oreilly.com*.

O'Reilly Online Learning

 For more than 40 years, *O'Reilly Media* has provided technology and business training, knowledge, and insight to help companies succeed.

Our unique network of experts and innovators share their knowledge and expertise through books, articles, and our online learning platform. O'Reilly's online learning platform gives you on-demand access to live training courses, in-depth learning paths, interactive coding environments, and a vast collection of text and video from O'Reilly and 200+ other publishers. For more information, visit *http://oreilly.com*.

How to Contact Us

Please address comments and questions concerning this book to the publisher:

O'Reilly Media, Inc.
1005 Gravenstein Highway North
Sebastopol, CA 95472
800-998-9938 (in the United States or Canada)
707-829-0515 (international or local)
707-829-0104 (fax)

We have a web page for this book, where we list errata, examples, and any additional information. You can access this page at *https://oreil.ly/ai-at-the-edge*.

Email *bookquestions@oreilly.com* to comment or ask technical questions about this book.

For news and information about our books and courses, visit *https://oreilly.com*.

Find us on LinkedIn: *https://linkedin.com/company/oreilly-media*.

Follow us on Twitter: *https://twitter.com/oreillymedia*.

Watch us on YouTube: *https://youtube.com/oreillymedia*.

Acknowledgments

This book wouldn't have been possible without the hard work and support of a large number of people to whom we are very grateful.

We've been honored with a foreword by the one and only Pete Warden (*https://pete warden.com*), who—beyond being a visionary technologist who deserves much of the credit for launching this field—is a wonderful human being and a great friend. Thank you so much for your support, Pete!

We extend our deep gratitude to Wiebke (Toussaint) Hutiri (*https://wiebketous saint.com*), who went truly above and beyond in helping shape and inform the responsible AI content in this book, including contributing a fantastic introduction to "Responsible Design and AI Ethics" on page 43. You are a star in your field.

We are indebted to our incredible panel of technical reviewers and advisors whose wisdom and insight has had such a huge impact on this book. Their names are Alex Elium, Aurélien Geron, Carlos Roberto Lacerda, David J. Groom, Elecia White, Fran Baker, Jen Fox, Leonardo Cavagnis, Mat Kelcey, Pete Warden, Vijay Janapa Reddi, and Wiebke (Toussaint) Hutiri. An additional big thanks to Benjamin Cabé for allowing us to feature his artificial nose project. Any inaccuracies are entirely the responsibility of the authors.

We'd also like to thank the amazing team at O'Reilly, especially Angela Rufino, who has shepherded us through the writing process with the utmost understanding and care. Major gratitude to Elizabeth Faerm, Kristen Brown, Mike Loukides, Nicole Taché, and Rebecca Novack.

This book would not exist without the support of our team at Edge Impulse, an all-star cast of absolute heroes. Special thanks to the founders, Zach Shelby and Jan Jongboom, for believing in our vision for this book, supporting us in making it happen, and creating a space where ideas can bloom. Much love to the entire team, which at the time of writing includes: Adam Benzion, Alessandro Grande, Alex Elium, Amir Sherman, Arjan Kamphuis, Artie Beavis, Arun Rajasekaran,

Ashvin Roharia, Aurelien Lequertier, Carl Ward, Clinton Oduor, David Schwarz, David Tischler, Dimi Tomov, Dmitry Maslov, Emile Bosch, Eoin Jordan, Evan Rust, Fernando Jiménez Moreno, Francesco Varani, Jed Huang, Jim Edson, Jim van der Voort, Jodie Lane, John Pura, Jorge Silva, Joshua Buck, Juliette Okel, Keelin Murphy, Kirtana Moorthy, Louis Moreau, Louise Paul, Maggi Yang, Mat Kelcey, Mateusz Majchrzycki, Mathijs Baaijens, Mihajlo Raljic, Mike Senese, Mikey Beavis, MJ Lee, Nabil Koroghli, Nick Famighetti, Omar Shrit, Othman Mekhannene, Paige Holvik, Raul James, Raul Vergara, RJ Vissers, Ross Lowe, Sally Atkinson, Saniea Akhtar, Sara Olsson, Sergi Mansilla, Shams Mansoor, Shawn Hanscom, Shawn Hymel, Sheena Patel, Tyler Hoyle, Vojislav Milivojevic, William DeLey, Yan Li, Yana Vibe, and Zin Kyaw. You make magic happen.

Jenny would like to thank her Texas family and friends for being super supportive over the years, and her cats Blue Gene and Beatrice for being the best coworkers. She especially would like to thank her dad, Michael Plunkett, who encouraged her to pursue electrical engineering at The University of Texas at Austin, and who inspired her lifelong curiosity in new technologies.

Dan would like to thank his family and friends for being supportive of every big adventure. He's deeply grateful to Lauren Ward for her love and partnership throughout all of our journeys. And he thanks Minicat for her calming feline presence—and permission to use her photographs in this book.

## CHAPTER 1

A Brief Introduction to Edge AI

Welcome on board! In this chapter, we'll be taking a comprehensive tour of the edge AI world. We'll define the key terms, learn what makes "edge AI" different from other AI, and explore some of the most important use cases. Our goal for this chapter is to answer these two important questions:

- What is edge AI, anyway?
- Why would I ever need it?

Defining Key Terms

Each area of technology has its own taxonomy of buzzwords, and edge AI is no different. In fact, the term *edge AI* is a union of two buzzwords, fused together into one mighty term. It's often heard alongside its siblings, *embedded machine learning* and *TinyML*.

Before we move on, we better spend some time defining these terms and understanding what they mean. Since we're dealing with compound buzzwords, let's deal with the most fundamental parts first.

Embedded

What is "embedded"? Depending on your background, this may be the most familiar of all the terms we're trying to describe. *Embedded systems* are the computers that control the electronics of all sorts of physical devices, from Bluetooth headphones to the engine control unit of a modern car. *Embedded software* is software that runs on them. Figure 1-1 shows a few places where embedded systems can be found.

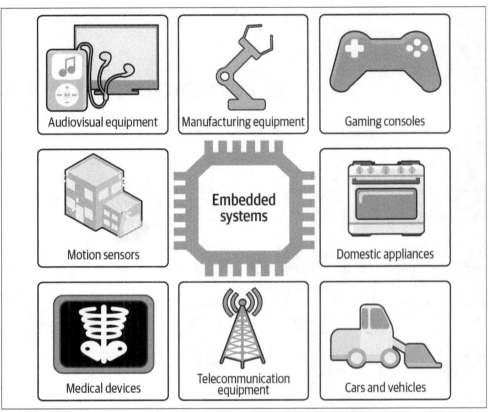

Figure 1-1. Embedded systems are present in every part of our world, including the home and the workplace

Embedded systems can be tiny and simple, like the microcontroller that controls a digital watch, or large and sophisticated, like the embedded Linux computer inside a smart TV. In contrast to general-purpose computers, like a laptop or smartphone, embedded systems are usually meant to perform one specific, dedicated task.

Since they power much of our modern technology, embedded systems are extraordinarily widespread. In fact, there were over 28 billion microcontrollers shipped in the year 2020[1]—just one type of embedded processor. They're in our homes, our vehicles, our factories, and our city streets. It's likely you are never more than a few feet from an embedded system.

---

1 As reported by Business Wire (*https://oreil.ly/xaOo-*).

It's common for embedded systems to reflect the constraints of the environments into which they are deployed. For example, many embedded systems are required to run on battery power, so they're designed with energy efficiency in mind—perhaps with limited memory or an extremely slow clock rate.

Programming embedded systems is the art of navigating these constraints, writing software that performs the task required while making the most out of limited resources. This can be incredibly difficult. Embedded systems engineers are the unsung heroes of the modern world. If you happen to be one, thank you for your hard work!

The Edge (and the Internet of Things)

The history of computer networks has been a gigantic tug of war. In the first systems—individual computers the size of a room—computation was inherently centralized. There was one machine, and that one machine did all the work.

Eventually, however, computers were connected to terminals (as shown in Figure 1-2) that took over some of their responsibilities. Most of the computation was happening in the central mainframe, but some simple tasks—like figuring out how to render letters onto a cathode-ray tube screen—were done by the terminal's electronics.

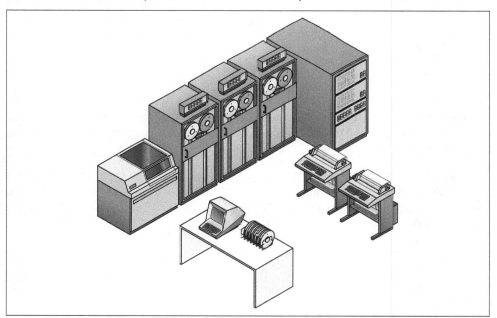

Figure 1-2. Mainframe computers performed the bulk of the computation, while simple terminals processed input, printed output, and rendered basic graphics

Over time, terminals became more and more sophisticated, taking over more and more functions that were previously the job of the central computer. The tug-of-war had begun! Once the personal computer was invented, small computers could do useful work without even being connected to another machine. The rope had been pulled to the opposite extreme—from the center of the network to the *edge*.

The growth of the internet, along with web applications and services, made it possible to do some really cool stuff—from streaming video to social networking. All of this depends on computers being connected to servers, which have gradually taken over more and more of the work. Over the past decade, most of our computing has become centralized again—this time in the "cloud." When the internet goes down, our modern computers aren't much use!

But the computers we use for work and play are not our only connected devices. In fact, it is estimated that in 2021 there were 12.2 billion assorted items connected to the internet,[2] creating and consuming data. This vast network of objects is called the Internet of Things (IoT), and it includes everything you can think of: industrial sensors, smart refrigerators, internet-connected security cameras, personal automobiles, shipping containers, fitness trackers, and coffee machines.

 The first ever IoT device was created in 1982. Students at Carnegie Mellon University connected a Coke vending machine to the ARPANET (*https://oreil.ly/B510Z*)—an early precursor to the internet—so they could check whether it was empty without leaving their lab.

All of these devices are embedded systems containing microprocessors that run software written by embedded software engineers. Since they're at the edge of the network, we can also call them *edge devices*. Performing computation on edge devices is known as *edge computing*.

The edge isn't a single place; it's more like a broad region. Devices at the edge of the network can communicate with each other, and they can communicate with remote servers, too. There are even servers that live at the edge of the network. Figure 1-3 shows how this looks.

---

2 Expected to grow to 27 billion by 2025, according to IoT Analytics (*https://oreil.ly/yMRAF*).

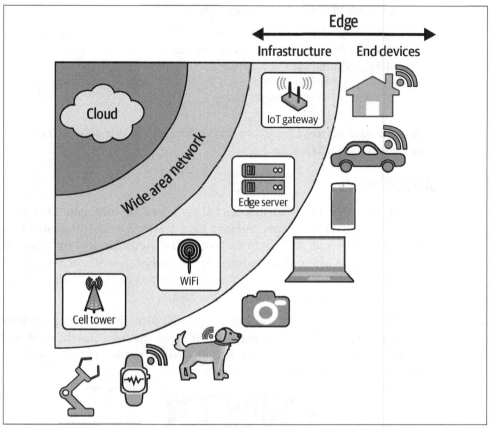

Figure 1-3. Devices at the edge of the network can communicate with the cloud, with edge infrastructure, and with each other; edge applications generally span multiple locations within this map (for example, data might be sent from a sensor-equipped IoT device to a local edge server for processing)

There are some major benefits to being at the edge of the network. For one, it's where all the data comes from! Edge devices are our link between the internet and the physical world. They can use sensors to collect data based on what is going on around them, be that the heart rate of a runner or the temperature of a cold drink. They can make decisions on that data locally and send it to other locations. Edge devices have access to data that nobody else does.

Are Mobile Phones and Tablets Edge Devices?

As portable computers that live at the edge of the network, mobile phones, tablets, and even personal computers are all edge devices. Mobile phones were one of the first platforms to feature edge AI: modern mobile phones use it for many purposes, from voice activation to smart photography.[3]

We'll come back to edge devices later (since they're the focus of this book). Until then, let's continue to define some terms.

Artificial Intelligence

Phew! This is a big one. Artificial intelligence (AI) is a very big idea, and it's terribly hard to define. Since the dawn of time, humans have dreamed of creating intelligent entities that can help us in our struggle to survive. In the modern world we dream of robot sidekicks who assist with our adventures: hyperintelligent, synthetic minds that will solve all of our problems, and miraculous enterprise products that will optimize our business processes and guarantee us rapid promotion.

But to define AI, we have to define intelligence—which turns out to be particularly tough. What does it mean to be intelligent? Does it mean that we can talk, or think? Clearly not—just ask the slime mold (see Figure 1-4), a simple organism with no central nervous system that is capable of solving a maze.

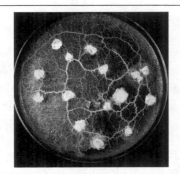

Figure 1-4. Slime molds are single-celled organisms that have been documented as being able to solve mazes in order to locate food, via a process of biological computation— as shown in "Slime Mould Solves Maze in One Pass Assisted by Gradient of Chemo-Attractants" (https://oreil.ly/Ecrq9) (Andrew Adamatzky, arXiv, 2011)

---

3 Embedded engineering and mobile development are typically separate disciplines. Even within a mobile device, the embedded firmware and operating system are distinct from mobile applications. This book focuses on embedded engineering, so we won't talk much about building mobile apps—but we will cover techniques that are relevant in both cases.

Since this isn't a philosophy book, we don't have the time to fully explore the topic of intelligence. Instead, we want to suggest a quick-and-dirty definition:

Intelligence means knowing the right thing to do at the right time.

This probably doesn't stand up to academic debate, but that's fine with us. It gives us a tool to explore the subject. Here are some tasks that require intelligence, according to our definition:

- Taking a photo when an animal is in the frame
- Applying the brakes when a driver is about to crash
- Informing an operator when a machine sounds broken
- Answering a question with relevant information
- Creating an accompaniment to a musical performance
- Turning on a faucet when someone wants to wash their hands

Each of these problems involves both an action (turning on a faucet) and a precondition (when someone wants to wash their hands). Within their own context, most of these problems sound relatively simple—but, as anyone who has used an airport restroom knows, they are not always straightforward to solve.

It's pretty easy for most humans to perform most of these tasks. We're highly capable creatures with *general* intelligence. But it's possible for smaller systems with more *narrow* intelligence to perform the tasks, too. Take our slime mold—it may not understand why it is solving a maze, but it's certainly able to do it.

That said, the slime mold is unlikely to also know the right moment to turn on a faucet. Generally speaking, it's a lot easier to perform a single, tightly scoped task (like turning on a faucet) than to be able to perform a diverse set of entirely different tasks.

Creating an artificial *general* intelligence, equivalent to a human being, would be super difficult—as decades of unsuccessful attempts have shown. But creating something that operates at slime mold level can be much easier. For example, preventing a driver from crashing is, in theory, quite a simple task. If you have access to both their current speed and their distance from a wall, you can do it with simple conditional logic:

```
current_speed = 10 # In meters per second
distance_from_wall = 50 # In meters
seconds_to_stop = 3 # The minimum time in seconds required to stop the car
safety_buffer = 1 # The safety margin in seconds before hitting the brakes

# Calculate how long we've got before we hit the wall
seconds_until_crash = distance_from_wall / current_speed

# Make sure we apply the brakes if we're likely to crash soon
```

```
if seconds_until_crash < seconds_to_stop + safety_buffer:
    applyBrakes()
```

Clearly, this simplified example doesn't account for a lot of factors. But with a little more complexity, a modern car with a driver assistance system based on this conditional logic could arguably be marketed as AI.[4]

There are two points we are trying to make here: the first is that intelligence is quite hard to define, and many rather simple problems require a degree of intelligence to solve. The second is that the programs that implement this intelligence do not necessarily need to be particularly complex. Sometimes, a slime mold will do.

So, what is AI? In simple terms, it's an artificial system that makes intelligent decisions based on some kind of input. And one way to create AI is with machine learning.

Machine Learning

At its heart, machine learning (ML) is a pretty simple concept. It's a way to discover patterns in how the world works—but automatically, by running data through algorithms.

We often hear AI and machine learning used interchangeably, as if they are the same thing—but this isn't the case. AI doesn't always involve machine learning, and machine learning doesn't always involve AI. That said, they pair together very nicely!

The best way to introduce machine learning is through an example. Imagine you're building a fitness tracker—it's a little wristband that an athlete can wear. It contains an accelerometer, which tells you how much acceleration is happening on each axis (x, y, and z) at a given moment in time—as shown in Figure 1-5.

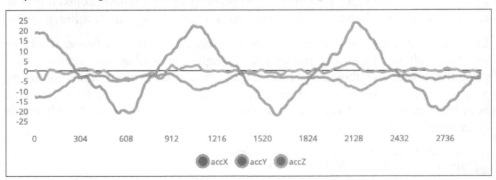

Figure 1-5. The output of a three-axis accelerometer sampled at 6.25 Hz

---

4 For many years it was hoped that artificial general intelligence could be achieved by complex conditional logic, hand-tuned by engineers. It has turned out to be a lot more complicated than that!

To help your athletes, you want to keep an automatic log of the activities they are doing. For example, an athlete might spend an hour running on Monday and then an hour swimming on Tuesday.

Since our movements while swimming are quite different from our movements while running, you theorize that you might be able to tell these activities apart based on the output of the accelerometer in your wristband. To collect some data, you give prototype wristbands to a dozen athletes and have them perform specific activities—either swimming, running, or doing nothing—while the wristbands log data (see Figure 1-6).

Now that you have a dataset, you want to try to determine some rules that will help you understand whether a particular athlete is swimming, running, or just chilling out. One way to do this is by hand: analyzing and inspecting the data to see if anything stands out to you. Perhaps you notice that running involves more rapid acceleration on a particular axis than swimming. You can use this information to write some conditional logic that determines the activity based on the reading from that axis.

Analyzing data by hand can be tricky, and it generally requires expert knowledge about the domain (such as human movements during sport). An alternative to manual analysis might be to use machine learning.

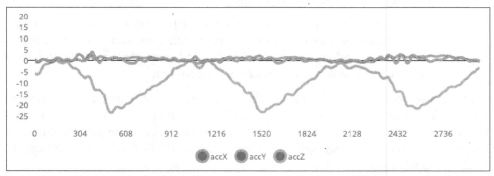

Figure 1-6. The output of a three-axis accelerometer showing a different activity than in Figure 1-5; each activity can be characterized by a pattern of changes in acceleration on each axis over time

With an ML approach, you feed all of your athletes' data into a training algorithm. When provided with both the accelerometer data and information about which activity the athlete is currently performing, the algorithm does its best to learn a mapping between the two. This mapping is called a *model*.

Hopefully, if the training was successful, your new machine learning model can take a brand new, never-seen-before input—a sample of accelerometer data from a particular window in time—and tell you which activity an athlete is performing. This process is known as *inference*.

This ability to understand *new* inputs is called *generalization*. During training, the model has learned the characteristics that distinguish running from swimming. You can then use the model in your fitness tracker to understand fresh data, in the same way that you might use the conditional logic we mentioned earlier.

There are lots of different machine learning algorithms, each with their own strengths and drawbacks—and ML isn't always the best tool for the job. Later in this chapter we'll discuss the scenarios where machine learning is the most helpful. But a nice rule of thumb is that machine learning really shines when our data is really complex.

Edge AI

Congratulations, we've made it to our first compound buzzword! Edge AI is, unsurprisingly, the combination of edge devices and artificial intelligence.

As we discussed earlier, edge devices are the embedded systems that provide the link between our digital and physical worlds. They typically feature sensors that feed them information about the environment they are close to. This gives them access to a metaphorical fire hose of high-frequency data.

We're often told that data is the lifeblood of our modern economy, flowing throughout our infrastructure and enabling organizations to function. That's definitely true—but all data is not created equally. The data obtained from sensors tends to have a very high volume but a relatively low informational content.

Imagine the accelerometer-based wristband sensor we described in the previous section. The accelerometer is capable of taking a reading many hundreds of times per second. Each individual reading tells us very little about the activity currently taking place—it's only in aggregate, over thousands of readings, that we can begin to understand what is going on.

Typically, IoT devices have been viewed as simple nodes that collect data from sensors and then transmit it to a central location for processing. The problem with this approach is that sending such large volumes of low-value information is extraordinarily costly. Not only is connectivity expensive, but transmitting data uses a ton of energy—which is a big problem for battery-powered IoT devices.

Because of this problem, the vast majority of data collected by IoT sensors has usually been discarded. We're collecting a ton of sensor data, but we're unable to do anything with it.

Edge AI is the solution to this problem. Instead of having to send data off to some distant location for processing, what if we do it directly on-device, where the data is being generated? Now, instead of relying on a central server, we can make decisions locally—no connectivity required.

And if we still want to report information back to upstream servers, or the cloud, we can transmit just the important information instead of having to send every single sensor reading. That should save a lot of cost and energy.

There are many different ways to deploy intelligence to the edge. Figure 1-7 shows the continuum from cloud AI to fully on-device intelligence. As we'll see later in this book, edge AI can be spread across entire distributed computing architectures—including some nodes at the very edge, and others in local gateways or the cloud.

As we've seen, artificial intelligence can mean many different things. It can be super simple: a touch of human insight encoded in a little simple conditional logic. It can also be super sophisticated, based on the latest developments in deep learning.

Edge AI is exactly the same. At its most basic, edge AI is about making some decisions on the edge of the network, close to where the data is made. But it can also take advantage of some really cool stuff. And that brings us nicely to the next section!

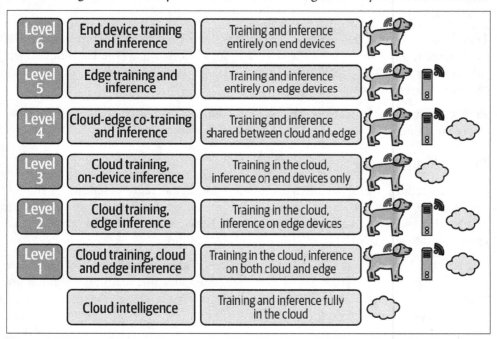

Figure 1-7. The continuum between cloud intelligence and fully on-device intelligence; these six levels were described by "Edge Intelligence: Paving the Last Mile of Artificial Intelligence with Edge Computing" (https://oreil.ly/8uWK-) (Zhou et. al., Proceedings of the IEEE, 2019)

Embedded Machine Learning and Tiny Machine Learning

Embedded ML is the art and science of running machine learning models on embedded systems. Tiny machine learning, or TinyML,[5] is the concept of doing this on the most constrained embedded hardware available—think microcontrollers, digital signal processors, and small field programmable gate arrays (FPGAs).

When we talk about embedded ML, we're usually referring to machine learning inference—the process of taking an input and coming up with a prediction (like guessing a physical activity based on accelerometer data). The training part usually still takes place on a conventional computer.

Embedded systems often have limited memory. This raises a challenge for running many types of machine learning models, which often have high requirements for both read-only memory (ROM) (to store the model) and RAM (to handle the intermediate results generated during inference).

They are often also limited in terms of computation power. Since many types of machine learning models are quite computationally intensive, this can also raise problems.

Luckily, over the past few years there have been many advances in optimization that have made it possible to run quite large and sophisticated machine learning models on some very small, low-power embedded systems. We'll learn about some of those techniques over the next few chapters!

Embedded machine learning is often deployed alongside its trusty companion, *digital signal processing*. Before we move on, let's define that term, too.

Digital Signal Processing

In the embedded world we often work with the digital representations of signals. For example, an accelerometer gives us a stream of digital values that correspond to acceleration on three axes, and a digital microphone gives us a stream of values that correspond to sound levels at a particular moment in time.

Digital signal processing (DSP) is the practice of using algorithms to manipulate these streams of data. When paired with embedded machine learning, we often use DSP to modify signals before feeding them into machine learning models. There are a few reasons why we might want to do this:

- Cleaning up a noisy signal
- Removing spikes or outlying values that might be caused by hardware issues

---

5 The term *TinyML* is a registered trademark of the TinyML Foundation.

- Extracting the most important information from a signal
- Transforming the data from the time domain to the frequency domain[6]

DSP is so common for embedded systems that often embedded chips have super fast hardware implementations of common DSP algorithms, just in case you need them.

We now share a solid understanding of the most important terms in this book. Figure 1-8 shows how they fit together in context.

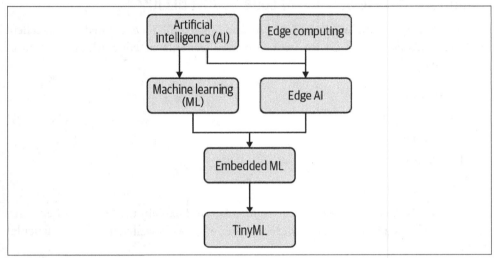

Figure 1-8. This diagram shows some of the most important concepts in edge AI in context with each other—from most general at the top to most specific at the bottom

In the next section, we'll dive deep into the topic of edge AI and start to break down what makes it such an important technology.

Why Do We Need Edge AI?

Imagine that this morning you went on a trail run through Joshua Tree National Park, a vast expanse of wilderness in the Southern California desert. You listened to music the whole time, streamed to your phone via an uninterrupted cellular connection. At a particularly beautiful spot, deep in the mountains, you snapped a photograph and sent it to your partner. A few minutes later you received their reply.

In a world where even the most remote places have some form of data connection, why do we need edge AI? What is the point of tiny devices that can make their own

---

6 This will be explained in "Spectral analysis" on page 91.

decisions if the internet's beefy servers are only a radio burst away? With all of the added complication, aren't we just making life more difficult for ourselves?

As you may have guessed, the answer is no! Edge AI solves some very real problems that otherwise stand in the way of making our technology work better for human beings. Our favorite framework for explaining the benefits of edge AI is a rude-sounding mnemonic: BLERP.

To Understand the Benefits of Edge AI, Just BLERP

BLERP? Jeff Bier, founder of the Edge AI and Vision Alliance, created this excellent tool (*https://oreil.ly/UY-DG*) for expressing the benefits of edge AI. It consists of five words:

- Bandwidth
- Latency
- Economics
- Reliability
- Privacy

Armed with BLERP, anyone can easily remember and explain the benefits of edge AI. It's also useful as a filter to help decide whether edge AI is well suited for a particular application.

Let's go through it, word by word.

Bandwidth

IoT devices often capture more data than they have bandwidth to transmit. This means the vast majority of sensor data they capture is not even used—it's just thrown away! Imagine a smart sensor that monitors the vibration of an industrial machine to determine if it is operating correctly. It might use a simple thresholding algorithm to understand when the machine is vibrating too much, or not enough, and then communicate this information via a low bandwidth radio connection.

This already sounds useful. But what if you could identify patterns in the data that give you a clue that the machine might be about to fail? If we had a lot of bandwidth, we could send the sensor data up to the cloud and do some kind of analysis to understand whether a failure is imminent.

In many cases, though, there isn't enough bandwidth or energy budget available to send a constant stream of data to the cloud. That means that we'll be forced to discard most of our sensor data, even though it contains useful signals.

Bandwidth limitations are very common. It's not just about available connectivity—it's also about power. Networked communication is often the most energy-intensive task an embedded system can perform, meaning that battery life is often the limiting function. Some machine learning models can be quite compute intensive, but they tend to still use less energy than transmitting a signal.

This is where edge AI comes in. What if we could run the data analysis on the IoT device itself, without having to upload the data? In that case, if the analysis showed that the machine was about to fail, we could send a notification using our limited bandwidth. This is much more feasible than trying to stream all of the data.

Of course, it's also quite common for devices to have no network connection at all! In this case, edge AI enables a whole galaxy of use cases that were previously impossible. We'll hear more about this later.

Latency

Transmitting data takes time. Even if you have a lot of available bandwidth it can take tens or hundreds of milliseconds for a round-trip from a device to an internet server. In some cases, latency can be measured in minutes, hours, or days—think satellite communications, or store-and-forward messaging.

Some applications demand a faster response. For example, it might be impractical for a moving vehicle to be controlled by a remote server. Controlling a vehicle as it navigates an environment requires constant feedback between steering adjustments and the vehicle's position. Under significant latency, steering becomes a major challenge!

Edge AI solves this problem by removing the round-trip time altogether. A great example of this is a self-driving car. The car's AI systems run on onboard computers. This allows it to react nearly instantly to changing conditions, like the driver in front slamming on their brakes.

One of the most compelling examples of edge AI as a weapon against latency is in robotic space exploration. Mars is so distant from Earth that it takes *minutes* for a radio transmission to reach it at the speed of light. Even worse, direct communication is often impossible due to the arrangement of the planets. This makes controlling a Mars rover very hard. NASA solved this problem by using edge AI—their rovers use sophisticated artificial intelligence systems (*https://oreil.ly/iQr8t*) to plan their tasks, navigate their environments, and search for life on the surface of another world. If you have some spare time, you can even help future Mars rovers navigate (*https://oreil.ly/RATTg*) by labeling data to improve their algorithms!

Economics

Connectivity costs a lot of money. Connected products are more expensive to use, and the infrastructure they rely on costs their manufacturers money. The more bandwidth required, the steeper the cost. Things get especially bad for devices deployed on remote locations that require long-range connectivity via satellite.

By processing data on-device, edge AI systems reduce or avoid the costs of transmitting data over a network and processing it in the cloud. This can unlock a lot of use cases that would have previously been out of reach.

In some cases, the only "connectivity" that works is sending out a human being to perform some manual task. For example, it's common for conservation researchers to use camera traps to monitor wildlife in remote locations. These devices take photos when they detect motion and store them to an SD card. It's too expensive to upload every photo via satellite internet, so researchers have to travel out to their camera traps to collect the images and clear the storage.

Because traditional camera traps are motion activated, they take a lot of unnecessary photos—they might be triggered by branches moving in the wind, hikers walking past, and creatures the researchers aren't interested in. But some teams are now using edge AI to identify only the animals they care about, so they can discard the other images. This means they don't have to fly out to the middle of nowhere to change an SD card *quite* so often.

In other cases, the cost of connectivity might not be a concern. However, for products that depend on server-side AI, the cost of maintaining server-side infrastructure can complicate your business model. If you have to support a fleet of devices that need to "phone home" to make decisions, you may be forced into a subscription model. You'll also have to commit to maintaining servers for a long period of time—at the risk of your customers finding themselves with "bricked" devices if you decide to pull the plug.[7]

Don't underestimate the impact of economics. By reducing the cost of long-term support, edge AI enables a vast number of use cases that would otherwise be infeasible.

Reliability

Systems controlled by on-device AI are potentially more reliable than those that depend on a connection to the cloud. When you add wireless connectivity to a device, you're adding a vast, overwhelmingly complex web of dependencies, from link-layer communications technologies to the internet servers that may run your application.

Many pieces of this puzzle are outside of your control, so even if you make all the right decisions you will still be exposed to the reliability risk associated with technologies that make up your distributed computing stack.

---

7 Not all edge AI applications are immune to this since it's often necessary to monitor devices and push updates to algorithms. That said, there are certainly many cases where edge AI can reduce the burden of maintenance.

For some applications, this might be tolerable. If you're building a smart speaker that responds to voice commands, your users might understand if it stops recognizing their commands when their home internet connection goes down. That said, it can still be a frustrating experience!

But in other cases, safety is paramount. Imagine an AI-based system that monitors an industrial machine to make sure that it is being operated within safe parameters. If it stops working when the internet goes down, it could endanger human lives. It would be much safer if the AI is based entirely on-device, so it still operates in the event of a connectivity problem.

Reliability is often a compromise, and the required level of reliability varies depending on use case. Edge AI can be a powerful tool in improving the reliability of your products. While AI is inherently complex, it represents a different type of complexity than global connectivity, and its risk is easier to manage in many situations.

Privacy

Over the past few years, many people have begrudgingly resigned themselves to a trade-off between convenience and privacy. The theory is that if we want our technology products to be smarter and more helpful, we have to give up our data. Because smart products traditionally make decisions on remote servers, they very often end up sending streams of sensor data to the cloud.

This may be fine for some applications—for example, we might not worry that an IoT thermostat is reporting temperature data to a remote server.[8] But for other applications, privacy is a huge concern. For example, many people would hesitate to install an internet-connected security camera inside their home. It might provide some reassuring security, but the trade-off—that a live video and audio feed of their most private spaces is being broadcast to the internet—does not seem worth it. Even if the camera's manufacturer is entirely trustworthy, there's always a chance of the data being exposed through security vulnerabilities.[9]

Edge AI provides an alternative. Rather than streaming live video and audio to a remote server, a security camera could use some onboard intelligence to identify that an intruder is present when the owners are out at work. It could then alert the owners in an appropriate way. When data is processed on an embedded system and is never transmitted to the cloud, user privacy is protected and there is less chance of abuse.

---

8 Even in this innocuous example, a malicious person accessing your thermostat data could use it to recognize when you're on vacation so they can break into your house.

9 This exact scenario unfolded in 2022 with the Ring home security system, which was found to be vulnerable to an attack ("Amazon's Ring Quietly Fixed Security Flaw That Put Users' Camera Recordings at Risk of Exposure" (*https://oreil.ly/Mf2LH*), TechCrunch, 2022).

The ability of edge AI to enable privacy unlocks a huge number of exciting use cases. It's an especially important factor for applications in security, industry, childcare, education, and healthcare. In fact, since some of these fields involve tight regulations (or customer expectations) around data security, the product with the best privacy is one that *avoids* collecting data altogether.

Using BLERP

As we'll start to see in Chapter 2, BLERP can be a handy tool for understanding whether a particular problem is well suited for edge AI. There doesn't have to be a strong argument for every word of the acronym: even meeting just one or two criteria, if compelling enough, can give merit to a use case.

Edge AI for Good

The unique benefits of edge AI provide a new set of tools that can be applied to some of our world's biggest problems. Technologists in areas like conservation, healthcare, and education are already using edge AI to make a big impact. Here are just a few examples we're personally excited about:

- Smart Parks (*https://www.smartparks.org*) is using collars running machine learning models (*https://oreil.ly/nyVIm*) to better understand elephant behavior in wildlife parks around the world.
- Izoelektro's RAM-1 (*https://oreil.ly/hR-US*) helps prevent forest fires caused by power transmission hardware by using embedded machine learning to detect upcoming faults.
- Researchers like Dr. Mohammed Zubair Shamim from King Khalid University in Saudi Arabia are training models that can screen patients for life-threatening medical conditions such as oral cancer (*https://oreil.ly/ktZq_*) using low-cost devices.
- Students across the world are developing solutions for their local industries. João Vitor Yukio Bordin Yamashita, from UNIFEI in Brazil, created a system for identifying diseases that affect coffee plants (*https://oreil.ly/gSv-J*) using embedded hardware.

The properties of edge AI make it especially well-suited for application to global problems. Since reliable connectivity is expensive and not universally available, many current generation smart technologies only benefit people living in industrialized, wealthy, and well-connected regions. By removing the need for a reliable internet connection, edge AI increases access to technologies that can benefit people and the planet.

When machine learning is part of the mix, edge AI generally involves small models—which are often quick and cheap to train. Since there's also no need to maintain expensive backend server infrastructure, edge AI makes it possible for developers with limited resources to build cutting-edge solutions for the local markets that they know better than anyone. To learn more about these opportunities, we recommend watching "TinyML and the Developing World" (*https://oreil.ly/csz6p*), an excellent talk given by Pete Warden at the TinyML Kenya meetup.

As we saw in "Privacy" on page 17, edge AI also creates an opportunity to improve privacy for users. In our networked world, many companies treat user data as a valuable resource to be extracted and mined. Consumers and business owners are often required to barter away their privacy in order to use AI products, putting their data in the hands of unknown third parties.

With edge AI, data does not need to leave the device. This enables a more trusting relationship between user and product, giving users ownership of their own data. This is especially important for products designed to serve vulnerable people, who may feel skeptical of services that seem to be harvesting their data.

TinyML for Developing Countries

If you're interested in the global benefits of edge AI, the TinyML for Developing Countries (TinyML4D) (*https://oreil.ly/Bd2np*) initiative is building a network of researchers and practitioners who are focused on solving developing world challenges using edge AI.

As we'll see in later sections, there are many potential pitfalls that must be navigated in order to build ethical AI systems. That said, the technology provides a tremendous opportunity to make the world a better place.

> If you're thinking about using edge AI to solve problems for your local community, the authors would love to hear from you. We've provided support for a number of impactful projects and would love to identify more. Send an email to the authors at *hello@edgeaibook.com*.

Key Differences Between Edge AI and Regular AI

Edge AI is a subset of regular AI, so a lot of the same principles apply. That said, there are some special things to consider when thinking about artificial intelligence on edge devices. Here are our top points.

Training on the edge is rare

A lot of AI applications are powered by machine learning. Most of the time, machine learning involves *training* a model to make predictions based on a set of labeled data. Once the model has been trained, it can be used for *inference*: making new predictions on data it has not seen before.

When we talk about edge AI and machine learning, we are usually talking about *inference*. Training models requires a lot more computation and memory than inference does, and it often requires a labeled dataset. All of these things are hard to come by on the edge, where devices are resource-constrained and data is raw and unfiltered.

For this reason, the models used in edge AI are often trained before they are deployed to devices, using relatively powerful compute and datasets that have been cleaned and labeled—often by hand. It's technically possible to train machine learning models on the edge devices themselves, but it's quite rare—mostly due to the lack of labeled data, which is required for training and evaluation.

There are two subtypes of on-device training that are more widespread. One of these is used commonly in tasks such as facial or fingerprint verification on mobile phones, to map a set of biometrics to a particular user. The second is used in predictive maintenance, where an on-device algorithm learns a machine's "normal" state so that it can act if the state becomes abnormal. There'll be more detail on the topic of on-device learning in "On-Device Training" on page 119.

The focus of edge AI is on sensor data

The exciting thing about edge devices is that they live close to where the data is made. Often, edge devices are equipped with sensors that give them an immediate connection to their environments. The goal of an edge AI deployment is to make sense of this data, identifying patterns and using them to make decisions.

By its nature, sensor data tends to be big, noisy, and difficult to manage. It arrives at a high frequency—potentially many thousands of times per second. An embedded device running an edge AI application has a limited time frame in which to collect this data, process it, feed it into some kind of AI algorithm, and act on the results. This is a major challenge, especially given that most embedded devices are resource-constrained and don't have the RAM to store large amounts of data.

The need to tame raw sensor data makes digital signal processing a critical part of most edge AI deployments. In any efficient and effective implementation, the signal processing and AI components must be designed together as a single system, balancing trade-offs between performance and accuracy.

A lot of traditional machine learning and data science tools are focused on tabular data—things like company financials or consumer product reviews. In contrast, edge

AI tools are built to handle constant streams of sensor data. This means that a whole different set of skills and techniques is required for building edge AI applications.

ML models can get very small

Edge devices are often designed to limit cost and power consumption. This means that, generally, they have much slower processors and smaller amounts of memory than personal computers or web servers.

The constraints of the target devices mean that, when machine learning is used to implement edge AI, the machine learning models must be quite small. On a midrange microcontroller, there may only be a hundred kilobytes or so of ROM available to store a model, and some devices have far smaller amounts. Since larger models take more time to execute, the slow processors of devices can also push developers toward deploying smaller models.

Making models smaller involves some trade-offs. To begin with, larger models have more capacity to learn. When you make a model smaller, it starts to lose some of its ability to represent its training dataset and may not be as accurate. Because of this, developers creating embedded machine learning applications have to balance the size of their model against the accuracy they require.

Various technologies exist for compressing models, reducing their size so that they fit on smaller hardware and take less time to compute. These compression technologies can be very useful, but they also impact models' accuracy—sometimes in subtle but risky ways. "Compression and optimization" on page 117 will talk about these techniques in detail.

That said, not all applications require big, complex models. The ones that do tend to be around things like image processing, since interpreting visual information involves a lot of nuance. Often, for simpler data, a few kilobytes (or less) of model is all you need.

Learning from feedback is limited

As we'll see later, AI applications are built through a series of iterative feedback loops. We do some work, measure how it performs, and then figure out what's needed to improve it.

For example, imagine we build a fitness monitor that can estimate your 10K running time based on data collected from onboard sensors. To test whether it's working well, we can wait until you run an actual 10K and see whether the prediction was correct. If it's not, we can add your data to our training dataset and try to train a better model.

If we have a reliable internet connection, this shouldn't be too hard—we can just upload the data to our servers. But part of the magic of edge AI is that we can deploy intelligence to devices that have limited connectivity. In this case, we might not have the bandwidth to upload new training data. In many cases, we might not be able to upload anything at all.

This presents a big challenge for our application development workflow. How do we make sure our system is performing well in the real world when we have limited access to it? And how can we improve our system when it's so difficult to collect more data? This is a core topic of edge AI development and something we'll be covering heavily throughout this book.

Compute is diverse and heterogeneous

The majority of server-side AI applications run on plain old x86 processors, with some graphics processing units (GPUs) thrown in to help with any deep learning inference. There's a small amount of diversity thanks to Arm's recent server CPUs, and exotic deep learning accelerators such as Google's TPUs (tensor processing units), but most workloads run on fairly ordinary hardware.

In contrast, the embedded world includes a dizzying array of device types:

- Microcontrollers, including tiny 8-bit chips and fancy 32-bit processors
- System-on-chip (SoC) devices running embedded Linux
- General-purpose accelerators based on GPU technology
- Field programmable gate arrays (FPGAs)
- Fixed architecture accelerators that run a single model architecture blazing fast

Each category includes countless devices from many different manufacturers, each with a unique set of build tools, programming environments, and interface options. It can be quite overwhelming.

The diversity of hardware means there are likely to be multiple suitable systems for any given use case. The hard part is choosing one! We'll cover this challenge over the course of the book.

"Good enough" is often the goal

With traditional AI, the goal is often to get the best possible performance—no matter the cost. Production deep learning models used in server-side applications can potentially be *gigabytes* in size, and they lean on powerful GPU compute to be able to run in a timely manner. When compute is not an obstacle, the most accurate model is often the best choice.

The benefits of edge AI come with some serious constraints. Edge devices have less capable compute, and there are often tricky choices involved with trading off between on-device performance and accuracy.

This is certainly a challenge—but it's not a barrier. There are huge benefits to running AI at the edge, and for a vast number of use cases they easily outweigh the penalty of a little reduced accuracy. Even a small amount of on-device intelligence can be infinitely better than none at all.

The goal is to build applications that make the most of this "good enough" performance—an approach described elegantly by Alasdair Allan as Capable Computing (*https://oreil.ly/W4gDl*). The key to doing this successfully is using tools that help us understand the performance of our applications in the real world, once any performance penalties have been factored in. We'll be covering this topic at length.

Tools and best practices are still evolving

As a brand-new technology that has only begun to reach mass adoption, edge AI still depends on tools and approaches that were developed for large-scale, server-side AI. In fact, the majority of AI research is still focused on building large models on giant datasets. This has a couple of implications.

First, as we'll see in Chapter 5, we'll often find ourselves using existing development tools from the fields of data science and machine learning. On the positive side, this means we can draw from a rich ecosystem of libraries and frameworks that is proven to work well. However, few of the existing tools prioritize things that are important on the edge—like small model sizes, computational efficiency, and the ability to train on small amounts of data. We often have to do some extra work to make these the focus.

Second, since edge AI research is fairly new we're likely to see extremely rapid evolution. As the field grows, and more researchers and engineers turn to focus on it, new approaches for improving efficiency are emerging—along with best practices and techniques for building effective applications. This promise of rapid change makes edge AI a very exciting field to work in.

Summary

In this chapter, we've explored the terminology that defines edge AI, learned a handy tool for reasoning about its benefits, explored how moving compute to the edge can increase access to technology, and outlined the factors that make edge AI different from traditional AI.

From the next chapter onward, we'll be dealing with specifics. Get ready to learn about the use cases, devices, and algorithms that power edge AI today.

## CHAPTER 2

Edge AI in the Real World

We now have a basic understanding of what edge AI means and what makes it—in theory—a useful set of technologies. In this coming chapter, we'll see what that theory looks like when it makes contact with the real world. We'll start by examining some actual products that are out in the field today. After that, we'll explore the top application areas for edge AI products. Finally, we'll learn more about the ethical considerations required to make any product a success.

Common Use Cases for Edge AI

As we learned in the previous chapter, edge AI is especially valuable for devices with an abundance of sensor data but a lack of compute or connectivity. Luckily for us, these conditions can be found nearly everywhere.

In modern cities, it can feel like we're never very far from a power socket or a wireless access point. But even when high bandwidth network connections and reliable power are available, there are huge advantages to limiting the communications and power consumption of devices. As we saw in "To Understand the Benefits of Edge AI, Just BLERP" on page 14, the pursuit of desirable features such as portability, reliability, privacy, and cost can drive product development toward devices that are designed to minimize the use amount of connectivity and energy usage.

Despite our seemingly global internet, there are plenty of places on the planet that are limited in connectivity or power. At the time of writing, 50% of the Earth's land is relatively untouched by human development (*https://oreil.ly/ASced*). Only a small percentage of the planet's surface has cellular or wireless coverage, and billions of people do not have reliable access to power (*https://oreil.ly/kly86*).

But beyond the obviously remote regions, there are plenty of hidden corners in our most built-up regions that fall into this category. In our modern industrial supply chains, there are places where it's impractical to provide hardwired DC power for embedded devices—making efficient, battery-powered devices the perfect fit (see Figure 2-1).

Figure 2-1. There are many places on our planet where battery power is required

At the same time, sensors are becoming cheaper, more sophisticated, and less power hungry. Often, even simple embedded devices ship with highly capable sensors that remain underutilized due to the challenges in getting the data off the system for remote processing. For example, imagine a basic fitness wearable that uses an accelerometer to count steps. Even this simple device might be equipped with a sensitive multiaxis accelerometer that has a very high sample rate, capable of recording the most subtle movements. Unless the device's software is equipped to interpret this data, most of it will be thrown away: it would be too energy intensive to send the raw data to another device for processing.

Greenfield and Brownfield Projects

Conditions such as those discussed above produce nearly endless opportunities for deploying edge AI. In practical terms, it can be helpful to group these opportunities into two categories: *greenfield* and *brownfield*. These terms are borrowed from urban planning. A greenfield project is one that takes place on a site that has yet to be developed and is still a grassy, green field. A brownfield project takes place on a site that has already been developed and may have some existing legacy infrastructure.

In the edge AI world, greenfield projects are ones where the hardware and software are designed together from the ground up. Since there's no existing hardware, greenfield projects can make use of the latest and greatest innovations in compute and sensing—which we'll learn more about later in this chapter. The developers have more freedom to design the ideal solution for the use case they are trying to target. For instance, modern cellphones are designed to include dedicated low-power digital signal processing hardware so that they can continually listen out for a wake word (such as "OK, Google" or "Hey, Siri") without draining the battery. The hardware is chosen with the specific wake word–detection algorithm in mind.

In contrast, brownfield edge AI projects begin with existing hardware that was originally designed for a different purpose. Developers must work within the constraints of the existing hardware to bring AI capabilities to a product. This reduces developers' freedom, but it avoids the major costs and risks associated with designing new hardware. For example, a developer could add wake word detection to a Bluetooth audio headset that is already on the market by making use of spare cycles in the device's existing embedded processor. This new functionality could even be added to existing devices with a firmware update.

Greenfield projects are exciting because they allow us to push the limits of what is possible by pairing the latest edge AI hardware and algorithms. On the other hand, brownfield projects allow us to bring new capabilities to existing hardware, delighting customers and making the most of existing designs.

Real-World Products

The best way to understand a technology is to see how it's applied in the real world. We're still in the early days of edge AI, but it's already being used across a huge range of applications and industries. Here are three brief overviews of real-world systems that have been developed using edge AI. Perhaps your own work will be featured in a future edition of this book!

Preventing forest fires using power line fault detection

Power lines transmit electricity across vast swathes of wilderness, including Europe's ancient forests. Equipment failure can potentially ignite vegetation and cause wildfires. With thousands of miles of towers and power lines, often in very remote areas, electrical equipment can be difficult to monitor.

Izoelektro's RAM-1 (*https://www.ram-center.com*) device uses edge AI to help solve this problem (Figure 2-2). A package of sensors monitors conditions at each electrical pylon, including temperature, inclination, and voltage, and uses a deep learning classification model (Chapter 4) to identify when a fault may be developing. Technicians can visit the pylon and make a repair before there is any danger of fire. The device has a rugged construction designed to withstand extreme weather conditions over many years of service.

Figure 2-2. Izoelektro's RAM-1 device (Credit: Izoelektro (https://www.ram-center.com))

There are two main factors that make this a perfect application for edge AI. The first is the lack of connectivity in wilderness locations. It would be prohibitively expensive to transmit raw sensor data from thousands of remotely located pylons in real time. Instead, the elegant solution is to interpret the sensor data at the source and transmit *only when a fault is predicted*—a maximum of around 250 kilobytes per month. The device is able to understand which data is crucial enough to require immediate attention, sending less important information in periodic batch transmissions.

This selective communication helps with the second, slightly unintuitive factor. Although the RAM-1 is mounted on an electricity pylon, it actually makes use of battery power. This ensures it keeps working even if there's a fault in the power lines, and it reduces the cost and complexity of installation. Since radio transmission uses a lot of energy, the RAM-1's ability to avoid unnecessary transmission helps it preserve battery life. In fact, with the help of edge AI, its battery can last for twenty years.

Here's how the RAM-1 fits the BLERP model:

Bandwidth
　　Connectivity is limited in remote locations where RAM-1 is deployed.

Latency
　　It's critical to identify failures as soon as they happen, as opposed to waiting for a periodic data transmission.

Economics
　　Avoiding unnecessary communication saves money and means the device can run on battery power, which reduces the cost of installation.

Reliability
　　The ability to run on battery power improves reliability.

Privacy
Not a major consideration for this use case.

Protecting first responders with intelligent wearables

The nature of their work means that firefighters are often exposed to high temperatures, and the extreme heat conditions can have a major impact on their long-term health. In fact, according to FEMA the leading cause of firefighter line-of-duty deaths is sudden cardiac events (*https://oreil.ly/lG6Hk*).

SlateSafety's BioTrac Band (*https://oreil.ly/mAWs1*) is a wearable device designed for workers, like firefighters, who are exposed to extreme conditions (Figure 2-3). It provides an early warning system that can help alert individuals and teams to conditions that may result in heat strain and overexertion. The BioTrac Band uses an embedded machine learning model alongside heuristic algorithms[1] to analyze data from multiple sensors—including signals from the wearer's body—and predict when an injury is about to happen. This intelligence made the device one of *Time* magazine's 100 best inventions of 2021 (*https://oreil.ly/cUy-b*).

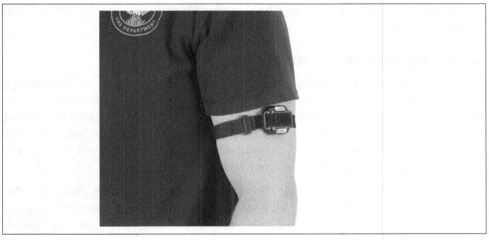

Figure 2-3. SlateSafety's BioTrac Band (Credit: SlateSafety (https://slatesafety.com))

The extreme environments that the BioTrac Band is deployed in make it a fantastic use case for edge AI. By analyzing data on-device, the band can continue to function and warn its wearer even when connectivity becomes limited or unavailable during the course of an emergency. In addition, the ability to interpret data on-device means that unnecessary transmission of data can be avoided—which saves energy and

---

1 We'll learn about these soon, in "Conditionals and heuristics" on page 101.

improves battery life, while allowing the size and weight of the device to be kept to a minimum. It also saves costs, which means the device can be more widely adopted.

Here's how the BioTrac Band fits the BLERP model:

Bandwidth
Connectivity is limited in extreme environments where firefighters work.

Latency
Health issues are time-critical and must be identified immediately.

Economics
Streaming raw data from sensors would require expensive high bandwidth connections.

Reliability
The device can continue to warn firefighters of potential risks even if connectivity drops, and it can function for a long time on a small battery.

Privacy
Raw biosignal data can be kept on-device, with only critical information being transmitted.

Understanding elephant behavior with smart collars

With increased pressure on their natural habitat, wild elephants are increasingly coming into contact with human beings. These interactions often end badly for the animals, with poaching or conflict with farmers and other people frequently leading to injury and death. To reduce the likelihood of these events, conservation workers and scientists are trying to learn more about elephant behavior and the types of conditions that lead to dangerous encounters.

ElephantEdge (*https://oreil.ly/Hehxr*) is an open source project to create a tracking collar (*https://oreil.ly/OHig1*) designed to help researchers understand elephant behavior (Figure 2-4). The collar, fit around the neck of an elephant, can provide insight into the animal's location, health, and activities using a combination of embedded sensors and machine learning models. This data can be used for scientific study—and it can also be used to alert humans to the presence of animals so that conflict can be avoided.

Since the device is attached to a wild elephant, replacing the battery is a difficult task! Edge AI technology helps by minimizing the amount of energy consumed by the device. Instead of transmitting large amounts of raw sensor data, the machine learning–equipped collar is able to transmit high-level information about the animal's activities—for example, whether it is walking, eating, drinking, or engaging in other behaviors. The models that allow it to do this were prototyped by a community of citizen scientists working with public datasets.

Figure 2-4. The OpenCollar Edge tracking collar being fitted to a sedated elephant (Credit: IRNAS (https://www.irnas.eu))

These low bandwidth requirements mean the collar can take advantage of an extremely low-power wireless communication technology named LoRa.[2] The collar is able to communicate with LoRa-equipped satellites that pass over once per day, sending a summary of the animal's activities since the last transmission. This means that the system can work reliably even in places with no traditional connectivity, but the battery can last for an estimated five years.

Here's how the OpenCollar Edge fits the BLERP model:

Bandwidth

Connectivity is limited in elephant habitats; on-device analysis enables use of low-energy wireless technologies.

Latency

Even though the device only transmits once per day, this is very frequent compared to traditional tracking collars that require manual downloading.

Economics

The device saves money by replacing traditional methods for monitoring elephants, which are labor intensive.

Reliability

Infrequent transmission means the battery can last for years, and makes satellite technology economically viable, increasing range.

---

2 LoRa is a trademark derived from the phrase "long range," since it is designed for long-range, low-power communications.

Privacy
> Tracking of elephants directly is less intrusive to local people than setting up cameras to monitor animal activity, which is another proposed solution.

These three use cases represent a tiny sample of what is possible. In the next section, we'll talk through some general high-level categories of applications.

Types of Applications

There are opportunities to deploy edge AI across every part of our modern world, from heavy industry to healthcare, agriculture to art. The possibilities are nearly endless! To make things easier to discuss, the roles that edge AI technologies play within these applications can be grouped into a few high-level categories:

- Keeping track of objects
- Understanding and controlling systems
- Understanding people and living things
- Generating and transforming signals

Let's walk through each of these categories and understand where edge AI fits.

Keeping Track of Objects

From vast container ships to individual grains of rice, our civilization depends on the movement of objects from one place to another. This might occur in the controlled conditions of a warehouse, where items are moved carefully from storage to shipment. It may also occur under the most extreme conditions, like the motion of weather systems across the face of the planet.

Tracking and interpreting the state of objects, both man-made and natural, is a key application area for edge AI. Intelligent sensors can help encode the state of the physical world in a form computers can understand, allowing us to do a better job of coordinating our activity.

Table 2-1 discusses edge AI use cases that involve keeping track of objects.

Table 2-1. Edge AI use cases for keeping track of objects

Use case	Key sensors
Monitoring shipments using smart packaging to detect damage during transit	Accelerometer, vibration, GPS, temperature, humidity
Counting products on store shelves using embedded cameras, so items can be restocked before they run out	Vision
Analyzing the movement of plastic waste in the ocean so it can be cleaned up	Vision

Use case	Key sensors
Identifying and tracking obstacles at sea to help ships avoid collisions	Radar
Locating buried natural resources using geophysical sensors	Electromagnetic, acoustic

---

Deep Dive: Monitoring Shipments Using Smart Packaging

It's common for manufactured products to travel thousands of miles on their way to a customer—and they don't always make it in one piece. Damage during shipping costs businesses money, but when a shipment arrives damaged after a long voyage, it isn't always easy to figure out what happened.

With edge AI, a logistics company could attach a device to high-value shipments that can recognize when an expensive item is at risk of damage. For example, if equipped with an accelerometer, the device could use a machine learning model to distinguish between normal bumps and jolts and specific types of rough handling that might lead to damage. Any rough handling event could be logged, along with a timestamp and a GPS location.

The logs could be uploaded periodically, whenever the device is able to get a wireless connection. Upon arrival, if there is any damage, the company could analyze the logs to discover the time and place where the damage happened—allowing them to find and fix the cause of the issue.

What makes this a good use case for edge AI? Let's think about it in terms of BLERP:

Bandwidth
> To detect sudden bumps, the accelerometer data would have to be quite high frequency. This makes it difficult to transmit from low-power wireless radios, which are generally low bandwidth. By processing data on-device, we can massively lower the bandwidth requirements.

Latency
> Not a major consideration for this use case.

Economics
> It's expensive to transmit data wirelessly, especially since the device could be anywhere in the world. Using edge AI helps conserve data and lower costs.

Reliability
> Shipments in transit are unlikely to have reliable connectivity, so it's important that the device can keep logging even when out of range. If we don't have to store raw data, we can log all the interesting events in a small amount of memory.

Privacy
> Not a major consideration for this use case.

Key benefits for object tracking

Object tracking tends to make use of the connectivity and cost-related benefits of edge AI. The world has many objects, and they're not always in convenient places. Cheap edge AI sensors making use of low-cost, opportunistic connectivity can provide high-resolution visibility into gaps in the supply chain that would otherwise be too expensive to monitor.

Of course, the exact benefits of deploying edge AI vary from project to project. For example, a system using cameras to monitor stock on store shelves might use edge AI for privacy. If internet-connected cameras were used to monitor store shelves, employees might feel like they are under constant scrutiny by HQ. But a stock tracking system that works offline, solely for the benefit of the store's team, could be a welcome aid.

Understanding and Controlling Systems

Our modern world is built on millions of complex, interconnected systems—everything from production lines to transportation networks, climate control to smart home appliances. The well-being of our economies is tied intimately to these systems. A breakdown in production can cost vast amounts of time and money and improvements in efficiency can lead to huge savings in costs, labor, and emissions.

The monitoring, control, and maintenance of complex systems is a vast opportunity for edge AI. The ability to make rapid, reliable decisions at the edge can improve the responsiveness and resilience of our systems, and fine-grained insights into system state can help us better plan for the future.

Some edge AI use cases that involve understanding and controlling systems can be found in Table 2-2.

Table 2-2. Edge AI use cases for understanding and controlling systems

Use case	Key sensors
Monitoring an oil rig for signs that it needs maintenance, avoiding downtime and reducing leaks and spillage	Accelerometer, vibration, load, temperature, audio, vision, and more
Autonomously driving a combine harvester, helping a farmer quickly harvest their crops	Vision, GPS
Understanding and shaping traffic flow on a busy highway, using variable speed limits to keep cars moving	Vision, magnetometer
Directing a mechanical tool using sensor feedback	Accelerometer, vibration, load
Identifying faulty items on a production line using computer vision, improving quality control and quickly recognizing issues	Vision
Cleaning a carpet using a robot vacuum, saving time for the owner of the home	Vision, proximity, touch, current[a]
Fetching items in a warehouse using robots, reducing labor costs and workplace health risks	Vision, proximity, touch, light

Use case	Key sensors
Detecting intrusions in computer networks using traffic analysis, automatically responding to security threats	Network logs[b]
Estimating vehicle tire wear based on vibration during motion	Accelerometer

[a] Analysis of motor current can be used to identify when a robot's wheels or cleaning tools are stuck.

[b] Edge AI doesn't always require sensor data: any locally available data streams can be used as input to algorithms.

This is a truly enormous category of applications, including many of the things we associate with our vision of "the future": self-driving vehicles, industrial robots, and smart factories. What they have in common is the use of edge AI to monitor the state of a complex system and to provide feedback and control when change is required.

Key benefits for understanding and controlling systems

A broad category, the automated monitoring and control of systems makes use of most of the benefits of edge AI. Economics and reliability are particularly important to many business use cases, and the benefits of low-bandwidth, low-latency solutions provide further justification where otherwise a server-side system might be used.

Deep Dive: Predictive Maintenance at an Oil Rig

If a piece of industrial equipment suddenly fails, the resulting downtime and disruption to processes can cost tremendous amounts of money. In some cases, it may also pose a threat to the health of human beings and the environment. Predictive maintenance is the art of identifying when a system is starting to fail—so that steps can be taken before it does.

An oil well is an incredibly complicated piece of machinery that operates under extreme conditions. Due to its precarious position in the middle of the ocean, faults can result in more than just costly downtime—the lives of the rig's crew are at stake, and oil spills can contaminate the ocean environment.

Using edge AI, sensor-equipped devices can be deployed to monitor key components of an oil rig, measuring factors such as vibration, temperature, and noise. They can learn the "normal" state of each part of the system, building a model of what a nominal operation looks like. If conditions start to deviate, they can alert a maintenance team to investigate further. Particularly sophisticated predictive maintenance systems might even have some control over the equipment, automatically halting operation if a dangerous situation is detected.

To understand why this is a good fit for edge AI, we can use the BLERP model:

Bandwidth
    Most oil rigs rely on satellites for connectivity, making it challenging to stream large amounts of sensor data from thousands of rig components into the cloud. Further, there are places within a drilling operation that have *very* limited

---

connectivity—for example, a drilling bit might be miles beneath the ocean floor! On-device predictive maintenance can turn a vast stream of noisy data into a lightweight sequence of events that are easy to transmit.

Latency
It's expensive to pay expert human beings to travel to an oil rig and inspect equipment. This means that inspection happens periodically, limiting how quickly a problem can be identified. With constant monitoring from an edge AI system, issues can be identified and addressed as soon as they present.

Economics
Predictive maintenance can save vast amounts of money that might otherwise be lost to downtime. In addition, monitoring via AI-equipped smart sensors is a lot cheaper than paying humans to perform the dangerous work of inspecting heavy machinery.

Reliability
In the extreme off-shore environment, you can't always depend on reliable transportation or communications. Using edge AI, insight into equipment health can continue even when usual operations are disrupted.

Privacy
Not a major consideration for this use case.

Understanding People and Living Things

The biological world is complex, messy, and can change quickly. There's huge value in being able to understand and react to it in real time. This category includes human-oriented technologies, like fitness tracking watches and educational toys, as well as systems for monitoring nature, agriculture, and the microscopic world.

These applications help bridge the gap between biology and technology, allowing our rigid computer systems to interface with the dynamic and flexible world of life on Earth. As our understanding of biology improves, this field will continue to grow.

Table 2-3 shows examples of edge AI use cases that help people and computers understand one another.

Table 2-3. Edge AI use cases involving people

Use case	Key sensors
Alerting workers in a dangerous environment when they are missing protective equipment	Vision
Understanding human gestures to control a video game	Vision, accelerometer, radar
Identifying when an intensive care patient's health is deteriorating and notifying a medical attendant	Biosignals, medical equipment

Use case	Key sensors
Recognizing when a thief has broken into a home and alerting the authorities	Vision, audio, accelerometer, magnetic sensors
Categorizing physical activities using sensors in a smart watch	Accelerometer, GPS, heart rate
Recognizing a user's voice commands and controlling an appliance	Audio
Counting the number of people who are waiting at a bus stop	Vision
Warning a driver when they are falling asleep at the wheel of a car	Vision

Our world is filled with plants, animals, and other living things. Table 2-4 shows examples of edge AI use cases that help us make sense of them.

Table 2-4. Edge AI use cases involving living things

Use case	Key sensors
Informing researchers when wildlife of interest is spotted by a remote trail camera	Vision, audio
Diagnosing crop diseases in a remote rural location with no cellphone coverage	Vision, volatile organic compound
Recognizing sounds made by marine mammals to track their movements and understand their behavior	Acoustic
Warning villagers of an approaching elephant so they can avoid human-animal conflict	Thermal imaging, vision
Categorizing farm animal behavior using a smart collar to understand health	Accelerometer
Cooking food to perfection by monitoring and controlling a sensor-equipped kitchen appliance	Vision, temperature, volatile organic compound[a]

[a] Volatile organic compound (VOC) sensors can detect various types of gases.

Key benefits for understanding people and living things

Another large area, applications involving people and living things, makes use of every aspect of the BLERP model. That said, this is a category where privacy can be especially important. There are many applications that are technically feasible using server-side AI, but only become socially acceptable when done on-device.

The most widespread example of this is digital personal assistants, such as Apple's Siri or Google's Google Assistant. As discussed earlier, personal assistants work by using on-device models to constantly listen for wake words. Only after the wake word is detected is any audio streamed to the cloud. Without the on-device component, the assistant would have to constantly stream audio to the service provider. This would be incompatible with most people's expectations around privacy.

By moving functionality onto devices, and avoiding the transmission of data, we unlock massive possibilities—especially in vision, which until recently required large models that could only be run in the cloud.

Deep Dive: Spotting Rare Wildlife with Trail Cameras

A trail camera, or camera trap, is a special type of camera designed for monitoring wildlife. It has a tough, weatherproof housing, a high-capacity battery, and a motion sensor. Installed with a view of a trail, it automatically snaps photos whenever it detects motion.

Researchers who are monitoring specific species install camera traps in remote locations and leave them for months at a time. When they return, they download the photos from the camera and use them to better understand their target species; for example, they may try to estimate how many individuals exist.

There are some significant problems with camera traps that cost a lot of time and money:

- Most of the photos captured do not feature the target species. Instead, the capture was triggered by nontarget species or by random motion in the field of view.

- Due to the high number of false positives, it would not be helpful to send notifications of captures via a network connection. Instead, researchers must travel out to the remote location to collect the saved photos. This is extremely expensive and can result in missing data if the memory card gets full, or unnecessary trips if nothing interesting has been photographed.

- Researchers must trawl through thousands of useless photographs to find the few that matter.

Using edge AI, camera traps can be equipped with deep-learning vision models trained to identify target species and reject any images that do not contain them. This means that researchers no longer have to worry about filling up memory cards with useless images. Even better, it means that cameras can potentially be equipped with low-power or cellular radio transmitters that allow them to report back on animal sightings without anyone having to visit the field. This can massively reduce the cost of a study and increase the amount of scientific work that can be done.

The BLERP model can tell us exactly why this is a great application for edge AI:

Bandwidth
> Camera traps are often deployed in remote areas with low connectivity—perhaps with expensive, low-bandwidth satellites as the only option. With edge AI, the number of photos taken can be reduced enough to make it possible to transmit them all.

Latency
> Without edge AI, the latency involved with sending a researcher to collect photos from camera traps could be measured in months! With edge AI and a low-power

radio connection, it's possible to analyze photos immediately and obtain useful information without having to wait.

Economics
Avoiding trips out into the field saves large amounts of money; so does avoiding unnecessary use of expensive satellite radios.

Reliability
If useless photos can be discarded, the memory card will take longer to fill up.

Privacy
An edge AI camera can discard photos of humans on the trail, preserving the privacy of other trail users (such as local people or hikers).

Transforming Signals

To a computer, our world is made up of signals: time series of sensor readings that each describe a small fragment of a situation or environment. Our previous categories of applications are mostly focused on interpreting these signals and responding to them accordingly. Data from one or more sensors is assimilated, and a simple output is constructed that either facilitates human interpretation or can be used as a control signal for an automated system.

This final category is a little different. Sometimes, rather than converting a raw signal into an instantaneous decision, we simply want to transform one signal into another (Table 2-5). As discussed in "Digital Signal Processing" on page 12, digital signal processing is an important part of embedded applications. In these use cases, which go much further than the traditional DSP pipeline, it is the end goal rather than a side effect.

Table 2-5. Edge AI use cases for transforming signals

Use case	Signal type
Filtering background noise to improve call quality on a cell phone	Audio
Removing noise from photographs captured with a smartphone camera	Vision
Generating music to accompany a musician during practice	Audio
Blurring the background of a video stream during a remote work meeting	Vision
Generating realistic human speech from text	Audio
Translating one written language into another using a smartphone camera	Vision, text
Upsampling low-resolution audio so that it sounds better to the human ear	Audio
Compressing video using deep learning so that it can be transmitted via a low bandwidth connection	Video
Creating a spoken representation of a visual scene for visually impaired people	Audio
Transcribing a spoken conversation into text for convenience of note-taking	Audio
Using data from cheap sensors to simulate the output of an expensive one	Time series

Key benefits for transforming signals

Since digital signals are expressed over time, applications in this area tend to benefit from the latency benefits of edge AI. Bandwidth is also particularly important, since access to the original signal is required; transmitting the transformed signal often requires the same amount of bandwidth, if not more.

Deep Dive: Blurring the Background During a Remote Work Meeting

With the growth of remote work and videoconferencing, employees have had to get used to their previously private home spaces being broadcast to their coworkers. To help maintain some privacy, many videoconferencing tools now support blurring the background of a video stream while leaving the subject of the video intact.

These tools depend on a technique named *segmentation*, which uses deep learning models to identify the pixels in a stream of video that belong to one category or another. In this case, the model is trained to distinguish between a person and their background scenery. The input is the raw stream of video from a camera. The output is a stream of video with the same resolution but with the background pixels blurred together, making it hard to see what is there.

To preserve privacy, it's important that this technique uses edge AI—otherwise, the unblurred video would be transmitted outside of the user's home. Instead, the segmentation and blurring is performed on-device before the data is transmitted.

Here's how this use case maps onto our BLERP model:

Bandwidth
> The transformation works best if it happens on the high-resolution original video stream rather than a compressed, low-resolution version that may contain visual artifacts. It's often not feasible to transmit high-resolution video, so the transformation must be done on-device.

Latency
> Performing the transformation on a remote server may add additional latency versus directly sending the video stream to a peer. Performing it on-device removes this potential extra step.

Economics
> It's cheaper to perform the required computation on the device sending video as opposed to in the cloud, where the service provider would have to pay for it.

Reliability
> With a cloud server as a middleman, the video streaming pipeline is more complex and has a higher probability of outages. By processing on-device, the pipeline is simpler and may be less likely to fail.

Privacy

When the data is transformed on-device, the user can be guaranteed that nobody will ever see the original video.

Another interesting application for transforming data is the concept of a *virtual sensor*. In some situations, engineering or cost constraints may prevent you from outfitting a device with all of the sensors you would like to. For example, perhaps your design would benefit from a particularly accurate sensor—but that sensor is too expensive for production use.

To get around this problem, it may be possible to create a virtual sensor—an artificial stream of data that provides signals that are almost as good as the real thing. To do this, an edge AI algorithm might process other signals (for example, it could combine readings from several cheaper sensors) and attempt to reconstruct the signal of the desired sensor based on the information they contain.

For example, in monocular depth estimation (*https://oreil.ly/LMBbU*) a model is trained to estimate the distance of objects from a simple image sensor. This would usually require a more expensive solution, such as a stereoscopic camera or a laser-based distance sensor.

We've now explored the four high-level categories that most edge AI applications can be grouped into. As edge AI technologies continue to evolve, we'll see many more potential use cases open up. But technological feasibility does not automatically make something a good idea. In the next section, we'll talk about the importance of responsible design—and learn some of the pitfalls that can result in edge AI applications that cause more harm than good.

Building Applications Responsibly

The first part of this chapter has covered some of the most interesting potential applications for edge AI, and the next chapter will provide a framework for breaking down problems and deciding whether they are a good fit for edge AI to solve.

But as we heard in "Responsible, Ethical, and Effective AI" on page xix, it's vital that any project is analyzed at every step along the way to make sure that its design and use are responsible. This isn't some warm-and-fuzzy process where we pat ourselves on the back for ticking some boxes and then continue with our work. Poorly designed technology products can be life-destroying, career-ending disasters—for the end users of the products, the businesses selling them, and the developers creating them.

An example of this is Uber's self-driving car division (*https://oreil.ly/UMkXa*). The rideshare company launched an aggressive drive toward developing a self-driving car, hiring industry luminaries, and investing billions of dollars. In its rush to test a system on real streets, the company's flawed safety procedures and ineffective software led to the tragic death of a pedestrian. This disaster resulted in the shutdown of Uber's self-driving program, layoffs of hundreds of employees, and the fire sale of the self-driving car division to another business.[3]

Building a self-driving car, if done well, could result in safer roads and reduced emissions. It seems like a noble mission. But the complex environment of edge AI can lead to potential pitfalls that are challenging to navigate. When these risks are factored in, a well-intentioned technology project can become a deadly minefield.

In Uber's case, their self-driving car was subject to an incredibly common failure mode of machine learning systems: it was incapable of understanding situations that had not appeared in its training dataset. According to the National Transportation Safety Board, Uber's self-driving car lacked "the capability to classify an object as a pedestrian unless that object was near a crosswalk" (*https://oreil.ly/A-URg*).

There are many factors that contribute to a catastrophic failure like this. On the part of the developers, it shows incompetence and negligence to drive a self-driving car on public roads when it was not tested for its ability to handle even the most common operating conditions. In Uber's case, this led directly to the death of a human being and the failure of a company division. We may assume that the team behind Uber's self-driving software were intelligent, capable people—they were recruited as the best in the business. So how can it be that capable people miss the obvious when building and deploying technology?

The unfortunate truth is that building technology well is hard, and it's difficult to solve complex problems with technologies that—by nature—can only reflect partial considerations. Beyond the fundamental technical challenges, it's your responsibility as a professional to know the limits of your technology, to scrutinize your processes, ruthlessly evaluate your work, and be willing to shut down a project if it doesn't seem to be going the right way. A product that unintentionally harms people is a bad product, no matter how brilliant the team that designed it.

In a business setting, you may be fighting against organizational inertia that is more concerned with shipping something than making sure it is safe. But you should always remember that, at the end of the day, your livelihood, reputation, and freedom are on the line if you neglect your professional responsibilities. Even worse, you could build a product that ruins the lives of others and regret it for the rest of your days.

---

3 The head of the division, Anthony Levandowski, was later sentenced to eighteen months in prison for theft of intellectual property—suggesting that ethical issues were a systemic problem.

Responsible Design and AI Ethics

Responsible design is critical to building effective products. To make sure it receives the introduction it deserves, the authors invited Wiebke (Toussaint) Hutiri (https://wieb ketoussaint.com), PhD researcher in the Cyber Physical Intelligence Lab at the Technical University of Delft, to write the following section. Wiebke does interdisciplinary research at the intersection of applied machine learning and edge computing, with a focus on designing trustworthy machine learning systems for the Internet of Things.

Harmful AI failures, as described earlier in this chapter, have made AI ethics an important consideration for most companies integrating AI into their products. For developers, ethics are important, but it is often very difficult to know what ethics are and how to put them into practice. Scrutinizing the values that underpin the product development process (see the following sidebar) is one way of connecting ethics to edge AI development in a practical way. With values as a foundation, the next step is to practice responsible design.

Values in Design

Products cannot be divorced from the context in which they are used. This means that a product is only good if it is useful for doing the task for which it was designed. Of course, products can be repurposed for unexpected alternative uses that expand beyond the initially intended design. However, for a developer, it is a very risky undertaking to hope for unpredictable repurposing, rather than doing good engineering.

In reality, it is seldom enough for products to be only useful. Utility only presents the lowest bar of what users expect from a product. Depending on the context, products also need to be safe to use, have longevity, have low manufacturing and operating costs, and avoid creating harmful waste throughout production, use, and at the end of their life. These are just a few *nonfunctional* requirements (i.e., requirements that do not contribute to technical performance) that are as important for product success as technical performance.

The work of developers is difficult, because oftentimes multiple requirements cannot be met simultaneously and pose trade-offs. Navigating and prioritizing these trade-offs is a key aspect of what engineering design is all about. Individual people typically navigate trade-offs based on their values. Values, like sustainability, democracy, safety, privacy, or equality, are principles that you apply, often unconsciously, to guide decisions in your life (e.g., if privacy is one of your core values, you may be really motivated to learn about edge AI because you don't want your personal data to be shared with third parties).

It is only natural that developers bring their values into the edge AI design process. But there is a big caveat to doing this. Values are personal and vary across people and cultures. You thus cannot rely on your own decision-making heuristics, or on those of a team of developers who all have the same perspective of life, to result in a successful product that addresses the needs of diverse users. Having a process for reaching consensus on how and which values should guide your design decisions is important and should be part of your development process.

This breakout is only a teaser, and you can learn more about designing for values in Design for Values—An Introduction (*https://oreil.ly/Y7BHu*), from Delft University of Technology.

To design responsibly, a developer needs to know the limits of their "construction" materials and master their tools. Moreover, they need to measure and evaluate whether their product meets the set of functional and nonfunctional requirements they set out to achieve. That's where machine learning is nothing like any of the hardware or software applications that you have developed before. In ML, data are your "bricks" and your "thermometer" at the same time. This has unique consequences for edge AI.

Data is your "bricks": For machine learning models in edge AI applications, your training data is your building blocks. The quality of your data affects the quality of your product. Put simply, if it's not in the training data, you cannot predict it. If it is underrepresented in the training data, you cannot predict it reliably. If it is overrepresented in the training data, you'll mostly predict it, rather than other things. When you look at representation, it is important to consider the distribution of subgroups across target labels, not only subgroup representation. It is also important to look at the quality of target labels across subgroups, as mislabeled training samples will affect the quality of your models.

Data is your "thermometer": Where training data is your bricks, evaluation data is the "thermometer" that measures your models. Using evaluation datasets that do not represent your application scenarios is like using an uncalibrated thermometer to measure the temperature. Having high-quality evaluation data is important. In statistics, small sample sizes require special treatment. The common metrics that are used to evaluate ML models assume sufficient sample representation. For evaluation data, it is important that all categories are represented sufficiently across labels, so that your evaluation is statistically meaningful. If a category is not evaluated across all target labels, the limits of the models are not known.

There are many implications of using data to build and evaluate models. For example, data is historic and represents the past, not the future. Data only represents a snapshot in time, while the world is changing. Data is specific to the location where it is collected and to the entity that has been measured. All of this implies that data is only a sample and never complete. Incomplete data is a major cause of bias and discrimination in AI, which has harmed people and caused scandals.

We'll take a deep dive into datasets, explaining all of these concepts from scratch, in Chapter 7.

Important Concepts in Responsible Design

Here are some of the key terms used in machine learning fairness that are very relevant to responsible design:

Bias

> In its most general sense, bias means a slanted or skewed perspective. In algorithmic systems, like AI, bias also describes a system that systematically produces outputs that favor some and are prejudiced against other groups or categories. Bias does not have to refer to people. Unless your application targets a particular group or category, bias is usually not a good thing.

Discrimination

> Discrimination refers to outcomes of decision-making processes that treat individuals or groups of people differently, based on protected or sensitive attributes. The law provides formal definitions for which attributes are protected in which applications. Sensitive attributes can also be defined informally, based on what a community or society deems as worthy of protecting to ensure equality.

Fairness

> Fairness is the most difficult concept to define. This is because no universal definition of fairness exists. Instead, fairness is highly context dependent and influenced by the type of application and its context, the risks and harms that can result from failure, and the stakeholders' values. People often value fairness alongside other values like equity, equality, and inclusiveness. Bias can result in unfairness, and many people consider discrimination to be unfair.

To mitigate bias, avoid discrimination, and evaluate potential unfairness, you need to understand the context in which your design will be used:

- Who will use your design, and how will they use it?
- What gap does your design fill?
- What are the environmental conditions your design will operate in?
- Are there adversaries who may seek to disrupt your product's operation?
- What can go wrong if your design doesn't work as intended?

Metaphorically speaking, are you building edge AI from bricks of unfired clay in a town where it rains for 200 days a year? Or have you carefully considered the context, and collected training data that allows you to build a structure suitable for the environment? Is your evaluation data a broken piece of equipment, or a carefully calibrated thermometer?

To wrap up this brief introduction to responsible design and AI ethics, you can think of a responsible developer as someone who is *skilled at using their tools to craft their materials into a form that fills a gap that stakeholders want to have filled in accordance with the values agreed on by all that are affected by the project.*

It is easy to get started with responsible design. Know the limits of your data. Know the limits of your models. Talk to the people who will use your product. If there's only one takeaway for you from this section, it should be this: *KUDOs (Know Ur Data, Obviously) to those that develop responsible edge AI.*

—Wiebke (Toussaint) Hutiri, Technical University of Delft

Black Boxes and Bias

There are two aspects of edge AI that make it especially prone to causing unexpected harm in practice: *black boxes* and *bias*.

The term *black box* is a metaphor for a system that is opaque to analysis and understanding. Data goes in, decisions come out, but the processes within it that lead to those decisions are inscrutable. This is a common criticism of modern AI, especially deep learning models, which are famously difficult to dissect. Some algorithms, like random forests, are quite easy to interpret—if you have access to the model, you can read its internals to understand why it makes certain decisions. But things are very different on-device.

Edge devices are often, by design, invisible. They are intended to merge into the background of our built environments; they're embedded in our buildings, products, vehicles, and toys. They are literal black boxes; their contents are invisible, often protected by layers of security to avoid any detailed inspection.

Once an AI algorithm—no matter how simple—is deployed to an edge device, it becomes a black box to anyone who is using it. And if the device is deployed in different real-world conditions to those anticipated by its original developers, even they may have little insight into why it is behaving the way it does.

This is dangerous in several ways, depending on who you are. The device's users—the people who bought and installed it—are now reliant on a system they do not fully understand. They may trust the device to make the right decisions, but they don't have any guarantees that this trust is warranted.

In the example of Uber's self-driving car, the test driver was supposed to be able to intervene in a dangerous situation. Ultimately, however, it's not feasible for a human operator to be able to reliably compensate for a faulty automated system, no matter their training. The experiment's reliance on human intervention to avoid tragedy was an irresponsible design decision.

The pedestrian, an innocent bystander who just happened to be crossing the road, was also a victim of the black box nature of the model. If they had been alerted that the car approaching was an unreliable self-driving prototype, they may not have chosen to cross. But the edge AI system, hidden inside an ordinary-looking car, provided no inherent warning. There was no reason for a pedestrian to assume that the car would not behave like human-driven cars.

Finally, the black box nature of edge AI creates a risk for its developers. For example, imagine an edge AI camera trap being used to monitor the population of an invasive species. It might turn out that the camera suffers from false negatives—it fails to recognize one in every three invasive animals that come past. If the camera trap is deployed in a remote location, it may not be possible to validate the camera's output against reality. The researchers will get an underestimate of the animals' population—but they will have no way of knowing, since the raw data may no longer exist.

Unlike server-side AI, which can be deployed and monitored alongside the raw data it processes, edge AI is often deployed specifically in situations where raw data cannot be captured. In practice, this means that there's sometimes no direct way for developers to measure whether an edge AI application is performing correctly once it is in the field.

In practice, conservation researchers solve this dilemma by storing all of the photos captured and performing manual reviews when the memory card is collected, until confidence is built in the system—but this costs time and money. If there's no equivalent mechanism available to monitor an application, or if it isn't feasible to implement one within the available budget, it may not be possible to deploy the application responsibly.

Black Boxes and Explainability

The opposite of a black box system is an *explainable* one. Some AI algorithms are more explainable than others, as we'll learn in "Classical machine learning" on page 103. Even systems using relatively opaque algorithms can be designed in a way that makes them more explainable—although this can come at the cost of reduced performance or increased complexity. The right trade-off is unique to each application.

Explainability is increasingly a legal requirement for certain projects.[4] It's worth exploring if this is the case in your regulatory environment.

---

4 As described in "Impact of Legal Requirements on Explainability in Machine Learning" (*https://creil.ly/ jNZ6m*) by Adrien Bibal et al. (arXiv, 2020).

The hazards of *black boxes* are compounded by the dangers of *bias*. Bias, in edge AI systems, results in the system being equipped with a model of its application area that does not represent the real world. Bias is very likely to occur in systems if developers do not pay attention to well-known sources of bias. The most common sources of bias are:

Human bias
All humans are biased toward a certain worldview based on their experiences (i.e., not appreciating that pedestrians may disregard traffic rules[5]).

Data bias
Datasets reflect the data collection process, not reality (i.e., a dataset may only contain examples of people crossing the street at crosswalks).

Algorithmic bias
All AI algorithms have innate limitations,[6] and their selection and tuning can result in bias (i.e., the selected algorithm may not perform well on small, faint objects like distant pedestrians at night).

Testing bias
Because real-world testing is difficult and expensive, it often only covers common cases, leading to biased test coverage (i.e., doing exhaustive testing on an artificial test course is expensive, and developers wished to reduce costs, so a critical scenario was not tested).

Bias can be hard to avoid in AI systems. While we tend to associate the term with deliberate, intentional forms of discrimination (such as deliberate sexism in hiring processes), in technology projects, it most commonly occurs due to a lack of understanding of the application context, which is then amplified by the limitations of our resources.

To mitigate bias, a development team needs access to relevant domain experts, a carefully collected dataset (even if it cannot reflect the exact conditions of the real world), an algorithm that is appropriate for the task, and a sufficient budget for real-world testing. In reality, many developer teams only pay attention to these after they experience costly failures due to bias.

When coupled with black box edge AI products, bias creates a risky situation. As described earlier, users are likely to assume that a system *works*. They will trust in

---

5 Crossing a street outside of a crosswalk is illegal in many parts of the US, where the Uber experiment was performed.

6 Machine learning models have a property known as inductive bias (*https://oreil.ly/TiRok*), which reflects the internal assumptions they make about how the world works. This inductive bias is required in order for models to work—so selecting the appropriate model is very important.

the correct, safe, and reasonable operation of a product. With no way to inspect its mechanism of operation, they are unable to test this assumption themselves. The responsibility is entirely on developers to meet and manage user expectations.

A successful AI project must be aware of its own limitations and provide the necessary structure to protect users and the public from its potential failure. It's critical for the team behind a product to define the parameters within which the product will function—and to make sure that its users are aware of these parameters.

Over the course of this book, we'll learn a framework for ensuring this awareness and for putting the brakes on projects that are not safe to deploy. It's an ongoing process, and one that must run from conceptualization until end of life. Many projects will run into an ethical quagmire as their true effectiveness is revealed—but some projects are just wrong from the start.

Technology That Harms, Not Helps

Surveillance systems have become pervasive in our modern world, and the public has been forced to adapt to their presence without being asked for consent. The application of AI to surveillance is a complicated topic. While edge AI can potentially be used to preserve privacy, it can also be used to infringe on human rights.

In November 2019, it was discovered that a major supplier of video surveillance cameras, Hikvision, was marketing a surveillance camera designed to classify the race of individuals (*https://oreil.ly/06M6r*), including that of Uyghurs, a Chinese minority who have been subject to vicious repression by their government. *The New York Times* reported that Chinese government authorities are attempting to use edge AI technology to identify Uyghur people by their appearance and "keep records of their comings and goings for search and review" (*https://oreil.ly/u2vfr*).

While Uber's self-driving experiment resulted in a tragedy caused by bad engineering, Hikvision's racial profiling technology is—to the authors of this book, who believe in a democratic society that promotes personal freedom and equality for all—fundamentally wrong.

When functioning perfectly, the system is designed to enforce a societal bias against a subgroup of people. There is no way to limit the system's bias; in fact, the bias is present as part of the design. While it may be argued that morality is subjective and that different societies have different values, the fact is that the millions of Uyghur people being tracked by this system have had no choice in the matter—and would likely reject it if asked.

Such clear violations of moral expectations may seem obvious, but human psychology—naivety, arrogance, or greed—makes it easy for a group of intelligent people to cross moral boundaries without considering the harm they might cause. One example of this is the service HireVue. Designed to reduce the cost of interviewing job candidates, companies use HireVue's product to analyze recorded videos where candidates answer specific questions. The company claims to use AI algorithms to rate the likelihood of a candidate being successful in a given role.

Naively, the developers of HireVue did not consider the impact of human, data, algorithmic, and testing biases on their work. Their product, built to use audio-visual information in hiring decisions, inevitably incorporated the voice, accent, and appearance of candidates when making hiring decisions. The clear risk of discrimination this created led to a lawsuit and a backlash from the public, resulting in HireVue having to scrap features of their product and conduct a third-party audit of their algorithms (*https://oreil.ly/R7Dy3*).

A further aspect to consider is that an edge AI technology may be used by customers for purposes other than those for which they were designed—and these purposes may be unethical. For example, consider an edge AI camera trap designed for spotting an endangered species. While intended for scientific research, the camera trap might easily be repurposed by poachers as a tool for locating animals that they wish to capture and sell on the black market. It's important to consider these potential "off-label" uses when designing an application, since the risk may be so high that it outweighs the potential benefits of the product.

The costs of negligence

Technologies that use artificial intelligence are often designed to integrate deeply into our world, shaping the day-to-day interactions we have with our homes, places of work, businesses, governments, and each other. This means that the failure of these systems can have a profound impact on people.

There isn't space in this book for a full discussion of the myriad ways this can happen, but here are a few examples:

Violations due to negligence
Medical hardware could misdiagnose patients, affecting their treatment.

Surveillance equipment could direct enforcement against some groups of people more than others, leading to unequal justice.

Educational toys could perform better for some children than others, reducing access to learning opportunity.

Safety devices could fail due to lack of testing with different user groups, leading to bodily harm.

Unsecured devices could be compromised by criminals, facilitating crime.

Deliberate ethical violations

Pervasive AI-powered surveillance could impact personal privacy.

Smart sensors could be used by poachers to target endangered wildlife.

Weapons augmented with edge AI could increase conflict deaths and disrupt the global balance of power.

Mitigating societal harms

The framework provided throughout this book will encourage you to take time during the development process to understand the societal implications of what you are building and to make go/no-go decisions based on your findings. Responsible design is very context specific, and mitigating societal harm should be done systematically and continuously to ensure you are on the right path.

A best practice for building responsible applications of AI is to assemble a product team with diverse perspectives in both technical expertise and lived experience. Human biases amplify technical biases, and a diverse team is less likely to have blind spots in their collective worldview. If you have a small team, it's important to budget time and money for diversity, and to reach out to the wider community to find people who are willing to help evaluate your ideas and provide feedback, adding their perspectives to the mix.

Psychological Safety and Ethical AI

Your team's insight is crucial in identifying potential harms, so it's vital that they feel like they have the ability to speak up and make their voices heard throughout the development process. Even in the best working environments it can feel risky for employees to speak up when they think their feedback may disadvantage them.

For example, imagine an employee who notices a potential risk but feels unable to mention it because they feel hesitant to derail an important project. In reality, the employee may save the company time, money, and reputation by pointing out a significant issue. However, if the employee feels afraid of a potential negative impact on their career, reputation, or the team's morale, they may choose not to say anything until it is too late.

Psychological safety is the feeling of being able to speak up and discuss issues without fearing negative consequences. This, along with a culture that reinforces the importance of ethics in AI, are necessary conditions for building successful AI projects. Some valuable resources on this topic are covered in "Diversity" on page 126.

There is no way to benchmark the "ethicality" of a system.[7] Instead, we need to understand the values underlying the creation of a system—including what those values are, who they belong to, and in which context they are intended to apply. This awareness allows us to shape our work into useful products that bring benefit, not harm.

Various companies and services exist to help guide teams through the process of developing AI responsibly, or to audit existing applications for potential harms. If you are concerned about harmful "off-label" use of your work, there are also some legal tools at your disposal. Responsible AI Licenses (*https://www.licenses.ai*) (RAIL) are technology licenses designed to help developers restrict the legal use of artificial intelligence products for harmful applications.

By attaching a RAIL to their product, developers create legal grounds to prevent its misuse in a specific list of applications, which can be extended to include any categories the developer would like to include. Some of the default prohibited options include surveillance, crime prediction, and generating fake photography. Of course, this only helps prevent ethical usage by entities that consider themselves bound by legal agreements.

Finally, there are many free, high-quality online resources that you can use to learn more about ethical and responsible AI and evaluate the work you are doing. To get you started, here's a short list:

- Berkeley Haas' guide, Mitigating Bias in Artificial Intelligence (*https://oreil.ly/8uXGZ*)
- Google's recommended practices for responsible AI (*https://oreil.ly/SBP-3*)
- Microsoft's responsible AI resources (*https://oreil.ly/ZOvEm*)
- PwC's responsible AI toolkit (*https://oreil.ly/zZl1N*)
- Google Brain's "People + AI Research (PAIR)" (*https://oreil.ly/bco24*)

For a detailed high-level summary of current approaches to principles in AI, we also recommend reading "Principled Artificial Intelligence: Mapping Consensus in Ethical and Rights-Based Approaches to Principles for AI" (*https://oreil.ly/8BM54*) (J. Fjeld et al., Berkman Klein Center Research Publication, 2020).

---

[7] Travis LaCroix and Alexandra Sasha Luccioni, "Metaethical Perspectives on 'Benchmarking' AI Ethics" (*https://oreil.ly/RS4p1*), arXiv, 2022.

Summary

In this chapter, we've developed a solid understanding of how edge AI fits into our world. We know the top use cases, the key benefits, and the critical ethical considerations that need to be applied.

We're now ready to dive into some of the technical details. In the next chapter, we'll learn about the technology that makes edge AI work.

## CHAPTER 3

The Hardware of Edge AI

It's now time to meet the devices, algorithms, and optimization techniques that power edge AI applications. This chapter is designed to provide a broad overview of the most important technical elements of the field. By the end of it, you'll have the building blocks necessary to start the high-level planning of an edge AI product.

Sensors, Signals, and Sources of Data

Sensors are electronic components that give devices the power to measure their environments and detect human input. They range from extremely simple (trusty old switches and variable resistors) to mind-blowingly sophisticated (light detection and ranging [LIDAR] and thermal imaging cameras). Sensors provide our edge AI devices with the streams of data that they use to make decisions.

Beyond sensors, there are other sources of data that our devices can tap into. These include things like digital device logs, network packets, and radio transmissions. Although they have a different origin, these secondary data streams can be just as exciting as sources of information for AI algorithms.

Different sensors provide data in different formats. A few data formats are commonly encountered in edge AI applications. They can be summarized as follows:

Time series

Time series data represents the change in one or more values over time. A time series may contain multiple values from the same physical sensor—for example, a single sensor component may provide readings of both temperature and humidity. Time series data is often collected by polling a sensor at a specific rate, such as a certain number of times per second, to produce a signal. The rate of polling is known as the sampling rate, or frequency. It is common that the individual readings (known as samples) are collected within a constant period, so the time interval between two samples is always the same.

Other time series may be aperiodic, meaning the samples are not collected at a constant rate. This might happen in the case of a sensor that detects specific events—for example, a proximity sensor that toggles a pin when something comes within a certain distance. In this case, it is common to capture the exact time when an event happened alongside the sensor value itself.

Time series may represent summary information. For example, a time series could consist of the number of times something happened during the interval since the last value.

Time series data is the most common form of sensor data for edge AI. It is particularly interesting because, in addition to the sensor values, the signal includes information about the timing of the values. This provides useful information when attempting to understand how a situation is changing. In addition to timing information being useful, time series data is valuable because it contains multiple readings from the same sensor, reducing the impact of momentary anomalous readings.

There is no typical frequency for a time series—it can range from a single sample a day to millions of samples per second.

Audio

A special case of time series data, audio signals represent the oscillation of sound waves as they travel through the air. They are generally captured at a very high frequency—thousands of times per second. Since hearing is a human sense, huge amounts of research and development have gone into innovations that make it easier to work with audio data on edge devices.

These technologies include special signal processing algorithms that make it easier to process audio data, which in its raw form is typically captured at an extremely high frequency. As we will see later, audio signal processing is so common that a lot of embedded hardware comes with built-in functionality for performing it efficiently.

One of the most widespread uses of edge AI audio processing is in speech detection and classification. That said, audio doesn't even have to be in the spectrum of human hearing. Sensors used by edge AI devices can potentially capture ultrasound (higher than audible by human hearing) and infrasound (lower than audible by humans) data.

Image

Images are data that represent the measurements taken by a sensor that captures an entire scene, as opposed to a single point. Some sensors, like cameras, use an array of tiny elements to capture data from the entire scene in one go. Other sensors, like LIDAR, build up an image by mechanically sweeping a single sensor element across the scene over a period of time.

Images have two or more dimensions. In their typical form, they can be thought of as a grid of "pixels," where the value of each pixel represents some property of the scene at the corresponding point in space. A basic example of this is shown on the left side of Figure 3-1. The size of the grid (for example, 96x96 pixels) is known as the *resolution* of the image.

A pixel may have multiple values, or channels. For example, while a grayscale image only has one value per pixel, representing how light or dark the pixel is, a color image may have three values per pixel (in the RGB model), representing three colors (red, blue, and green) that can be mixed to represent any other color in the visible spectrum. This structure is shown on the right side of Figure 3-1.

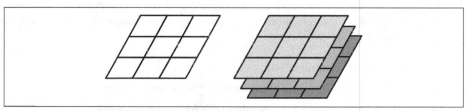

Figure 3-1. The diagram on the left represents the pixels of a single channel image; the diagram on the right represents the structure of a three-channel image, such as an RGB photograph

The typical representation of images, as an *n*-dimensional grid, means that they contain spatial information about the relative proximity of different aspects of a scene to one another. This information is extremely valuable in understanding what a scene contains. There are entire classes of *image processing* and *computer vision* algorithms that make use of this information.

Images don't have to represent visible light, or even light at all. They can represent infrared light (often used to measure the temperature of parts of a scene), time of flight (in the case of LIDAR, which measures how long it takes light to bounce back from each part of a scene), or even radio waves (think of data collected by a radio telescope, or on a radar screen).

Video

Technically another special case of time series data, video deserves its own category due to its distinct utility. A video is a sequence of images, each representing a snapshot of a scene at a point in time. As a time series, video has a sampling rate—although in the case of video it is typically referred to as the frame rate, since each individual image in the sequence is known as a frame.

Video is a very rich format—it contains both spatial information (within each frame) and temporal information (between each frame). This richness means that it tends to occupy a lot of memory, so it tends to require more capable computing devices.

How Are Values Represented?

All of the preceding categories represent individual sensor readings using single numeric values. For example, a time series is a sequence of individual readings, and an image is a grid composed of individual readings.

Each reading is a number and can be represented on a computer in a variety of different ways. For example, here are some typical numeric types used to represent sensor data in C++:

- Boolean (1 bit): a number with two possible values
- 8-bit integer: a nondecimal number with 256 possible values
- 16-bit integer: a nondecimal number with 65,536 possible values
- 32-bit floating point:[1] can represent a wide range of numbers with up to seven decimal places, with a maximum of 3.4028235×10^{38}

By varying the numeric type used to represent a value, developers can trade numerical precision for reduced memory usage and computational complexity.

Types of Sensors and Signals

There are thousands of different types of sensors on the market. A nice way of grouping them is by their *modality*. According to Carnegie Mellon University, modality refers to the way in which something happens or is experienced (*https://oreil.ly/WaiBM*). From a human perspective, our senses of sight, hearing, or touch all have different modalities.

---

1 As described by the IEEE 754 (*https://oreil.ly/oGnUz*) standard.

There's no strictly defined list of sensor modalities, and the best way to describe them may vary between industries and applications. In the following section, we'll explore some groupings that make sense from a broad edge AI perspective:

- Acoustic and vibration
- Visual and scene
- Motion and position
- Force and tactile
- Optical, electromagnetic, and radiation
- Environmental, biological, and chemical

There are also many nonsensor data sources available to edge devices—we'll go through those, too.

Acoustic and Vibration

The ability to "hear" vibrations allows edge AI devices to detect the effects of movement, vibration, and human and animal communication at a distance. This is done with acoustic sensors, which measure the effect of vibrations that are traveling through a medium that might range from air (in the case of microphones, like the one in Figure 3-2) to water (hydrophones) or even the ground (geophones and seismometers). Some vibration sensors are designed specifically for use with heavy industrial machinery.

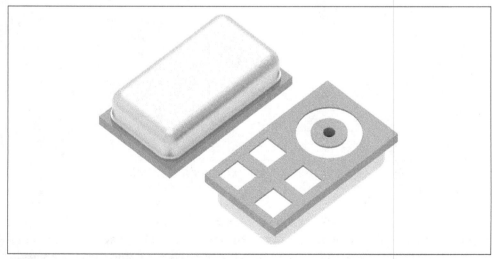

Figure 3-2. A 3D rendering of a surface-mount microelectromechanical systems (MEMS) microphone, found in many modern products

An acoustic sensor typically provides a time series that describes the variation of pressure in its medium. Acoustic signals contain information across various frequencies—for example, the high and low notes of a singing voice. Acoustic sensors generally operate in a certain frequency range, and they may not have a linear response to frequencies even within that range.

In addition to their nonlinear frequency response, the ability of acoustic sensors to capture high frequencies depends on their sample rate. To accurately capture a high-frequency signal, an acoustic sensor must have a sufficiently high sample rate. When building an edge AI application for acoustics, make sure you understand the properties of the signal you are trying to measure, and choose sensor hardware that is a good fit.

Visual and Scene

It is common for edge AI applications to need to understand the scenery around them in a passive manner, without reaching out to touch it. The most common sensors used for this task are image sensors, ranging from tiny, low-power cameras (as seen in Figure 3-3) to super high-quality, multimegapixel sensors. As described previously, the images obtained from image sensors are represented as arrays of pixel values.

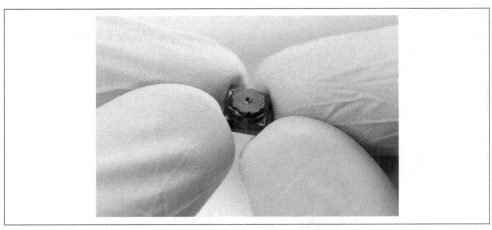

Figure 3-3. A tiny image sensor, the type of form factor that might be used in an embedded device

Image sensors capture light using a grid of sensor elements. In a camera, light from a scene is focused onto the sensor by a lens. The area that can be imaged by a camera is known as its field of view, and it depends on the size of the lens and the image sensor.

Some common variations in image sensors:

Color channels
> For visual light, sensors can commonly capture data in grayscale or color (red, green, and blue, or RGB).

Spectral response
> The wavelengths of light the image sensor is sensitive to, which may exceed the range of human vision. This can even include infrared radiation, allowing sensors known as thermal cameras to "see" heat.

Pixel size
> Larger sensors can capture more light per pixel, increasing their sensitivity.

Sensor resolution
> The more elements on a sensor, the finer detail it can capture.

Frame rate
> How frequently a sensor can capture an image, typically in frames per second.

Since illumination of a scene is sometimes required, it is common to pair image sensors with light emitters—in both visible and invisible ranges of the spectrum. For example, an infrared LED can be used with an infrared-sensitive camera to illuminate dark scenes without disturbing humans or animals with visible light.

Larger, higher resolution sensors typically require more energy. High-resolution sensors produce large amounts of data, which can be difficult to process on smaller edge AI devices.

A relatively new group of image sensors, known as event cameras, work slightly differently. Instead of capturing the entire visual field at a specific frame rate, each pixel in the camera responds individually to changes in brightness but remains silent if nothing is happening. The result is a time series of individual pixel changes that can be easier for edge AI devices to process than a large sequence of full frames.

Another interesting type of image sensor is known as range imaging sensors. These allow devices to image their surroundings in three dimensions—often by emitting light and measuring how long it takes to bounce back, a technique known as "time of flight." A common time-of-flight sensor technology is known as LIDAR. LIDAR sensors work by scanning their surroundings with a laser beam, measuring how much of the light is reflected back to the sensor. This allows them to visualize an area in three dimensions, as shown in Figure 3-4.

Figure 3-4. This image from the PandaSet (https://pandaset.org) open source LIDAR dataset shows a typical LIDAR "point cloud," with each point in the 3D visualization representing a distance that was measured by the laser; the inset photograph at the top right shows the same scene from the perspective of an image sensor

LIDAR and other time-of-flight sensors are typically much larger, more complex, expensive, and energy intensive than standard image sensors. The large amounts of data they generate can be difficult to process and store on edge devices, which also limits their utility. LIDAR is typically used for mapping environments—including to help self-driving vehicles navigate the world.

Radar, or radio detection and ranging, is also occasionally used by edge devices to understand the position of surrounding objects in three dimensions, potentially at long range. Like LIDAR, it is complex and has high energy requirements—but is definitely an option if your use case requires it.

Motion and Position

It can be useful for edge AI devices to understand both where they are and where they might be headed. Fortunately, there are many different types of sensors that can help. This is a broad category, ranging from the simplest (mechanical tilt switches) to the most complicated (the satellite-enabled GPS [Global Positioning System]). As a whole, they allow devices to understand their position and motion within the world.

Here's a list of typical motion and position sensors for edge AI applications:

Tilt sensor
A mechanical switch that is on or off depending on its orientation. Super cheap and easy to use.

Accelerometer

Measures the acceleration (the change in velocity over time) of an object across one or more axes, often at a high frequency. Accelerometers are the Swiss Army knives of motion sensing, used for everything from recognizing the characteristic motions of sporting activities (in smart watches) to sensing the vibrations of industrial equipment (in predictive maintenance). They also always know which way is down, thanks to the pull of gravity.

Gyroscope

Measures the rate of rotation of an object. Often paired with an accelerometer to give a picture of the motion of an object in 3D space.

Rotary or linear encoder

Measures the exact position of either a shaft or axle (rotary) or a linear mechanism (like the position of an inkjet printer head). Often used in robotics to capture the positions of robots' wheels, limbs, and other appendages.

Time of flight

A sensor that uses an electromagnetic emission (light or radio) to measure the distance from a sensor to whatever object is directly in its line of sight.

Real-time locating systems (RTLS)

Systems that use multiple transceivers in fixed locations around a building or site to track the position of individual objects, such as pallets in a warehouse.

Inertial measurement unit (IMU)

A system that uses multiple sensors to approximate the current position of a device based on its motion as measured from an internal frame of reference (as opposed to using external signals such as GPS).

Global Positioning System (GPS)

A passive system that uses radio signals from satellites to determine the location of a device, down to a few meters. Requires line of sight from the device to several satellites.

Motion and position are typically represented as a time series of sensor readings. Given the number of sensor types in this category, there are options for every cost and energy budget. Typically, the more confidence in absolute position required, the more cost and complexity involved.

Force and Tactile

From switches to load cells, force and tactile sensors help edge AI devices measure the physicality of their environment. They can be helpful in facilitating user interaction, understanding the flow of liquids and gases, or measuring the mechanical strain on an object.

Here are some typical force and tactile sensors:

Buttons and switches
Traditional switches used as simple buttons for human interaction, but also serve as sensors that provide a binary signal that indicates when a device is colliding with something.

Capacitive touch sensors
Measure the amount that a surface is being touched by a conductive object, like a human finger. This is how modern touchscreens work.

Strain gauges and flex sensors
Measure how much an object is being deformed, which can be interesting for detecting damage to objects and for building tactile human interface devices.

Load cells
Measure the precise amount of physical load that is applied to them. They come in a wide range of sizes, from tiny (useful for measuring the weight of small objects) to gigantic (measuring strain in bridges and skyscrapers).

Flow sensors
Designed to measure the rate of flow in liquids and gases, such as water in a pipe.

Pressure sensors
Used to measure pressure of a gas or liquid, either environmental (such as atmospheric pressure) or inside a system (such as inside a car tire).

Force and tactile sensors are typically simple, low energy, and easy to work with. Their measurements are easy to represent as time series. They are especially useful when building tactile user interfaces or detecting when a robot (or other device that can move around) has hit something.

Optical, Electromagnetic, and Radiation

This category includes sensors that are designed to measure electromagnetic radiation, magnetic fields, and high energy particles, in addition to basic electrical properties such as current and voltage. This may sound exotic, but it includes familiar things like measuring the color of light.

Here are some typical optical, electromagnetic, and radiation sensors:

Photosensor
A category of sensor that detects light at various wavelengths, both visible and invisible to the human eye. This can be useful for many things, from measuring ambient light levels to detecting when a beam of light has been broken.

Color sensor

Uses photosensors to measure the precise color of a surface, which can be helpful for recognizing different types of objects.

Spectroscopy sensor

Uses photosensors to measure the way that various wavelengths of light are absorbed and reflected by materials, giving an edge AI system insight into their composition.

Magnetometer

Measures the strength and direction of magnetic fields. A subtype of magnetometer is a digital compass, which can indicate the direction of north.

Inductive proximity sensor

Uses an electromagnetic field to detect nearby metal. It is commonly used to detect vehicles for traffic monitoring.

Electromagnetic field (EMF) meter

Measures the strength of electromagnetic fields. This includes those emitted incidentally, for example by industrial equipment, or those intentionally emitted by radio transmitters.

Current sensor

Measures the flow of current through a conductor. This can be useful in monitoring industrial equipment since fluctuations in current can provide information about the functioning of the equipment.

Voltage sensor

Measures the amount of voltage across an object.

Semiconductor detector

Measures ionizing radiation, which is composed of extremely fast-moving particles, typically created by the decay of radioactive substances.

As with many other sensors, this category generally provides a time series of measurements. While useful for measuring ambient conditions, the sensors described here can also be useful in arrangements where they detect emissions that are produced deliberately by a device. For example, a photosensor can be paired with a light emitter on the other side of a hallway to detect when someone is moving past.

Environmental, Biological, and Chemical

A loose category that includes many different types of sensors; environmental, biological, and chemical sensing allows edge AI devices to sniff the composition of the world around them. Some common types of sensors include:

Temperature sensor
Measures temperature, either of the device itself or of a distant source of infrared emissions.

Gas sensor
Many different sensors exist to measure concentrations of different gases. Common gas sensors include humidity sensors (which measure water vapor), volatile organic compound (VOC) sensors, which measure a selection of common organic compounds, and carbon dioxide sensors.

Particulate matter sensor
Measures the concentration of tiny particles in a sample of air and are commonly used to monitor pollution levels.

Biosignals sensor
Covers a vast range of signals that are present in the bodies of living things—for example, measurement of electrical activity in the human heart (electrocardiography) and brain (electroencephalography).

Chemical sensor
Many different sensors available that are designed to measure the presence or concentration of specific chemicals.

This category of sensors generally provides a time series of readings. Due to their need to interact chemically and physically with the environment, they can sometimes be difficult to work with—for example, calibration against known quantities of chemicals is often required, and sometimes sensors require a warm-up period before they can take a reliable reading. It is common for environmental sensors to degrade over time and require replacement.

Other Signals

In addition to gathering signals from the physical world, many edge AI devices have access to a rich feed of virtual data. This can be split roughly into two groups: introspective data, about the state of the device itself, and extrospective data, about the systems and networks that the device is connected to.

Depending on the device, various types of internal state may be available. These could include:

Device logs
These track the lifecycle of the device since it was powered up. This could provide information about many different things: configuration changes, duty cycle, interrupts, errors, or anything else you choose to log.

Internal resource utilization

This might include available memory, power consumption, clock speed, operating system resources, and usage of peripherals.

Communications

A device can keep track of its physical connections, radio communications, networking configuration and activity, and the resulting energy usage.

Internal sensors

Some devices have internal sensors; for example, many system-on-chip devices include a temperature sensor to monitor their CPU.

One interesting usage of introspective data is in preserving battery life. Lithium rechargeable batteries can lose capacity if they are continually held at 100% charge while plugged in. Apple's iPhone uses an edge AI feature known as Optimized Battery Charging (*https://oreil.ly/rWJbA*) in order to avoid this problem. It uses an on-device machine learning model to learn the user's charging routine, then uses this model to minimize the amount of time the battery spends full—while ensuring the battery is still charged when the user needs it.

Extrospective data streams, which come from outside the device, can be extremely rich in information. Here are some possible sources:

Data from connected systems

It's common for edge AI devices to be deployed in a network, and data forwarded by adjacent devices can be used as input to AI algorithms. For example, an IoT gateway could use edge AI to process and make decisions based on the data collected by its nodes.

Remote commands

An edge AI device might receive control instructions from another system or user. For instance, the user of a drone could request that it move to a certain coordinate in 3D space.

Data from APIs

An edge AI device can request data from remote servers to feed into its algorithms. For example, a home heating system equipped with edge AI might request weather forecast data from an online API and use the information to help decide when to turn the heating on.

Network data

This might include network structure, routing information, network activity, and even the contents of data packets.

Some of the most interesting edge AI systems make use of all of these data streams together. Imagine an agricultural technology system that helps a farmer take care of crops. It might include remote sensors out in the fields, connections to important online data sources (like the weather forecast, or the price of fertilizer), and a control interface used by the farmer. As an edge AI system, it could potentially operate without an internet connection—but if it had one, it could make use of valuable information.

In more complex system architectures, edge AI also pairs nicely with server-side AI; we'll learn more about that later in this chapter.

Processors for Edge AI

One of the most exciting parts of edge AI is the vast—and growing—array of hardware that applications can make use of. In this section, we'll explore the high-level categories of hardware and learn what makes each one suited to a particular niche.

We're in the midst of a Cambrian explosion of edge AI hardware, so in the time since this book was published it is likely that there are even more options than what is printed here. With a spectrum that runs from cheap, low-power microcontrollers (so-called "thin edge" devices) to lightning-fast GPU-based accelerators and edge servers (known as "thick edge"), developers can find hardware that is the perfect fit for almost any application.

Edge AI Hardware Architecture

The *architecture* of a hardware system is the way its components connect to each other. Figure 3-5 shows the typical hardware architecture of an edge device.

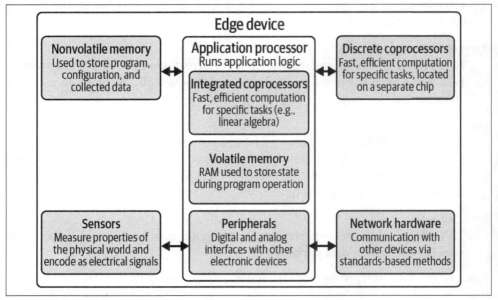

Figure 3-5. Architecture of an edge device

The beating heart of the device is the *application processor*. This is the general-purpose processor that coordinates the application and, by default, runs all of the algorithms and logic that make up its program.

In many cases, the application processor will have *integrated coprocessors*: built-in additional hardware that is highly efficient at performing certain computations. For example, many processors have a built-in floating-point unit (FPU) designed to quickly perform floating-point calculations. Medium- and high-end MCUs increasingly have integrated hardware that can accelerate functions relevant to edge AI, such as digital signal processing and linear algebra.

The application processor also integrates the *volatile memory* (such as RAM) that is used as working memory during program execution. That said, it's also common to have additional RAM that is external to the processor itself and lives on a separate chip.

On Die Versus Off Die

A computer system typically consists of integrated circuits (ICs) made from silicon chips attached to a printed circuit board (PCB). For example, the application processor is an IC. A silicon chip consists of a literal piece of silicon, upon which is etched a series of complex patterns that make up a processor. This piece of silicon is known as a *die*.

When referring to a processor and the other components it integrates with, it's common to hear the terms *on die* and *off die*. On-die components are located on the same piece of silicon as the processor itself, whereas off-die components are located in separate ICs attached to the same PCB.

Because on-die components are physically closer to the main processor, they're typically faster and more energy efficient: it takes less time and energy to send data back and forth between them. However, the more items located on the same die, the bigger the die has to be—and large dies tend to be expensive and power hungry.

Every embedded hardware design has to strike a balance between what is included on die and off die. For example, if efficiency is the highest priority it may make sense to choose a processor with on-die features. If cost is more important, off die may be the way to go.

Many designs make use of both on-die and off-die components. For example, a system may have a small amount of on-die RAM for program execution combined with a larger amount of off-die RAM used to buffer raw sensor data that is waiting to be processed.

RAM is very fast memory, but it uses a lot of energy, and the contents of RAM are lost when the device shuts down. It's quite expensive and takes up a lot of physical space, so it's often a very limited resource.

The application processor is connected to *nonvolatile memory*, commonly known as ROM (read-only memory) or flash,[2] which can similarly be located either on die or off die (in Figure 3-5 it is shown off die). Nonvolatile memory is used to store things that don't often change and need to be preserved when the system is shut down. This might include software programs, user configuration, and machine learning models. It's slow to read and extremely slow to write.

Many designs have *discrete coprocessors*. Similar to integrated coprocessors, these exist to perform fast and efficient mathematics for specific purposes. Unlike integrated coprocessors, they are located off die. They may be far more powerful (and power hungry) than the application processor: for example, a low-power SoC may be combined with a powerful GPU.

The *peripherals* of the processor provide its interface with the rest of the world, via various standards.[3] The most common things peripherals are used to connect with are *sensors* and *network hardware*.

Microcontrollers and Digital Signal Processors

It could be argued convincingly that microcontrollers are the foundation of our modern world. They're the tiny, cheap computers that animate everything from car engines to smart appliances. Microcontrollers are manufactured in astonishing volume; it's projected that 26.89 billion of them will be shipped in 2022 (*https://oreil.ly/d4KPy*)—that's three and a half for every human being on the planet.

> **MCUs**
>
> Microcontrollers are often referred to as MCUs, an acronym for microcontroller units.

Microcontrollers are typically used for single-purpose applications, like controlling a piece of machinery. This means that they can get away with being a lot simpler than other types of computers that need to run multiple programs—for example, they generally do not use an operating system.

---

2 While flash memory can be reprogrammed, it's still referred to as ROM in an embedded context.

3 Peripheral interfaces, such as GPIO, I2C, SPI, and UART, are important when designing hardware but are beyond the scope of this book. Most modern embedded processors have decent peripheral support.

Instead, their software (known as *firmware*) is run directly on the hardware and incorporates the low-level instructions necessary to drive any peripherals.[4] This can make software engineering for microcontrollers quite challenging, but it gives developers a lot more control over exactly what is going on when their programs run.

One of the distinguishing characteristics of microcontrollers is that the majority of their components are implemented on a single piece of silicon; this is key to their relatively low cost. In addition to a processor, a microcontroller is generally equipped with flash memory (for storing programs and other useful data), RAM (for storing state during program execution), and various technologies for communicating with other devices (such as sensors) using either digital or analog signals.

The microcontroller world is incredibly diverse—part of the reason they are so valuable is that they are available in variants to suit every imaginable situation. For the purposes of this book, we'll divide them into three main categories: low-end, high-end, and digital signal processors.

Low-end MCUs

Many MCUs are designed specifically for low cost, small size, and energy efficiency. The trade-off is that they have limited computational resources and capabilities. Here are some typical specifications:

- 4-bit to 16-bit architecture
- <100 MHz clock speed
- 2 KB to 64 KB of flash memory
- 64 bytes to 2 KB of RAM
- Digital input and output
- Current draw: single digits to tens of milliamps at ~1.5–5 volts when running, and microamps when sleeping while waiting for input
- Cost: one or two dollars per unit when bought in large volumes

---

4 Another characteristic of firmware is that, unlike an operating system, firmware is not typically intended to be modified by the end user.

> ## A Note on Power
>
> The amount of energy that a microcontroller consumes depends on many factors, most of which are in the developers' hands to control. Among other things, you can decrease power consumption by running the processor at a reduced speed, switching off features when not in use, and putting the entire microcontroller into idle mode when it is not currently processing data.
>
> This flexibility, coupled with the general diversity of the microcontroller market, makes it tricky to quote exact numbers for power consumption. If you're designing against tight power constraints, you'll want to evaluate the hardware and measure energy use for yourself.

Many low-end MCUs used today are based on designs that have been in use since the 1980s.[5] While technology has continued to improve, there's always a need for simple, low-cost and low-power hardware, so these chips are here to stay. They are extremely common across many industries.

Low-end MCUs have some significant disadvantages when it comes to edge AI. Since they lack memory and compute, they aren't well suited to dealing with large amounts of data or complex signal processing. They generally do not have any hardware implementation of floating-point arithmetic, meaning calculations involving rational numbers can be incredibly slow. These attributes limit the types of edge AI algorithms they can run.

The typical applications for low-end MCUs play to their benefits: high-reliability automotive and medical devices and low-cost appliances, gadgets, and infrastructure. One popular low-end MCU is the Atmel 8-bit AVR platform (*https://oreil.ly/Buwcj*). While they are an important part of the MCU world, their computational limitations mean that low-end MCUs probably shouldn't be your first choice of target for an edge AI application.

That said, as we mentioned in the first section of the book, edge AI programs don't always have to be computationally challenging. Low-end MCUs are perfectly capable of running complex conditional logic, which may be enough for what you need to do. They can also form part of a network of connected devices that makes use of edge AI—for example, a low-end MCU could capture sensor data and forward it to a more sophisticated device for decision making.

---

5 The Intel 8051 (*https://oreil.ly/5DV2e*) was first developed in 1980 and is still in use today.

High-end MCUs

At the other end of the MCU spectrum, today's most powerful microcontrollers have enough compute to give a '90s vintage personal computer a run for its money. In many cases, they still manage to be highly energy efficient. Here are some typical specs:

- 32-bit architecture
- <1000 MHz clock speed
- 16 KB to 2 MB of flash
- 2 KB to 1 MB of RAM
- Optional hardware support for faster math
- Floating-point unit (FPU)
- Single instruction, multiple data (SIMD) instructions
- Optional multiple processor cores
- Digital and analog input and output
- Current draw: low single digits to high tens of milliamps at ~1.5–5 volts; micro-amps while sleeping
- Cost: from low single digits to low tens of dollars per unit

High-end MCUs provide a big jump in performance, thanks to faster clock speeds and a 32-bit architecture.[6] In addition, many models of MCUs have hardware support for some neat tricks that increase computation speed. One of these, SIMD, allows the processor to run several computations in parallel—which can be extremely helpful when running signal processing and machine learning applications, which involve a lot of computation.

Increasingly, high-end MCUs are designed with edge AI applications in mind. It's common for vendors to offer software and libraries that help optimize edge AI code to run efficiently on-device. Another big benefit is a trend toward providing larger amounts of flash and RAM—very helpful for manipulating data and storing large machine learning models.

High-end MCUs are used in a huge range of use cases, from sensing and IoT to digital gadgets, smart appliances, and wearables. At the time of writing, they represent the sweet spot for cost, energy usage, and computational ability for embedded machine learning. They have just enough power to run capable deep learning

---

6 A 32-bit processor can operate on twice the data in one go as a 16-bit processor can. This means data can be processed more quickly. It also supports a larger amount of RAM.

models—including deep learning models that can process visual information—but they remain simple enough to embed very cheaply into a wide range of applications.

Microcontrollers based on Arm's Cortex-M cores (*https://oreil.ly/nuhBH*) are extremely popular, such as the Nordic nRF52840 (*https://oreil.ly/uZfax*) and the STMicroelectronics STM32H743VI (*https://oreil.ly/SGkdC*). There are also popular options based on the RISC-V (*https://oreil.ly/YpH2r*) architecture, such as the Expressif ESP32 (*https://oreil.ly/OzsLd*).

As edge AI becomes more important, it's increasingly common to pair general-purpose, high-end microcontrollers with purpose-built coprocessors designed to accelerate deep learning workloads. We'll cover that more in "Deep Learning Accelerators" on page 77.

Performance Characteristics

An average high-end microcontroller can process audio using deep learning in near real time, and low-resolution video at a second or so per frame.

Digital signal processors (DSPs)

An interesting subcategory, DSPs are special microcontrollers that are designed to be highly efficient at transforming digital signals. Instead of general-purpose computation, their architecture is designed to run specific algorithms and mathematical operations as quickly as possible—including things like multiply–accumulates and Fourier transforms, which we'll encounter in Chapter 4.

As luck would have it, many of those mathematical operations are very helpful in edge AI, both for processing data and for running machine learning models. This can make DSPs a valuable tool. The downside of DSPs is that they are not designed for general-purpose compute, meaning that they may not be suitable for running the non–edge AI parts of your application.

Today's high-end MCUs often have some of the features of DSPs, such as SIMD instructions that can help increase throughput for signal processing tasks—in fact, some are described as "digital signal controllers" in order to highlight these abilities. However, dedicated DSPs can still be useful. For example, many smartphones that include voice assistants (such as the Google Assistant) include a DSP chip in order to run an always-on keyword-spotting model without hurting battery life.

Heterogeneous Compute

Hardware designers aren't limited to choosing a single microcontroller for a given application. It's actually quite common to combine multiple microprocessors in a single product. For instance, an edge AI device may include a small, low-power MCU to run its basic operations—alongside a large, powerful MCU that is used for occasional signal processing and machine learning workloads.

This type of setup is known as heterogeneous compute, and it's increasingly important in edge AI because it enables true concurrency: the ability to perform more than one task at a time. One of the big challenges with heterogeneous compute is deciding how to split a computational workload between two processors in order to maximize efficiency. If you can do it right, there are major rewards.

Some architectures for edge AI application, such as those that use cascading models (see "Cascading flow" on page 283), lend themselves particularly well to heterogeneous compute. The rise of deep learning accelerators (see section "Deep Learning Accelerators" on page 77) is making it an increasingly important concept.

System-on-Chip

After microcontrollers, the next most common type of edge compute comes in the form of system-on-chip (SoC) devices. While a microcontroller is a stripped-down, optimized version of a computer with all the fat trimmed away, SoC devices attempt to squeeze all of the functionality of an entire traditional computer system into a single chip.

Unlike microcontrollers, whose software interacts directly with the hardware, SoC devices run traditional operating systems that abstract away a lot of the hardware so that developers can focus entirely on their application code. Developers can use the same tools and environments they use to write server and desktop applications, including high-level languages like Python (modern microcontrollers are typically programmed in C or C++).

There are two costs associated with this ease of use: efficiency and complexity. SoCs are generally a lot less energy efficient than microcontrollers, which limits their fields of application. They are still an order of magnitude more efficient than traditional computer systems with separate peripherals, but they're nowhere near as good as microcontrollers for keeping energy usage to a minimum. This additional energy usage may also introduce heat management issues.

The additional complexity represented by an operating system is another burden on SoC devices. With huge amounts of OS code being run alongside a developer's application, it's more difficult to guarantee reliability in the field.

SoCs tend to be a lot more powerful than microcontrollers, and they have a lot more features. Here are some typical stats:

- 64-bit architecture
- >1 GHz clock speed
- Multiple processor cores
- External RAM and flash (generally multiple gigabytes)
- 2D or 3D graphics processing unit
- Wireless networking
- High-performance digital input and output
- Current draw: hundreds of milliamps at ~5 volts
- Cost: tens of dollars per unit

Performance Characteristics

An average SoC can process audio and high-resolution video using deep learning in near real time.

Despite being far less efficient than microcontrollers, SoCs have been revolutionary. They allow the power of a formidable general-purpose computer to be deployed in an extremely small form factor. In the modern world, SoCs are pervasive—they power our mobile phones, televisions, car entertainment systems, industrial hardware, security systems, IoT gateways, and pretty much anything else that requires flexible computational power in a small package.

Their power, flexibility, and ease of use makes them especially valuable for edge AI. Developers can use familiar tools to develop applications that run on SoCs, and they have enough memory and processing power to run complex algorithms, such as relatively large deep learning models. There are very few types of edge AI algorithm that will not run on an SoC. Ease of use makes SoCs a great choice for prototyping edge AI applications even if the end goal is to move to cheaper or more efficient hardware.

Well-known SoC products include the Qualcomm Snapdragon (*https://oreil.ly/b0Va-*) and the Broadcom BCM58712 (*https://oreil.ly/ZbqES*), which is used in the Raspberry Pi development board (mentioned in the sidebar "Boards and Devices" on page 79). Many popular SoCs are based on Arm Cortex-A (*https://oreil.ly/GyNNz*) processor cores.

Embedded Linux

Linux has become a very common choice of operating system for SoC devices. It's open source, which means it's free to use, and has a lot of community support. Being able to use familiar Unix development tools makes it easy for those with Unix experience to work with embedded Linux systems.

Deep Learning Accelerators

Both microcontrollers and SoCs are typically general-purpose computers—they are designed to be as flexible as possible. However, if you're willing to sacrifice some flexibility, it's possible to design integrated circuits that run certain operations *extremely* fast.

With the advent of deep learning (see "Deep learning" on page 106) on embedded devices, semiconductor companies have started to produce accelerators that can be paired with microcontrollers and SoCs to allow deep learning models to be run faster and more efficiently. The mathematics of deep learning is based around linear algebra, so deep learning accelerators—also known as *neural processing units* (NPUs)—are designed to perform linear algebra efficiently.

There are various types of deep learning accelerators with their own trade-offs between energy use and flexibility. At one end of the spectrum, devices like Syntiant's NDP10x series (*https://oreil.ly/XDxoQ*) have hardware implementations of specific deep learning model architectures (we'll learn more about these later) that can run quickly with incredibly low energy. Since the algorithm itself is baked into the silicon, these devices are not very flexible—but they can be extremely efficient.

At the other end of the spectrum, devices based on graphics processing unit (GPU) technology, like Nvidia's Jetson (*https://oreil.ly/MVga8*) and Google's Coral (*https://coral.ai/products*), offer a huge amount of flexibility and can run basically any type of deep learning model. The trade-off for this flexibility is that they are nowhere near as energy efficient.

Between the two ends of the spectrum are many different types of devices with varying degrees of flexibility and efficiency—like Syntiant's NDP120 (*https://oreil.ly/Y9ZeL*) or Arm's Ethos-U55 (*https://oreil.ly/KS_Dv*) design.

Some types of accelerator use alternatives to traditional deep learning mathematics. For example, BrainChip's Akida (*https://oreil.ly/JgaIv*), described as a neuromorphic processor, uses spiking neural networks (see "Compression and optimization" on page 117) to deliver a unique set of trade-offs, including greater energy efficiency.

Performance Characteristics

Deep learning accelerators tend to be extremely fast—you can expect enough computational power to process audio and video in real time. Some devices can even process multiple streams in parallel.

Generally, deep learning accelerators are paired with either microcontrollers or SoCs. The conventional processor runs the application logic, and the accelerator runs the deep learning workload. Many designs combine the microprocessor and accelerator in a single package and provide special tools to help developers split the processing between them.

Early deep learning accelerators provided very little freedom of choice with regards to the types of deep learning models that are supported, but as the field matures devices are becoming more flexible. We're still in the very early days, so you can expect big advances and efficiency gains over time. In the long term, expect absurdly capable devices with miniscule power budgets—real-time video processing or language transcription that can run for years on a small battery.

FPGAs and ASICs

For the ultimate performance and efficiency benefits, designing your own processor circuit is an option. It's difficult, time consuming, and expensive, so it isn't something to be taken lightly, but for certain applications it might make sense.

Field programmable gate arrays, or FPGAs, are silicon integrated circuits that can be reprogrammed on demand to implement custom hardware designs. They allow engineers to create a custom processor design that implements a specific algorithm as efficiently as possible, then load it onto a device for deployment. The designs are created using special programming languages called hardware description languages, or HDLs.

Application-specific integrated circuits, or ASICs, are integrated circuits that are customized for particular applications. Unlike FPGAs, they can't be reprogrammed—their logic is permanently written into silicon. You can buy predesigned ASICs designed for specific purposes, such as Himax's WE-I Plus (*https://oreil.ly/oI4bv*), or design your own.

Development with FPGAs is substantially cheaper than with ASICs, but the per-device cost is higher, as is the power consumption. It's common for companies to use FPGAs for prototypes or small production runs and ASICs for high volume. The engineering cost of creating an ASIC puts them out of reach for the majority of companies.

FPGA developer tools are becoming easier to use and more accessible, but they're still a relatively niche option in edge AI. Researchers are working on tooling that can automatically convert deep learning models into efficient FPGA implementations, so it's likely that FPGAs will play an increasingly large role in edge AI over time. Here are some interesting projects in the space at the time of publication:

- Google's CFU Playground (*https://oreil.ly/Fhf-9*), which helps developers create deep learning accelerators using FPGAs

- Tensil.ai (*https://www.tensil.ai*), a machine learning model compiler and hardware generator for FPGAs

Boards and Devices

A processor isn't much use by itself—it needs to be mounted onto a board along with the other components that make up a full device—power supply, sensors and peripherals, and connectors. Most mass-produced edge AI products use custom printed circuit boards designed for their specific application.

Since these custom boards take time to design and produce, a lot of early engineering work is done with *development boards*, also known as *dev boards*. These are ready-to-use devices, sold by hardware manufacturers, that feature a given processor along with everything needed to connect to it and develop software (see Figure 3-6).

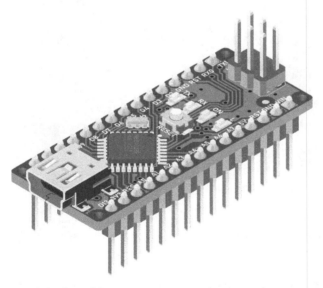

Figure 3-6. A typical dev board features a processor, power supply, input and output pins, connectors, and often some sensors that are connected to the processor and ready to use

They allow embedded engineers to evaluate various processors for a particular use case, and to rapidly build prototypes.

The computational requirements of edge AI algorithms means there's an interplay between hardware and algorithm choice, which makes development boards extremely valuable. With access to a few development boards, developers can quickly test their algorithms on real processors and find the ideal balance between performance, energy usage, and cost.

While traditionally only used during early prototyping, some manufacturers have realized the potential benefits of development boards for production use. If you're making a small batch of hardware, it may not be worth the extra cost and time to design a custom printed circuit board—which would only be economical if produced at large volume. Instead, you might choose to use a predesigned platform such as the Arduino Portenta (*https://oreil.ly/_ezK6*), which features an MCU and a flexible set of inputs and outputs that allow you to easily integrate it into other systems.

These types of devices are available for SoCs and accelerators, too—for example, Raspberry Pi (*https://www.raspberrypi.com*) produce a range of fully integrated single board computers (SBCs) (see Figure 3-7) based on powerful SoCs, and Nvidia's Jetson accelerators (*https://oreil.ly/t0—j*) allow developers to quickly run code on accelerator hardware. Many of these platforms provide a range of compatible devices, so you can prototype using a single board computer and then deploy to a system on module (SOM) designed to integrate into your own hardware without any code changes.

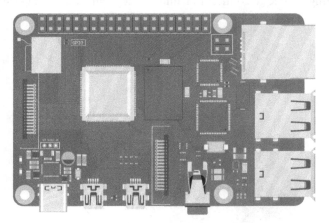

Figure 3-7. A single board computer includes a processor, memory, power supply, input and output connectors, network interfaces, and everything else required for plug and play use

Dev boards are typically just bare circuit boards without any enclosure, so they can't be used in the field without at least a bit of design work. If you'd prefer a fully finished device, industrial IoT gateways place SoCs in rugged enclosures with standard I/O ports, networking hardware, and power supply. They can be fairly expensive, but they may save time and money versus designing and manufacturing a full piece of hardware.

The most common type of prebuilt edge AI device—by far—is the smartphone. There are entire books on integrating AI into smartphone apps, such as Laurence Moroney's *AI and Machine Learning for On-Device Development* (O'Reilly, 2021), so we won't be covering that topic here. More within our scope is the use of MCUs and DSPs to power specific smartphone features, such as digital assistants that wake up when specific keywords are spotted.

Beyond their integrated edge AI, smartphones can be a handy tool for edge AI developers who are prototyping applications. Since they are battery powered and have great connectivity, they can be useful for collecting initial data or testing out early versions of machine learning models during the initial stages of development, when proving feasibility is the most important thing.

Edge Servers

At the other end of the spectrum from custom silicon, it's possible to run conventional server hardware—the same that might be deployed in a data center—at the edge of the network. These powerful computers run full-scale server operating systems (typically Linux or Windows) and can be treated in the same way as any other cloud server. If they have access to AI-specific acceleration, it's likely in the form of GPUs. Some edge servers are sold in ruggedized form factors that are better suited to industrial settings (like a factory floor) than their data center dwelling equivalents.

The power of edge servers means that they can provide many of the benefits of cloud compute while maintaining the security, privacy, and convenience that comes with keeping data on-site. For some applications, they can provide the best of both worlds—high-capability hardware, low latency, reduced risk of data leakage, and economic use of bandwidth.

Another benefit of edge servers is that they can be treated as essentially just another piece of standard IT infrastructure. This means they can fit neatly into the procedures and skillsets of an existing IT department. In fact, it wasn't long ago that *all* commercial compute was done with on-premises servers. Edge compute used to be the norm for every business.

Edge servers have two major downsides: they use huge amounts of energy and they are very large. If you need vast amounts of compute located conveniently on-site, these trade-offs can be worth it. However, they are typically limited to fixed locations such as buildings and factories where there is spare room and a reliable power supply.

If full-sized edge servers feel like overkill for your application (and they probably are), Linux SoCs offer a great compromise. As standard Linux boxes, an IT department can treat them like any other server—but they are available in tiny, power-efficient forms.

Multi-Device Architectures

Edge AI applications aren't always implemented directly on the devices that host the actual sensors. Sometimes, it makes sense to use a multi-device architecture. For example, sensors on a fleet of shipping pallets might use low-power radio to report data back to a gateway device mounted in a truck. The gateway, with less constraints on energy use and insight into the data from multiple pallets, could run the sophisticated edge AI logic that makes decisions with the data. Figure 3-8 shows how this might look.

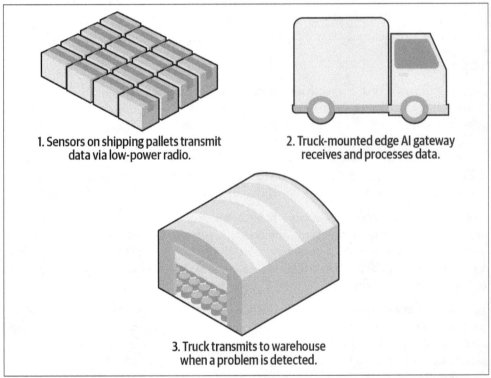

1. Sensors on shipping pallets transmit data via low-power radio.

2. Truck-mounted edge AI gateway receives and processes data.

3. Truck transmits to warehouse when a problem is detected.

Figure 3-8. It's common to see architectures involve multiple devices

Things can get even funkier with heterogeneous compute (see the sidebar "Heterogeneous Compute" on page 75) in the mix. A single device might contain multiple types of processors: for example, one for running application code and another for running ML algorithms. A complete system might be composed of many devices, some with multiple processors, that collect and process data at many different points depending on which BLERP benefits are needed. This type of solution can even involve cloud computation.

A great example of this type of architecture is a smart speaker with a voice assistant. Typically, they have at least two processors. The first is a low-power, always-on chip that runs DSP and a machine learning model to listen for wake words without using too much energy.

The second is an application processor, which is woken up by the always-on chip when the wake word is detected. The application processor might run a more sophisticated model to try to catch any false positives that got past the always-on chip. Together, these two processors can identify wake words without violating user privacy by streaming private conversations to the cloud.

Once the wake word has been confirmed, the application processor streams the audio to a cloud server, which performs speech recognition and natural language processing in order to come up with an appropriate response. The general flow is shown in Figure 3-9.

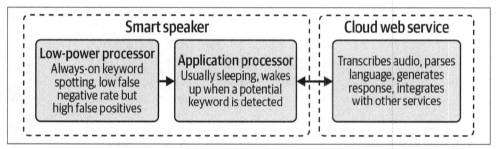

Figure 3-9. The low-power processor aims to catch as many potential keywords as possible; the application processor wakes up to evaluate any possible matches and invokes the cloud web service if a match is confirmed

When designing a system, don't be afraid to consider using multiple devices to tackle some of the trade-offs involved with different device types. Some common situations where it can be helpful are:

- Monitoring large numbers of individual entities: this can get expensive if high-end AI-capable hardware is used on every entity.

- Reducing energy use: sensors are battery powered and need to last a long time.

- Protecting privacy: sending data directly to a large device or cloud server might violate privacy norms.

- Integrating with legacy equipment: existing sensors or gateways might be supplemented with edge AI devices rather than being replaced.

Devices and Workloads

It's important to understand what each type of device is capable of. Table 3-1 provides a quick reference you can use to break down which types of devices are capable of processing which types of data. It shows the level of support for each data type on a given device: *Full*, *Limited*, or *None*.

However, bear in mind that each category is broad, and every individual device is unique. Not all high-end MCUs are the same. It's also worth noting that the state of the art moves *fast* and that this reference may quickly become outdated!

Table 3-1. Data types and devices

Device type	Low-frequency time series	High-frequency time series	Audio	Low-resolution image	High-resolution image	Video
Low-end MCU	Limited	Limited	None	None	None	None
High-end MCU	Full	Full	Full	Full	Limited	Limited
High-end MCU with accelerator	Full	Full	Full	Full	Full	Limited
DSP	Full	Full	Full	Full	Limited	Limited
SoC	Full	Full	Full	Full	Full	Full
SoC with accelerator	Full	Full	Full	Full	Full	Full
FPGA/ASIC	Full	Full	Full	Full	Full	Full
Edge server	Full	Full	Full	Full	Full	Full
Cloud	Full	Full	Full	Full	Full	Full

Summary

This chapter has introduced the key hardware that hosts artificial intelligence on the edge and the sensors that keep it fed with data. In the next chapter, we'll learn about the algorithms that make it work.

## CHAPTER 4

Algorithms for Edge AI

There are two main categories of algorithms that are important in edge AI: feature engineering and artificial intelligence. Both types have numerous subcategories; in this chapter we're going to explore a cross-section of them.

The goal is to provide an overview for each algorithm type from an engineering perspective, highlighting their typical usage, strengths, weaknesses, and suitability for deployment on edge hardware. This should give you a place to start when planning real-world projects, which we'll walk through in the coming chapters.

Feature Engineering

In data science, feature engineering is the process of turning raw data into inputs usable by the statistical tools we use to describe and model situations and processes. Feature engineering involves using your domain expertise to understand which parts of the raw data contain the relevant information, then extracting that signal from the surrounding noise.

From an edge AI perspective, feature engineering is all about transforming raw sensor data into usable information. The better your feature engineering, the easier life is for the AI algorithms that are attempting to interpret it. When working with sensor data, feature engineering naturally makes use of digital signal processing algorithms. It can also involve chopping the data into manageable chunks.

Working with Data Streams

As we've seen, the majority of sensors produce time series data. The goal of an edge AI application is to take these streams of time series data and make sense of them.

The most common way to manage streams is to chop a time series into chunks, often called windows, then analyze the chunks one at a time.[1] This produces a time series of results that you can interpret in order to understand what is going on. Figure 4-1 shows how a window is taken from a stream of data.

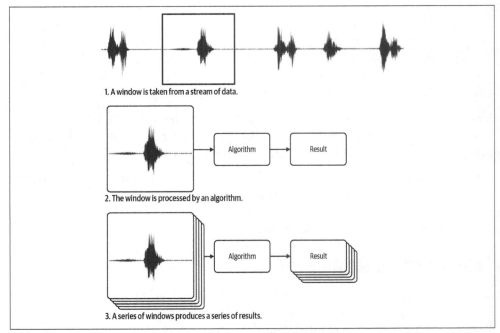

Figure 4-1. A time series is often broken into chunks, called windows, which are analyzed one at a time

It takes a certain amount of time to process a single chunk of data—we can call this the *latency* of our system. This limits how often we can take and process a window of data. The rate at which we can capture and process data is known as the *frame rate* of a system, often expressed in the number of windows that can be processed per second. Frames may be sequential or they may overlap, as shown in Figure 4-2.

---

1 The chunks can be discrete or overlapping, or even have gaps between them.

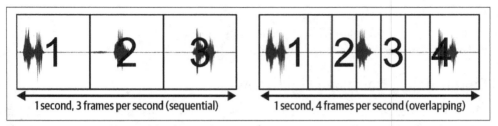

1 second, 3 frames per second (sequential) | 1 second, 4 frames per second (overlapping)

Figure 4-2. Depending on the frame rate, windows can potentially overlap; overlapping is desirable for data that contains events because it increases the chance that an entire event will fall within a window, rather than being cut short

The lower the latency, the more windows of data can be analyzed in a given period of time. The more analysis you can do, the more reliable the results. For example, imagine we are using a machine learning model to recognize a command. If the windows are too far apart, we might miss critical parts of a spoken command and not be able to recognize it (see Figure 4-3).

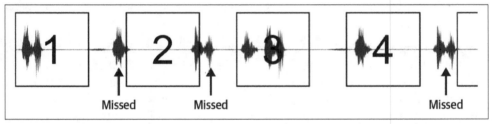

Missed   Missed   Missed

Figure 4-3. If the frame rate is too low, some parts of the signal will not be processed; if you are trying to detect short-lived events, this might mean that some events are missed

The choice of window size is very important. The larger the window, the longer it takes to process the data within it. However, larger windows contain more information about the signal—meaning they may make life easier for the signal processing and AI algorithms being used. The trade-off between window size and frame rate is an important thing to explore when you are developing a system.

As we'll see later, there are many different AI algorithms—and some of them are more sensitive to window size than others. Some algorithms (typically those that maintain an internal memory of what is occurring in a signal) are able to work well with very small window sizes, while others require large window sizes in order to properly parse a signal. Algorithm choice also impacts latency, which also constrains window size. It's a complex system of trade-offs between window size, latency, and algorithm choice.

Windowing also applies to video streams: in this case, each "window" of the video is a certain number of still images—typically a single one, but some AI algorithms can potentially analyze several images at the same time.

More sophisticated techniques for dealing with streams of data fall into the category of digital signal processing. These techniques can be combined with windowing in order to create data that feeds AI algorithms.

Digital Signal Processing Algorithms

There are hundreds of different signal processing algorithms that can help digest the signals produced by sensors. In this section, we'll cover some of the DSP algorithms that are most important for edge AI.

Resampling

All time series signals have a sample rate (also known as a frequency), often described in terms of the number of data samples per second (Hz). It's often necessary to change the sample rate of a signal. For example, you might want to reduce the rate of a signal (known as *downsampling*) if it is producing data faster than you can process it. On the other hand, you may want to increase the rate of a signal (*upsampling*) so that it can be conveniently analyzed alongside another signal that has a higher frequency.

Downsampling works by "throwing away" some of the samples in order to achieve the target frequency. For example, if you threw away every other frame of a 10 Hz (10 samples per second) signal it would become a 5 Hz signal. However, due to a phenomenon called aliasing, reducing the frequency in this way can lead to distortion in the output. To help combat this, signals must have some high-frequency information removed before they are downsampled. This is achieved using a low-pass filter, described in the next section.

Upsampling works in the opposite way—new samples are created and inserted to increase the frequency of a signal. For example, if an extra sample was inserted after every sample in a 10 Hz signal, it would become a 20 Hz signal. The difficult part is knowing what to insert! There's no way to know what would actually have been happening during the time between two samples, but a technique known as *interpolation* can be used to fill in the blanks with an approximation.

In addition to time series, images can also be upsampled and downsampled. In this case, it's the spatial resolution (pixels per image) that is being increased or decreased. Like time series resampling, the resizing of images also requires anti-aliasing or interpolation techniques.

Both upsampling and downsampling are important, but downsampling is more commonly encountered in edge AI. It's typical for sensors to produce an output at a set frequency, leaving it to the developer to downsample and obtain the frequency that best suits the rest of their signal processing pipeline.

For edge AI applications, upsampling is mostly useful if you wish to combine two signals with different frequencies into a single time series. However, this can also be achieved by downsampling the higher frequency signal, which might be computationally cheaper.

Resizing and Cropping Images

Different models of image sensors output images with varying sizes and shapes, and edge AI algorithms (such as deep learning vision models) often require images of very specific sizes. Cropping and resizing is commonly used to make images compatible with models and can involve both downsampling and upsampling, as well as throwing chunks of an image away.

Figure 4-4 shows some common ways that images are resized and cropped to fit a required input shape.

Fit shortest axis (crop)

Original image

Fit longest axis

Squash to fit

Figure 4-4. Three different ways that a rectangular image can be made to fit a square input shape

Filtering

A digital filter is a function that, applied to a time series signal, transforms it in certain ways. Many different types of filters exist, and they can be very useful in preparing data for edge AI algorithms.

Low-pass filters are designed to allow low-frequency elements of a signal to pass through, while removing high-frequency elements. The *cutoff frequency* of the filter describes the frequency beyond which high-frequency signals will be affected, and the *frequency response* describes how much those signals will be affected.

High-pass filters are the same thing in reverse, allowing frequencies *above* a cutoff frequency to pass, and attenuating (reducing) those below. A band-pass filter combines the two, allowing frequencies within a certain *band* but attenuating those outside of it.

The purpose of filtering in edge AI is to isolate the useful parts of a signal, removing parts that do not contribute to solving the problem. For example, a speech recognition application could use a band-pass filter to allow frequencies in the normal range of human speech (125 Hz to 8 kHz) while rejecting information in other frequencies. This could make it easier for a machine learning model to interpret the speech without being distracted by other information in the signal.

Filtering Noise

All signals from sensors contain some level of noise: random fluctuations in the data that happen due to slight inaccuracies in measurement. The background hum in audio recordings, or the speckles in a digital camera photograph taken at night, are typical examples of noise.

If the noise is present at specific frequencies, which is quite common, filters can be very useful in removing it. This can make it easier for some AI algorithms to interpret signals. However, some types of algorithms—such as deep learning models—are naturally able to cope with noise, so it isn't always necessary to filter it.

Filters can be applied to any type of data. For example, if a low-pass filter is applied to an image, it has a blurring or smoothing effect. If a high-pass filter is applied to the same image, it will "sharpen" details.

One type of low-pass filter is a *moving average filter*. Given a time series, it calculates a moving average of values within a certain window. In addition to smoothing the data, it has the effect of making a single value represent information from a wide range of time.

If several moving averages are calculated and stacked together, each with differing window lengths, a momentary snapshot of the signal (containing several different moving averages) contains information about changes in the signal across a window of time and a number of different frequencies. This can be a helpful technique in feature engineering, since it means an AI algorithm can observe a broad window of time using relatively few data points.

Filtering is an extremely common signal processing operation. Many embedded processors provide hardware support for some types of filtering, which reduces latency and energy usage.

Spectral analysis

A time series signal can be said to be in the *time domain*, meaning it represents how a set of variables change over time. Using some common mathematical tools, it's possible to transform a time series signal into the *frequency domain*. The values obtained through transformation describe how much of the signal lies in various frequency bands over a range of frequencies—a spectrum.

By slicing a signal into multiple, thin windows and then transforming each window into the frequency domain, as shown in Figure 4-5, it's possible to create a map of how the signal's frequencies change over time. This map, known as a spectrogram, serves as a very effective input to machine learning models.

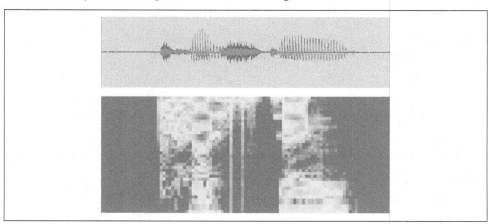

Figure 4-5. The same clip of audio represented as a waveform in the time domain (top) and a spectrogram in the frequency domain (bottom)

Spectrograms are commonly used in real-world applications, especially around audio. Separating the data into windowed frequency bands allows relatively small and simple models to interpret it.[2] It's also possible for humans to visually distinguish one word from another while looking at spectrograms—some people have even learned to read them.

There are many algorithms that can transform a signal from the time to the frequency domain, but the most common is the Fourier transform. It's a very common operation, and there's often hardware support (or at least optimized implementations) available for performing Fourier transforms on embedded devices.

There are a huge number of algorithms and techniques for digital signal processing and time series analysis; they're major fields of engineering and study. Some great resources on the subjects are:

- *The Scientist and Engineer's Guide to Digital Signal Processing* (*https://oreil.ly/jo0UJ*), by Steven W. Smith (California Technical, 1997)
- *Practical Time Series Analysis*, by Aileen Nielsen (O'Reilly, 2019)

Image feature detection

A whole subset of signal processing algorithms are concerned with the extraction of useful features[3] from images. These have traditionally been referred to as *computer vision* algorithms. Some common examples include:

Edge detection
    Used to identify boundaries in an image (see Figure 4-6)

Corner detection
    Used to find points in an image that have an interesting two-dimensional structure

Blob detection
    Used to identify regions of an image that have something in common

Ridge detection
    Used to identify curves within an image

---

2 One reason for this is that the raw audio shown in Figure 4-5 consists of 44,100 samples, while the equivalent spectrogram only has 3,960 elements. The smaller input means a smaller model.

3 In image processing, a feature is a particular piece of information about an image, such as the positions of certain visual structures. The Wikipedia page titled "Feature (computer vision)" (*https://oreil.ly/-EC-T*) lists many common image features.

Figure 4-6. Edge detection algorithms find boundaries between areas with different colors or intensities

Image feature detection reduces a big, messy image into a more compact representation of the visual structures that are present within it. This can potentially make life easier for any AI algorithms that are operating downstream.

Feature detection is not always necessary when working with images. Typically, deep learning models are able to learn their own ways of extracting features, reducing the utility of preprocessing. However, it's still common to perform feature detection when interpreting image data using other types of edge AI algorithm.

The OpenCV project (*https://opencv.org*) provides a set of libraries for feature detection (and other image-processing tasks) that will run on most SoC devices. For microcontrollers, OpenMV (*https://openmv.io*) provides an open source library of feature detection algorithm implementations along with hardware designed to run them.

Combining Features and Sensors

There's nothing stopping you from combining several different features and signals as the input to your AI algorithms. For example, you could calculate several moving averages of a time series over several different windows and pass them all into a machine learning model together. There are no hard-and-fast rules, so feel free to experiment and be creative with the way you slice and dice your data. The following chapters will provide a framework for experimentation.

Going beyond combining features from the same signal, *sensor fusion* is the concept of integrating data from multiple sensors together. For example, an edge AI fitness tracker could combine information from an accelerometer, gyroscope, and heart rate sensor to try to detect which sport a wearer is playing.

In a more complex edge AI scenario, the sensors don't even have to be integrated with the same device. Imagine a smart climate control system that makes use of temperature and occupancy sensors distributed throughout a building to optimize air conditioning usage.

There are three categories of sensor fusion:

Complementary
> Where multiple sensors combine to deliver a more complete understanding of a situation than would be possible with a single sensor—for example, the various sensors on our hypothetical fitness tracker.

Competitive
> Where multiple sensors measure the same exact thing in order to reduce the likelihood of bad measurements—for example, multiple redundant sensors monitoring the temperature of a critical piece of equipment.

Cooperative
> Where information from multiple sensors combines to create a signal that was not otherwise available—for example, two cameras producing a stereo image that provides depth information.

The challenge inherent in sensor fusion is how to combine multiple signals that may even occur at different rates. You should consider the following:

1. Aligning the signals in time. For many algorithms, it's important that all of the signals we intend to fuse are sampled at the same frequency, and that the values reflect simultaneous measurements. This can be achieved through resampling—for example, upsampling a low-frequency signal so that it has the same rate as the high-frequency signal it is being fused with.

2. Scaling the signals. It's critical that the signals' values are on the same scale, so that a signal with typically large values does not overwhelm a signal with typically smaller ones.

3. Numerically combining the signals. This can be done using simple mathematical operations (addition, multiplication, or averaging) or with more sophisticated algorithms such as the Kalman filter (covered later)—or simply by concatenating the data together and passing it into the algorithm as a single matrix.

You can perform sensor fusion before or after other stages of feature engineering. For an arbitrary example: if you intended to fuse two time series, you might choose to run a low pass over one of them first, then scale them to the same scale, combine the two through averaging, and transform the combined values into the frequency domain. Don't be afraid to experiment!

Feature Scaling

A stream of data from a sensor can have a wide range of values. For example, if the sensor returns measurements as 16-bit unsigned integers, their value could be anywhere from 0 to 65,535.

Big ranges like this can make things tricky for some AI algorithms. For example, deep learning models can have a hard time training when their input values have a large magnitude.

Additionally, it can be hard to get good results from machine learning models when passing in features that have wildly different scales. The larger values outweigh the smaller ones, which reduces the benefit of having multiple input features. This is also a problem for sensor fusion.

To get around the issue, it's a very good idea to scale your inputs before combining them or sending them into AI algorithms. A common way to do this is called *normalization*. There are a few different varieties of normalization. In the simplest, known as *rescaling*, you determine the maximum and minimum values for a specific feature in a representative sample of your input data (typically using your training data, if you're working with machine learning models). You can then calculate the normalized values using the following formula:

```
normalized_value = (raw_value - minimum) / (maximum - minimum)
```

This will provide a value between 0 and 1, which can be conveniently compared and combined with other normalized values on the same scale.

Some other common scaling methods include *mean normalization* and *standardization*. The Wikipedia article "Feature Scaling" (*https://oreil.ly/hhzyc*) provides a general overview.

One thing to note is that the values you encounter in the real world may turn out to have a different range from those in your training data. To avoid issues, you should clip any that are out of the expected range.

We now have some serious tools for processing data. In the next section, we'll explore the AI algorithms that will help us understand it.

Artificial Intelligence Algorithms

There are two ways to think about AI algorithms. One is based on functionality: what are they designed to do? The other is based on implementation: how do they work? Both aspects are important. Functionality is critical to the application you are trying to build, and implementation is important when thinking about your constraints—which generally means your dataset and the device you will be deploying to.

Algorithm Types by Functionality

First up, let's look at the most important types of algorithm from a functional perspective. Mapping the problem you are trying to solve to these algorithm types is known as *framing*, and we'll be diving deep into framing in Chapter 6.

Classification

Classification algorithms try to solve the problem of distinguishing between various *types*, or *classes*, of things. This could mean:

- A fitness monitor with an accelerometer classifying walking versus running
- A security system with an image sensor classifying an empty room versus a room with a person present
- A wildlife camera classifying four different species of animal

Figure 4-7 shows a classifier being used to determine whether a forklift truck is idle or moving, based on data collected by an accelerometer.

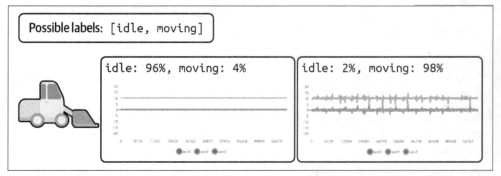

Figure 4-7. A classifier typically outputs a probability distribution including each possible class

Classification can be categorized in a few different ways, depending on the task:

Binary classification
    The input belongs to one of two classes.

Multiclass classification
    The input belongs to one of more than two classes.

Multilabel classification
    The input belongs to zero or more of any number of classes.

The most common forms of classification are binary and multiclass. With these forms of classification, you always need at least two classes. Even if there's only one thing you care about (for example, a person in the room), you also need a class that represents everything that you *don't* care about (for instance, rooms that don't have people in them). Multilabel classification is comparatively rare.

Regression

Regression algorithms try to come up with numbers. This could mean:

- A smart thermostat that predicts the temperature in an hour's time
- A virtual scale that estimates the weight of a food product using a camera
- A virtual sensor that estimates a motor's speed of rotation based on its sound

Virtual sensors, like the latter two examples, are a particularly interesting case of regression. They can use available sensor data to predict measurements from different types of sensor—without actually requiring those sensors to be present.

Object detection and segmentation

Object detection algorithms take an image or video and identify the locations of specific objects within them, often by drawing *bounding boxes* around them. They combine classification and regression, identifying specific types of objects and predicting their numeric coordinates—as seen in Figure 4-8.

Figure 4-8. A common output for object detection models consists of bounding boxes drawn around detected objects, each with an individual confidence score

Specialized object detection algorithms exist for particular types of objects. For example, pose estimation models are designed to recognize human body parts and identify their locations within an image—as shown in Figure 4-9.

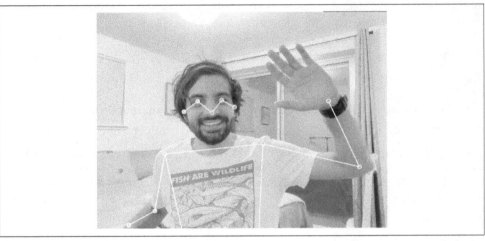

Figure 4-9. Pose estimation identifies key points on a human body, the position of which can be used as input for other processes

Segmentation algorithms are similar to object detection algorithms, but they classify images at a pixel level. This results in a *segmentation map*, as seen in Figure 4-10, which attempts to label areas of the input with their content.

Figure 4-10. This street scene has been labeled with a segmentation map. Different areas, such as people and the road surface, are shown in different shades. A segmentation algorithm aims to predict which pixels belong to which type of object.

Here are some example use cases for object detection and segmentation:

- A farm monitor that uses cameras to count the number of animals in a field
- A home fitness system that gives people feedback on their form during workouts
- An industrial camera that measures how much of a container is filled with product

Anomaly detection

Anomaly detection algorithms recognize when a signal has deviated from its normal behavior. They are useful in many applications:

- An industrial predictive maintenance system that can recognize when a motor has started to break down by its current draw
- A robot vacuum that can identify when it is driving on an unusual surface using an accelerometer
- A trail camera that knows when an unknown animal has walked past

Anomaly detection algorithms are very useful for predictive maintenance. They're also very helpful when paired with machine learning models. Many machine learning models will produce spurious, random results if they are presented with an input that isn't in their training set.

To avoid this, an ML model can be paired with an anomaly detection algorithm that tells it when something is *out of distribution* so that its spurious results can be discarded. Some types of models can also be *calibrated* so that their output represents a true probability distribution that can be interpreted to recognize when the model is uncertain.

Clustering

Clustering algorithms try to group inputs by similarity and can recognize when an input is not similar to what it has seen before. They are often used when an edge AI device needs to learn from its environment, including for anomaly detection applications. For example, consider:

- A voice assistant that learns which voice belongs to each of its users
- A predictive maintenance application that learns a "normal" state of operation and can detect deviations from it
- A vending machine that can recommend drinks based on a user's previous choices

A clustering algorithm can either learn its clusters on the fly (after deployment) or have them configured ahead of time.

Dimensionality reduction

Dimensionality reduction algorithms take a signal and produce a representation of it that contains equivalent information but takes up a lot less space. The representations of two signals can then be compared to one another easily. Here are some example applications:

- Compression of audio, to make it cheaper to transmit sounds from a remote device
- Fingerprint recognition, ensuring a fingerprint matches the owner of a device
- Facial recognition, recognizing individual faces in a video feed

Dimensionality reduction tends to be used alongside other AI algorithms, as opposed to being used on its own. For example, it can be used in conjunction with a clustering algorithm to identify similar signals in complex data types, like audio and video.

Transformation

Transformation algorithms take one signal and output another. Here are some examples:

- Noise-canceling headphones that identify and remove specific noises in a signal
- A car reversing camera that enhances the image in dark or rainy conditions
- A speech recognition device that takes an audio signal and outputs a transcription

The input and output of transformation algorithms can be extremely different. In the case of transcription, the input is a stream of audio data and the output is a sequence of words.

Combining Algorithms

There's no reason you can't mix different types of algorithms in the same application. Later in this section we'll explore techniques for combining algorithms (see "Combining algorithms" on page 113).

Algorithm Types by Implementation

Exploring algorithms by functionality helps us understand what they are used for, but from an engineering perspective it's important to get a sense for the different ways these functionalities can be implemented. There are hundreds of different ways to build a classification algorithm, for example, resulting from decades of computer science research. Each method has its own unique strengths and weaknesses that are amplified by the constraints posed by edge AI hardware.

In the following section, we'll explore the most important ways that edge AI algorithms are implemented. Bear in mind that this isn't an exhaustive list—we're focused on edge AI, so we're focused on technologies that work well on-device.

Conditionals and heuristics

The simplest type of AI algorithms are based on conditional logic: simple if statements that result in decisions. Let's look back at the code snippet we explored in "Artificial Intelligence" on page 6:

```
current_speed = 10 # In meters per second
distance_from_wall = 50 # In meters
seconds_to_stop = 3 # The minimum time in seconds required to stop the car
safety_buffer = 1 # The safety margin in seconds before hitting the brakes

# Calculate how long we've got before we hit the wall
seconds_until_crash = distance_from_wall / current_speed

# Make sure we apply the brakes if we're likely to crash soon
if seconds_until_crash < seconds_to_stop + safety_buffer:
    applyBrakes()
```

This simple algorithm does a basic calculation using some human-defined values (seconds_to_stop, etc.) and decides whether to apply a car's brakes. Does this count as AI? It's a question that might stimulate debate—but the answer is emphatically yes.[4]

The common understanding of artificial intelligence is that it's a quest to create machines that can think like human beings. The engineering definition is much more realistic: AI allows computers to do tasks that typically require human intelligence. In this case, controlling a car's brakes to avoid a collision is definitely something that has typically required human intelligence. It would have been considered extremely impressive twenty years ago, but automatic braking is a common feature in modern vehicles.

---

4 There's a well-documented phenomenon known as the "AI effect" (*https://oreil.ly/hcR8Q*), where the moment AI researchers figure out how to make a computer do a task, critics no longer consider that task representative of intelligence.

Before you laugh at the idea that if statements can be artificial intelligence, consider that *decision trees*—one of the most popular and effective categories of machine learning algorithms—are just if statements under the hood. These days, even deep learning models can be implemented as binary neural networks, which are essentially conditional logic. Intelligence comes from the application, not the implementation!

The conditional logic in our car braking algorithm is actually an implementation of classification. Given an input (the speed of the car and the distance from a wall), the algorithm classifies the situation into one of two types: safe driving or impending crash. Conditional logic is naturally used for classification since its output is categorical; an if statement gives us either one output or another.

Conditional logic is connected to the idea of *heuristics*. A heuristic is a handcrafted rule that can be applied to a situation in order to help understand or react to it. For example, our car braking algorithm uses the heuristic that if we have less than four seconds before hitting a wall, we should apply the brakes.

Heuristics are designed by human beings using domain knowledge. This domain knowledge can be built on data that has been collected about a real-world situation. In that respect, our seemingly simple car braking algorithm might actually represent some deep, well-researched understanding of the real world. Perhaps the value of seconds_to_stop was arrived at after millions of dollars' worth of crash tests and represents the ideal value for the constant. With this in mind, it's easy to see how even an if statement can represent a significant amount of human intelligence and knowledge, captured and distilled into a simple and elegant piece of code.

Our car braking example is very simple—but when paired with signal processing, conditional logic can make some quite sophisticated decisions. For example, imagine you are building a predictive maintenance system that aims to alert workers of the health of an industrial machine based on the sounds it makes. Perhaps the machine makes a characteristic high-pitched whine when it is about to break down. If you capture audio and translate it into the frequency domain using a Fourier transform, you can use a simple if statement to determine when the whine is happening and let the workers know.

Beyond if statements, you can use more complex logic to interpret situations based on known rules. For example, an industrial machine may use a handcoded algorithm to avoid damage by varying its speed based on measurements of internal temperature and pressure. The algorithm might take the temperature and pressure and directly calculate an RPM, using human insight that is captured in the code.

If it works for your situation, conditional logic and other handcoded algorithms can be amazing. It is easy to understand, easy to debug, and easy to test. There's no risk of unspecified behavior: the code either branches one way or another, and all paths can be exercised with automated tests. It runs incredibly fast and will work on any imaginable device.

There are two major downsides of heuristics. First, developing them may require significant domain knowledge and programming expertise. Domain knowledge is not always available—for example, a small company might not have the resources to conduct the expensive research necessary to understand the fundamental mathematical rules of a system. In addition, even given domain knowledge, not everyone has the expertise required to design and implement a heuristic algorithm in efficient code.

The second big downside is the idea of *combinatorial explosion*. The more variables that are present in a situation, the more difficult it is to model with traditional computer algorithms. A good example of this is the game of chess: there are so many pieces, and so many possible moves, that deciding what to do next requires a vast amount of computation. Even the most advanced chess computers built using conditional logic can easily be beaten by expert human players.

Some edge AI problems are *far* more complex than games of chess. For example, imagine trying to handwrite conditional logic that can determine whether a camera image shows an orange or a banana. With some tricks ("yellow means banana, orange means orange") you might succeed for some categories of images—but it would be impossible to make it generalize beyond the simplest of scenes.

A good rule of thumb for handcoded logic is that the more data values you have to deal with, the more difficult it is going to be to get a satisfactory solution. Fortunately, there are plenty of algorithms that can step in when a handcoded approach fails.

Classical machine learning

Machine learning is a special approach to creating algorithms. Where heuristic algorithms are created by handcoding logic based on known rules, machine learning algorithms discover their own rules—by exploring large amounts of data.

The following description, taken from the book *TinyML*, introduces the basic ideas behind machine learning:

> To create a machine learning program, a programmer feeds data into a special kind of algorithm and lets the algorithm discover the rules. This means that as programmers, we can create programs that make predictions based on complex data without having to understand all of the complexity ourselves. The machine learning algorithm builds a *model* of the system based on the data we provide, through a process we call *training*. The model is a type of computer program. We run data through this model to make predictions, in a process called *inference*.
>
> —*TinyML* (O'Reilly, 2019)

Machine learning algorithms can perform all of the functional tasks described earlier in this chapter, from classification to transformation. The key requirement for using machine learning is that you have a *dataset*. This is a large store of data, generally collected under real-world conditions, that is used to train the model.

Typically, the data needed to train a machine learning model is gathered during the development process, aggregated from as many sources as possible. As we'll see in later chapters, a large and varied dataset is critical for working with edge AI—but especially machine learning.

Since machine learning depends on large datasets, and because *training* a machine learning model is computationally expensive, the training part generally happens before deployment, with *inference* happening on the edge. It's certainly possible to train machine learning models on-device, but the lack of data combined with the small amount of compute make it a challenge.

In edge AI, there are two main ways to work with machine learning datasets:

Supervised learning
> Where the dataset has been *labeled* by an expert to assist the machine learning algorithm in understanding it

Unsupervised learning
> Where the algorithm identifies structures in the data without human help

Machine learning has a major dataset-related drawback. ML algorithms depend entirely on their training data to know how to respond to inputs. As long as they are receiving inputs that are similar to their training data, they should work well. However, if they receive an input that is significantly dissimilar from their training dataset—known as an *out-of-distribution* input—they will produce an output that is completely useless.

The tricky part is that there is no obvious way of telling, from the output, that an input was out of distribution. This means that there's always a risk that a model is providing useless predictions. Avoiding this problem is a core concern when working with machine learning.

There are many different types of machine learning algorithms. *Classical* machine learning encompasses the vast majority of them used in practice, with the major exception of *deep learning* (which we'll explore in the next section).

Interpretability and Explainability

When a machine learning model makes a prediction, it's great if we can also understand *why* it made that particular prediction—as opposed to a different one. The property of making human-comprehensible decisions is known as *interpretability* or *explainability*.

Some machine learning algorithms are more interpretable than others. Whether this is important or not depends on your use case. For example, if a machine learning model is being used to assist with medical diagnosis, doctors may not trust it if it can't explain its predictions.

Interpretable algorithms are easier to work with, since debugging them is straightforward—if they produce an incorrect output, you can directly understand why and attempt to address it.

Here are some of the most useful types of classical ML algorithms for edge AI. The title indicates whether they are supervised or unsupervised algorithms:

Regression analysis (supervised)
> Learns the mathematical relationships between input and output to predict a continuous value. Easy to train, fast to run, low data requirements, and highly interpretable, but can only learn simple systems.

Logistic regression (supervised)
> A classification-oriented type of regression analysis, logistic regression learns the relationship between input values and *categories* of output—for relatively simple systems.

Support vector machine (supervised)
> Uses fancy mathematics to learn much more complex relationships than basic regression analysis. Low data requirements, fast to run, can learn complex systems, but difficult to train and low interpretability.

Decision trees and random forests (supervised)
> Uses an iterative process to construct a series of if statements that predict an output category or value. Easy to train, fast to run, highly interpretable, can learn complex systems but may require a lot of training data.

Kalman filter (supervised)
> Predicts the next datapoint given a history of measurements. Can factor in multiple variables to improve precision. Often trained on-device, low data requirements, fast to run, easy to interpret, but can only model relatively simple systems.

Nearest neighbors (unsupervised)
> Classifies data by how similar it is to known data points. Often trained on-device, low data requirements, easy to interpret, but can only model relatively simple systems and can be slow with lots of data points.

Clustering (unsupervised)
> Learns to group inputs by similarity but does not require labels. Often trained on-device, low data requirements, fast to run, easy to interpret, but can only model relatively simple systems.

Classical ML algorithms are an incredible set of tools for interpreting the output of your feature engineering pipeline and making decisions with data. They cover the spectrum from highly efficient to highly flexible, and they can perform many functional tasks. Another major benefit is that they tend to be very explainable—it's easy to understand how they are making their decisions. And depending on the algorithm, the data requirements can be quite low (deep learning typically requires very large datasets).

The diverse pool of classical ML algorithms (there are literally hundreds) are both a blessing and a curse for edge AI. On the one hand, there are algorithms well suited to many different situations, which makes it possible to find one that is—theoretically—ideal for a particular use case. On the other hand, the large constellation of algorithms can be challenging to explore.

While libraries like scikit-learn (*https://oreil.ly/EI2MV*) make it easy to try out many different algorithms, there's an art and a science to tuning each one to perform optimally, and to interpreting their results. In addition, if you're hoping to deploy to a microcontroller, you may have to write your own efficient implementation of an algorithm—there are not many open source versions available yet.

A major downside of classical ML algorithms is that they run into a relatively low ceiling in terms of complexity of the systems they can model. This means that to get the best results, they often have to be paired with heavy feature engineering—which can be complex to design and computationally costly. Even with feature engineering, there are some tasks—such as the classification of image data—where classical ML algorithms just don't perform well.

That said, classical ML algorithms are a fantastic set of tools for making on-device decisions. But if you hit their limitations, deep learning might help.

Deep learning

Deep learning is a type of machine learning that focuses on neural networks. These have proven such an effective tool that deep learning has grown into a gigantic field, with deep neural networks being applied to many types of application.

This book focuses on the important properties of deep learning algorithms from an engineering perspective. The underlying mechanics of deep learning are interesting, but they're not required knowledge for building an edge AI product. Using modern tools, any engineer can deploy deep learning models without a formal background in machine learning. We'll share some of the tools for doing that in the tutorial chapters later on.

Deep learning shares the same principles as classical ML. A dataset is used to train a model, which can be implemented on a device to perform inference. There isn't anything magical about a model—it's just a combination of an algorithm and a collection of numbers that are fed into it, along with the model's input, in order to produce the desired output.

The numbers in the model are called *weights*, or *parameters*, and they're generated during the training process. The term *neural network* refers to the way that the model combines its input with its parameters, which was inspired by the way neurons in an animal brain connect to one another.

Many of the most mind-blowing feats of AI engineering that we've seen over the past decade have made use of deep learning models. Here are some popular highlights:

- AlphaGo (*https://oreil.ly/ynHNq*), a computer program that used deep learning to beat the best players at Go (*https://oreil.ly/LZOWt*), an ancient game once thought impossible for computers to master
- GPT-3 (*https://oreil.ly/fADs3*), a model that can generate written language that is indistinguishable from human writing
- Fusion reactor control (*https://oreil.ly/7r9_5*), using deep learning to control the shape of plasma within a fusion reactor
- DALL•E (*https://oreil.ly/Gw5gq*), a model that can generate realistic images and abstract art based on text prompts
- GitHub Copilot (*https://copilot.github.com*), software that assists software engineers by automatically writing code

Beyond the fancy stuff, deep learning excels at all of the tasks in our subsections of algorithm types (see "Algorithm Types by Functionality" on page 96). It has proven to be flexible, adaptable, and an incredibly useful tool in allowing computers to understand and influence the world.

Deep learning models are effective because they work as *universal function approximators*. It's been mathematically proven that, as long as you can describe something as a continuous function, a deep learning network can model it (*https://oreil.ly/4xX1m*).

This basically means that for any dataset that shows various inputs and desired outputs, there's a deep learning model out there that can convert one into the other.

A really exciting result of this ability is that during training, deep learning models can figure out how to do their own feature engineering. If a special transformation is needed to help interpret the data, a deep learning model can potentially learn how to do it. This doesn't make feature engineering obsolete, but it definitely reduces the burden on the developer to get things exactly right.

The reason deep learning models are so good at approximating functions is that they can have very large numbers of parameters. With each parameter, the model gets a little bit more flexibility, allowing it to describe a slightly more complex function.

This property leads to the two major drawbacks of deep learning models. First, finding the ideal values for all of these parameters is a difficult process. It involves training a model with lots of data. Data is often a rare and precious resource, difficult and expensive to obtain, so this can be a major obstacle. Fortunately, there are many techniques that can help make the most of limited data—we'll cover them later in the book.

The second major drawback is the risk of *overfitting*. Overfitting is when a machine learning model learns a dataset *too* well. Instead of modeling the general rules that lead from outputs to inputs in its dataset, it memorizes the dataset completely. This means that it won't perform well on data that it hasn't seen before.

Overfitting is a risk with all machine learning models, but it's especially a challenge for deep learning models because they can have so many parameters. Each additional parameter provides the model with slightly more ability to memorize its dataset.

There are a lot of different types of deep learning models. Here are some of the most important for edge AI:

Fully connected models
> The simplest type of deep learning model, fully connected models consist of stacked *layers* of *neurons*. The input of a fully connected model is fed directly in as a long series of numbers. Fully connected models are capable of learning any function, but they are mostly blind to spatial relationships in their inputs (for example, which values in an input are next to one another).
>
> In an embedded context, this means they work well for discrete values (for example, if the input features are a set of statistics about a time series) but they aren't as great with raw time series or image data.
>
> Fully connected models are very well supported on embedded devices, with hardware and software optimizations commonly available.

Convolutional models

Convolutional models are designed to make use of the spatial information in their inputs. For example, they can learn to recognize shapes in images, or the structures of signals within time series sensor data. This makes them extremely useful in embedded applications since spatial information is important in so many of the signals we deal with.

Like fully connected models, convolutional models are very well supported on embedded devices.

Sequence models

Sequence models were designed originally for use on sequences of data, like time series signals or even written language. To help them recognize long-term patterns in time series, they often include some internal "memory."

It turns out that sequence models are very flexible, and there's increasing evidence that they can be very effective on any signal where spatial information is important. Many people believe they will eventually take over from convolutional models.

Sequence models are currently less well supported than convolutional and fully connected models on embedded devices; there are few open source libraries that provide optimized implementations for them. This is more due to inertia than technical limitations, so the situation is likely to change over the next couple of years.

Embedding models

An embedding model is a pretrained deep learning model that is designed for dimensionality reduction—it takes a big, messy input and represents it as a smaller set of numbers that describes it within a certain context. They are used in the same way a signal processing algorithm would be: they produce features that can be interpreted by another ML model.

Embedding models are available for many tasks, from image processing (turning a big messy image into a numeric description of its contents) to speech recognition (turning raw audio into a numeric description of the vocal sounds within it).

The most common use for embedding models is *transfer learning*, which is a way of reducing the amount of data required to train a model. We'll learn more about that later.

Embedding models can be fully connected, convolutional, or sequence models, so their support on embedded devices varies—but convolutional embedding models are the most common.

Model Architectures

Deep learning models are flexible and modular—they are composed of *layers* and *operations* (also known as *ops*) that can be stacked and combined in an infinite number of ways.

Different arrangements are known as *architectures*, and many architectures have been designed that are optimized for different tasks. You'll often see references to deep learning model architectures in online articles and scientific literature.

Some noteworthy architectures for edge AI include:

- MobileNet and EfficientNet, families of architectures designed to run efficiently on mobile devices
- YOLO, a family of architectures designed to perform object detection
- Transformers, a family of architectures designed to translate between sequences of data

It's only in recent years that deep learning models have been brought to edge AI hardware. Since they are often large and involve significant computation to run, it's been the advent of high-end MCUs and SoCs with relatively powerful processors and large amounts of ROM and RAM that have enabled them to make the leap.

It's possible to run a small deep learning model using just a few kilobytes of memory, but for models that do more complex things—from audio classification to object detection—it is common for models to require dozens or hundreds of kilobytes as a minimum.

This is already impressive since traditional server-side machine learning models can be anywhere from tens of megabytes to several terabytes in size. Using clever optimization, and by limiting scope, embedded models can be made much smaller— we'll introduce some of these techniques shortly.

There are various ways to run a deep learning model on an embedded device. Here's a quick summary:

Interpreters
> Deep learning interpreters, like TensorFlow Lite for Microcontrollers (*https://oreil.ly/4Q7xN*), use an interpreter to execute a model that is stored as a file. They are flexible and easy to work with, but they come with some computational and memory overhead, and they don't support every type of model.

Code generation
> Code generation tools, like EON (*https://oreil.ly/SmT-s*), take a trained deep learning model and translate it into optimized embedded source code. This

is more efficient than an interpreter-based approach, and the code is human-readable so it can still be debugged, but it still doesn't support every possible model type.

Compilers

Deep learning compilers, like microTVM (*https://oreil.ly/0JTaR*), take a trained model and generate optimized bytecode that can be included into embedded applications. The implementation they generate can be highly efficient, but it's not as easy to debug and maintain as actual source code. They can support model types not explicitly supported by interpreters and code generation. It's common for embedded hardware vendors to provide custom interpreters or compilers to assist with running deep learning models on their hardware.

Handcoding

It's possible to implement a deep learning network by writing code by hand, incorporating the parameter values from a trained model. This is a difficult and time-consuming process, but it allows full control over optimization and allows you to support any model type.

The environment for deploying deep learning models is very different between SoCs and microcontrollers. Since SoCs run full, modern operating systems, they also support most of the tools that are used to run deep learning models on servers. This means that pretty much any type of model will run on a Linux SoC. That said, the latency of the model will vary depending on the architecture of the model and the SoC's processor.

There are also interpreters designed specifically for SoC devices. For example, TensorFlow Lite (*https://oreil.ly/pNs5W*) provides tools that allow deep learning models to be run more efficiently on SoCs—typically those that are used in smartphones. They include optimized implementations of deep learning operations that make use of features available in some SoCs, such as GPUs.

The SoCs that have integrated deep learning accelerators are a special case. Typically, the hardware vendor will provide a special compiler or interpreter that allows the model to make use of hardware acceleration. Accelerators typically only accelerate certain operations, so the amount of speedup depends on the architecture of the model.

Since microcontrollers don't run full operating systems, the standard tools for running deep learning models aren't available. Instead, frameworks like TensorFlow Lite for Microcontrollers provide a baseline of model support. They tend to lag behind the standard tools a little in terms of operator support, meaning they will not run some model architectures.

Operators and Kernels

In edge machine learning, an *operator*, or *kernel*, is an implementation of a particular mathematical operation used to run a deep learning model. These are overloaded terms with different meanings in other fields, including elsewhere in deep learning.

Typical high-end microcontrollers have hardware features such as SIMD instructions that will drastically improve the performance of deep learning models. TensorFlow Lite for Microcontrollers includes optimized implementations of operators, making use of these instructions, for several vendors. Like with SoCs, the vendors of microcontroller-based hardware accelerators often provide custom compilers or interpreters that allow models to run on their hardware.

The core advantages of deep learning are its flexibility, reduced requirements for feature engineering, and ability to make use of large amounts of data due to the high parameter counts of models. Deep learning is noteworthy for its ability to approximate complex systems, going beyond simple prediction to perform tasks such as generating art and accurately recognizing objects in images. Deep learning provides a lot of freedom, and researchers have only just begun to explore its potential.

The core disadvantages are its high data requirements, its propensity toward overfitting, the relatively large size and computational complexity of deep learning models, and the complexity of the training process. Additionally, deep learning models can be hard to interpret—it can be challenging to explain why they make one prediction over another. That said, there are tools and techniques that help mitigate most of these drawbacks.

Why Not Always Use Deep Learning?

Since deep learning is so capable, you may wonder why we would use any other machine learning algorithms. Deep learning is a powerful general-purpose tool that can model pretty much any relationship between input and output variables. However, just because it *can* doesn't mean it's always the *best* at it. Depending on the situation, classical ML algorithms can outperform deep learning in terms of:

Explainability
  Nothing beats the interpretability of a decision tree, if your use case allows it.

Efficiency
  Classical ML algorithms are typically much easier to compute than deep learning models.

Portability
  Since they are simpler, classical ML algorithms can be deployed to the most basic devices (such as low-end MCUs).

Effectiveness
> Some classical algorithms work better than deep learning in certain situations, especially when there is not much data available.

On-device training
> Deep learning training is difficult to perform on-device, while some classical algorithms are easy to train in the field.

It all comes down to your individual use case. That said, if you were only going to take a deep dive into one technique for edge AI algorithm development, then it would probably make sense to choose deep learning.

Combining algorithms

A single edge AI application can make use of multiple different types of algorithms. Here are some typical ways this is done:

Ensembles
> An *ensemble* is a collection of machine learning models that are fed the same input. Their outputs are combined mathematically in order to make a decision. Since every ML model has its own strengths and weaknesses, an ensemble of models is often more accurate together than its constituent parts. The downside of ensembles is the additional complexity, memory, and compute required to store and run multiple models.

Cascades
> A *cascade* is a set of ML models that are run in sequence. For example, in a cellphone with a built-in digital assistant, a small, lightweight model is run constantly to detect any signs of human speech. Once speech is detected, a larger, more computationally expensive model is woken up in order to determine what was said.
>
> Cascades are a great way of saving energy since they allow you to avoid unnecessary computation. In a heterogeneous compute environment, where multiple types of processor are available, the individual components of a cascade can even be run on different processors.

Feature extractors
> As we learned earlier, embedding models take a high-dimensional input, like an image, and distill it down to a set of numbers that describe its content. The output of an embedding model can be fed into another model, designed to make predictions based on what the embedding model describes about the original input. In this case, the embedding model is being used as a *feature extractor*.
>
> If a pretrained embedding model is used, this technique—known as *transfer learning*—can massively reduce the amount of data required to train a model.

Instead of learning how to interpret the original high-dimensional input, the model only needs to learn how to interpret the simple output returned by the feature extractor.

For example, imagine you wish to train a model to identify different species of birds from photographs. Rather than train an entire model from scratch, you could use the output of a pretrained feature extractor as the input to your model. This could reduce the amount of data and training time required in order to get good results.

Many pretrained deep learning feature extractors are available under open source licenses. They are commonly used for image related tasks, since large public image datasets are available for pretraining.

Multimodal models

A *multimodal model* is a single model that takes inputs of multiple types of data simultaneously. For example, a multimodal model might accept both audio and accelerometer data together. This technique can be used as a mechanism for sensor fusion, using a single model to combine disparate data types.

Postprocessing algorithms

On edge AI devices, we typically work with streams of data—for example, a continuous time series of audio data. When we run an edge AI algorithm on that stream of data, it will produce a second time series that represents the outputs of the algorithm over time.

This poses a problem. How do we interpret this second time series in order to decide? For example, imagine we are analyzing audio to detect when somebody says a keyword so that we can trigger some functionality on a product. What we *really* want to know is when did we hear the keyword?

Unfortunately, the time series of inference results is not ideal for this purpose. First, it contains many events that do not represent a keyword being detected. To clean these up, we can ignore any whose confidence that a keyword was spotted is below a certain threshold.

Second, the model may occasionally (and briefly) detect a keyword when a keyword was not actually spoken. We need to filter out these blips to clean up our output. This is equivalent to running a low-pass filter on the time series.

Finally, instead of telling us *each* time the keyword was spoken, the raw time series tells us at a set rate whether the keyword is *currently* being spoken. This means we need to do some output gating to get the information we really want.

After cleaning up the raw output, we now have a signal that tells us when a keyword was actually spotted. This is something we can use in our application logic to control our device.

This sort of postprocessing is extremely common in edge AI applications. The exact postprocessing algorithm used, and its particular parameters—for example, the threshold for considering something a match—can be determined on a case-by-case basis. Tools like Edge Impulse's Performance Calibration (covered in "Performance Calibration" on page 337) allow developers to automate discovery of the ideal postprocessing algorithm for their application.

Fail-safe design

There are many things that can go wrong with an edge AI application, so it's critical that there are always safeguards in place to protect against unexpected issues.

For example, imagine a wildlife camera that uses a deep learning model to identify when an animal of interest has been photographed and uploads the animal's image via a satellite connection. Under normal operation, it may send a few photographs a day—not costing very much in data fees.

But out in the field, a physical problem with the camera hardware—such as dirt or reflections on the lens—might result in images being taken that are very different from those in the original training dataset. These out-of-distribution images could lead to unspecified behavior from the deep learning model—which could mean that the model begins to constantly report that the animal of interest is present.

These false positives, caused by out-of-distribution inputs, might result in hundreds of images being uploaded via satellite connection. Not only would the camera be rendered useless, but it could potentially cost large amounts in data transfer fees.

In real-world applications, there's no way to avoid things like damage to sensors or unexpected behavior from algorithms. Instead, it's important that you design your application to be fail-safe. This means that if part of the system were to fail, the application would minimize harm.

The best way to do this varies between situations. In the case of a wildlife camera, it could be wise to build in a rate limit that kicks in if an unreasonable number of photographs are being uploaded. In another application, you might shut a system down entirely rather than risk harm being caused.

Building fail-safe applications is an important part of responsible AI—and good engineering in general. It is something to think about from the very beginning of any project.

Optimization for Edge Devices

With machine learning models, and particularly deep learning models, there's often a trade-off between how well a model performs its task and how much memory and compute the model requires.

This trade-off is extremely important for edge AI. Edge devices are typically computationally constrained. They are designed to minimize cost and energy usage, not to maximize compute. At the same time, they are expected to deal with real-time sensor data, often at high frequencies, and potentially react in real time to events in the data stream.

Larger machine learning models tend to be better at complex tasks, since they have more capacity—which is helpful for learning complicated relationships between inputs and outputs. This extra capacity means they may require more ROM and RAM, and it also means they take longer to compute. The additional compute time results in higher power consumption, as we'll learn in "Duty cycle" on page 333.

Finding the correct balance between *task performance* and *computational performance* is essential in any application. It's a matter of juggling constraints. On the one hand, there's a minimum standard for performance at a given task. On the other hand, hardware choices create hard limits on available memory, latency, and energy.

Managing this trade-off is one of the difficult—but fascinating—parts of edge AI development. It's part of what makes the field uniquely interesting, and why tools for things like AutoML (which we'll learn about in "Automated machine learning (AutoML)" on page 150) need to be redesigned for edge AI.

Here are some of the factors that can help us minimize compute requirements while maximizing task performance.

Choice of algorithm

Every edge AI algorithm has a slightly different profile of memory usage and computational complexity. The constraints of your target hardware should inform your choice of algorithm. Typically, classical ML algorithms are smaller and more efficient than deep learning algorithms.

However, it's commonly the case that feature engineering algorithms use vastly more compute than either, making the choice between classical ML and deep learning less significant. The exception to this rule is the analysis of image data, which typically requires little feature engineering but relatively large deep learning models.

Here are some common ways to reduce the latency and memory required by your choice of algorithms:

- Reduce the complexity of feature engineering. More math means higher latency.
- Reduce the amount of data that reaches the AI algorithm.
- Use classical ML instead of deep learning.
- Trade complexity between feature engineering and machine learning model, depending on which runs more efficiently on your device.
- Reduce the size (the number of weights and layers) of deep learning models.
- Choose model types that have accelerator support on your device of choice.

Compression and optimization

There are many optimization techniques designed to reduce the amount of data and computation required by a given algorithm. Here are some of the most important types:

Quantization

One way to reduce the amount of memory and computation required by an algorithm or model is to decrease the precision of its numeric representations. As mentioned in "How Are Values Represented?" on page 58, there are many different ways to represent numbers in computation—some that have more precision than others.

Quantization is the process of taking a set of values and reducing their precision while preserving the important information they contain. It can be done for both signal processing algorithms and ML models. It's especially useful for deep learning models, which by default tend to have 32-bit floating-point weights. By reducing the weights to 8-bit integers you can reduce a model to 1/4th its size—typically without much reduction in accuracy.

Another advantage of quantization is that the code to perform integer math is faster and more portable than the code for floating-point math. This means that quantization results in a significant speedup on many devices, and that quantized algorithms will run on devices that lack floating-point units.

Quantization is a lossy optimization, meaning that it typically reduces the task performance of the algorithm. In ML models, this can be mitigated by training at a lower precision so that the model learns to compensate.

Operator fusion

In operator fusion, a computation-aware algorithm is used to inspect the operators that are used when a deep learning model is run. When certain groups of operators are used together, it's possible to replace them with a single *fused* implementation that has been written to maximize computational efficiency.

Operator fusion is a lossless technique: it improves computational performance without causing any reduction in task performance. The downside is that fused implementations are only available for certain combinations of operators, so its impact depends greatly on the architecture of a model.

Pruning

Pruning is a lossy technique applied during the training of a deep learning model. It forces many of the model's weights to have a value of zero, creating what is known as a *sparse* model. In theory, this should allow for faster computation since any multiplication involving a zero weight will invariably result in a zero.

However, at this point in time there is very little edge AI hardware and software designed to take advantage of sparse weights. This will change over the next few years, but for now the main benefit of pruning is that sparse models are easier to compress, due to their large blocks of identical values. This is helpful when models need to be sent over the air.

Knowledge distillation

Knowledge distillation is another lossy deep learning training technique that enables a large "teacher" model to help train a smaller "student" model to reproduce its functionality. It takes advantage of the fact that there is typically a lot of redundancy in the weights of a deep learning model, meaning that it's possible to find an equivalent model that is smaller but performs almost as well.

Knowledge distillation is a bit fiddly, so it's not yet a common technique—but it's likely to become a best practice over the next few years.

Binary neural networks (BNNs)

BNNs are deep learning models where every weight is a single binary number. Since binary arithmetic is extremely fast on computers, binary neural networks can be very efficient to run. However, they are a relatively new technology and the tooling for training and running inference with them is not yet in broad use. Binarization is similar to quantization and is therefore a lossy technique.

Spiking neural networks (SNNs)

A spiking neural network is an artificial neural network where the signals transmitted through the network have a time component. As "neuromorphic" systems, they are designed to more closely resemble the way biological neurons work. They have different trade-offs compared to traditional deep learning models, offering improved performance and efficiency for some tasks. However, they require specialized hardware (in the form of an accelerator) in order to offer a benefit.

SNNs can either be trained directly or be created from a traditional deep learning model in a conversion process. This process may be lossy.

Model compression has two major downsides. The first is that running compressed models often requires specific software, hardware, or a combination of the two. This can limit the devices that a compressed model can be deployed to.

The second downside is more dangerous. The lossy nature of compression often results in a subtle degradation of a model's predictive performance that can be difficult to spot. The reduction in precision can bias a model to perform well in common cases, but to lose performance in the "long tail" of less frequently encountered inputs.

This problem can amplify the biases inherent in datasets and algorithms. For example, if a dataset collected for training an ML-powered health wearable contains fewer examples from people in minority groups, model compression may lead to degraded performance for people in these groups. Since they are a minority, the impact on the model's overall accuracy might be hard to spot. This makes it extremely important to evaluate your system's performance on every subgroup within your dataset (see "Collecting Metadata" on page 223).

There are two excellent scientific papers on this topic from researcher Sara Hooker et al. One is "What Do Compressed Deep Neural Networks Forget?" (*https://oreil.ly/v3Bvl*), and the other is "Characterising Bias in Compressed Models" (*https://oreil.ly/V_cTk*).

On-Device Training

In the vast majority of cases, machine learning models used in edge AI are trained before being deployed to a device. Training requires large amounts of data, typically annotated with labels, and involves significant computation—the equivalent of hundreds or thousands of inferences per data point. This limits the utility of on-device training, since by nature edge AI applications are subject to severe constraints in memory, compute, energy, and connectivity.

That said, there are a few scenarios where on-device training makes sense. Here's an overview:

Predictive maintenance

A common example of on-device training happens in predictive maintenance when a machine is being monitored to determine whether it is functioning normally. A small on-device model can be trained with data that represents a "normal" state. If the machine's signals start to deviate from that baseline, the application can notice and take action.

This use case is only possible when it can be assumed that abnormal signals are rare, and that at any given moment the machine is likely to be operating normally. This allows the device to treat the data being collected as having an implicit "normal" label. If abnormal states were common, it would be impossible to make assumptions about the state at any given moment.

Personalization

Another example where on-device training makes sense is when a user is asked to deliberately provide labels. For example, some smartphones use facial recognition as a security method. When the user sets up the device, they are asked to enroll images of their face. A numeric representation of these facial images is stored.

These types of applications tend to use carefully designed embedding models that convert raw data into compact numeric representations of their content. The embeddings are designed in such a way that the Euclidean distance between two embeddings[5] corresponds to the similarity between them. In our face recognition example, this makes it easy to determine whether a new face matches the representations stored during setup: the distance between the new face and the enrolled face is calculated, and if it is sufficiently close then the faces are considered the same.

This form of personalization works well because, typically, the algorithm used to determine embedding similarity can be very simple; either a distance calculation or a nearest neighbors algorithm. The embedding model has done all the hard work.

Implicit association

A further example of on-device training is when labels are available by association. For example, battery management features such as Apple's Optimized Battery Charging (*https://oreil.ly/OzgdM*) train models on-device to predict what time a user is likely to be using their device. One way to do this would be to train a forecasting model to output a probability of usage at a specific time, given a log of the previous few hours' usage.

In this case, it's easy to collect and label training data on a single device. Usage logs are collected in the background, and labels are applied according to some metric (such as whether the screen was activated). The implicit association

---

5 An embedding can be thought of as a coordinate in a multidimensional space. The Euclidean distance between two embeddings is the distance between the two coordinates.

between time and log content allow the data to be labeled. A simple model can then be trained.

Federated learning

One of the obstacles to training on-device is a lack of training data. In addition, on-device data is often private and users are not comfortable with it being transmitted. Federated learning is a way of training models in a distributed manner, across many devices, while preserving privacy. Instead of raw data being transmitted, partially trained models are passed around between devices (or between each device and a central server). The partially trained models can be combined and distributed back to devices once they are ready.

Federated learning often seems attractive since it appears to provide a way for models to learn and improve while in the field. However, it has some serious limitations. It is computationally expensive and requires large amounts of data transfer, which runs counter to the core benefits of edge AI. The training process is very complex and requires both on-device and server-side components, which increases project risk.

Since data is not stored globally, there is no way to validate that the trained model is performing well across the entire deployment. The fact that models are uploaded from local devices presents a vector for security attacks. Finally, and most importantly, it does not solve the problem of labels. If labeled data is not available, federated learning is useless.

Over-the-air updates

Although not actually an on-device training technique, the most common way to update models in the field is via over-the-air updates. A new model can be trained in the lab, using data collected from the field, and distributed to devices via firmware updates.

This depends on network communication, and it doesn't solve the problem of obtaining labeled data, but it's the most common way to keep models up to date over time.

Summary

We've now learned about the key AI algorithms that make edge AI possible, along with the hardware that runs them. The next chapter will walk through the tools—and the skills—that are needed to bring everything together.

## CHAPTER 5

Tools and Expertise

The edge AI development workflow includes many highly technical tasks, and most projects will require skills and expertise pooled by a team of experts.

The first section of this chapter is a guide to building the team that will turn your ideas into reality. Even if you're still at an early stage, it's helpful to understand the types of skills that will be important and the challenges you can expect to encounter. AI is all about automating human insights, so it's vital that you have the right insights on your team.

The second part of the chapter, starting with "Tools of the Trade" on page 136, is designed to help get you to grips with the key technical tools for working with edge AI. If you're still early in your product development journey, you may want to skim over some of the details—and then use this chapter as a reference once you've come up with some concrete ideas and are ready to start.

Building a Team for AI at the Edge

Edge AI is a truly complete technology. As a topic, it makes use of knowledge from everything from the physical properties of semiconductor electronics all the way up to the engineering of high-level architectures that span devices and the cloud. It demands expertise in the most cutting-edge approaches to artificial intelligence and machine learning along with the most venerable skills of bare-metal embedded software engineering. It makes use of the entire history of computer science and electrical engineering, laid out end to end.

Nobody in the world holds deep expertise in every subfield of edge AI. Instead, the people working at the heart of the field rely on assembling networks of experts who they can look to for insight into other pieces of the puzzle. If you're building an edge AI product, you may have to do the same for yourself.

The best team for edge AI is one that has broad, cross-disciplinary knowledge, direct experience working on the problem domain, and comfort working in an iterative development process. The best executed products so far have come from teams with direct experience of the issue they are trying to solve: they've taken their existing knowledge and used it to inform their edge AI product.

It isn't necessary for a single team to have experts in every subfield of edge AI. The absolute bare minimum is probably two roles:

- A domain expert, who has deep insight into the problem to be solved
- An embedded engineer with experience developing for devices similar to the target

There's no reason why these two roles can't be filled by the same person. However, without experience working with machine learning or other AI algorithms, they'll have to rely very heavily on end-to-end platforms designed to guide non-ML experts through the process of algorithm creation.

If you're a solo developer without embedded development experience, you can level up your skills by building some non-AI projects on your target hardware. To make your life easier, you might consider sticking to SoC-level hardware, since embedded Linux development is much easier than bare metal. If you're using an end-to-end edge AI platform it should be relatively simple to deploy your model.

Determination and some scrappy improvisational skills can go a long way: we've seen plenty of scientific researchers build their own AI-powered hardware with relatively simple embedded skills.

While many problems can be solved by a minimal team, the most complex problems will require more heavy lifting. The remainder of this chapter lays out the roles and responsibilities that can potentially be important, which will hopefully give you a sense of what you need for your own team. It also talks through the challenges of hiring for edge AI.

Domain Expertise

Domain expertise, as we'll learn about in detail in "Datasets and Domain Expertise" on page 205, is by far the most essential component of your team. If you have nothing but domain expertise and a budget, you can still hire developers and get a product built. But if nobody on your team has a deep understanding of the problem you're trying to solve, it's very unlikely you'll be able to solve it. In fact, there is a fair chance you may end up trying to solve the wrong problem or creating a solution that nobody needs.

It would be difficult to build any kind of quality product without domain expertise but using AI is almost impossible. The goal of edge AI is to distill expert knowledge into a piece of software and use it to automate a process. As we learned earlier in the book, intelligence means knowing the right thing to do at the right time. But how can we build a system that does that if we do not know it ourselves?

If you aren't a domain expert yourself, your first job is to find someone who is. Your second job is to have them validate the solution that you are planning to build. Here are some of the questions to ask them:

- Does the problem you wish to tackle really exist?
- If it exists, is it a useful problem to solve?
- Are there solutions to the problem that already exist?
- Would your proposed solution actually help solve the problem?
- Does your proposed solution sound feasible to build?
- If you build your solution, would anybody in the field want to buy it?

You should hopefully be able to ask someone these questions without having to pay too much money: they're the basic questions that any genuine domain expert would be thinking about if you were to offer them a job. You should make sure you pay attention to their answers, even if you disagree. If a genuine expert is telling you something is a bad idea, there's likely some truth to it.

Domain expertise should be at the heart of your organization and part of your core team. Your experts will be involved with so many aspects of the project that it isn't feasible for them to be peripheral members. That said, the ideal situation is that you have domain expertise at every level of your organization. For example, in addition to your core expertise you may have engineers, board members, and advisors who all have experience in the relevant area. Their combined insight will help your team anticipate and mitigate risk.

If you are unable to find anyone with the required expertise, you should abort your project before it gets started. There's simply no way to work ethically if you don't have the appropriate knowledge. Your project may be violating some golden rule of the field—and you wouldn't have any way to know about it. It's not acceptable to test unqualified functionality on your customers, as Figure 5-1 makes clear. It's so difficult to establish a feedback loop with performance in the field that you likely won't know what's going wrong.

Figure 5-1. Using customers to validate your solution is a horrible idea (Twitter (https://oreil.ly/jI6HJ), 2022)

If you are truly convinced that you have a good idea, you may have to spend some time developing the required expertise yourself.

Diversity

In addition to domain expertise, the other essential property your team should aim for is diversity. As we discussed in "Mitigating societal harms" on page 51, one of the best defenses against societal issues is to build a team with diverse perspectives.

It can be helpful to think of workplace diversity in terms of four core areas:[1]

Internal
Internal diversity reflects the things that a person is born with and didn't choose for themselves. Some of these areas include age, nation of origin, race, ethnicity, sexual orientation, gender identity, physical ability, and personality types.

External
External diversity includes the things we pick up along the way, whether due to influence by external factors or due to conscious choices. Some examples are socioeconomic status, life experiences, education, personal interests, family status, location, and religious beliefs.

Organizational
Organizational diversity relates to a person's role within an organization. This might include their place of work, job function, level within a hierarchy, pay level, seniority, or employment status.

---

1 See "What Are the 4 Types of Diversity?" (*https://oreil.ly/SQ-P9*) for more information on the four core areas.

Worldview

Diversity in worldview relates to how a person sees the world. It can include things like ethical frameworks, political beliefs, religious beliefs, personal philosophy, and general outlook on life.

As a result of differences in these four areas, every person has a different set of experiences that make their perspective unique. This unique viewpoint means that they will see the same situation in different ways. As a team building technology products, a diversity of perspectives is incredibly valuable because it allows the organization to view the problem and the proposed solutions from a multitude of different angles.

This provides a significant advantage over organizations that lack diversity. You'll be more capable of identifying all the nuance in a given situation, which has huge benefits when mapping out the space of possible solutions. Perhaps someone's personal experiences will translate into an amazing idea that nobody else would have thought of.

Even more importantly, diverse perspectives will help you identify issues with your own product. For example, you may find that different people naturally come up with different axes on which to evaluate your product's performance. A person with kids is more likely to consider the need for a product to cope well with family life, and someone with a physical disability may be more likely to think about accessibility.

This isn't to say that the members of your team should stand in for domain experts in these areas: just because a person has a disability does not mean they are automatically your official accessibility expert, a role they may neither want nor be qualified for. However, the fact that your team has diverse perspectives hopefully means that they are more likely to consider the *need* to bring on an accessibility expert.

It's not enough to just have a diverse team: individuals have to be comfortable sharing their input, and the rest of the organization has to actually listen to them. The work of building that type of environment is beyond the scope of this book, but there's plenty of literature on the subject. A good place to start is this introduction to psychological safety from Google (*https://oreil.ly/rZYFL*), who have found that teams where individuals can confidently speak up are far more effective (*https://oreil.ly/2LD_i*).

Another key idea is that you should make use of perspectives from your entire organization. Beyond the people working directly on the product, you should draw feedback from everyone you can—from executives to entry-level workers. This will help you avoid blind spots in your insight. At many large tech companies, employees are encouraged to sign up to test new products that are still in development,[2] allowing development teams to access insight from across the entire company.

---

2 It's part of a strategy known as "dogfooding," covered in "Real-world testing" on page 321.

As with everything in iterative development, this process is all about building feedback loops that will help make your product over time. You should create systems to gather the perspectives of your diverse team from the very earliest stages when you're still sketching out ideas.

It's not always feasible for a single team to include all of the necessary diversity of perspectives. For example, you may need input on a product from young children, who are unlikely to be paid employees of your organization! One way to ensure these perspectives are included is to create a budget for having focus groups with these types of people throughout the course of your project.

Another way of broadening perspectives is to find a diverse group of advisors who can help inform your decisions. Assembling an advisory board that combines expertise in key areas with diverse representation is a powerful tool for helping you make the right decisions. They can act as a review board who can help you understand whether you are meeting your goals or veering off course.

Regardless of whether you have a large team, you should be relentless in seeking feedback from the people affected by your product—the most diverse group of all.

The Costs of Diversity

It's worth noting that diversity comes with some costs. Beyond the practical expense of compensating people for their time, diverse teams may find it harder to reach agreement on things like values and goals.

The leadership of a project needs to be prepared for this and may have to make some decisions that do not have full agreement. Documenting the reasoning behind any decisions, along with any dissenting views, is essential in ensuring a team can track its decision making and improve it over time.

That said, if there's fundamental disagreement on a particular issue, it can be a sign of significant risk.

Stakeholders

The stakeholders of your project are all of the people and communities who are potentially affected. This includes people within your organization, your customers, the end users of your system, and anybody who may be impacted—both directly and indirectly.

For a system to be effective, and for it to avoid causing harm, the needs and values of stakeholders must be considered. For example, if your system will come into contact with members of the public then it is important that they are considered as stakeholders, and that the project is designed with them in mind.

The best way to understand the needs and values of stakeholders is to ask them directly. They should be represented throughout your development workflow, from ideation to end of life.

Stakeholders can be identified using a well-established tool known as stakeholder mapping (*https://oreil.ly/t7Gv0*). You should make sure your team includes someone who is familiar with the process.

Roles and Responsibilities

Building a product takes a village full of people, and the next section of this chapter outlines some of the roles that are required. Your project may require roles that are not included here; these are just the most common ones that directly participate in the edge AI workflow.

 You don't need to hire an individual person for each role. It's perfectly possible for the same person to play multiple roles in a project, and early on it may be the case that all of your prototyping is done by a single person.

For ease of digestion, we'll divide up the roles by type.

Knowledge and understanding

The roles in this category are critical to understanding the problem and solving it in the right way:

Domain expert
> The starring role in the play, the domain expert brings a deep understanding of the project area. While a product manager's job is to understand how a project fits into the surrounding context (such as the market), a domain expert is the person who understands the science of the situation. For example, an industrial automation project might require a domain expert in the relevant industrial processes, and a healthcare project might need an expert in the related areas of medicine and biology.

Ethics and fairness expert
> The ethics and fairness role is required in order to avoid making the types of mistakes that often result in harmful or ineffective products. They need a strong understanding of the technologies that will be used to solve a problem, the types of pitfalls that can emerge, and the processes that need to be followed. Domain expertise is important, too, since ethical issues can be specific to a domain.

Planning and execution

These high-level roles are important in guiding the project down the right path as it travels from ideation to launch and long-term support:

Product manager

A product manager is responsible for making decisions about the product: what it should be, what it should do, and who it should serve. Their job is to deeply understand the problem and the market, and work with those in technical roles to design and implement an effective solution. They lead through influence, pulling together different threads to weave a product that fits the right requirements.

Project manager

The project management role involves coordinating the execution of complex tasks across groups of people. For example, a project manager may organize the collection of a dataset that will be used to build and create a product.

Program manager

Program managers coordinate high-level strategies that are made up of multiple projects. For instance, a company planning to incorporate edge AI into multiple parts of its business to make cost savings may use a program manager to coordinate the process.

Algorithm development

These roles are involved in the exploration of datasets and the design of algorithms—along with mechanisms for evaluation of the system that is being built. This work can increasingly be done by nonexpert users who are using end-to-end platforms, but it's always good to have some solid experience to draw on to avoid making rookie mistakes:

Data scientist

The data science role is responsible for gathering, maintaining, and understanding the data that underlies an edge AI project. They have skills in data cleaning, analysis, and feature engineering. This role may often encompass machine learning work, but it could just as easily be distinct.

DSP engineer

A DSP engineer develops and implements DSP algorithms. They typically have strong skills in both algorithm development and low-level programming. DSP is extremely important in most edge AI projects—with the exception of those that combine deep learning with image data, since images are typically input without much processing.

ML practitioner

Machine learning practitioners spend their time trying to solve problems with ML. An ML practitioner will try to frame a problem in terms of different types of learning algorithms. They will then work with a dataset, attempting to develop algorithms that solve the problem. A key part of their role is determining how to evaluate algorithms and their performance, both in the lab and in the field.

In an edge AI project, DSP engineers and ML practitioners work very closely together, since DSP is a sophisticated form of feature engineering—which is a key part of the ML workflow.

Product engineering

This set of roles leads development of the product itself. They create the hardware and application code, and they implement the algorithm in a form that works efficiently on-device:

Hardware engineer

A hardware engineer designs the hardware that powers a product. This design includes both the sensors that capture raw data and the processors that attempt to make sense of it, along with the design and layout of printed circuit boards.

It's critical for hardware engineers to work closely with those in algorithm development roles so that the hardware and algorithms support each other. This is a two-way street: algorithm design must be informed by hardware constraints, and hardware design must be informed by algorithm design.

Embedded software engineer

Embedded software engineers write the low-level code that brings a piece of hardware to life. Their code has to interface with sensors, run algorithms, and interpret their output in order to make decisions. They implement the embedded application itself.

Embedded ML engineer

Some embedded software engineers focus specifically on machine learning. Their job is to make sure that ML algorithms run as efficiently as possible on a particular piece of hardware. They may have deep knowledge of the mathematics behind machine learning, along with experience with low-level software optimization. They aren't necessarily an expert in data science, although they can likely train simple ML models.

This is a very new role, but it's growing in step with the edge AI space.

Industrial designer

An industrial designer creates the physical design of the product. This is relevant to edge AI in that the physical design dictates many of the realities of sensor data collection: moving a sensor to another location on a product can completely change its typical output and make a dataset instantly obsolete. This means there needs to be significant communication between industrial design, electronics engineering, and algorithm development.

Software engineer

Many projects involve software engineering outside of the embedded space. For example, a lot of edge AI projects involve a server-side component. Writing this backend code requires different skills to developing embedded applications, so a different type of engineer is needed.

Technical services

These supporting roles help keep the technical side of the development process running smoothly and manage the tools that keep the team productive and safe:

MLOps engineer

An MLOps engineer is responsible for building and maintaining the MLOps solutions that are used by the rest of the team. It's essentially a DevOps role (*https://oreil.ly/kEFI-*), but it requires strong understanding of the processes and demands of the edge AI workflow.

Security practitioner

This role attends to the security needs of the team, its data, and the products that are produced. It is both a consulting role—helping other roles understand how to be secure in what they do—and a proactive role, putting measures in place that help reduce security risk.

Quality assurance engineer

This role helps design and implement testing plans that put a product through its paces, allowing a team to understand whether the product is meeting its design goals. There's more about quality assurance in "Real-world testing" on page 321.

Hiring for Edge AI

A significant challenge of edge AI development is that as a very new field, there are not many people out there with experience working on it. At the time of writing, it is almost impossible to hire an engineer who has existing experience with edge AI: there are likely only a few hundred in the world, and most are still working on their first exciting edge AI projects and haven't had long enough to get itchy feet.

Fortunately, the fact that this is a new field means that even the most experienced engineers only have a couple of years' advantage. Recent advances in edge AI tooling, particularly in the form of end-to-end platforms, have massively reduced the barriers to entry. Hiring for edge AI has two main fronts where very specific knowledge is required: algorithm development and embedded engineering.

In the case of algorithm development, you'll likely be in the market for data scientists and ML practitioners. Some practitioners have backgrounds in applied engineering, solving practical problems in industry. Others may have a more academic background, investigating the principles underlying machine learning and coming up with new techniques.

Applied practitioners will have more experience with problem framing, which is very important in edge AI. This makes them a desirable choice, especially as an initial or solo hire. That said, academic researchers can still be a good fit for edge AI projects. They are less likely to have experience working within a typical software development environment and may take longer to ramp up. On the other hand, they are easier to hire than applied practitioners: there are simply more of them.

 ML research is very different from applied ML, and some ML researchers may feel bored routinely applying existing techniques rather than attempting to come up with new ones. Make sure that it's clear to candidates what the expectations are around a role to avoid disappointment on both sides.

One difficulty is that not many people in data science and machine learning have much experience with sensor data. While vision is a common modality, audio is less so, and time series sensor data is likely to be a mystery to most practitioners: while time series analysis is common in data science, it's not typically the type of high-frequency time series that are produced by electronic sensors.

Fortunately, DSP engineers have a similar workflow and toolchain to ML practitioners, and they are already experts in feature engineering for sensor data. The skills and experience of DSP engineers makes them well suited to learning embedded ML, so one potential avenue is to recruit DSP engineers and have them learn the basics of machine learning. A team composed of both DSP engineers and ML practitioners will have a much easier time than either role alone.

In terms of embedded engineering, the challenges vary. While working with deep learning interpreters (or code generated by a deep learning compiler) is often simply a matter of library integration, embedded engineers may sometimes have to dig into the internals to figure out when something is going wrong. In these cases, some knowledge and understanding of deep learning is definitely helpful. Embedded engineers may also end up being responsible for the onerous task of converting a model into the appropriate form to use on-device, which is definitely easier with some ML insight.

Another common task for embedded engineers is to implement classical ML models in software. There isn't yet a great embedded-specific C++ library for this but porting them is usually easy: there are reference implementations in higher-level languages that are simple to understand.

Unfortunately, finding an embedded engineer with existing ML knowledge is going to be a challenge for a while. That said, end-to-end platforms make things a lot easier, and eventually the number of experienced embedded ML engineers will grow. For now, it shouldn't be a blocker: a competent embedded engineer should be able to learn today's tools without too much trouble.

Learning Edge AI Skills

Over the last few years, some great resources have emerged for learning about AI at the edge. Like with most fields, there are two sides: theory and practice. Theory content will be most interesting to those who wish to contribute to advancing the field, while practical content is more helpful for those who wish to build products.

A word of caution: don't get lost in the weeds. Many people who wish to build AI products end up getting paralyzed by learning, exploring every rabbit hole they can rather than actually getting started on their projects. The reality is that this is a massive field, and you're never going to be able to learn it all. Be oriented toward action, learn enough to take your next step, and then reevaluate. Successful hardware products require teams, so figure out the minimum you need to know and then bring some experts on board.

Here are our top recommendations for both practical and theoretical content.

Practice

The final three chapters of this book, starting with Chapter 11, will walk through the edge AI workflow end to end with three real-world use cases: wildlife monitoring, food quality assurance, and consumer products.

Once you're done with that, here's some further content:

Introduction to Embedded Machine Learning (https://oreil.ly/ouQyM) (Coursera course)
   A highly rated online course intended as a practical introduction to the subject.

Computer Vision with Embedded Machine Learning (https://oreil.ly/LgjmK) (Coursera course)
   A follow-up to the first course, focused specifically on vision.

Applied Machine Learning (TinyML) for Scale (https://oreil.ly/jX-m1) (HarvardX course)
>This brilliant collection of courses focuses on the applied skills and big-picture expertise required for working with embedded ML.

TinyML Cookbook, a book by Gian M. Iodice (Packt, 2022)
>A practical book based around useful "recipes" that demonstrate various concepts within embedded ML.

TinyML, a book by Pete Warden and Daniel Situnayake (O'Reilly, 2020)
>A working introduction to embedded ML on microcontrollers, with examples focused on TensorFlow Lite for Microcontrollers.

Designing Machine Learning Systems, a book by Chip Huyen (O'Reilly, 2022)
>A fantastic book about the machine learning development workflow, geared toward server-side applications but still very relevant.

Making Embedded Systems, a book by Elecia White (O'Reilly, 2011)
>The best available practical introduction to developing embedded systems.

Theory

This content is for people who want to dig deeper into the theory of embedded machine learning. Remember, it's not a prerequisite for successful product development—so don't feel intimidated or get lost down the rabbit hole of studying.[3]

Tiny Machine Learning (TinyML) (https://oreil.ly/cZoLK) (HarvardX course)
>This set of courses overlaps with Applied Tiny Machine Learning (TinyML) for Scale, referenced earlier, but starts with the absolute fundamentals—which may not be necessary if you want to get building as quickly as possible.

The Scientist and Engineer's Guide to Digital Signal Processing, a book by Steven W. Smith (California Technical, 1997)
>A truly comprehensive guide to digital signal processing, available for free and as a hardcover book. A good resource for any non-DSP engineer who will be working seriously with DSP algorithms.

Hands-On Machine Learning with Scikit-Learn, Keras, and TensorFlow, a book by Aurélien Géron (O'Reilly, 2022)
>A wonderful introduction to practical machine learning concepts and skills. A good resource for any non-ML engineer who will be working with ML algorithms.

---

3 Remember, the best way to learn is to build! Don't fall into the common trap of thinking you need to memorize all of the theory first. This field develops so rapidly that you can never hope to learn it all.

Deep Learning with Python, a book by François Chollet (Manning, 2021)
Another fantastic introduction to ML, specifically focused on deep learning algorithms.

TinyML Foundation (https://oreil.ly/AdXwm) (YouTube channel)
The TinyML Foundation hosts regular presentations on embedded ML. Typically highly technical, this content reflects the cutting edge of research and engineering.

TinyML papers and projects (https://oreil.ly/P1YbW) (GitHub repository)
This repo is a goldmine of papers and resources related to the field.

Tools of the Trade

The story of edge AI is a story of tooling. In terms of raw technology, most of the basic ingredients required for putting artificial intelligence on edge devices have existed for a decade or more. However, these technologies—from capable embedded processors to deep learning models—tend to have a steep learning curve when they first become available.

Over time, however, our global technology ecosystem evolves tooling designed to manage the complexity and improve the usability of even the most challenging technologies. A rich combination of open source and commercial libraries, frameworks, and products have brought edge AI into the toolbox of the average embedded engineer.

A lot of this work has happened in the past two or three years, with libraries such as TensorFlow Lite for Microcontrollers (*https://oreil.ly/oowo5*)[4] and end-to-end development platforms like Edge Impulse (*https://edgeimpulse.com*)[5] bringing the technology over the threshold to enable mass adoption.

The following sections will walk through the tools that we think are most essential to AI at the edge. Successful teams will be at least passingly familiar with all of them.

End-to-End Platforms

End-to-end development platforms for edge AI incorporate many of the tools described in the following section, providing automated integration between them—along with a conscious, holistic design intended specifically for edge AI projects. They can massively reduce the complexity burden, making development much faster and less risky—and helping you avoid drowning in an ocean of unfamiliar tooling.

---

[4] Founded by Pete Warden, then at Google, who kindly wrote the foreword for this book.

[5] Which impressed this book's authors enough that we left jobs at Google and Arm to come and work on it.

End-to-end platforms are explained in their own section, "End-to-End Platforms for Edge AI" on page 162. While it's helpful to have a basic understanding of low-level tools, it's advisable to start with an end-to-end platform and only attempt to "roll your own" if the platform doesn't fully meet your needs. In that case, the best end-to-end platforms will integrate with other industry standard tools so that you can extend their functionality without losing the benefits.

Software Engineering

A large portion of edge AI involves software development, so modern software engineering tools are incredibly important. Here are some of the key contributors.

Operating systems

It's important to consider operating systems during both development and deployment. In development, your OS of choice will determine how easy it is to work with the extremely diverse set of software tools that make up the edge AI ecosystem. There's a bit of minor conflict between two different engineering traditions.

In embedded engineering it's historically common to use Windows as an operating system, and some embedded tools are written with this assumption. In contrast, the tools of data science and machine learning are typically best suited to a Unix-compatible environment such as Linux or macOS.

That said, this isn't a huge problem in practice. It's not strictly necessary for every member of a team to be able to run all of the tooling: for example, a machine learning engineer might train and optimize models with Linux and then hand them over to an embedded engineer who uses Windows. There are also plenty of tools for mixing environments, such as Windows Subsystem for Linux (*https://oreil.ly/VYaE6*). In addition, it's common for more recent embedded toolchains to work fine in Unix environments—although embedded engineers may still prefer Windows as a familiar environment. The entire team at Edge Impulse, including both embedded and ML engineers, uses a combination of macOS and Linux virtual machines.

In deployment, operating systems are sometimes used on edge devices themselves. These are typically either embedded Linux (stripped-down distributions of Linux compiled to run on SoCs) or real-time operating systems (RTOS), which are special embedded-specific operating systems designed to run with minimal overhead. Both of these options, plus the option of no OS at all[6] (which is the most common case for microcontrollers), are fully compatible with edge AI.

---

6 Known as "bare metal."

Programming and scripting languages

The two most important programming languages for edge AI are Python and C++. Python is overwhelmingly the current language of choice for machine learning, thanks to a vast array of open source mathematical and scientific computing libraries and nearly 100% adoption by the machine learning research community. Since Python is also a first-class language for general software engineering, it beats domain-specific languages such as R.[7] The two most important deep learning frameworks, TensorFlow and PyTorch, are both written in Python, as are the incredible tools we'll encounter in "Mathematical and scientific computing libraries" on page 143. Python has its quirks, but it's the right language to use for developing edge AI algorithms—from machine learning to DSP.

C++ (pronounced *C-plus-plus*) is a ubiquitous language in modern embedded software engineering. While some embedded platforms only support C (a simpler language than C++ that shares some characteristics), the high-end embedded devices that are typically used for edge AI are generally programmed with C++. The ecosystem around C++ features numerous tools and libraries that can make development easier, which is lucky—since it's the only game in town for most microcontroller-based systems.

C++ is a low-level language that provides a huge amount of control over the underlying hardware. It takes a skilled engineer to write good C++ code, but it can be much faster than the equivalent written in a higher-level language such as Python.

 It's interesting to note that most of the mathematical heavy lifting done by Python libraries is actually implemented in C++ under the hood: the Python code is just used as a convenient wrapper. This gives developers the best of both worlds.

You're also likely to use scripting languages, such as Bash, during the development process. They are used to chain together and automate the complex tools and scripts that help build applications and deploy them to devices.

In terms of targets, you can expect to almost always use C++ when working with microcontrollers. SoCs, which run full operating systems, are often a lot more flexible—you may be able to run high-level languages such as Python. The trade-off is that they are far more expensive and consume a lot more energy than smaller devices.

Since most targets require C++, you'll need to port any algorithms developed in higher-level languages (like Python) in order to deploy your work. There are some tools explained later that make this easier, but it's not always a simple process.

---

7 A popular language for statistical computing that is not typically used for purposes outside data analysis.

Dependency management

Modern software typically has a lot of dependencies, and AI development takes this to the next level. Data science and machine learning tools often require absurd numbers of additional third-party libraries; installing a major deep learning framework such as TensorFlow brings everything from web servers to databases along for the ride.

Things can get complex on the embedded side, too, since signal processing and machine learning algorithms commonly require sophisticated, highly optimized mathematical computing libraries. In addition, the compilation and deployment of embedded C++ code often requires a rat's nest of dependencies to be present on a machine.

All of these dependencies can be an absolute nightmare and managing them is truly one of the most challenging parts of edge AI development. Various techniques exist to make it easier, from containerization (see the next section, "Containerization" on page 139) to language-specific environment management.

For Python, one of the most helpful tools is called Poetry (*https://python-poetry.org*). It aims to simplify the process of specifying, installing, and isolating dependencies in multiple environments on a single machine.[8] Other essential tools include OS-specific package management systems like aptitude (*https://oreil.ly/aCq1n*) (Debian GNU/Linux) and Homebrew (*https://brew.sh*) (macOS).

One of the worst parts of dependency management comes when attempting to integrate different parts of a system together. For example, a model trained with one version of a deep learning framework may not be compatible with an inferencing framework released slightly later. This makes it extremely important to test systems end to end very early in the development process, to avoid nasty surprises later on.

Containerization

Containerization is the use of OS-level techniques to run software inside of sandboxed environments called *containers*. From inside, a container appears entirely distinct from the machine that is running it. It can have a different operating system and dependencies, and limited access to system resources.

Edge AI involves many different toolchains, used for everything from machine learning to embedded development. These toolchains often have mutually incompatible dependencies. For example, two toolchains might require entirely different versions of a language interpreter. Containerization is a powerful tool for enabling these incompatible toolchains to happily live side by side on a single machine.

---

8 The most common Python dependency management tools are pip (*https://oreil.ly/fV_w0*) and Conda (*https://conda.io*); Poetry is a relative newcomer but is highly recommended.

Containers are typically state-free and highly portable. This means that you can treat an entire painstakingly configured machine—described in a special syntax—as a command-line program that does a specific task. You can chain these together in order to perform useful work, and you can easily run them on different machines for a distributed computational environment.

It's also possible to run containers on embedded devices, typically within embedded Linux on an SoC. This can be an interesting way to package your software and its dependencies for distribution, although there is some overhead involved.

The most popular tools for containerization are Docker (*https://www.docker.com*) and Kubernetes (*https://kubernetes.io*). Docker is typically used locally on a development workstation, while Kubernetes is used to run clusters of containers within distributed computing infrastructure.

Distributed computing

Distributed computing is the idea of running different processes on different machines, potentially located anywhere in the world and connected via the internet. It's a more flexible way to approach computation than the use of single, high-powered mainframes and supercomputers, and it's the architectural style underlying the majority of modern computing.

Distributed compute is important to edge AI for many reasons. First, edge AI is an example of distributed computing! Computation is performed at the edge, where the data is created, and the results are either used locally or sent across the network.

Second, managing datasets, developing algorithms, and training machine learning models can be highly compute and storage intensive. This makes distributed computing a good fit for these parts of the process. For example, it's common to rent a highly capable remote server in order to train deep learning models—as opposed to having to buy and maintain a powerful machine for your office.

The task of organizing and controlling distributed computing infrastructure is called *orchestration*. There are many open source orchestration tools available, designed for different tasks. Kubeflow (*https://www.kubeflow.org*) is an orchestration framework designed for running machine learning workloads across multiple machines.

Cloud providers

Businesses like Amazon Web Services (*https://aws.amazon.com*), Google Cloud (*https://cloud.google.com*), and Microsoft Azure (*https://oreil.ly/zXZeB*) provide on-demand distributed computing resources that are available to anyone willing to pay for them. This type of distributed compute is known as "cloud compute," since diagrams of computer networks typically use a cloud symbol to signify resources that are located outside of the local network.

Cloud providers host most of the world's websites. They take care of the physical hardware and the network configuration, allowing developers to focus on building applications rather than managing equipment. They make heavy use of containerization to allow many different workloads to live side by side on the same infrastructure.

It's common for edge AI projects to use cloud compute for storing datasets, training machine learning models, and providing a backend from which edge devices can send and receive data. In some cases, such as "Cascade to the cloud" on page 288, AI algorithms running on cloud servers work in unison with those on edge devices in order to provide a service.

Working with Data

Data is a key ingredient of edge AI applications, and many tools exist for collecting, storing, and processing data.

Data capture

Obtaining data from the field can be difficult since there's often limited connectivity available at remote locations. Two useful tools are data loggers (*https://oreil.ly/0Tl46*) and mobile broadband modems (*https://oreil.ly/xl0eZ*).

Data loggers are small devices designed to capture and log data collected by sensors in the field. They typically have a large amount of persistent storage for collecting sensor readings and can either be battery powered or connected to a permanent power source. The benefit of using a data logger is that you can begin collecting data immediately, before designing and building any of your own hardware. The downside is that data needs to be collected manually, by physically connecting to the logger.

Mobile broadband modems provide a wireless internet connection, typically via cellular networks—although satellite connections are also available. They can potentially transmit data from almost anywhere in the world, although connectivity depends on local availability and conditions. They offer the convenience of immediate data availability. However, data rates can be quite expensive, and wireless communication consumes a lot of energy, so they are not feasible for use in all situations.

IoT device management

Many platforms exist for communicating with IoT devices, managing their operation, and collecting data from them. Using them typically involves integrating either libraries or APIs into your embedded software. The software then connects with a cloud server that you can use to control the device.

These platforms can be convenient for collecting sensor data, especially in brownfield deployments where device management software may already be in use.

Data storage and management

As you collect your dataset, you'll need somewhere to store it. This can be as simple as comma-separated files on a hard disk—or as complex as a time series database designed specifically for storing and querying time series data. We will cover some of these options in "Storing and Retrieving Data" on page 220.

Data storage solutions are designed for various purposes. Some are intended to be extremely fast at real-time querying of data, while others are designed to be as robust as possible against data loss. For edge AI applications, you're typically dealing with data in a "batch" mode, so performance isn't usually the most important factor. Instead, you should aim for a simple solution that fits the type of data you are collecting.

It's pretty common for AI datasets to be stored in the filesystem, without any type of database at all. Filesystems are designed for this type of data, and filesystem tools such as those available for the Unix command line can be helpful in manipulating it efficiently. Python's scientific computing ecosystem includes a lot of tools that are great at reading data from disk and helping you explore and visualize it.

While a fancy database isn't necessary, storing data in the right format is still important. As we will learn in "Formatting" on page 246, sensor readings themselves should be stored in an efficient, compact binary representation such as CBOR (*https://cbor.io*), NPY (*https://oreil.ly/FdGWo*), or perhaps TFRecord (*https://oreil.ly/ 5HZPO*)—which is specifically designed for high performance during machine learning training. Metadata about readings should be stored in separate files (known as *manifest files*) or in a simple database. Separating data from metadata in this way allows you to efficiently explore and manipulate datasets without reading massive files into memory.

Data pipelines

A data pipeline is a process that takes raw data and transforms it for use in a task, such as training a machine learning model. It's the way that data engineers automate things like data cleaning and wrangling. A typical data pipeline might take raw sensor data, filter it, combine it with other data, and write it into the correct format for training a machine learning model.

Many tools exist for defining data pipelines, some more complex than others. Edge AI data pipelines tend to involve very large amounts of relatively simple data, so avoid tools that are designed for working with structured data (such as data stored in relational databases). Instead of querying capabilities, look for high throughput and enough flexibility to run arbitrary signal processing algorithms.

Many cloud providers have features for running data pipelines in their distributed infrastructure. Some end-to-end platforms for edge AI make data pipelines a core feature and are designed specifically for the characteristics of sensor data.

Algorithm Development

Algorithm development is where most of the tooling complexity lives; there's a real galaxy of software available to help with the process. Some software is better suited to edge AI than others.

Mathematical and scientific computing libraries

The Python community has created some legitimate marvels of software engineering in the form of various open source libraries for performing mathematics and analysis of numbers. Some of the most important ones are:

NumPy (https://numpy.org)
> NumPy describes itself as "the fundamental package for scientific computing with Python," and it's absolutely true. It provides the high-performance backbone for most Python-based numerical computing, and it has a wonderful API that lets you do complex things to large arrays of numbers with minimal effort. Its file format, NPY, is a convenient way to store sensor data.

pandas (https://pandas.pydata.org)
> What NumPy is to arrays, pandas is to tables of data. It provides an almost magically intuitive syntax for querying and transforming any information that can be organized into rows and columns. Pandas works with NumPy, so you can use it to help explore your sensor data; it's super-fast.

SciPy (https://scipy.org)
> SciPy provides a collection of fast implementations of algorithms that are essential to scientific computing. It's used heavily in developing DSP algorithms, and it's the magic that powers many other tools.

scikit-learn (https://scikit-learn.org/stable)
> The library scikit-learn, built using NumPy and SciPy, provides a huge library of implementations of machine learning algorithms, along with the tools needed to feed them with processed data and evaluate their performance. Its API is designed so that you can plug its components together interchangeably, meaning you can easily compare and combine different algorithms. It's the gold standard for classical machine learning in Python, and its data processing and evaluation tools are often used even when training deep learning models with other frameworks.

Data visualization

When working with data, visualization is an essential tool—especially when the data concerned is digital signals. Graphs and charts allow us to represent and interpret numeric information that would otherwise be incomprehensible. The Python ecosystem has some fantastic libraries for visualizing data. They can be quite complex to get to grips with—especially if you want to customize visualizations beyond the provided defaults—but once you get the hang of them they can quickly turn rows of numbers into clear insight.

The two most common libraries are Matplotlib (*https://matplotlib.org*) and seaborn (*https://seaborn.pydata.org*). Matplotlib provides a million different ways to create data visualizations; it's commonly used to create the figures in scientific publications. Its syntax can be a little challenging, but it's so popular that a quick web search will usually help you figure out what you're trying to do.

Seaborn is built on top of Matplotlib and is designed to tame some of the complexity, making it easier to build attractive visualizations like the one in Figure 5-2 without getting tangled in difficult APIs. It's made specifically to pair well with pandas.

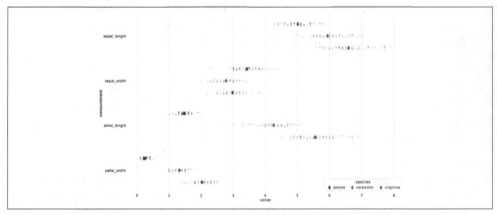

Figure 5-2. This plot shows the ranges and means for various columns in a dataset of plant measurements; it's one of the visualizations in seaborn's example gallery (https:// oreil.ly/uPOl0)

Seaborn and Matplotlib output image files—but some visualization libraries, such as Plotly (*https://plotly.com/python*), produce interactive visualizations that can be explored dynamically.

Interactive computing environments

Edge AI development involves a lot of exploration that lives outside of the context of routine software engineering. Exploratory data analysis, digital signal processing, and machine learning all have a workflow that involves trying different ideas and quickly visualizing the results.

Various interactive environments exist for this purpose. Rather than just running a script and writing the results to a file or having to build an entire web application just to express information visually, interactive computing environments allow code and visualizations to exist side by side in the same editor.

The most important interactive environment for Python code is called Jupyter Notebook (*https://jupyter.org*). Inside a notebook you can write and run Python code, and the output of the code is displayed alongside. This includes any visualizations you generate using libraries such as Matplotlib—as seen in Figure 5-3.

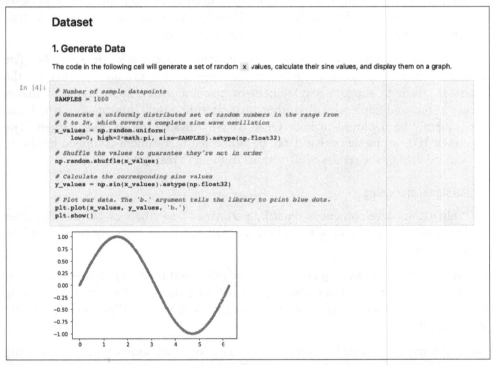

Figure 5-3. A screenshot from a Jupyter Notebook, showing a mixture of rich text, code, and the output of the code; the featured notebook is from the TensorFlow Lite for Microcontrollers Hello World example (https://oreil.ly/a976F)

This allows you to build interactive living documents that contain both the implementation of algorithms and the results of running them. They're valuable as both an interactive tool for experimentation and as documentary evidence of the work that you've done. A common workflow is to experiment with algorithms in a notebook until you find the best candidate, then port the code into regular Python scripts once you know it works well.

Jupyter can be run locally, but there are also Jupyter-based hosted environments. One of these is Google Colab (*https://oreil.ly/eA4Mb*), and another is Amazon SageMaker (*https://oreil.ly/GxOs-*). Both can be used without cost but will provide additional compute for a fee.

Another common environment for interactive computing is MATLAB (*https://oreil.ly/NJ7Pr*), which combines a similar interactive environment with its own programming language. It's common in academia and engineering, but as a closed-source commercial product that costs money to license, it's less popular with software engineers. It's quite likely that those with a background adjacent to electrical engineering are familiar with MATLAB, including DSP engineers.

There's even an interactive environment designed specifically for edge AI. The OpenMV IDE (*https://oreil.ly/f0-KB*) is an open source product created by the OpenMV team to support development of machine vision applications. It makes it easy to test and implement algorithms that interpret visual information, which can subsequently be deployed to both OpenMV's hardware, and to other targets. The OpenMV IDE is unique in that it can be connected to a camera-equipped hardware device and display the results of algorithms running in real time.

Digital signal processing

DSP algorithm development is typically performed in Python or MATLAB. Either environment can be used, with individual DSP engineers typically preferring one over the other.

In Python, SciPy's `scipy.signal` (*https://oreil.ly/UwJsO*) module provides implementations of a lot of important DSP algorithms. In MATLAB, the signal processing (*https://oreil.ly/X8umU*) and image processing (*https://oreil.ly/MYpwC*) toolboxes are very helpful.

MATLAB has some nice GUI-based tools that reduce the amount of programming required for algorithm development, but Python has the advantage of being directly compatible with the toolchains used for training machine learning models—as well as being free.

An increasingly popular third choice is GNU Octave (*https://www.octave.org*), designed to be a free, open source alternative MATLAB.

Deep learning frameworks

The ecosystem of deep learning tools is dominated by two wildly popular open source frameworks, written for Python: TensorFlow (*https://tensorflow.org*), created by Google, and PyTorch (*https://pytorch.org*), created by Meta.[9] Each framework originated as an in-house system for training deep learning models, and they both reflect the priorities of their respective sponsors.

Deep learning frameworks are different from typical software libraries (like NumPy or scikit-learn) in that they attempt to provide entire suites of tools under a single banner. TensorFlow and PyTorch both include systems for defining and training machine learning models, handling data, coordinating distributed systems, deploying to different types of compute, and much more.

Example 5-1. A simple deep learning model architecture being defined and trained using Keras, the high level API of TensorFlow

```
from tensorflow.keras.models import Sequential
from tensorflow.keras.layers import Dense

# Defining the model architecture
model = Sequential()
model.add(Dense(units=64, activation='relu'))
model.add(Dense(units=10, activation='softmax'))

# Setting up the training process
model.compile(loss='categorical_crossentropy',
              optimizer='sgd',
              metrics=['accuracy'])

# Training the model
model.fit(x_train, y_train, epochs=5, batch_size=32)

# Evaluating the model
loss_and_metrics = model.evaluate(x_test, y_test, batch_size=128)
```

The history of both tools has led to TensorFlow being the primary framework for industry, while PyTorch is the preferred tool of deep learning researchers.[10] A big part of this is due to the TensorFlow ecosystem having more options available for model deployment, and this is especially relevant for edge AI.

At the time of writing, the majority of tools for optimizing models for efficiency and deploying them to edge devices have been written to integrate with the TensorFlow

---

9 Back when they were known as Facebook.

10 The history and comparison between the two frameworks is quite interesting, and this fantastic blog post from AssemblyAI (*https://oreil.ly/6c6ta*) does a great job of summarizing it.

ecosystem. TensorFlow and PyTorch have different formats for storing models, and while there are ways to convert between them, it isn't a straightforward process.[11] This means that the majority of ML engineers working in edge AI currently use TensorFlow.

Since PyTorch is the framework of choice for researchers, many of the newest model architectures are available first in a PyTorch format. This can be frustrating for industry developers who are using TensorFlow for its deployment capabilities. Fortunately, most of the researchers focusing on producing smaller, more efficient models that are suited for edge deployment are doing so within the TensorFlow ecosystem. The area where model incompatibility is most frustrating is in visual object detection since the training code for object detection models tends to be complex and difficult to port from one framework to another.

At the time of writing, TensorFlow is the best choice of framework for edge AI development. Developers using PyTorch will struggle with a complex and unreliable conversion process when they attempt to deploy their models. It will be interesting to see how this evolves over time as the PyTorch ecosystem matures.

Model compression and optimization

Edge devices typically require small, efficient models—especially in a deep learning context, where parameter count and computational requirements can scale up fast. In "Compression and optimization" on page 117, we learned about the various techniques available for improving the performance of models. Some of them are applied during training, while others happen afterwards.

Compression and optimization tools are generally available either as part of deep learning frameworks or by hardware vendors whose hardware supports particular optimizations. The TensorFlow Lite converter (*https://oreil.ly/P5VHY*) has become the de facto standard for operator fusion and basic quantization, with the TensorFlow Lite model file format becoming close to a standard in the industry.[12] Still in the TensorFlow ecosystem, the TensorFlow Model Optimization Toolkit (*https://oreil.ly/ASl_h*) provides a collection of open source tools that cover other types of optimization and compression.

It's worth remembering that most optimization approaches also require special tooling at inference time, covered later in the sidebar "Inference and Model Optimization" on page 156. At the time of writing the best supported optimization approach is quantization, with 8-bit quantized operator implementations widely available. Other

---

11 In fact, it can be an absolute nightmare even for the most experienced developers.

12 Other formats are in use, such as ONNX (*https://onnx.ai*), but the TensorFlow Lite format is by far the most popular.

techniques are less well supported, with sparsity being the biggest red herring: it sounds impressive, but there's currently very little hardware that supports it.

Experiment tracking

Algorithm development is an iterative, exploratory process, and over the course of a project you're likely to make hundreds or thousands of different attempts at getting something that works acceptably well. It's important to keep things scientific, testing ideas systematically rather than just making random changes and hoping for the best. To achieve this, you'll need some kind of system for tracking experiments.

A typical experiment might involve taking a specific set of data samples, applying a particular DSP algorithm, using the features to train a machine learning model with a unique set of hyperparameters, and then testing the model on a standard test dataset. This situation has a lot of variables: the choice of samples, the DSP algorithm, the model, and its parameters.

Experiment tracking tools are designed to keep a log of which experiments are run, how their variables are set up, and what the results are. They try to organize what would otherwise be an unreliable, informal process of taking notes in a notebook and trying not to forget any details. Experiment trackers can also store the artifacts that result from experiments: training scripts, datasets, and trained models. This is helpful in understanding and reproducing your work at a later stage.

Experiment trackers are available as both open source packages and hosted commercial products. One of the simplest options is TensorBoard (*https://oreil.ly/nOaGP*), an official part of the TensorFlow ecosystem.[13] TensorBoard provides a simple web interface for visualizing and comparing the logs collected during training runs, along with some very powerful tools for optimizing and debugging training code. It's useful for keeping track of basic experiments, although it isn't designed as a persistent datastore that will last the lifetime of a project, and it doesn't work well if you are running very large numbers of trials.

A more sophisticated open source option is MLflow (*https://mlflow.org*). It's a complex web application, backed by a database that can track experiments, store trained models, and package data science code so that experiments can be reproduced easily. It's better suited to long-term use than TensorBoard, and it can scale to track many thousands of experiments. It doesn't have the same optimization and debugging features as TensorBoard, which remains the tool of choice for improving the computational performance of training.

Many commercial products exist to help with experiment tracking. A notable option is Weights & Biases (*https://wandb.ai/site*), which has a simple API and a

---

13 TensorBoard works with both TensorFlow and PyTorch.

well-designed web interface (along with many features that fit into the MLOps category, which we'll explore in "Machine learning operations (MLOps)" on page 151). A nice benefit of commercial tools is that you don't have to host them on your own infrastructure; you just pay a monthly fee and someone else performs the setup and maintenance and makes sure they are secure.

Automated machine learning (AutoML)

Once you begin tracking experiments using software, it's a simple step to start running them from software, too. AutoML tools are designed to automate the process of iteratively exploring a design space. Given a dataset and some constraints, they'll design experiments to test different combinations of variables in order to try and find the best model or algorithm.

This process is called *hyperparameter optimization*,[14] and it's a highly effective way to find the best model for a particular dataset. There are many different algorithms that guide hyperparameter optimization, from a simple grid search (where every possible combination of variable is tried in turn) to named algorithms such as Hyperband (*https://oreil.ly/OOeNa*) that aim to intelligently control the process for maximum efficiency.

AutoML isn't a magic wand that will solve problems for you. It still takes domain expertise to frame a problem and set up the design space in the correct way. What AutoML *can* do is take the guesswork and tedium out of the ML workflow: it's a way to automate the trial and error while you focus on more productive things.

Some AutoML systems just take a design space as input and output a list of experiments to run, while others take it a step further toward the MLOps world (see the next section, "Machine learning operations (MLOps)" on page 151) by orchestrating the process of running the experiments using distributed computing techniques. A particularly complex flavor of AutoML is neural architecture search (NAS), which incorporates machine learning into the process of exploring the design space.

In terms of specifics, we recommend Ray Tune (*https://oreil.ly/8eGs9*) as a popular open source framework for hyperparameter tuning that is able to orchestrate the task of running hyperparameter optimization within your distributed infrastructure. Sweeps by Weights & Biases (*https://oreil.ly/-tRCq*) is a commercial, hosted product that helps orchestrate experiments on your own hardware.

AutoML is especially powerful for edge AI. This is because models designed for edge devices tend to be small and quick to train, which makes it easy to try a lot of different options. It's also especially important, since in edge AI we are optimizing for

---

14 Or *hyperparameter tuning.*

more than just model accuracy: we also need to find the smallest, fastest, and lowest power-consuming models that we can.

Typical AutoML tools don't account for these things, but some end-to-end edge AI platforms do.[15]

Machine learning operations (MLOps)

The machine learning workflow has a lot of moving parts, and MLOps is the art and science of keeping track of them all. It encompasses many of the types of tools that we've covered in this chapter, from data storage systems to experiment tracking and AutoML capabilities.

As an engineer on an ML project, you're doing MLOps whether you're conscious of it or not. Even in the simplest projects, keeping track of your dataset, training scripts, and your current best model can be a challenge. In more complex projects, where every part of the workflow is constantly evolving as the result of feedback loops, keeping a handle on what is going on can be nearly impossible without effective tools.

ML Pipelines

One of the key pieces of functionality that makes up an MLOps solution is the ability to define and run ML pipelines. An ML pipeline is a scripted process that takes data, applies transformations (including signal processing or any other feature engineering), uses it to train a machine learning model, and evaluates the results. It's an extension of a data pipeline that includes the ML parts, too.

While initial experimentation often takes place in a notebook or in local scripts, it's common to start defining a formal pipeline once you want to begin automating the process of training a model. For example, pipelines make it easier to run repeated experiments to try different hyperparameters, and they are convenient if you are continually adding fresh data and want to automatically train and compare new models.

The simplest ML pipelines are implemented using scripting languages, either Python or Bash, and run on a single machine. More complex pipelines may be designed to run in distributed infrastructure, potentially with steps running in parallel to improve performance. It's common for sophisticated ML pipelines to make use of containerization (see "Containerization" on page 139): each step of the pipeline may be defined in a separate container that contains all of its required dependencies, and the containers are invoked one after the other.

---

15 Introduced in "End-to-End Platforms for Edge AI" on page 162.

An MLOps system can be built from individual components: you may choose one tool for dataset management, another tool for experiment tracking, and a different tool to store your best models. It is equally common to use comprehensive frameworks that take care of every stage in the process. It's also possible to use a mixture of comprehensive frameworks and whichever individual tools fit your specific needs.

MLOps is a big area that encompasses many categories of tools, including some that we've seen earlier in this chapter. The website *ml-ops.org*, a great resource for understanding MLOps, says that MLOps includes the following tasks:[16]

- Data engineering
- Version control of data, ML models, and code
- Continuous integration and continuous delivery pipelines
- Automating deployments and experiments
- Model performance assessment
- Model monitoring in production

Since edge AI is a new field, most MLOps systems are designed with the assumption that models will be "served" by web services, not deployed to edge devices. The unique nature of edge AI development involves some additional tasks, including:

- Capture of data from devices and sensors
- Digital signal processing and rule-based algorithms
- Estimation of on-device performance[17]
- Model compression and optimization
- Conversion and compilation for edge device support
- Tracking which model versions are currently in the field

A great way to think about MLOps is as a "stack": a set of software tools that work together to enable development, deployment, and maintenance of an edge AI system. The company Valohai created the idea of an MLOps stack template (*https://oreil.ly/MKaon*): a diagram that shows how all of the components of the MLOps stack fit together. Their original stack template is based on a server-side context, but Figure 5-4 shows the idea adapted to suit edge ML.

---

16 Listed in State of MLOps (*https://oreil.ly/aGKfQ*) at *ml-ops.org*.

17 Including both model quality and computational performance.

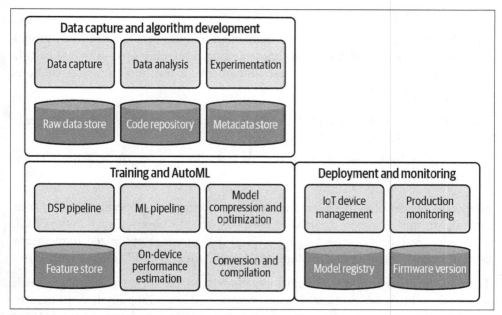

Figure 5-4. A stack template for ML at the edge; you'll need a solution for each of the boxes, and probably some others depending on your particular use case

Over the course of development, you might choose to incrementally assemble your stack from various software components. On the other hand, you may benefit from working with a comprehensive MLOps platform that is designed specifically for edge AI, as we'll encounter in "End-to-End Platforms for Edge AI" on page 162.

MLOps is a massive topic, too extensive to cover fully in a book about edge AI. If you're looking to dig deeper, we recommend the following resources—with the caveat that most MLOps content is written with server-side models, not edge AI, in mind:

- The website *ml-ops.org*.
- *Introducing MLOps*, a book by Mark Treveil et al. (O'Reilly, 2020).
- Google Cloud's introduction to MLOps (*https://oreil.ly/ang28*), an excellent technical article.

Running Algorithms On-Device

Designing algorithms and training models requires one set of tools, while another is needed to run them efficiently on-device. These include both general-purpose C++ libraries and highly efficient implementations that are optimized for specific hardware architectures.

Math and DSP libraries

Various implementations of common mathematical operations are available, providing functionality for both DSP algorithms and deep learning ops—it would be time consuming to have to implement these fundamental algorithms from scratch. Some notable examples are:

- Fast Fourier transforms, used heavily in DSP, such as KISS FFT (*https://oreil.ly/BPyFl*) and FFTW (*https://www.fftw.org*).
- Matrix multiplication libraries such as gemmlowp (*https://oreil.ly/6hCG3*) and ruy (*https://oreil.ly/WSrv4*).

Hardware devices often have features designed to improve the performance of common algorithms. These are available in hardware-specific libraries, such as the CMSIS DSP Software Library (*https://oreil.ly/PkVwj*) that provides optimized implementations of many popular DSP algorithms for Arm's Cortex-M and Cortex-A hardware.

There are similarly optimized implementations available for deep learning kernels, such as the CMSIS NN Software Library (*https://oreil.ly/dLOXy*). Equivalents exist for many modern processor architectures, including microcontrollers and SoCs. When choosing hardware, you should investigate the availability of optimized kernels, since they can make a huge (10–100x) difference in latency.

Machine learning inference

One way to run inference on an edge device is to write a custom program that implements a specific deep learning model in code that is hand-optimized for the target architecture. However, this would be time consuming and inflexible: you wouldn't be able to reuse your code for new applications or with different hardware, and if you made any changes to your model you would have to change your entire program.

Developers have come up with various solutions to avoid this problem.[18] The most common approaches are as follows:

Interpreters
An interpreter (or *runtime*) is a program that reads a file describing a model, including both its operations and its parameters, and then uses a set of prewritten operators to execute the model's operations one after the other. Interpreters are very flexible: using an interpreter, an identical few lines of code can be used to run any model interchangeably. The trade-off is that the process of reading and interpreting a model introduces some operational overhead beyond what

---

18 Pete Warden has an excellent blog post (*https://oreil.ly/UbDtm*) that outlines the technical challenges in this area.

is required for the model's operations. Interpreters consume additional RAM, ROM, and CPU cycles.

The most widely used interpreters are both from the TensorFlow ecosystem. TensorFlow Lite (*https://oreil.ly/vc3-p*) was originally designed for cellphones but works on many popular SoCs, and TensorFlow Lite for Microcontrollers (*https://oreil.ly/OHQ9a*) works well on microcontrollers and DSPs. Both of them are implemented in C++, but TensorFlow Lite provides Python and Java APIs for convenience. They both benefit from operator fusion and quantization provided by the TensorFlow Lite converter (*https://oreil.ly/_ryR8*).

The kernels used by interpreters can be switched out depending on the device being targeted, so highly efficient optimized kernels can be used where available. These are readily available for several common devices and architectures.

Code generation compilers

With a code generation approach, a code-generating compiler takes a model file as input and transforms it into a program that implements it. For operator support, the program relies on a library of prewritten operators, calling them in the correct order and passing the appropriate parameters.

Code generation provides many of the same benefits as an interpreter-based approach but eliminates the majority of the overhead associated with the interpreter itself. Code generation may even make use of the wide array of prewritten operators available for interpreters: for example, Edge Impulse's EON Compiler (*https://oreil.ly/GN5oT*) is compatible with TensorFlow Lite for Microcontrollers kernels.

Bytecode compilers

It's possible for a compiler with knowledge of a target to directly generate the bytecode that implements a model, applying target-specific optimizations along the way. This results in a highly efficient implementation that makes use of whatever performancing-enhancing features are available on the silicon. For example, Synaptics' TENSAI Flow neural network compiler (*https://oreil.ly/1bP6V*) is designed to compile models for deployment to Synaptics Katana Edge AI processors.

Virtual machines

The big downside of the bytecode compiler approach is that a compiler has to be written for each device that is going to be targeted, and writing a compiler is a difficult task. To get around this problem, some compilers target a so-called *virtual machine*: an abstraction layer that sits directly above the hardware and provides instructions that map to various low-level processor capabilities.

The abstraction layer slightly reduces the efficiency, but the benefits can outweigh the drawbacks—although the virtual machine still has to be ported to new processors. This approach is used by Apache TVM (*https://tvm.apache.org*), which also uses an on-device runtime that can iteratively test different implementations to find the most efficient.

Hardware description language

A newly emerging trend is the use of special compilers to generate hardware description language (HDL), the code that describes processor architectures and is used to program FPGAs and ASICs. Using these techniques, it is possible to implement a model directly in hardware, which can be extremely efficient.

CFU Playground (*https://oreil.ly/SzHbP*) and Tensil (*https://www.tensil.ai*) are both open source tools that aim to make it easier to design custom accelerators using this approach.

Alternative methods

Some accelerator chips are programmed using systems that fall outside of the normal workflow of code and compilation. For example, some chips with hardware implementations of neural network kernels provide an interface via which a model's weights are written directly to a special memory buffer, separately from any application code.

Inference and Model Optimization

The optimization of kernels for high performance on specific devices is distinct from the optimization of *models* through compression and other techniques. Model optimizations tend to require their own kernel—and sometimes hardware—support.

For example, to run a quantized model, kernels compatible with the specific level of quantization must be available. A model quantized to 8-bit integer precision requires kernels designed to support it, and the same is true of other quantization levels. In fact, specific kernels are required depending on the data type used, whether that might be `int8`, `uint8`, `int16`, or so on.

The same is true of other optimization techniques. For example, pruning results in models that have a large amount of sparsity: they have lots of zeros. By itself, this doesn't make any difference to execution time—the model has to be run using special kernels or hardware that can make use of the sparsity to reduce computation time. These kernels and hardware have yet to enter wide availability, so pruning remains of limited utility in the field.

On-device learning

As we learned in "On-Device Training" on page 119, the data and computational requirements of deep learning training means that on-device training remains of limited utility. Most of the time, "on-device training" means a simple approach that involves calculating the distance between embedding vectors, for example if determining whether the embeddings of two fingerprints are a match.

It's very rare for actual deep learning training to happen on an edge device. If you do have a device with the required amount of storage and compute—typically an SoC or mobile telephone— TensorFlow Lite provides some functionality (*https://oreil.ly/WDBo7*).

The problem remains that it is incredibly difficult to understand whether a model trained on-device is actually performing well. On-device deep learning is best avoided unless you have an extremely good reason to require it.[19]

Federated learning remains a topic of fascination for many people, but as we learned earlier in the book it is not a particularly good fit for the vast majority of problems. In addition, the tooling around federated learning is still primitive and experimental.[20] Many people feel drawn to follow the federated learning rabbit hole and end up wasting time: the chance that a project really needs it is very slim. However, if you really feel compelled to dig deeper, TensorFlow Federated (*https://oreil.ly/6dxOr*) is a good resource.

Embedded Software Engineering and Electronics

Edge AI is a subfield of embedded software engineering, which is closely tied to the practical disciplines of electrical engineering and electronics. Each of these areas involves multitudes of tools and techniques—there's no way we'd have space in this book to cover them all.

Instead, we'll step through the parts that specifically matter for developing AI at the edge.

---

19 Pete Warden's blog post, "Why Isn't There More Training on the Edge?" (*https://oreil.ly/vo7-R*) does a great job of illuminating this topic.

20 Although it will invariably improve over time.

Just Getting Started

If you're prototyping your own edge AI project but don't have much embedded experience, Arduino (*https://www.arduino.cc*) and Arduino Pro (*https://www.arduino.cc/pro*) products are a great place to start. Arduino has created an embedded development environment that is easy for beginners to use but still powerful enough for building real applications—perfect if you're an ML engineer beginning to work with edge devices, or a newcomer to both fields. The Arduino team have understood the potential of the edge AI movement since the very beginning and have contributed a lot to its growth.

Embedded hardware tools

Developing embedded software is challenging due to the nature of embedded devices. Software is harder to debug when it's running on a separate device, especially one with limited ways to display its internal state. Embedded programs must take care of everything from basic hardware integration—it's common to have to write your own drivers for hardware such as sensors—to the complex handshakes of low-level communications protocols.

As such, embedded development requires some tools that would appear unusual to other software engineers. Some of these items include:

- Device programmers, which are pieces of hardware that allow a developer to upload new programs to an embedded device. They are often device specific.

- Debug probes, hardware devices that connect to embedded processors and allow analysis of a program at runtime. They are also device specific.

- USB to UART adapters, which send and receive arbitrary data between the developer's workstation and the embedded device. They are generic.

- Multimeters, which measure voltage, current, and resistance and can be used to understand the state of an embedded circuit as it is being controlled by a program.

- Oscilloscopes, which measure signals on the device or PCB, expressed as voltage over time.

These tools are necessary in order to reach into, manipulate, and understand the states of embedded devices. For example, to test a program is running correctly you might have it toggle a specific pin on the processor when it gets to a certain point. You would then use a multimeter to measure whether the pin has been toggled. Another common way to communicate with an embedded device is via a serial (UART) cable, which can send and receive data at a relatively low frequency—but still high enough to transfer sensor data in a reasonable timeframe.

Development boards

An embedded processor on its own is just a little piece of sand, wrapped in plastic. In order to actually do anything, it requires a small constellation of other electronic components to be wired up to it. As we saw in "Boards and Devices" on page 79, development boards (or dev boards) provide a convenient ready-to-go platform that includes an embedded processor and various inputs and outputs, often including some sensors.

The goal of a dev board is to allow embedded engineers to evaluate a particular chip for suitability for a project, and allow software development to proceed without being blocked by the hardware development process. Once a working iteration of the product's own hardware is ready, development can move there. The exception is with rapid prototyping platforms, such as Arduino Pro (*https://www.arduino.cc/pro*), which are designed for use in small-batch production designs.

Dev boards are available for most families of embedded processors. When deciding on hardware, it's a good idea to obtain a few different dev boards to experiment with. For example, you might try to run an early version of your deep learning model on a few different dev boards to understand their relative performance.

Some end-to-end platforms (see "End-to-End Platforms for Edge AI" on page 162) provide deep integration with dev boards, allowing you to capture data from their sensors or deploy and evaluate models without writing a single line of code. This can be extremely useful in development and testing.

Embedded software tools

For the purposes of edge AI, embedded software engineering generally means C++ development. This can be done in your text editor of choice, but it's also common for embedded processor vendors to provide their own integrated development environments (IDEs) that integrate neatly with their hardware and make it easier to upload and debug code.

Vendors will often provide SDKs, drivers, and libraries that can be used on their hardware to help you access various processor features—but they are not always great quality, often provided more as a proof of concept than as production-quality code.

To reduce the amount of boilerplate code you need to write, you may choose to use a real-time operating system (RTOS). An RTOS provides the functionality of a simple operating system, but it arrives as a bunch of library code that you compile alongside your own program. You can then call the RTOS APIs to do things such as controlling peripherals or performing network communication.

Embedded development frequently involves complex toolchains: programs and scripts that are supplied by the hardware vendor and are used to take code from a text file, turn it into a program, and "flash" it onto a hardware device.

The workflow generally looks like this:

1. Make changes to your source code.

2. Run a compiler (supplied by the processor vendor) and linker to transform your code into a binary.

3. Run a script to flash your code onto the embedded device.

4. Use a serial connection to communicate with the device and test your code.

When your code is running on-device, you can often use a hardware tool called a *debug probe* to inspect it from your development machine. This allows you to debug as if you were running the code locally, setting break points, examining variables, and stepping through code.

Some parts of your code will be generic C++, and you'll be able to run it on your development machine with no problem, perhaps in the form of unit tests. However, you'll also end up with plenty of code that integrates with the specific hardware APIs of your processor. It's not possible to run that on your development machine—so you can either shrug your shoulders and test it on-device only, or you can attempt to use an emulator.

Emulators and simulators

An *emulator* is a piece of software that aims to reproduce a processor virtually, running on your development machine, so that you can execute your embedded code without having to flash it to the device. It will never be a perfect representation of the real hardware—for example, it won't necessarily run at the exact same speed as the program on real hardware—but it can be close enough to be a valuable tool.

If you need to determine how fast a program will run, for example in order to estimate the latency of an AI algorithm, a cycle-accurate simulator will allow you to determine the exact number of clock cycles that will run on the real hardware. You can divide this number by the clock rate to give you a precise estimate of latency. The emulator won't actually *run* at that speed, but it will give you the information you need to create an estimate.

Simulation is the use of software to simulate an entire device, including an emulated processor plus all of the other devices it may be attached to—including sensors and communications hardware. Some simulators can even represent multiprocessor boards, or entire networks of interconnected devices.

Emulators aren't available for all processors, but Renode (*https://renode.io*) is a powerful emulation and simulation environment for many common processor architectures, and Arm Virtual Hardware (*https://oreil.ly/iXED4*) allows you to emulate Arm processors in the cloud.

Embedded Linux

Most of the specialized embedded tools we've mentioned so far are intended for working with microcontrollers and other bare-metal devices. SoCs and edge servers are another story: with enough computing power and memory to host a full-blown operating system, SoC development is much more similar to development for personal computers and web servers. This is one of their major benefits: developers don't need quite so many specialized skills.

A typical SoC will run a distribution of Linux, with all the helpful tools and libraries that that implies. Programming can be done in nearly any language, with the same trade-offs as on any other platform: low-level languages like C++ are fast and efficient, while high-level languages like Python are flexible and easy to use.

Google provides a TensorFlow Lite runtime (*https://oreil.ly/VAk82*) that is prebuilt for some popular platforms, and you'll have the benefit of being able to use Python computing libraries directly: for example, you can use SciPy's digital signal processing functions within your application.

Embedded Linux devices can even make use of containerization for deployment: embedded applications can be packaged as Linux containers, making them easy to install and use.

With SoCs, it's relatively common to use an off-the-shelf board in a production installation. Many vendors exist who design and sell SoC-based platforms designed for specific applications. For example, you can buy devices in ruggedized housing designed for industrial deployments. To deploy, you just connect whatever sensors are required and install your application.

One challenge working with SoCs is that despite the familiar Linux environment, prebuilt packages are not always available. You may have to get used to building libraries from source in order to make your applications work, which can get a little involved at times.

It's important to think about security when working with devices that have fully fledged operating systems. The embedded Linux running on an SoC needs to be locked down as tightly as any other machine on your network to avoid it becoming a vector for attacks. Insecure IoT devices are notorious for being compromised by hackers and used to attack other systems.

Automated hardware testing

Modern software engineering best practices encourage the use of continuous integration tests: every code change is put through its paces by a suite of automated tests. Creating automated tests for embedded applications can be difficult, since code that interacts with hardware can't be tested on a development machine; it can only be tested on the target device itself.

However, it's easy for an embedded device to get into a state where it is unable to run tests. For example, if the program crashes it may not be possible to restart the device without physically interacting with it. Similarly, uploading new firmware may require physical intervention.

To get around this problem, developers build automated hardware testing systems that can interact with embedded devices to facilitate easier testing. These systems are a combination of software and hardware that can do things like flash new code, power cycle devices between tests, and even provide input to I/O ports or sensors.

Automated hardware testing systems are usually custom built. They are based around a host system (perhaps an embedded device itself) that is connected to whatever continuous integration tools the team is using, as well as being connected to the devices that are intended to run the code.

If integration with a sensor needs to be tested—for example, a microphone that is supposed to be detecting a keyword—the host system might even feature a speaker that can issue keywords on demand.

End-to-End Platforms for Edge AI

In an ideal world, any team with expertise in a certain domain would be able to capture its knowledge and deploy as edge AI. People with deep insight into diverse fields like healthcare, agriculture, manufacturing, and consumer technology should be able to take what they know and use it to build amazing AI-powered products.

Unfortunately, with so many moving parts and so much to learn, it's easy to feel overwhelmed by the edge AI development process. A huge amount of the workflow is focused not on domain knowledge but on the arcane engineering skills required to build a complex product across multiple fronts, including machine learning, digital signal processing, and low-level software engineering on embedded hardware.

In the early days, only a small number of technologists—who happened, by accident, to have all of the required skills—were able to work with edge AI technology. However, over the past few years a vibrant ecosystem of tools has sprung up that is designed to reduce the barriers to entry and make it possible for people without backgrounds in machine learning or embedded systems to build fantastic new products.

End-to-end edge AI platforms are designed to assist developers with the entire process of developing an application: collecting, managing, and exploring datasets; performing feature engineering and digital signal processing; training machine learning models; optimizing algorithms for embedded hardware; generating efficient low-level code; deploying to embedded systems; and evaluating systems' performance on real-world data. This flow is summarized in Figure 5-5.

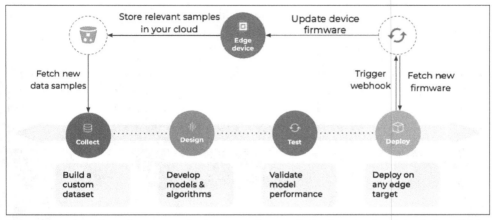

Figure 5-5. A major advantage of using an end-to-end platform is that it includes all of the components required for an iterative, data-driven feedback loop; that said, the most flexible platforms provide points for integration with external tools (Image courtesy of Edge Impulse Inc.)

End-to-end platforms are designed to apply the principles of MLOps to the specific process of creating algorithms that will run on embedded devices. As highly integrated tools, they are able to take most of the friction out of the development process: far less time is wasted in getting different parts of a toolchain to work together, and a holistic view of the entire process allows for helpful guidance that massively reduces exposure to risk.

For example, an end-to-end platform can analyze a dataset in order to help a user select the type of ML model best suited to it, or it might provide estimates of on-device performance that can help the developer choose an algorithm or embedded processor. A platform may perform AutoML with the goal of finding the best possible combination of signal processing and model that will fit on a specific device, within a maximum specified latency, or within a limited power budget.[21] A wide range of ready-to-deploy algorithms or architectures are typically available, preoptimized for various processors.

Platforms can also help teams collaborate. For instance, a cloud-based edge AI platform can act as a central repository for a team's datasets and workflow artifacts. APIs and configurable ML pipelines allow teams to automate routine tasks: so, for example, a new version of a model might be trained, tested, and deployed whenever new data is available. And visualizations and low-code user interfaces make it possible for

---

21 The paper by Kanav Anand et al., "Black Magic in Deep Learning: How Human Skill Impacts Network Training" (*https://oreil.ly/-TlS9*) (arXiv, 2020), shows that prior experience can have a strong impact on performance when tuning ML models by hand, which suggests the value of AutoML tools.

anyone on a team to contribute insight, not just those with existing data science or embedded engineering skills.

Cloud-based platforms also allow developers to benefit from distributed compute without having to administer their own systems. For example, data processing and model training might occur on powerful cloud servers that are managed by the platform, not by the user. This simplifies the process of running AutoML, where experiments may be run in parallel—as shown in Figure 5-6.

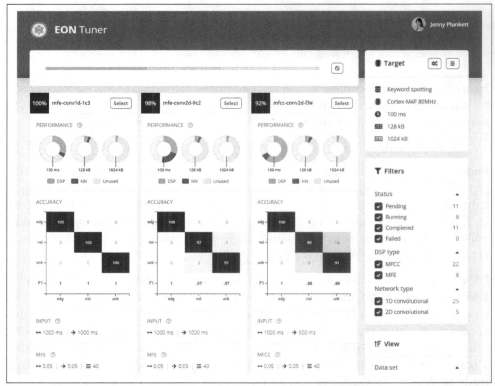

Figure 5-6. An AutoML sweep conducted using Edge Impulse's EON Tuner (https:// oreil.ly/QP1pZ); with end-to-end platforms, optimization of signal processing and machine learning algorithms can occur hand in hand, incorporating estimates of on-device latency and memory use

The best end-to-end platforms have a focus on tightening all the feedback loops in the edge AI workflow. They make it possible to iterate rapidly, moving back and forth between development and testing with minimal overhead. This makes it far easier to build a successful product, since you're able to immediately detect and course-correct on any issues.

Traditionally, getting an algorithm to run on-device for the first time—using real sensor data—has been a tricky process. Some end-to-end platforms provide prebuilt firmwares for popular development boards, allowing you to capture sensor data and deploy and test models without writing any code. This enables you to close the loop between model development and real-world testing.

Another big benefit provided by end-to-end platforms is the ability to conveniently try out a variety of hardware to find the best fit. The same model can potentially be deployed in an optimized form to a multitude of microcontrollers, SoCs, and ML accelerators with a couple of clicks, allowing a development team to compare performance and determine the right choice for their application. Done by hand, this process could take weeks.

The AI ecosystem is built on top of open source tools, and good end-to-end platforms will allow you to continue using them however you want; they will integrate with industry standard technologies throughout the workflow and won't rely on vendor lock-in to keep you as a customer. You should be able to easily export your data, models, and training code, and it should be simple to create a mixed MLOps stack that incorporates parts of multiple solutions.

End-to-End or Roll Your Own?

You may be wondering which is a better choice: using an end-to-end platform or assembling your own custom set of tools from different sources. At the time of writing, it's pretty clear that the vast majority of projects will benefit from the productivity, structure, and cross-workflow integration provided by an end-to-end platform.

Even if you have strong existing skills in data science, signal processing, or embedded engineering, the process of setting up your own toolchain from scratch can be extremely tough. Depending on your target, you may find that you aren't even able to install the required tools side by side without resorting to containerization in order to isolate dependencies.

Beyond startup costs, individual tools on their own won't provide the type of immediate feedback and seamless iterative workflow required to build a successful project. You'll have to create your own automation between tools, which will result in countless scripts—and further dependencies—that need to be tracked, maintained, and scaled to serve your whole team.

In addition, end-to-end platforms are designed to provide the appropriate guidance to fill in your blind spots. Almost nobody has all of the required skills to build an edge AI application on their own. For example, someone with deep domain expertise is unlikely to also have a strong intuition about which deep learning model architectures are most efficient on a specific model of embedded processor.

The teams developing end-to-end platforms for edge AI have spent years building and improving them—so while it's certainly possible for a sufficiently large enterprise organization to build their own internal platform, it would be a multimillion dollar investment in time and resources. It's very unlikely that the cost-benefit analysis would make sense, which is why some of the world's biggest, most sophisticated organizations—from government organizations like NASA to industrial giants like Bosch—are users of end-to-end platforms.

A major, valid concern is around flexibility and openness. If a company decides to use an end-to-end platform, what happens if they need to use techniques—for example, specific algorithms—that aren't available in the platform?

Fortunately, the best platforms already account for this and provide easy integration points for interoperability. New algorithms, data stores, deployment targets, and evaluation methods can be connected seamlessly, and APIs allow end-to-end platforms to be interwoven with other tools, including existing internal systems and alternative open source AI tooling.

Another concern is cost. End-to-end platforms are typically supported by an enterprise subscription fee that includes technical support and compute time, with many products also offering a free tier for individual projects. One platform, Edge Impulse, has a large, active community of free users who provide support to one another, including sharing example projects for inspiration and technical guidance.

If you don't have a budget, it's absolutely possible to use a product's free tier to build a successful project. If you do have a budget, platforms are typically quite affordable—especially when compared to the time cost of setting up and managing your own environment. The subscription cost typically buys you the type of heavy duty functionality that is required when dealing with big enterprise datasets and large teams.

Given the absurd complexity of the edge AI toolchain, it's very easy to recommend end-to-end edge AI platforms as the best starting point for the vast majority of projects. In the uncommon case that you require a feature that isn't supported, high-quality platforms make it simple to integrate with external tools—so you can use the platform as a foundation and extend it however you need.

At this point, it's worth addressing the fact that the authors of this book, Daniel and Jenny, are part of the team that has designed and developed Edge Impulse (*https://edgeimpulse.com*), an extremely popular end-to-end edge AI development platform. It's always important to take recommendations with a pinch of salt when the people doing the recommendation have a vested interest! Since we work on an end-to-end tool, how can we be expected to recommend anything else?

Hopefully, the history of this book provides some reassurance. One of the authors, Dan, was coauthor of *TinyML*—a book that helped introduce the field of embedded machine learning to a wider audience. *TinyML* introduces the process of building edge AI software using open source tools. At about 500 pages, it's not a short guide—but it only covers the absolute basics, and it relies on its readers learning both Python and C++. Working directly with low-level tools is not a productive way to go.

Writing *TinyML* inspired both of its authors to try and make life easier for developers. Dan went on to join Edge Impulse as its founding engineer, inspired by a demo where the company's CEO built and deployed a deep learning model for activity classification live in under ten minutes. The other coauthor of *TinyML*, Pete Warden, is working to simplify machine learning deployment by integrating sensors and ML as closely as possible.

Machine Learning Sensors

Building an effective edge AI product requires a lot of difficult work and specialized knowledge. Another concept that could help make the task easier is the idea of *machine learning sensors*. Proposed in a 2022 paper[22] by a team led by Pete Warden, ML sensors are designed to be as simple to work with as ordinary sensors—but to include a dash of intelligence.

For example, a "person detector" ML sensor might be provided as a single chip that includes an image sensor, a processor, and a deep learning model that can identify human beings from images. As an interface, the ML sensor could expose a single digital pin that toggles high when a person is detected or low when there is nobody there.

Integrating with an ML sensor would be far easier than training and incorporating a machine learning model (along with all of the required dependencies) into an embedded application, making it trivial to add intelligence to devices. The trade-off is reduced flexibility—although if required, models could be customized via integration with end-to-end platforms.

At the time of writing, Pete's company Useful Sensors (*https://usefulsensors.com*) is selling the Person Sensor, a small, low-power device that can detect and locate human faces. You can find more general information at ML Sensors (*https://mlsensors.org*).

Summary

We've now encountered the people, skills, and tools that are prerequisites to successful edge AI projects. From the next chapter onward, we'll be taking a journey through the iterative development workflow that real-world teams use to build applications.

---

22 Pete Warden et al., "Machine Learning Sensors" (*https://oreil.ly/xOtDp*), arXiv, 2022.

## CHAPTER 6

Understanding and Framing Problems

The next five chapters provide a roadmap for working with edge AI. We'll establish best practices for:

- Viewing the problems you want to solve through the lens of edge AI
- Building datasets that allow you to you train models and evaluate algorithms
- Designing applications that make use of edge AI technologies
- Developing effective applications through an iterative process
- Testing edge AI applications, deploying them, and monitoring them in the field

For this chapter in particular, we'll start by introducing a high-level, general workflow for edge AI projects. This should give you a sense of how everything will fit together. After that we'll learn how to evaluate projects to make sure they are a good fit for edge AI, then walk through the process of identifying which types of algorithms and hardware make sense for a given problem—and start to think about planning our implementation.

The Edge AI Workflow

Like any sophisticated engineering project, a typical edge AI project involves multiple tracks of work, some of which run in parallel. Figure 6-1 shows them in context.

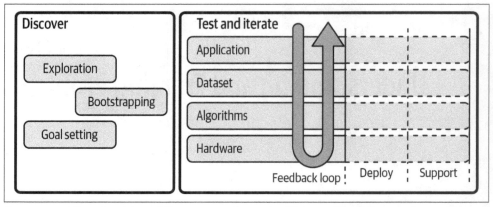

Figure 6-1. The edge AI workflow, grouped into the "discover" and "test and iterate" stages

The process can be split roughly into two chunks—labeled in the diagram as *discover* and *test and iterate*. The first chunk, *discover*, involves developing a deep understanding of the problem you are trying to solve, the resources you have at your disposal, and the space of possible solutions. This is where you do the up-front work of figuring out what you would like (and what is realistic) to achieve.

The second chunk, *test and iterate*, is a continual process of refinement that takes you from initial prototype through to a production-ready application. It spans time before and after development—in machine learning, your application is never truly *finished* but needs to be monitored, supported, and iterated on after being deployed in the field. This continual improvements happens across all parts of your project in parallel—application, dataset, algorithms, and hardware.

The most important part of this process is the *feedback loop* (see Figure 6-2) that enables continuous improvement. The more feedback you can create between different aspects of your project, the more successful your project will be. For example, the results of your model's performance on different types of data can be fed back into the data gathering process, helping you build a diverse and representative dataset that covers the entire space of potential inputs.

We'll be covering this whole workflow over the next few chapters. The *discover* stages are represented in Chapters 6, 7, and 8, while the *test and iterate* stages—including deployment and support—are covered in Chapters 9 and 10.

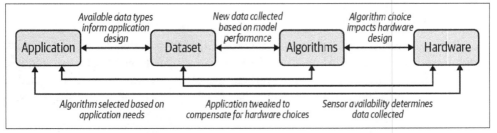

Figure 6-2. A few examples of possible feedback between application, dataset, algorithms, and hardware; the four parts will change and evolve as a project proceeds, and any change in one aspect will need to be reflected in another

Core to the success of any technology project (and arguably any project in general) is the task of managing risk. Edge AI projects are uniquely risky, thanks to their combination of hardware and software and their dependence on complex algorithms and data-driven development.

At each stage in the workflow, we'll learn techniques you can use to keep risk to a minimum and improve your chances of success.

Responsible AI in the Edge AI Workflow

As we've learned, AI applications are especially prone to propagating social harms. There are many types of issues that can lead to unexpectedly poor performance in the real world. This makes careful analysis of potential risks, and their likelihood of causing harm, a critical part of the edge AI development workflow.

It isn't enough to do a single ethical review at the start of a project, or a final one at the end. Since new information will come to light over the course of a project, and many decisions will be taken that have downstream effects, risk analysis needs to be happening at every stage along the way, giving you time to course-correct if required.

In this book we'll be reflecting on ethical design during every step of the process. You shouldn't think of this as an optional extra—it's a part of the core engineering and product management work that is necessary for a successful project. The nightmare scenario for teams working with edge AI is that issues are discovered only after a system has been deployed to production. Nobody wants to be responsible for a product recall or actual harm being caused.

By considering social factors in our risk analysis throughout the development process, we'll maximize our ability to identify challenges before they reach production—and increase the quality of our work.

Do I Need Edge AI?

Artificial intelligence and edge compute are both sophisticated technologies, each involving an entire landscape of considerations. Working with either of them involves making trade-offs between capability and complexity. For many projects, the burden of complexity may outweigh the benefits in capability that come from working with them.

With this in mind, for any potential application, it's very important to try to understand whether the risk is worth the reward. The answer depends heavily on context, including elements such as:

- The specific requirements of the application
- The skills of the team that will be building it
- The available budgets for engineering, data collection, and long-term support
- The amount of time available for delivery

In the following sections, we'll break down the questions that we need to ask in order to decide whether a project is a good fit for edge AI technologies. This is a great exercise to begin with since it will also shed light on many of the other necessary considerations for the discover phase of a project.

 While it can be exciting to try to find new opportunities for edge AI, it's important to approach problems with an open mind and not assume that a technological solution is the right answer. Instead of trying to fit edge AI into a problem from the beginning, focus on understanding the problem and designing the right solution to address it. This solution may involve edge AI or it may not.

Describing a Problem

Describing a problem is the first step in figuring out whether edge AI is a good fit to solve it. You should try to summarize a problem in a few sentences and bullet points—keep it short and to the point. A good description should include:

- A high-level summary of the scenario, including any existing solution
- Problems currently faced
- Constraints that must be worked around

In "Deep Dive: Spotting Rare Wildlife with Trail Cameras" on page 38, we discussed a possible application for edge AI in wildlife monitoring. Following is an example of how we might capture that use case as a problem description.

Problem Description: Trail Cameras

Summary: Wildlife researchers sometimes need to estimate animal population and activity in remote areas. One way of doing this is to install trail cameras in remote locations to monitor specific animal species. The devices typically use a passive infrared (PIR) motion sensor to detect motion, triggering a camera to take a photograph. Photographs are saved to a memory card. The memory card is collected periodically to obtain the photos, which are then analyzed by researchers.

Problems:

- The PIR can be triggered by nontarget species or moving vegetation, filling up the memory card with useless photos and reducing battery life.
- No animal activity data is available until the memory card has been collected and analyzed.
- It's time consuming and expensive to send somebody to collect a memory card from a remote location.
- If the memory card is collected too infrequently, it will fill up and important data will be missed.
- If the memory card is collected too frequently, then money is being wasted on travel expenses.

Constraints:

- Trail cameras run on battery power and must be energy efficient.
- High-bandwidth data connections are expensive in the field.
- Research budgets are typically low.

The exact format of your problem description doesn't matter as much as the content. By capturing the exact problems and constraints, we can consider them while evaluating possible solutions.

Do I Need to Deploy to the Edge?

At this point in the book, we're very familiar with the model in the section "To Understand the Benefits of Edge AI, Just BLERP" on page 14 for expressing the benefits of edge AI:

- Bandwidth
- Latency
- Economics

- Reliability
- Privacy

BLERP is the perfect tool to help us analyze our problem description and evaluate whether it might benefit from an edge architecture. A good way to do this is to create bullet points for each BLERP term.

To illustrate, let's explore *bandwidth*:

- Due to cost, trail cameras don't have access to much bandwidth. This makes doing work on-device important.
- If we could analyze photos on-device, we could send the resulting information (much smaller than raw images) up to the cloud.
- This could help avoid expensive trips into the field to collect memory cards.

By brainstorming the potential impact of each term, we start to understand whether BLERP benefits are important for this problem. Once you're done brainstorming and summarizing, you'll end up with something like the next BLERP analysis, taken from "Deep Dive: Spotting Rare Wildlife with Trail Cameras" on page 38.

BLERP Analysis: Trail Cameras

Bandwidth
> Camera traps are often deployed in remote areas with low connectivity—perhaps with expensive, low-bandwidth satellite as the only option. With edge AI, the number of photos taken can be reduced enough to make it possible to transmit them all.

Latency
> Without edge AI, the latency involved with sending a researcher to collect photos from camera traps could be measured in months! With edge AI and a low-power radio connection, it's possible to analyze photos immediately and obtain useful information without having to wait.

Economics
> Avoiding trips out into the field saves large amounts of money; so does avoiding unnecessary use of expensive satellite radio.

Reliability
> If useless photos can be discarded, the memory card will take longer to fill up.

Privacy
> An edge AI camera can discard photos of humans on the trail, preserving the privacy of other trail users (such as local people, or hikers).

In this case, there are clear and obvious benefits to deploying on the edge across multiple BLERP terms. In other cases, it may not be so evident—for example, there might not be benefits under every single term. That doesn't necessarily mean that edge deployment isn't a good fit. As long as there's enough compelling benefit in any category it is worth considering further.

Things that don't work well on the edge

In some situations, you may find that your problem does not fit BLERP very well at all. The following is an example description for a different problem.

Problem Description: Medical Imaging

A medical imaging device creates images that represent the interior of a patient's body. Specially trained doctors use these images to help diagnose certain medical conditions. The device is very large and is typically located in a major hospital. After scanning a patient, the device stores images on a hard disk attached to a computer network. Special software must be used to view the images.

Problems:

- Diagnosing medical conditions by looking at images is challenging and requires medical training.
- If trained doctors are not available, patients may have to wait for a diagnosis.
- Doctors can only view images on certain computers that have the imaging software installed.

Constraints:

- Images represent sensitive patient information that must be kept secure.
- Imaging devices are very large and cannot be moved around.
- Imaging devices are very expensive.

From the description, it's clear that there are some problems worth solving here: it's challenging for people to diagnose medical conditions based on imaging data, and patients may have to wait for a diagnosis depending on availability of equipment or experts. Perhaps there's some potential for AI to help doctors analyze images.

However, the question we need to answer is whether this is a good problem to try to solve using edge computing. To do this, let's try and brainstorm some potential benefits via BLERP (shown in the sidebar).

BLERP Analysis: Medical Imaging

Bandwidth
> None. The imaging devices are located in major hospitals that typically have good internet connections, and they are already connected to a computer network. No benefit from reducing bandwidth requirements.

Latency
> It would be helpful for patients to have faster access to the diagnosis.

Economics
> Performing analysis using AI would reduce reliance on doctors' time, which is expensive.

Reliability
> Doctors could use AI analysis to help improve their success at diagnosis.

Privacy
> AI analysis could reduce the need to expose sensitive patient data.

Superficially, these sound like compelling reasons. However, if we dig a little deeper, it's clear that most of these benefits are attainable *without* edge computing. Because the imaging device is located in a hospital, there's no major benefit to performing analysis on a potentially resource-constrained "edge" device. Instead, we could use a standard computer, either attached to the hospital's network or in the cloud.[1] Privacy concerns could be addressed using techniques such as federated learning without using any tools specifically associated with edge AI.

In this case, a single fact—that a reliable network connection is already available—makes it unnecessary to use edge compute. But why not use it anyway? Does it make a difference whether we run compute on the edge or not?

Disadvantages of edge compute

While edge compute can have some massive benefits, especially in conjunction with AI, there are some very good reasons why most compute has moved into the cloud over the past decade. If the BLERP framework doesn't highlight some very good reasons to do work on the edge, you may be better off doing your information processing on a cloud server.

Here are some things that can make edge applications a challenge:

---

1 While the case could be made that a computer on a hospital network is a form of edge device, many major hospitals have on-site data centers and are not subject to the typical constraints of edge computing.

Development complexity

Writing and maintaining embedded applications is difficult, especially with smaller targets. The simpler your embedded code, the better. Even if an embedded device is required in order to collect data, it may make sense to simplify engineering by hosting the more complex application logic in the cloud.

Staffing

Embedded development requires very specific skills, and while a cloud application can be built and maintained by many types of engineers, embedded engineering talent can be harder to find. If your organization doesn't have access to embedded engineering talent, it may make sense to de-risk a project by leaving compute in the cloud.

Limited compute

Even the most powerful edge devices are nowhere near as capable as a beefy cloud server with access to a GPU. Some applications require levels of compute that would be unreasonable to deliver in the field—for example, some language models are gigabytes in size and require a GPU to achieve low latency.

Deployment complexity

If you plan to update your application after it has been deployed, edge compute can create some problems. Updating edge firmware can be risky—devices can be "bricked" by a bug or a power outage at the wrong moment. Managing the application versions installed across a fleet of devices can also be a challenge. Working around these challenges is possible, but it requires engineering time. It may be simpler just to host your application logic in the cloud, where it can be updated with minimal fuss.

Hardware and support costs

Deploying and supporting a network of edge devices can be expensive. The expense can grow even higher if you require high-end devices with acceleration for machine learning workloads, or custom hardware designed for a specific purpose. Depending on the application, it may be cheaper to use less capable devices to collect data and send it to the cloud for processing.

Flexibility

If the workloads you wish to run outgrow your edge hardware, or your application changes substantially, you may need to buy new hardware to replace it. In contrast, cloud workloads can be scaled and modified at the click of a button.

Security

There is some security risk involved with allowing physical access to the implementations of your AI algorithms. In some cases, cloud compute may help reduce the risk. There'll be more on security later in the book.

As we saw in "Multi-Device Architectures" on page 82, it's possible to split compute between edge devices and the cloud. This can be a helpful way to blend the benefits of each, especially when devices are deployed within controlled environments where reliable connectivity and power are available, such as homes or factories. For instance, a smart speaker can preserve privacy by doing wake word detection on the edge while still benefiting from powerful cloud servers to run large, highly sophisticated transcription and NLP models. In an industrial setting, an edge computer vision system could identify potential manufacturing defects with extremely low latency before invoking a cloud model to precisely categorize the defects and determine the appropriate response.

Do I Need Machine Learning?

As we learned in Chapter 1, AI doesn't always require machine learning. As a category, ML algorithms have various benefits and drawbacks that make them ideal for some applications but of limited utility for others.

 It's important to identify whether your use case is a good fit for ML early on in the development process. ML-based projects involve a substantially different workflow, which will impact your timeline and budget.

For a given edge AI problem, you'll typically have to choose between a machine learning solution and a rule-based or heuristic solution. As we learned in "Conditionals and heuristics" on page 101, rule-based systems are designed by human beings using domain knowledge. They can make use of anything from basic arithmetic to incredibly complex physics equations. Here are some examples of applied heuristic algorithms in edge devices:

- A water kettle that shuts off when the temperature reaches the boiling point
- A diabetic insulin pump that dispenses precise doses of insulin based on blood glucose levels
- A driver assist feature that uses traditional computer vision (see "Image feature detection" on page 92) to identify lane markings and center a car between them
- The autopilot that flies a jumbo jet aircraft on international routes
- The guidance systems of a space rocket headed to Mars

Each of these examples, from simple to sophisticated, relies on domain knowledge. For example, the insulin pump's algorithm is based on knowledge of the human blood sugar regulation system, and the space rocket's guidance system is based on knowledge of physics, aerodynamics (at least for part of the trip), and the handling characteristics of the vehicle.

In each case, the systems involved are governed by strict rules. These rules may be complex, and their discovery might have taken thousands of years of human history, but at the end of the day they can be described with acceptable accuracy by engineers using mathematical formulas.

Often, digital signal processing algorithms are used in conjunction with rule-based systems. A little processing can go a long way in making it possible to react to input using simple rules. For example, a driver assist feature might use DSP in the form of image feature detection in order to reduce a complex image into a set of simple vectors representing lane markings. This makes it much easier to determine whether to steer the car left or right.

The nice thing about rule-based systems is that their limits are known exactly, meaning that it can be proven when they work. A heuristic algorithm is based on a system that is well understood. It's possible to establish the mathematical correctness of an algorithm with regards to the underlying rules it is designed to model. This makes them reliable, trustworthy, and safe.

If there's a rule-based solution to your problem, you should almost certainly choose it. Many problems can be solved in an elegant manner using rules and heuristics, and they can prove much easier to develop, support, and interpret than the machine learning alternative. They also tend to be far less demanding in terms of computational power.

ML sounds exciting, but it's risky to use it unless you have a clear need. Heuristics are what landed man on the moon; there's a fair chance your problem is easier than that.

Unfortunately, not all problems can be solved with rule-based algorithms. Back in "Conditionals and heuristics" on page 101, we encountered their two main weak points:

Problems with rules that are prohibitively difficult to discover.
    For instance, it could require a huge amount of research and development to discover the system of algorithms that underlies your complex, noisy, high frequency sensor data. Even if it's possible to describe a system mathematically, it could be out of reach given your budget and time frame.

Problems with large numbers of variables.
> For example, there may simply be too many inputs for a rule-based system to be feasible. This is a common problem with image data, which is incredibly highly dimensional and also very noisy. It's tough to write an equation that describes the appearance of a dog.

For nontrivial problems, good implementations of rule-based algorithms may depend on extensive research, domain knowledge, and relevant engineering skills. These are not always available for a given project. The weak spots for heuristics provide an opportunity for ML to shine.

Reasons to use ML

While rule-based systems often depend on a scientific understanding of the processes they interact with, ML algorithms can learn an approximation of the relationships between variables through exposure to the data itself.

This can certainly make life easier. Here are some situations where it could make sense to consider trying ML, in order of validity:

- Your situation and data are too complex or noisy to model by conventional means.
- Too much fundamental research would be required to find rule-based solutions.
- You do not have access to the domain expertise necessary to implement a rule-based system.[2]

If you find yourself in one of these situations, machine learning can be a huge help. The following sidebar provides a nice example.

Building an Artificial Nose

IoT engineer Benjamin Cabé wanted to build an artificial nose (*https://oreil.ly/f_7_8*) —a device that can identify objects and substances by their distinctive smell. His initial goal was to try and distinguish between different types of alcoholic spirits: vodka, rum, and Scotch (although it works for many foods and drinks, as you can see in Figure 6-3).

Benjamin had access to a cheap gas sensor designed to measure levels of several different types of gases. To build a rule-based algorithm for distinguishing between the spirits, he would have had to perform a chemical analysis of the various drinks,

---

2 As we'll see, domain expertise is still critical in training and evaluating ML models. However, ML-based approaches potentially enable experts with knowledge of a specific problem area to get good results without having to enlist as much outside help in other areas (such as signal processing).

---

understand their composition, and work backwards from there to determine which gases to look out for. He'd also have to account for any gases that might be present in the surrounding environment, since they might lead to false positives.

Figure 6-3. Benjamin's artificial nose (Credit: blog.benjamin-cabe.com (https://oreil.ly/ f_7_8))

This type of research was beyond the scope of his project. Fortunately for Benjamin, he was familiar enough with machine learning that he knew it might be able to help.

Benjamin used his gas sensor to capture a small dataset of samples from several different types of drinks. He used this data to train a simple machine learning classification model to identify which gas readings were associated with which drink. The project was a success! Benjamin's system was able to discern between different types of drinks—even to the level of telling one brand of whiskey from another.

The ability of machine learning to extract rules from data allowed Benjamin to build a successful project without having to invest in chemical analysis of the drinks, which could have been time consuming and expensive. It also allowed him to avoid writing the sensitive, hand-tuned logic required to account for other gases present in the environment, since the dataset—collected in the real world—already factored this in.

It turns out that complex, noisy data is very common. In fact, most real-world data is a bit of a mess! One of the strengths of machine learning, especially deep learning models, is that given enough data they can learn to account for noise. During training, the parameters of the model are tuned in such a way that they filter out the noise from the data, leaving just the important information—which can be used to make a decision.

In addition, machine learning models are great at identifying the hidden patterns that exist within their training data. Relationships that would be invisible to the human eye, or too complex for our handcoded rules to represent, can become quite clear to machine learning models when they are provided with enough training data.

These advantages make machine learning a great pick if you are confronted with a bunch of noisy data describing unclear relationships. However, ML's use of data can also provide some risk.

The drawbacks of ML

From an engineering perspective, there are three major drawbacks to machine learning: data requirements, explainability, and bias.

It's well known that today's ML depends heavily on data.[3] Large amounts of data are often required to train and test machine learning systems. Finding adequate data, and ensuring its quality, is the biggest challenge and expense associated with machine learning.

Data may seem plentiful—after all, don't we have "data warehouses" and "data lakes" filled with decades of IoT sensor data that has been carefully captured and logged? Unfortunately, raw data isn't enough. Most of today's machine learning techniques require data that has been *labeled*, meaning it has been tagged with information describing what it means. This tedious task often falls to humans, which makes it expensive and risky (since it's easy to get things wrong).

In addition, machine learning models can only make sense of situations they have seen before. This makes datasets highly context dependent. A model trained on a dataset collected using a specific type of sensor may not perform well if fed data captured by a different brand. A dataset of typical household items from one country may not be any help when trying to identify items from another.

Research is ongoing to mitigate these issues, and amazing progress is being made, but the fact remains that machine learning typically requires a lot of data. We'll learn more about this topic in the next chapter.

The second big drawback of machine learning, *explainability*, was mentioned already in "Interpretability and Explainability" on page 105. While there are some highly explainable ML models, the more sophisticated a model gets the more challenging it can be to pinpoint exactly why it is making the predictions it does.

This problem is compounded by the fact that, thanks to their origins in statistics, many types of ML models don't give definitive answers. Ask a question of a

---

3 The effort to reduce the data requirements of ML algorithms is one of the most important and fascinating strands of ML research.

rule-based system and it will give you a nice, firm response, with clearly visible workings that you can double-check and review. Ask the same question of deep learning model and you'll get a fuzzy probability distribution that indicates the *potential* answer. Trace the answer back through the system and you'll meet an inscrutable mess of linear algebra that is beyond the comprehension of a human mind.

Their probabilistic nature means that ML models are great for dealing with fuzzy situations and nonobvious rules. Unfortunately, this means that their output has some of the same properties. This can be a challenge for many applications.

For example, the code that powers safety-related devices in fields like medical technology, automotive, and aerospace is often expected (through best practices and government regulation) to be *provably* correct. It's very difficult to meet this bar with a probabilistic model whose internal rules can only be gleaned through probing and experimentation.

The third big drawback of ML, *bias*, is a direct result of the first two challenges. We encountered this issue back in "Black Boxes and Bias" on page 46. When we create ML models, we rely on our datasets to both train them and to validate their performance. Our goal is to produce a model that works well in the real world. However, the real world is a big place, and it's quite challenging to capture all of its possible variation in a finite dataset.

If our dataset only includes a subset of all possibilities, our model may fail to perform correctly on the others. Even worse, because we don't have any examples of those other possibilities in our dataset, we'll have no idea that this is even a problem. Our model may appear to be working great when in fact it has some major issues.

To compound the issue, our model won't necessarily even *tell us* when it is having trouble.[4] Instead, it will just make its best guess—which could be catastrophically wrong. Without data to test it, and without an easy way to analyze the internal rules of the model and understand where it might fall short, we'll have no way of knowing there is something wrong, beyond our application failing.

A Simple Example of ML Bias

Imagine you're building a system that uses audio to identify faults in an industrial machine. Working in your research and development lab, you collect a big dataset with thousands of audio samples representing correct and faulty operation. When you train and test the model in the lab, it works great. But when you deploy it to a customer's factory, it identifies far more faults than expected.

---

4 There are techniques that will help with this, such as those mentioned in "Anomaly detection" on page 99, though they may come with a burden of additional complexity.

On investigation, you discover that the model is detecting faults when *adjacent* machines are running. Because your dataset only contains data from your quiet lab, the model never learned to account for the ambient sounds of a factory floor. The model's biases reflect the lab conditions under which it was trained. It does not perform well in the real world.

Since we can never hope to sample the entire world in our dataset, bias is inevitable. However, we can manage the risk by rigorously understanding our application. In some situations, however, the consequences of bias may be so high that the application is not well suited to ML at all. The values held by many societies would not consider it appropriate for ML to be used to make certain life-or-death decisions, such as those resulting from the use of autonomous weapons systems. Similarly, there is much debate about the use of machine learning in automating judicial decisions, including sentencing.

Knowing when to use ML

There's a common saying about solving problems: "If all you have is a hammer, everything looks like a nail." Machine learning is far more exciting than the shiniest of hammers, and it's tempting to try to use it everywhere. Sadly, its complexity, limitations, and inherent risks make it a poor choice in many situations. Mat Kelcey, principal ML engineer at Edge Impulse, is fond of saying "the best ML is no ML at all."

There's no shame in using traditional algorithms to solve problems. As we saw in "Artificial Intelligence" on page 6, the *intelligence* part of AI comes from "knowing the right thing to do at the right time." It doesn't matter to your users whether this knowledge is embedded in the form of an `if` statement or in the form of a deep learning model.

With that in mind, here's a checklist you can use to help decide whether ML might be appropriate for your application:

- There is no existing rule-based solution, and you don't have the resources to discover one.
- You have access to a high quality dataset or collecting one is within your budget.
- Your system can be designed to make use of fuzzy, probabilistic predictions.
- You do not need to explain the exact logic behind your system's decisions.
- Your system will not be exposed to inputs beyond those reflected in its training data.
- Your application can tolerate a degree of uncertainty.

Machine learning models are never perfect. The reason we use them is that compared to human intelligence, they are cheap and they scale well. One big trade-off is that they can fail in unintuitive ways. The decision of whether to use ML is a question of both "Is it good enough?" and "Can we handle the types of errors it is likely to make?"

Automation Versus Augmentation

There's often an assumption that machine learning should be used to *automate* tasks: taking something that a person would have done and doing it automatically on the cheap. However, a slightly different approach to a problem can mitigate some of the risks associated with the strange ways that ML models can fail.

Rather than replacing a human role, it can be much more powerful to *augment* a person's ability to do their job. Instead of putting a model in charge, the model's output is provided as guidance for a person—who is able to combine it with their own insight, expertise, and common sense in order to decide how to act.

A combination of human and machine intelligence has been proven to work better than either technique alone in settings as complex as medicine.[5] While there are some risks, including automation bias (*https://oreil.ly/QHD74*), where people over-rely on automated systems and ignore their own intuition, augmentation can be an effective way to derive value from an imperfect system.

Practical Exercise

Here are three scenarios that might potentially call for the use of edge AI. For each one, come up with a problem description and then decide whether it might make sense to apply edge compute, machine learning, or both. You may have to do some online research to fully understand each scenario:

Scenario 1: Fertilizer application
> An agricultural producer wishes to save money and reduce environmental impact by applying less fertilizer to their crops. Rather than spraying a field uniformly with fertilizer, they would like to identify the areas within a field that would benefit the most from fertilizer (for example, due to variations in soil quality), and apply it there exclusively. They can understand whether fertilizer is needed by visually inspecting the growing plants.

Scenario 2: Hotel servicing
> Hotels traditionally clean guest rooms during the daytime when guests are likely to be out. However, if a guest is still present in their room they may not want to

---

5 As documented in "Human–Machine Partnership with Artificial Intelligence for Chest Radiograph Diagnosis" (*https://oreil.ly/147IG*), by Bhavik N. Patel et al. (National Library of Medicine, 2019).

be disturbed. A hotel chain would like to know whether any guest is present in a given room, so that their cleaning staff do not have to knock on the door and potentially disturb them.

Scenario 3: Tire life

Car tires wear out over time, and certain types of wear can indicate mechanical problems. This wear is usually spotted during periodic maintenance. A vehicle manufacturer would like their cars to identify some types of tire wear automatically, so that they can catch problems earlier.

There's no right or wrong answer for any of these prompts; they simply provide an opportunity to apply the analysis techniques we've learned so far.

Determining Feasibility

So, you have an idea for an edge AI project? Your first goal should be to determine its feasibility. There are many things to consider. Perhaps your project would be better served using server-side AI—or maybe your solution requires machine learning, but it's not feasible to collect a dataset. Alternatively, maybe it's the perfect fit!

The first step is to try and come up with an *ideal* solution to the problem in your problem description. If you try to forget about technological limitations and think at an extremely high level, what would you want the system to do?

Preconceived Notions

The purpose of our ideal solution is to give us something to aim for. If we constrain our search for ideas by what we think is feasible, we may miss promising solutions that are not immediately obvious. By keeping things *ideal*, we make sure we don't limit our own creativity.

The ideal solution also helps us avoid the temptation to use a certain technology because we are excited about it. It's a very common trap: we've just learned about some fascinating new technique and have been looking for an excuse to try it—so we overlook another method that would have given better results.

Once we have an ideal solution, we can consider feasibility from a few angles:

- Moral: Should it be done?
- Business: Is there value in doing it?
- Dataset: Do we have the raw materials?
- Technology: Can it be done?

For a project to be feasible overall, it needs to sit in the sweet spot of all four. Let's explore each of these angles one by one, using an example application to illustrate. In the real world, we would base our ideal solution on a detailed problem description. To keep things lightweight, we'll go with this simplified statement.

Edge AI for Warehouse Security

A warehouse filled with valuable products could be an attractive prospect to thieves. The first step in keeping the warehouse safe is to monitor it 24 hours per day.

Our ideal solution would be a system that is aware of every human being on the premises, understands contextually which of those people are *supposed* to be present, and informs a centralized authority of the location of any others.

There's no requirement that our solution is based on AI, or even uses technology. Depending on the context, the best system might be a team of human security guards. In the process of our feasibility investigation, we'll begin to determine the appropriate mix of human and technological abilities that will solve our problem in an elegant way.

Moral Feasibility

Ethical review is one of the most important parts of any feasibility analysis. A project that fails due to unaccounted technology risk may cost a lot of wasted money, but damage resulting from ethical issues is potentially unbounded—it can easily cost a company its reputation, trigger punitive regulatory measures, and cause direct harm to human beings.

"Building Applications Responsibly" on page 41 introduced some of the ethical issues that can affect AI products. As part of a feasibility analysis, it's critical to rigorously explore and document any potential ethical issues that could result from your application. Beyond the product itself, it's important to also understand any potential risks that come from the development process: data collection, deployment, and support.

This process needs to involve participation from the length and breadth of your team—driven by your ethical and domain experts. The material in "Diversity" on page 126 outlines the importance of maximizing the number of perspectives you are able to draw from.

Some key questions to ask include:

- To whom can the solution cause harm? *Example: Some products (such as AI weapons) are designed to directly cause harm, while others may cause harm indirectly or due to negligent engagement with human stakeholders.*

- Can the required data be obtained without violating the rights of individuals or communities? *Example: Some datasets may not be feasible to collect without violating user privacy.*

- Is it possible to test the product without harming or violating the rights of stakeholders? *Example: An application that provides medical advice may cause harm during testing if the advice given is not reliable.*

- Have the potential risks been documented? How can they be mitigated? *Example: What is the potential harm if an application produces incorrect predictions?*

- Does the application work for all of its potential users? *Example: A safety-related speech detection application might be ineffective with speakers who have regional accents.*

It can be very difficult to understand the potential for indirect harm resulting from a project. For example, what if jobs are placed at risk as a result of an AI project, or if there are trade-offs between profit and environmental impact? Having a broad pool of expert advisors will help you navigate the nuance.

Warehouse Security Application Ethical Feasibility Review

A good way to begin an ethical review is to brainstorm a list of potential issues. Here's an example brainstorm for our warehouse security application. This is not intended to be an exhaustive list!

- Is the product itself ethical? The product might cause harm if it labels innocent people as suspicious. The product might cause harm if it results in the security team being reduced in size.

- Can the required data be obtained ethically? Available datasets may include photographs of individuals who did not consent to being included. If data is collected at the warehouse, employees may not feel comfortable with being included.

- Is it possible to test the product ethically? False alarms could lead to harm if an innocent person is labeled as suspicious. The testing process could distract the security team and lead to security issues.

- Does the application work for all of its potential users? The application may classify people as suspicious at different rates depending on their appearance, not their intent. The application may be difficult to use for security guards who are unfamiliar with similar technology.

Ethics is all about people and processes. One way to reduce the risk of unforeseen ethical issues is to make sure the ethical review is conducted by a diverse group of people from a representative set of demographics, including professionals who have direct expertise in the ethical evaluation of AI systems.

In addition to your own team, this group should include representation of stakeholders potentially affected by the product, as described in "Stakeholders" on page 128.

While the feasibility analysis begins with understanding moral feasibility, your long-term goal should be to enable a process of continuous ethical review during product conceptualization, development, deployment, and support. The work you do at this stage will pay dividends by helping throughout your product lifecycle.

Business Feasibility

There are two main ways that organizational issues can impact the feasibility of a project. First, for an AI application to be successful it needs to provide some clear benefit. In a business context, this could be to customers, executives, or the balance sheet. In a scientific context, it might mean allowing more work to be done with the same budget. At the outset of any project, it is vital to make sure that the proposed work will, if successful, add real value.

Second, AI application development is limited by the practical constraints faced by organizations. For example, there may not be enough budget to collect a dataset of sufficient size to train an effective ML model. Other common constraints include time, expertise, and long-term support from stakeholders.

Proving benefit

One particularly effective way of proving (and demonstrating) the benefits of an edge AI application is called a *Wizard of Oz prototype*. In the story of *The Wizard of Oz*, the titular wizard is first introduced as an impressive supernatural being. However, he is later revealed to be a normal man, hidden behind a curtain, who is controlling the illusion remotely.

In Wizard of Oz prototyping, a mock version of an AI product is produced. It is superficially functional, but in reality its functionality is controlled by hidden human actions. The mock product can be tested and experienced by stakeholders, allowing people to get a sense for how it might work in the real world, and to compare it against other options.

Wizard of Oz Testing for Warehouse Security

To test our warehouse security concept, a basic mobile application is developed. A security guard, equipped with the application, is tasked with his normal patrol. Periodically, a notification is sent to the guard by a human tester in order to simulate what would happen if an AI system detected an intruder. The guard reacts by investigating the issue. He records the amount of time it takes for him to respond.

Subsequent analysis finds that, given the response time, the application is not helpful: in the large warehouse complex, it takes so long for the guard to reach the site that

---

any thief would have long departed. The expense of developing the application would not be worth it, and the money would be better spent hiring additional guards.

Alternatively, it may have been found that the guard was able to attend to each situation rapidly, and that an AI application would help improve their ability to protect the site. The findings help persuade management that the investment is worthwhile.

In either case, the outcome of the Wizard of Oz test helps the organization save money.

This can be an extremely helpful exercise. Even without the technology portion of the project, the user experience can be explored, analyzed, and refined. If the experience is impressive, it can go a long way toward convincing stakeholders that a project is worthwhile. If things do not work well even in an artificial form, it's a good signal that you should go back to the drawing board.

For any evaluation to be successful, it's important to get stakeholder agreement on what "good" looks like. In our warehouse example, this might mean setting the minimum time it takes for a single guard to respond to an intrusion. During the test, we set up instrumentation that helps us monitor these metrics, deploy a baseline version of our application (for example, the fake Wizard of Oz application), and then evaluate it.

During this process, it's really important to test out the *current* solution alongside the proposed ones. This will provide a clear signal as to whether the solutions being evaluated are genuinely beneficial. This is an important thing to check throughout the development process, not just at the start.

Since we've established a specific threshold for good, it may even turn out that the current solution is good enough to satisfy the stakeholders, in which case the organization can save money by *not* adopting an AI-based solution. But if we prove that there's a benefit, the project can proceed with confidence.

Understanding constraints

Of course, beyond Wizard of Oz prototyping, there are many ways that organizations work to determine the risk, reward, and benefit of new projects. AI projects are no different and establishing that your idea is a good fit for the needs of the organization you work within will be critical to ensuring its success.

Part of this is identifying your organizational constraints and making sure they will not pose any problems. Here are some of the top constraints when developing AI applications:

Expertise

Although AI engineering is increasingly accessible, having experienced AI experts on hand will help de-risk your project. Make sure the skills you need are available to you before you begin.

Timeline

AI development is a data-driven, iterative process, and it's even more challenging to produce accurate time estimates for than traditional software engineering. Make sure you have room for contingencies, such as discovering late in the process that you need to collect more data.

Budget

The three most expensive parts of AI development are payroll, data collection, and testing in the field. If you are an individual or a small organization, compute time for training can become significant—although it will typically not exceed more than a few thousand dollars, since edge AI models tend to be small.

Long-term support

As we'll see in Chapter 10, AI applications need long-term support to remain effective. As the world changes around them, ML models and hard-coded rules will need to be updated and refined. If your project will be deployed for more than a few months, it's important to know whether your organization can afford (and is willing) to support it.

You are the expert in the way your organization works, and it's up to you to understand whether it is capable of supporting the project you wish to develop.

Dataset Feasibility

Alongside technical feasibility, edge AI application development is constrained by data that is available. Machine learning is famously data hungry, but even hand-coded, rule-based approaches require substantial amounts of data to develop and test.[6]

Data collection is difficult, time consuming, and expensive, so it is challenging but vital to understand the data requirements of your project during the feasibility assessment stage. There are two steps to understanding data feasibility:

1. Estimating how much data is required to solve your problem

2. Understanding whether you will be able to obtain enough of it

---

6 Even if you are reproducing a well-known algorithm from a textbook, you'll still need to run data through it to make sure your application works end to end.

Both of these topics are covered in detail in Chapter 7. As we'll see, understanding data requirements involves both research and engineering work. This means that you won't know your actual data requirements until you have invested a significant amount of time in a project.

At this stage, it's OK just to have a ballpark idea, perhaps based on some precedents that you have found via research (as we will discover in Chapter 7). If it doesn't look like you will have enough data, your project may not be feasible. It's critical that you rule this out at an early stage to avoid wasted development effort.

Dataset Feasibility for Warehouse Security

Our security application revolves around detecting people in a warehouse. To begin understanding the data requirements, it's helpful to identify some similar applications in scientific literature. For example, some web searching around the topic of person detection might unearth a reference to the *Visual Wake Words dataset* (Chowdhery et al., 2019) (*https://oreil.ly/biJLy*), a dataset of 115,000 images of people in a wide range of contexts.

The literature shows it is possible to get >95% accurate performance on the dataset with a model that will run on a high-end MCU. This gives us at least some assurance that our use case might be feasible. In addition, the fact that it is publicly available means that we could potentially use it to help train our own model.

At this stage, this might be enough to convince us that our project is feasible from a dataset perspective. There's always some risk that things may not work out—for instance, we may discover that detecting people in a dark warehouse is more challenging than in the typical contexts that appear in the Visual Wake Words dataset. It's up to us to decide the level of risk we are willing to accept, and we can always reduce the risk through experimentation.

Data issues are one of the leading causes of ML project failure, so if you see negative signals during this part of your feasibility check, don't just cross your fingers and hope for the best.

Technological Feasibility

In Chapters 3 and 4 we took a long walk through the technologies most important to edge AI. That material will be a great resource as you try to understand the feasibility of your ideas.

The first step is to map your idea onto edge AI concepts and methodologies. Here are some of the key ones, all of which are featured earlier in the book:

Sensors
> How will you collect the data you need?

Data formats
> What kinds of signals will your sensors output?

Feature engineering
> What are the options available for processing raw signals?

Processors
> How much compute can you afford, budgeting by cost and energy usage?

Connectivity
> What type of communications are available to you?

Problem types
> Do you need to perform classification, regression, or something else?

Rule-based or ML
> Is it necessary to use machine learning, or can you get away with a rule-based or heuristic approach?

Choice of ML algorithm
> Will classical ML suffice, or do you need a deep learning model?

Application architectures
> Will you need a single edge device, or a more complex arrangement?

Finally, and most importantly, you'll need to consider the human element. Your eventual solution will be a system composed of people and technology, working together. Any technology decisions need to be viewed through a human lens.

At this point, it's still too early to try to answer all of these questions definitively. Instead, it makes sense to brainstorm a handful of possible solutions: start with four or five rough ideas, but feel free to capture more if they come easily to you. They don't all have to be fully thought out, but you should try to capture elements of the above.

An example in our warehouse security context is shown in the following sidebar.

Brainstorming Ideas for Warehouse Security

Even though we're trying to brainstorm an edge AI system, in most cases it's helpful to begin by establishing the simplest possible baseline. This gives us a known quantity to measure our other solutions against. You should also consider any incumbent solution that you are attempting to replace.

Solution 1: Security team

> The warehouse is staffed by a team of trained trustworthy security guards that is large enough to maintain 24-hour visibility over its contents.

> In some cases, a nontechnological baseline (or a non-AI solution) may turn out to be the best solution. You should always be open to this eventuality: our job here is to deliver value, not to find an excuse to use AI.

> Similarly, since *edge* AI comes with significant challenges, it's also a good idea to reason about possible *cloud-based* solutions. Of course, in some cases there may not *be* a cloud-based solution—but it's always worth thinking about.

Solution 2: Cloud AI

> The warehouse has numerous hardwired cameras, each streaming video to the cloud via networked internet access. A cloud server runs deep learning person detection on every video stream concurrently, messaging a security guard via an app if a person is detected in an unauthorized location.

> We now have a cloud-based system to reason about. Let's see what happens if we push some of the compute back down to the edge.

Solution 3: Edge server

> The warehouse has numerous hardwired cameras, each streaming video to an on-site edge server via a network. The edge server runs deep learning person detection on every video stream concurrently, messaging a security guard via an app if a person is detected in an unauthorized location.

> This sounds interesting! It sounds achievable, and there are certainly some technology benefits—for example, we're no longer reliant on an internet connection. Now let's see if we can push even *more* compute to the edge.

Solution 4: On-device compute

> The warehouse has numerous hardwired cameras, each of which is equipped with a high-end MCU. The MCU runs deep learning person detection on the camera's video stream, messaging a security guard via an app if a person is detected in an unauthorized location.

> In addition to edge versus cloud, there are many other axes we can explore for ideas. For example, how about varying up the sensor type?

Solution 5: On-device compute with sensor fusion

> The warehouse has numerous hardwired devices, each equipped with multiple sensors, including video, audio, and radar, along with a high-end MCU. The MCU uses sensor fusion to detect people, messaging a security guard via an app if a person is detected in an unauthorized location.
>
> We now have five possible solutions to explore. Each one has its own benefits and drawbacks that can be analyzed, compared, and debated. It's not always obvious which solution makes the most sense; the correct answer will vary depending on everything from business requirements to the skillset of an organization. The key is to produce a portfolio of ideas so that you can begin to explore the options.

Framing problems

In order to fully explore the technology requirements of any AI solution, we need to be able to *frame* our problem in terms of the tools available to us. In "Algorithm Types by Functionality" on page 96, we met an assortment of useful techniques:

- Classification
- Regression
- Object detection and segmentation
- Anomaly detection
- Clustering
- Dimensionality reduction
- Transformation

To solve any problem, we first need to break it down into chunks that can be addressed using these techniques. A given problem may require multiple techniques to solve. For example, identifying intruders in unauthorized locations might involve both object detection (for spotting people) and anomaly detection (to identify when a person is behaving unusually, like sneaking around a warehouse aisle at night).

Each technique may require a different type of algorithm: for example, object detection might require a deep learning model and anomaly detection could be done using classical ML. By breaking down a problem into these techniques, we can better understand the computational burden of the work that must be done—which will aid with brainstorming solutions and help inform our hardware choices.

Any given problem can typically be broken down (or framed) in many different ways, each with its own set of technology requirements. For example, it might also be possible to spot intruders in a warehouse using dimensionality reduction: we could use an embedding model to describe any people in view, then compare their embeddings to a database, allowing us to identify when a nonemployee is in the warehouse.

This would have different technology, data, business, and ethical considerations than an object detection-based system. As such, framing gives us another tool to explore the space of possible solutions and find something that fits our unique requirements.

Device capabilities and solution choice

For every edge AI project, there are innumerable hardware options. For instance, our warehouse security brainstorm resulted in solutions that could be implemented using MCUs, with an edge server, or in the cloud. Each individual solution has its own gigantic space of hardware choices—for example, for an MCU-based project we must select hardware from a list including dozens of silicon vendors, each with dozens of chips, all configurable in endless ways.

From a feasibility standpoint, we need to understand which of these hardware options are reasonable given the constraints of our problem—as described by our problem description. Constraints might include cost, in-house expertise, existing brownfield ("Greenfield and Brownfield Projects" on page 26) systems, or supply chain considerations. Capturing these constraints shrinks both the space of hardware options and the space of possible solutions.

After applying constraints, we might discover that there is no solution that fits. For example, in a brownfield project the only available hardware might not have enough memory to run an object detection model with suitable performance.

Table 3-1 provides a reference you can use to understand whether your application is in the ballpark of feasibility for the hardware options available to you. Remember, you can always split your application across multiple device types if you need additional flexibility. We'll cover this in depth in "Architectural Design" on page 278.

Making a Final Decision

At this point, we've reviewed the feasibility of our project from the perspective of ethics, business, dataset, and technology. We should have enough information to make a call. If none of the solution ideas we have brainstormed seem like a good fit, our next steps should be as follows:

1. Update the problem description with the new constraints that we have identified during the review process.

2. Perform a new brainstorm of solutions, coming up with a new set of possible solutions that factor in our newly identified constraints.

3. Go through the same feasibility review process with our new solutions.

As with everything in AI, this can be an iterative process. You may have to repeat these steps several times in order to clarify your understanding of the constraints and arrive at a solution that works. It's worth having patience and being willing to revisit your assumptions. You will likely end up with a potential solution, even if it isn't what you envisioned at the start.

That said, in some cases there may simply not be a good edge AI solution for the problem you are trying to solve. If that happens, take note of the reasons. Perhaps they are ethical, and a sign that the project is too ethically risky to consider. Alternatively, they may be purely technological—which could mean the project may become feasible at some point down the line, as new hardware and techniques become available.

In any case, even if you have not been able to identify a promising solution, the process of exploring the solution space from a feasibility standpoint will have been incredibly instructive. You now likely know more about this problem space, from an AI perspective, than anybody out there.

If a solution does not pass the feasibility test, resist the temptation to continue anyway. If you've proven that it is too risky, trying to develop the project will result in wasted time and potential harm.

 Even the knowledge that there is no reasonable edge AI solution to a problem is valuable information; the fact that you are aware of it is a form of competitive advantage. You may see other organizations wasting time pursuing it—but you will have the confidence to know that their efforts will fail and you will get better results focusing elsewhere.

If you have reached this point and your project seems feasible, congratulations—it's time to start making it a reality.

Planning an Edge AI Project

Edge AI development is a multistage process involving iterative development and potentially unbounded tasks (such as data collection, which as a process is never truly finished). With this in mind, it's important to come up with a plan before developing a solution.

In "The Edge AI Workflow" on page 169 we saw the various workflow stages and how they are connected by a multitude of feedback loops. As an iterative process, you can spend as long as you like on each section. The two most important aspects of planning are:

- Defining acceptable performance
- Understanding time and resource constraints

Defining acceptable performance

The very first stage of your planning process should be to come up with a set of concrete standards for what acceptable performance will look like for your system. This must be done in conjunction with stakeholders and ethical analysis since an underperforming system may create risks in these areas.

Your task during development will be to step through the iterative process until you have met your goals with regards to acceptable performance. Once they have been satisfied, your stakeholders can confidently sign off on the project knowing that it is working well enough. Your goals should be set realistically—they need to be achievable—but they should also be set in such a way that the project will genuinely deliver value if they are met.

We'll learn about some key performance metrics in "Useful Metrics" on page 322.

Understanding time and resource constraints

It's very important to understand both how much time you have and the resources you have available to help deliver a project—including funds, expertise, and hardware. Estimating development time is famously hard, and this is especially true with AI projects.

Due to the iterative nature of AI development, a traditional waterfall-style development model will not work well. Instead, you'll need to understand and manage risk as you move forward. A good approach is to aim to have something working end to end as rapidly as possible.

You can then iterate on the entire system as well as its individual components. Your very first version may be a Wizard of Oz prototype that uses off-the-shelf hardware and simple logic. You might iterate on this, training a simple ML model to replace the Wizard of Oz component and then creating a custom hardware design.

At every point during the process, your entire system should be tested end to end to determine whether it meets the performance standards you have defined. One benefit of this is that it removes the risk that you will spend all of your time on one stage of the project—for example, training a model—and not leave enough time for the remainder. Another benefit is that, sometimes, you may find that a simpler system than you originally envisioned is more than adequate to meet your performance goals.

We'll dig deeper into the topic of planning when we reach Chapter 9.

Hardware Is Hard

Hardware projects come with unique challenges, and it's often important to begin the process of hardware design early in the process, concurrently with any software work. Once you have identified a suitable processor, obtain a development board so that you can begin working directly with hardware as soon as possible. This will help reduce the risk of unexpected friction when you try to deploy your logic to the hardware.

Due to the realities of the hardware supply chain, you may find that you need to pull the trigger on hardware orders before you feel entirely confident in your application's requirements. This is a major source of risk, but it may be an unavoidable one. It's best managed by getting your application deployed onto some development hardware as quickly as possible. Most silicon manufacturers provide plenty of development boards for this exact purpose.

If you are particularly worried, it may be helpful to select hardware with some excess capacity, giving you some headroom if you underestimate the requirements of your application code. Once you've gone to market and proven your algorithm works, you can potentially design a second version that is more cost effective. Some processor lines are even "pad compatible," meaning you can start with a more capable processor but easily switch it out for a cheaper version without any changes to your circuit board.

Summary

We now understand the general workflow that applies to edge AI projects, and we've learned how to evaluate problems and generate promising solutions.

In the next chapter, we'll move forward with the first part of the edge AI workflow—collecting an effective dataset.

## CHAPTER 7

How to Build a Dataset

The dataset is the foundation of any edge AI project. With a great dataset, every task in the workflow becomes both easier and less risky—from selecting the right algorithm to understanding your hardware requirements and evaluating real-world performance.

Datasets are indisputably critical for machine learning projects, where data is used directly for training models. However, data is vital even if your edge AI application doesn't require machine learning. Datasets are necessary in order to select effective signal processing techniques, design heuristic algorithms, and test applications under realistic conditions.

Collecting a dataset is typically the most difficult, time-consuming, and expensive part of any edge AI project. It's also the most likely place you will make terrible, hard-to-detect mistakes that can doom your project to failure. This chapter is designed to introduce today's best practices for building an edge AI dataset. It's probably the most important section of this book.

What Does a Dataset Look Like?

Every dataset is made up of a bunch of individual items, known as *records*, each of which contains one or more pieces of information, known as *features*. Each feature may be a completely different data type: numbers, time series, images, and text are all common. This structure is shown in Figure 7-1.

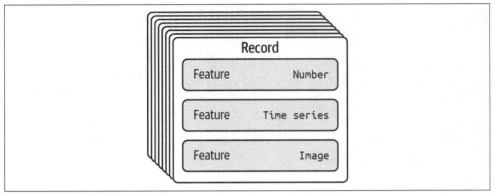

Figure 7-1. A dataset contains many records, each of which may contain many features; features can have different data types.

There are many different names for these components of datasets. Records are commonly referred to as *rows*, *samples*, *items*, *examples*, or *instances*. Features are also known as *columns* or *fields*.[1]

Many datasets also contain *labels*, which are a special kind of feature that indicates the desired output of a model trained on that dataset—for example, the class returned by a classifier, or the bounding boxes returned by an object-detection model.

It is common for datasets to include something called *metadata*. This is special data that describes the data itself. For example, a record may include metadata that indicates the exact model of sensor its features were collected with, the precise date and time it was captured, or the sampling rate of the signal that makes up one of its features.

 Datasets can be stored in many different ways: on a filesystem, in a database, in the cloud, or even in filing cabinets and cardboard boxes.

The structure of a dataset often evolves substantially during development. This may include changes in what its records and features represent. For example, imagine you are building a dataset of vibration data from industrial machines, since you wish to train a classifier to distinguish between different operational states.

---

1 Bear in mind that samples at the dataset level are not the same thing as samples in an arbitrary digital signal. One dataset-level sample (aka record) might contain a feature that consists of multiple samples. As a multidisciplinary field, edge AI has a ton of these confusing terminology collisions!

You may begin by capturing 24 hours of data from 10 different machines. In this case, each record represents a specific period of time from a particular machine. You might then divide these records up, splitting each 24-hour record into sections that correspond to different operational states, and then adding the appropriate labels. Next, you might perform feature engineering on each record, creating additional features that can be fed into a machine learning model.

The Ideal Dataset

An ideal dataset has the following properties:

Relevant

Your dataset should contain information that is useful for the problem you are trying to solve. For example, if you're building a system that uses heart rate sensor data to estimate athletic performance, you'll need a dataset that includes both heart rate sensor data and some measure of performance. If you're planning on using a particular type of sensor, it's typically important that your dataset was collected using a similar device. If you're trying to solve a classification problem, it's important that your dataset contains discriminative information about the classes you care about.

Representative

To be representative, a dataset must include information about all of the different, varied types of conditions that might be encountered in the real world. For example, a dataset to be used in a health monitoring application would need to include data from a wide enough range of individuals to cover all of the different types of people who might be using the application. Unrepresentative datasets will result in bias, as described in "Black Boxes and Bias" on page 46.

Balanced

Beyond being merely representative, ideal datasets contain a good *balance* of information from all of the relevant types of conditions. Many types of machine learning algorithms work best with balanced datasets, including deep learning models.

For example, in the US, 76% of commuters use a car to get to work, while only 10% of commuters use a bicycle.[2] If we were training a model to count vehicles driving across town, it would be important to use equal amounts of data for cars and bicycles—even though bikes would represent a minority of encounters. Otherwise, the model may perform better at identifying cars than bikes. This is another common way for bias to enter your system.

---

2 According to Statista Global Consumer Survey, 2022 (*https://oreil.ly/7qzc8*).

Reliable

An ideal dataset is consistently accurate. It contains as few errors as possible, and if there are errors, they exist uniformly across the data—as opposed to being concentrated in certain categories.[3] If there's noise in your data (which is common for sensor applications), it should be the same type and magnitude of noise that is present under real-world conditions. For example, we might want to train a classification model to identify different genres of music, using a dataset of music samples. In our dataset, it's important that each sample is labeled with the correct genre, and that the samples include a similar amount of background noise as the expected real-world conditions.

Well formatted

The same data can be formatted in numerous different ways. For example, images can be represented in an infinite variety of different formats, resolutions, and color depths. In an ideal dataset, the data is formatted in the way that best suits the tasks you are using it for. At the very least, it's helpful for a dataset to have consistent formatting throughout its samples.

Well documented

It's critically important to understand where a dataset came from, how it was collected, and what all of its fields mean. Without this information, you will not be able to determine if the dataset meets your requirements. For example, imagine you wish to use a dataset of sensor data sourced from the internet. Without good documentation, you will have no way of knowing whether the data is relevant: it may come from sensors that are not equivalent to the ones you intend to use.

Appropriately sized

A machine learning model can learn the hidden rules in almost any system—as long as it is provided with sufficient data. For example, you may wish to train a model to identify different types of tennis shots using accelerometer data. If the dataset only includes a few samples of each shot, the model may struggle to learn a general representation of what characterizes each one. To generalize, more samples for each shot type may be necessary—the more the better.

However, larger datasets result in longer training times, and they are more difficult to work with from a technical perspective. In addition, different problems require different amounts of data to solve, so for every project there is a point of diminishing returns for collecting further data. Your goal should be to collect enough data to solve your problem.

---

3 See "The Uneven Distribution of Errors" on page 234.

If you are mostly using your dataset for testing (versus training a model), you can get away with a smaller one—but it's important that your dataset is big enough to be representative and balanced.

As you might expect, it's tricky to create a dataset with all of these ideal properties. As you build your dataset, you will likely have to do some work to get it into shape.

Datasets for Evaluation

While building and testing an edge AI system in the lab requires one type of dataset, evaluating its performance under *real-world conditions* may require another. Chapter 10 will introduce several ways to evaluate edge AI systems and will explain how to collect the right types of data for the task.

Every AI project involves the distillation of domain expertise from a human mind into a computer system. The process of building a dataset is where the majority of this work happens. It must be conducted with care, intent, and careful consideration. The good news is that if you get it right, you'll massively increase your chances of success.

Datasets and Domain Expertise

Domain experts, also known as subject matter experts (SMEs), are the people with deep knowledge about the problem you are trying to tackle. No matter what the niche, there are people who have studied, experienced, and learned the subject inside out.

It's important to view domain expertise in your problem area as potentially distinct from the knowledge required to work with AI algorithms, signal processing, embedded engineering, or hardware design. While it's possible for a domain expert to also have skills in these areas, the fact that somebody is, say, a machine learning expert does not automatically make them qualified to design AI systems to solve any problem under the sun.

For example, imagine you are building an edge AI product for the healthcare market. In addition to hardware and software engineers, and people versed in building AI applications,[4] your team will need to include domain experts who have a genuine understanding of the healthcare problem you are trying to solve. Otherwise, you'll risk building a product that does not work in the way you expect it to.

---

4 Chapter 9 will talk more about the composition of the teams required to build edge AI products.

Datasets and domain experts are intimately connected. Every AI product reflects the dataset used to develop, train, and test it. When products use machine learning, the algorithms are dictated directly by the data. But even handcoded algorithms are only as good as the data that is used to test them.

This means that the outcomes of your entire project are dictated by the quality of your dataset. Moreover, the only people in your organization who are qualified to *understand* that quality are your domain experts. Their knowledge of the problem you are trying to solve must guide the construction and curation of your dataset. No matter how many talented data science experts you have on your team, their skills will be redundant without proper insight into the problem at hand.

In essence, your dataset acts as the main vector for domain expertise both within your product and your organization. Since it is constructed using knowledge from domain experts, it ends up being a representation of their knowledge in digital form—almost like an application programming interface (API) that provides access to their captured insights.

This encoded knowledge will be used by the rest of your team to help build your application. For example, the engineers working on your algorithms will use the dataset to tune or train them, and those responsible for testing your application will use it to ensure that it works well in all the situations you need it to.

All of this makes it critical that you have sufficient domain expertise on hand. In addition, since your domain experts may not necessarily be experts in building and assessing datasets, you will need them to work closely with the members of your team who have data science skills. It will take collaboration to build an effective dataset.

But what if you don't have access to domain expertise? The answer is frank and perhaps unwelcome. If your team lacks domain expertise in your problem area, it would be irresponsible for you to attempt to build a product. You will lack not only the knowledge to build an effective product but also the insight to understand whether you have built an *ineffective* one.

Data, Ethics, and Responsible AI

The quality of your dataset will shape your application's social consequences more than any other factor. No matter how carefully you have worked to investigate the ethical issues around your project, and to design an application that delivers benefit while being safe, the limitations of your dataset dictate your ability to understand and avoid unintentional harm.

From the perspective of responsible AI, your dataset provides two core things:

- The raw construction material for the system of algorithms that you are attempting to create
- Your most powerful tool for understanding the performance of your system

Your dataset is your only detailed representation of the real-world situation that your system is designed to interact with. Your entire application development feedback loop is mediated by it. As raw construction material, if your dataset is in any way lacking it will invariably and unavoidably lead to bad performance of your system. Even worse, the same failings will impact your ability to understand—or even notice—that the system is underperforming.

This is especially true for edge AI projects, since the nature of their edge deployment means that it is often challenging to capture information about how they are performing in the field. Your dataset often represents your only chance at evaluating your model's performance with any real precision.

With this in mind, it's beyond critical that you spend enough time on getting this part right.

Insufficient Data Causes a Tragic Death

In "Building Applications Responsibly" on page 41, we learned about a failure in Uber's self-driving car system that resulted in the death of a pedestrian. While the failure was systemic and involved the poor design of procedures and safety systems, the core issue was a lack of adequate training data.

The following quote, from a *Wired* article on the incident (*https://oreil.ly/p-zWi*), provides some illustration:

> The report says that the Uber vehicle, a modified Volvo XC90 SUV, had been in autonomous mode for 19 minutes and was driving at about 40 mph when it hit 49-year-old Elaine Herzberg as she was walking her bike across the street. The car's radar and lidar sensors detected Herzberg about six seconds before the crash—first identifying her as an unknown object, then as a vehicle, and then as a bicycle, each time adjusting its expectations for her path of travel…
>
> Herzberg, walking a bike loaded with plastic bags and moving perpendicular to the car, outside the crosswalk and in a poorly lit spot, challenged Uber's system. "This points out that (a) classification is not always accurate, which all of us need to be aware of," says Rajkumar, "and (b) Uber's testing likely did not have any, or at least not many, images of pedestrians with this profile."
>
> —Aarian Marshall and Alex Davies, *Wired*

Human beings are good at something called "zero-shot learning," the ability to recognize and identify objects we have not seen before based on our prior understanding of

---

the world. At present, it's very challenging to build AI systems that are capable of this. If a human driver had seen Elaine Herzberg as she was crossing the road, they would have immediately understood that they were seeing a person wheeling a bicycle and could have applied the brakes immediately.

In some locations it is relatively rare to see a person wheeling a bike loaded with plastic bags across the street, so it was unlikely that Uber's self-driving dataset would include many instances of it. However, as we learned earlier, an ideal dataset is *balanced*: even if a situation is rare, the dataset will still contain sufficient instances of it to be able to train a model—or at least to be able to evaluate the model and show that it is ineffective in that situation.

Since Uber's self-driving algorithms weren't capable of zero-shot learning, they depended on their dataset in order to learn about situations such as Elaine Herzberg's crossing of the road. But since the dataset was imbalanced, it didn't contain sufficient examples of that type of situation for the model to be able to learn to recognize it.

This tragedy highlights one of the greatest challenges in dataset construction. The real world is varied to an almost absurd degree. There are a near infinite variety of human beings, bicycles, plastic bags, roads, and lighting conditions. It's impossible for a dataset to ever capture all of the possible combinations of these things.

Further, there are so many possible combinations of variations that even a domain expert may be unaware of some of them. For example, even if an expert on urban traffic was tasked with identifying objects that are critical for inclusion in a self-driving dataset, they may not have thought of including a bicycle loaded with plastic bags.

Minimizing Unknowns

As in Donald Rumsfeld's infamous quote, in dataset creation there are both "known unknowns" and "unknown unknowns." The only way to build an effective dataset is to minimize both of them. There are two main ways to do this.

The first, and most effective, is to limit the scope of the situation your model is going to interact with. A general-purpose, self-driving system could be considered a nightmare scenario for dataset construction. Self-driving cars must navigate across vast distances of messy reality, from city streets to country roads, encountering almost anything that can possibly be imagined. There's no possible way you can build a dataset that is representative of all that variety.

In contrast, consider a self-driving golf cart that is restricted to driving around a golf course. While it's still possible that it might encounter a bicycle as it roams around the fairways, it's quite unlikely—so it may be easier to build a dataset that is representative of the typical set of circumstances that exist in normal use. In the case of a self-driving car, the principle of limited scope may guide you to limit vehicle operation to the geographic area that its algorithms were trained on.

The second way to avoid unknowns is to improve your domain expertise. The more expert knowledge available about a situation, the less "unknown unknowns" there may be. If Uber had employed a more effective panel of urban transportation experts to help build and evaluate their dataset, then they might potentially have averted a tragedy.

On a practical level, we can also derive a firm rule from this insight: we should never build edge AI applications for real-world usage in areas where we do not have access to domain expertise. Without domain expertise, the field of "unknown unknowns" is unbounded in size. It's almost guaranteed that we will run into them.

Ensuring Domain Expertise

The amazing tools that now exist to assist with training machine learning models have massively lowered the barriers to entry. Unfortunately, this creates the temptation for developers to build applications in areas where they lack domain expertise.

During the COVID-19 pandemic, thousands of well-meaning researchers and engineers created projects designed to diagnose infection using medical imagery. A 2021 review published in *Nature Machine Intelligence*[5] identified 2,212 such studies. Of these, only 62 passed a quality review, and not a single model was recommended for potential clinical use. The majority of issues found could likely have been resolved had clinical and machine learning domain expertise been applied.

The peer review system of academia provides a mechanism to analyze and critique attempts to solve problems with AI. However, in industry there is no such system. Models are deployed inside black box systems, with no accompanying documentation, and are allowed to interact with real-world systems in an unmediated and unmonitored way. This massively increases the chance that a catastrophic issue may make it into production.

Those of us who work in edge AI have a profound responsibility to build systems for ensuring adequate quality, both internally within organizations and through cross-organizational collaboration. A focus on dataset quality, and the corresponding deployment of domain knowledge, must be at the heart of any serious effort.

---

5 Michael Roberts et al., "Common Pitfalls and Recommendations for Using Machine Learning to Detect and Prognosticate for COVID-19 Using Chest Radiographs and CT Scans," *Nat Mach Intell* 3(2021): 199–217, *https://doi.org/10.1038/s42256-021-00307-0.*

Data-Centric Machine Learning

Traditionally, machine learning practitioners have focused on selecting the best combination of feature engineering and learning algorithm to get good performance on a particular task. In this framework, datasets are considered fixed elements that are rarely manipulated beyond some basic cleanup. They provide an input, and a reference for correctness, but they are not considered something to be tuned and tweaked.

In recent years, it has been increasingly recognized that datasets should not be thought of as static objects. The makeup of a dataset has a strong impact on the performance of models that are trained on it, and practitioners have begun to modify datasets in order to achieve better performance on tasks.

This new way of thinking is referred to as "data-centric machine learning." In a data-centric workflow, more emphasis is placed on improving the quality of datasets—as opposed to tweaking the parameters of algorithms.

Data-centric ML follows the age-old computing principle of "garbage in, garbage out" (*https://oreil.ly/NJ8I2*)—the idea that it is unreasonable to expect a computer program to make good decisions if it is provided with poor-quality input.

Data-centric workflows and tools help developers understand the quality of their data and how to remedy issues within it. This could involve:

- Fixing or removing mislabeled samples
- Removing outliers
- Adding specific data to improve representation
- Resampling data to improve balance
- Adding and removing data to account for drift

It's important to acknowledge that all of these tasks require domain knowledge. In some respects, the shift toward data-centric ML is a recognition of the importance of domain knowledge in getting satisfactory performance from machine learning systems.

 Drift is the idea that the real world changes over time. Datasets and models must be continually updated to account for it. We'll cover drift in detail later in this chapter.

The data-centric approach considers datasets to be living entities that require regular maintenance. This maintenance is worthwhile because it both reduces the amount of algorithm work that needs to be done to train an effective model and reduces the amount of data that is required. A high-quality dataset with fewer samples is often superior to a low-quality dataset that has more.

Successful real-world projects often combine a data-centric approach with modern tools that automate the discovery of effective algorithmic parameters (such as AutoML systems, which we learned about in "Automated machine learning (AutoML)" on page 150). Presented with high-quality data, these tools can do an excellent job of exploring the design space and coming up with effective models.

This is the approach recommended by this book. It empowers domain experts to focus on the data that reflects their areas of expertise, while handing the grunt work of algorithm tuning to an automated system. These automated systems rely on high-quality data in order to evaluate models and select the best one for a task. By focusing on dataset quality, developers simultaneously improve both the raw inputs to the system and the mechanism for evaluating it.

Estimating Data Requirements

The most common question that people ask during the initial stages of an edge AI project is "How much data do I need?" Unfortunately, this isn't a simple question to answer. Data requirements vary massively from project to project.

Typically, the data requirements of machine learning projects are much higher than those that rely only on signal processing, heuristics, and other handcoded algorithms. In these cases, you will primarily use data for testing—so while you will still need enough to guarantee that your dataset is representative, you won't need the vast numbers of examples of each type of condition that is required by many machine learning algorithms.

The best way to know the data requirements for a problem is to look for precedents. Are there examples of this type of problem being solved that give you a sense of how much data is required?

The web is your best friend in this regard. A quick search will turn up scientific papers, benchmarks, open source projects, and technical blog posts that can provide a ton of insight. For example, the website Papers with Code (*https://oreil.ly/P8opj*) has a "State-of-the-Art" section that lists benchmark datasets for various tasks and the performance that has been attained on them over time.

If we were developing a keyword-spotting application, we could take a look at the results for the Google Speech Commands dataset (*https://oreil.ly/OuLiV*), which at the time of writing has been solved with 98.37% accuracy. Digging into the dataset itself (*https://oreil.ly/gLy_i*) tells us that the task involves classifying among 10 keywords, and that the dataset has 1.5–4k utterances for each keyword. If our task is sufficiently similar, these numbers give us a ballpark figure for how much data we might need.

Another good idea is to explore tools in your problem domain that are specifically designed to work with minimal data. Deep learning models can be especially data hungry: are there classical ML alternatives that could fit your use case? If your problem requires deep learning, are there any pretrained feature extractors available that might fit your use case, via transfer learning, or could you train one using an existing dataset?

For example, in the keyword-spotting domain, a paper from researchers at Harvard, "Few-Shot Keyword Spotting in Any Language" (*https://oreil.ly/3conT*) (Mazumder et al., 2021), provides evidence that a keyword-spotting model can be trained with only five examples of a keyword, along with a substantially larger dataset to verify its performance.

Table 7-1 provides a relative indication of how much data is required to train machine learning models for some common tasks.

Table 7-1. Data requirements for common tasks

Task	Relative data requirements	Notes
Time series classification	Low	DSP can do a lot of the hard work, making this task easier to train.
Time series regression	Medium	This is more challenging than classification due to finer-grained labels.
Nonvoice audio classification	Medium	Varied data is required to account for the diversity of background noise and environmental acoustics.
Voice audio classification	Low or High	This typically demanded many hours of data, but new few-shot techniques reduce this.
Image classification in visible spectrum	Low	Transfer learning using models trained on public datasets makes this a relatively simple task.
Object detection in visible spectrum	Medium	Transfer learning is available, but this is more challenging than classification.
Vision models for nonvisible spectrum	High	Transfer learning is not typically available, increasing data requirements.

It's important to remember that even these relative requirements are highly approximate—they may vary greatly from project to project, which is why it's difficult to give exact amounts. Data requirements will continue to evolve as new tooling and technology becomes available. The more common a task, the more likely there are signal processing or learning techniques that can help reduce data requirements.

The largest datasets in machine learning are the massive text datasets used for training language models from scratch. This is typically not a required task in edge AI, which limits the upper bounds of datasets that we're required to deal with.

A Practical Workflow for Estimating Data Requirements

After our initial research, the next step is to dig out the tools and start doing some experimentation. Our core task here is to understand whether, given sufficient data, the feature engineering and machine learning pipeline we have selected will be able to achieve good enough results.

This task naturally ends up as part of the iterative approach to application development, which we'll be covering in more detail in Chapter 9. For now, we'll go over the relevant tasks at a high level.

 Defining what "good enough results" means for our project is an important step that will be explored in "Scoping a Solution" on page 271.

Here is the basic process for estimating data requirements:

1. Capture and refine a small dataset. To be effective in estimating data requirements, this dataset should meet all the requirements of the ideal dataset described earlier in the chapter, aside from being appropriately sized. The rest of this chapter will help you understand the processes required to get it into good shape.

2. Based on your research into potential model types, select a candidate model. It's a good idea to begin with the simplest model that seems reasonable, since simpler models are typically easiest to train. Don't fall into the trap of wanting to try a hot new technology without having ruled out the simple and elegant alternatives.

3. Divide your dataset into multiple, same-sized chunks. Each chunk should have close to the same balance and distribution as the original dataset. To achieve this, you should use stratified random sampling.[6] Begin with approximately eight chunks.

4. Train a simple model on one chunk of the dataset and record the resulting performance metrics. It may be helpful to use a hyperparameter optimization tool, as described in "Automated machine learning (AutoML)" on page 150, to rule out the effects of hyperparameter selection.

5. Add another chunk to your training data, so it's now made up of two chunks worth of data. Train the same model again, from scratch (continuing to use hyperparameter optimization if you decided to use it) and record the metrics again.

---

6 This term is explained in "How is data split?" on page 258.

6. Continue the process, adding a chunk of data, training the model, and collecting the performance metrics, until you are using the entire dataset.

7. Plot the performance metrics on a chart. It will look something like one of the charts in Figure 7-2.

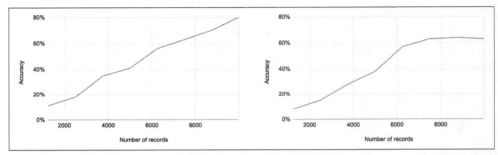

Figure 7-2. Each chart shows how a performance metric (in this case, accuracy) changes with the number of records. The chart on the left shows a situation where adding more data would likely result in better performance. The chart on the right shows a plateau: adding more data of the same type would be unlikely to result in much performance improvement.

In both charts, we can see that the model's performance increases every time we add more data. By looking at the shape of the curve, we can understand the impact that new samples are having. In the lefthand chart, the curve indicates that performance would likely continue to increase if we were to add more data. The trend line provides a way to approximately estimate how much data would be required to achieve a given performance.

In the righthand chart we can see that the model has already reached a performance plateau. Adding more of the same type of data is unlikely to have any effect. In this case, it may be worth testing a different machine learning model or algorithm, or trying to improve on our feature engineering. You might also consider improving your dataset in ways beyond just increasing its size: perhaps it contains a lot of noise that could be reduced.

Of course, this technique depends entirely on the assumption that our dataset is "ideal." In reality, there are likely to be issues with your dataset—and limitations of your feature engineering and machine learning algorithm—that prevent the real-world performance from matching the trend line as data is added. However, it's still useful to obtain a ballpark figure—it can help you plan for the effort of collecting more data.

This technique will *not* tell you whether your dataset is representative, balanced, or reliable. These parts are entirely up to you.

Getting Your Hands on Data

A large part of the challenge of constructing a high-quality dataset is sourcing the data itself. These are some of the typical ways that data can be obtained:[7]

1. Collecting an entirely new dataset from scratch
2. Outsourcing the collection of data to another team or a third party
3. Using data from a public dataset
4. Repurposing existing data from a partner or collaborator
5. Repurposing existing data from an internal data store
6. Reusing data from a previous successful AI project

As you can see, there are a range of potential options. However, it's unlikely that all of them will be available for a given project. For example, if this is your first edge AI project you may not have any existing data to repurpose.

Each of these sources represents a different compromise between two important things: risk of quality issues and effort (which translates into cost). Figure 7-3 shows how each of them compare.

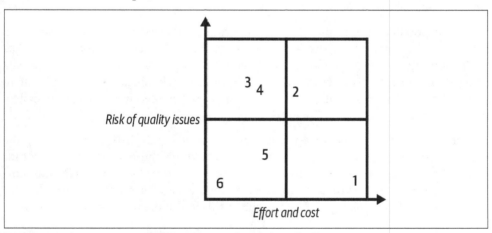

Figure 7-3. Data sources organized by quality risk and effort/cost.

The more control of the data collection process you have, the better you can guarantee quality. By far, the best option is being able to reuse data that you have used successfully in the past (6). If you're lucky enough to be able to take this option, you'll

---

7 Additionally, you may find yourself combining data from two or more of these sources.

already know the quality of the data, and you won't have to invest much effort to reuse it—as long as it remains relevant.

It's quite common for organizations to have existing stores of data that can be reused for AI projects (5). In these cases, it's potentially possible to understand the quality of the data since it was collected internally. However, it may require a bit of effort to get it into the form required for your AI project. For example, a manufacturer may already be collecting machine data using an existing IoT system. In this case, the data's provenance and the collection techniques are known, which helps reduce risk. However, the data may not be in a ready-to-use form and will likely require some cleanup. Existing data often lacks labels, which are expensive to add.

Often, data may be available from a partner organization or collaborator (4). In this case, since someone else has collected the data, there's no way to guarantee quality—and some cleanup may be required to make it usable.

The same is true for public datasets (3), which are typically used for academic research. Public datasets have the advantage of being scrutinized by many pairs of eyes, and may have useful benchmarks available, but they tend to either be cobbled together from low-quality data sources and contain a lot of errors or be very small. They may require significant cleanup to be usable, and they may contain biases that are not documented or obvious.[8]

It may be possible to outsource data collection to another team in your organization, or to a third party (2)—there are entire companies that exist to assist with data collection and labeling. While in theory you have significant control over the data collection process, this may still involve significant risk, since it's very difficult to guarantee that the third party will follow the correct procedures. This is typically a costly approach.

The approach that has the lowest risk is getting your hands dirty and collecting the data yourself (1). When the people who are designing the dataset and algorithms are the same ones who are leading the data collection effort, the risk of miscommunication or undetected error is minimized (assuming they have the required domain knowledge to do the job right). Unfortunately, this is also the most costly approach.

---

8 That said, even messy public datasets can be helpful in *evaluating* algorithms—they can be a good source of interesting corner cases.

Overcoming Data Limitations

It's often challenging to obtain enough data. If you run into data constraints, a good way to unblock your progress is to determine whether a slightly simpler approach to solving your problem might still work.

For example, imagine you're building a predictive maintenance system for a production line. Your initial goal might be to identify when a specific fault is likely to occur soon so that you can schedule preemptive repairs.

As you begin development, you might discover that no data is available that shows the specific fault you care about, and that you don't have the budget to collect any. Rather than give up on your project, you could instead modify your goals.

Instead of predicting when a specific fault is likely to occur, you might decide to create a more general system that identifies when *any* sort of change has happened. This system could be trained on nominal data, which may be easier to collect.

This general system might result in more false positives but depending on the situation it could potentially still help solve your maintenance issue and solve costs overall. By simplifying your goals, you're able to reduce data requirements and make the project feasible.

The Unique Challenges of Capturing Data at the Edge

The more common the use case, the more likely you are to find an easily accessible dataset that has been reviewed for quality. This makes life difficult for many edge applications, since there's a massive variety of niche use cases and exotic sensors. In addition, commercial entities don't tend to share their datasets since they represent potential competitive advantage.

If you need to collect your own data, there are some specific challenges to navigate:

Connectivity and bandwidth
> Edge compute is often used in applications where bandwidth and connectivity is limited. This means that it can be difficult to collect data in the field. For example, if you are building an AI-powered camera for monitoring the movement of farm animals, you might wish to collect images of animals from the field. However, this may not be possible given the remote locations of many farms and the lack of connectivity.
>
> To get around this issue, you could temporarily install networking hardware on-site (for example, a satellite connection might be used in remote regions)—or

rely on *sneakernet* capabilities.[9] This is very expensive, but it may only need to be done temporarily, at the beginning of a project.

Brownfield hardware

As we learned in "Greenfield and Brownfield Projects" on page 26, it's quite common to deploy edge AI applications on existing hardware. Unfortunately, the hardware was not always designed with data collection in mind. To succeed at data collection, brownfield hardware needs sufficient memory to store samples, sufficient networking capability to upload them, and sufficient energy budget to permit the process to occur frequently.

To work around this problem, it may make sense to temporarily install new hardware on-site that is better suited to the challenge of collecting data. Dedicated industrial data loggers (*https://oreil.ly/3qfG1*) exist for this purpose, and industrial-grade rapid IoT development platforms like Arduino Pro (*https:// www.arduino.cc/pro*) can be convenient to use.

Greenfield hardware

If an edge AI project involves the creation of new hardware, working hardware is likely not available until some time has passed. This can be a major challenge since it's important to make progress with dataset and algorithm development in parallel with the hardware development process. It's tricky to even know what hardware is required until at least some algorithm development has been done.

In this case, it's important to try and get some representative data as quickly as possible. Similar to the brownfield case, it could make sense to use a rapid IoT development platform to start collecting data before your production hardware is ready.

Sensor differences

Sometimes, the sensor hardware currently available in the field may not be identical to the hardware you plan to use in a new device. In some cases, even the placement of a sensor may be different enough to cause problems.

If you suspect sensor differences might be a challenge, you should try as early as possible to evaluate the sensor data side by side and determine whether it is different enough to present a problem. If so, you can use the same approach recommended for working with inadequate brownfield hardware.

Labeling

One of the biggest challenges in working with edge AI data is the availability of labels. For example, imagine you are collecting accelerometer data from the

---

9 The age-old practice of transmitting data by carrying a storage device from one place to another. See this Wikipedia article (*https://oreil.ly/gqK1e*).

ear tag of a farm animal with the goal of classifying how it is spending its time between eating, walking, and sleeping. Even in a situation where it is trivial to collect the raw sensor data, it may be challenging to correlate this data with the actual activity of the animal. If you could already identify the animal's activity using the data, your project would not be necessary!

To work around this problem, you can try to collect additional data that may not be available during the normal operation of the device you are designing. For example, during initial data collection, you may choose to collect both accelerometer data and video from a camera that shows the animal's activity, with timestamps for both. You can then use the video to help you label the data.

Synthetic Data

Depending on your application, it may be possible to add *synthetic data* to your dataset. This is data that is created artificially rather than being captured. If it's realistic enough, it may help you meet your data requirements.

Here are some types of synthetic data:

- Simulation-based (e.g., time series from virtual sensors in a physics-based simulation of a machine)

- Procedural (e.g., algorithmically generated audio designed to simulate environmental noise)

- Generated images (e.g., realistic 3D renders, or images output directly from sophisticated deep learning models)

Synthetic data is typically helpful as a way to extend a dataset that contains real data. For example, artificially generated background noise could be mixed with real captured audio to help train a classifier to distinguish between background noise and human speech.

The concept of training a model on entirely simulated data, and then applying it to solve real-world tasks is known as *Sim2Real*.[10] It is considered one of the most important and challenging tasks in robotics and is an area of ongoing research.

There are various software tools designed to help create synthetic data, or you can write your own with the help of a domain expert. At the time of writing, tools for generating artificial data are rapidly improving and available with commercial support.

---

10 In Sim2Real projects, synthetic data is used for training, and real-world data is used for testing.

Storing and Retrieving Data

As you begin to collect data, you'll need somewhere to store it. You'll also need a mechanism for getting data from devices into your data store, and from your data store to your training and testing infrastructure.

Storage requirements vary massively depending on how much data you expect your dataset to contain. The more data you have, the more sophisticated your solution needs to be. That said, edge AI datasets are typically relatively small and are unlikely to require technologies designed to operate at massive scale.

When choosing a solution, it's always preferable to go with the simplest you can get away with. If you're dealing with a quantity of data that can fit happily on a single workstation, there's no need to invest in fancy technology. The more direct access you have to your data for easy exploration and experimentation, the better—so from a convenience perspective, the ideal option is always your local filesystem.

Data Forms

Data tends to live in many different places throughout an organization's infrastructure. Some typical locations (which you may or may not have encountered) include:

- Production SQL databases
- Time series databases
- Log files
- Data lakes
- Data warehouses
- Cloud services
- IoT platforms

It's absolutely fine for data to live in different stores along its journey to become a part of your dataset. For example, you might find it convenient to store raw sensor data in one place, cleaned sensor data in another, and labels in a totally separate store.

When you're building a dataset for an AI project, you'll typically need to pull data from all of these disparate locations into a single place. You'll also need to reformat the data so it is compatible with the formats that are expected by the tools commonly used for developing signal processing and AI algorithms: Python-based software such as NumPy, pandas, scikit-learn, TensorFlow, and PyTorch, plus engineering software like MATLAB (see Chapter 5).

While there is no single standard, these tools typically expect data to be stored in simple, efficient, and filesystem-based formats. Even when training is done at massive

---

scale, in complex distributed infrastructure, the data itself is usually stored on disk in a relatively simple manner.

As such, you should expect to set up a pipeline for extracting data from your organizational data stores and transforming it into a simple format for training and evaluation. We'll learn about how to do this later.

Table 7-2 provides a quick reference to a variety of data storage solutions, with the advantages and disadvantages of each.

Table 7-2. Data storage solutions

Storage type	Advantages	Disadvantages
Local filesystem	Fast, simple, and easy to work with	No API, no backups, no distributed training; upper limit of a few terabytes
Network or cloud filesystem	Accessible by multiple machines; can store massive datasets	Slower than local filesystem; complex to set up mounts
Cloud object storage	Simple APIs for reading and writing data; massive scale	Data must be downloaded to use
Feature store	Data can be versioned and tracked; can store metadata; can query data	Data must be downloaded to use; more complex and costly than simple storage
End-to-end platform	Designed specifically for edge AI; data exploration tools built in; tight integration with data capture, training, and testing	More costly than simple storage

Data stored on a local filesystem is incredibly easy to use and can be accessed very fast. Even when using sophisticated cloud storage, data is typically copied to the local filesystem before training a model.

However, it's risky to store all of your valuable data on a single machine without a backup. It's also inconvenient if the data needs to be accessed by multiple people. Network shares, including cloud-based filesystems—like Amazon FSx, Azure Files, and Google Cloud Filestore—address this issue. However, they are relatively complex to access—they must be mounted as drives within an operating system.

Cloud object storage services—like Amazon S3, Azure Blob Storage, and Google Cloud Storage—provide HTTP APIs that make it much easier to get data in and out. These APIs can even be used by embedded devices to upload data from the edge, assuming the hardware is capable enough. However, they have slower access speeds than drive mounts, so data is typically downloaded to a local disk before it is used.

Feature stores are a relatively new trend in dataset storage. They are designed to offer simple APIs for data access and storage, along with additional features such as data versioning and the ability to query data. Feature store offerings from major providers include Amazon SageMaker Feature Store, Azure Databricks Feature Store, and Google Cloud Vertex AI Feature Store. There are also open source equivalents you can host on your own infrastructure, such as Feast.

There are now several end-to-end platforms designed specifically for creating edge AI applications. Some of these include their own data storage solutions. These are typically equivalent to feature stores, but with the benefit of being designed specifically for edge AI projects. They may include tools for exploring and understanding sensor data or provide integration points with embedded software development tools. They are designed to integrate tightly with the other stages in the deep learning workflow. We learned more about these tools in "Tools of the Trade" on page 136.

Data Versioning

In modern software engineering, it's expected that all source code is *versioned*—it exists within a system that keeps track of how it changes over time. It's important to know which version of code is deployed to production, or to a particular embedded device, so that problems can be traced back to the source.

In addition to code, machine learning systems are built using datasets. This means it makes a lot of sense to version your data, too. Data versioning tools allow you to record which data was used to train a given model. They can also help you understand where your data came from, which allows you to trace problems in production back to individual samples of data.

Data versioning is a powerful tool for data-centric ML, since it allows you to test different versions of your dataset and understand which performs better in the field. It is part of the practice of machine learning operations, described in "Machine learning operations (MLOps)" on page 151.

Getting Data into Stores

If you're capturing sensor data for a project, how do you get it into your data store? The answer depends on your particular circumstances:

There is good connectivity on-site
> If you have enough connectivity, bandwidth, and energy to send data directly from the edge, you can push data directly to APIs from your edge devices. This is easiest if you're using an end-to-end platform for edge AI that has APIs designed specifically for on-device use.
>
> Another good option is to use an IoT platform. You can upload data to the platform using its purpose-built APIs, and then use another system to copy the data from the IoT platform into your dataset.

It's generally not a great idea to try to upload data directly to a cloud object store from an embedded device. Since the APIs were not designed for embedded use, they tend to use inefficient data structures, and their client libraries may not fit on small targets. This is less of an issue when working with embedded Linux devices, which have greater capabilities and access to a full OS.

There is poor or no connectivity on-site

If you lack decent connectivity, or you don't have the energy budget to send data from the very edge of the network, you may have to install some hardware to allow data to be stored at the edge and collected periodically.

This could mean modifying your existing hardware to add data storage. It might also mean adding another independent system, situated nearby, that is able to receive and store data from the device that is generating it. This separate system could be equipped with better connectivity, or it could be physically collected on a periodic basis.

Collecting Metadata

As we learned earlier, an ideal dataset is well documented. When designing your system for collecting data, you should be sure to capture as much information as possible about the context in which the data is being collected.

This additional information, known as metadata, can be included in your dataset alongside the sensor data itself. It may include things such as:

- The date and time that data was captured
- The specific device that collected the data
- The exact model of sensors used
- The location of the device on the data collection site
- Any people involved with the collection of the data

Metadata can be relevant to an entire dataset, to any subset of its records, or to individual records themselves. The paper "Datasheets for Datasets" (*https://oreil.ly/8cF1f*) (Gebru et al., 2018) defines a standard for collecting documentation that describes a dataset in aggregate, along with subsets of its records. While this is extremely valuable and should be considered a best practice, there are major benefits to collecting metadata on a more structured, granular, and machine-readable basis.

In many cases, you will be collecting samples of data that relate to individual entities. For example, you might be monitoring vibrations from a specific machine, capturing samples of keywords spoken by particular human beings, or logging biosignal data from individual farm animals.

In these cases, it's crucially important to capture as much relevant metadata as possible about each individual entity. In the case of a machine, you might capture:

- The exact make and model
- The machine's production run
- The place the machine is installed
- The work the machine is being used for

In the case of a person who is speaking keywords, you might try and capture any conceivable property that might affect their voice. For example:

- Physical characteristics, such as age, gender, or medical conditions
- Cultural characteristics, such as accent, race, or nationality
- Personal characteristics, such as profession or income level

You should attach this metadata to the individual samples that it relates to. This will allow you to split your dataset into subgroups according to metadata. You can use this ability to understand two things in great depth:

- During algorithm development, you will understand the makeup of your dataset and where you are missing representation and balance.
- During evaluation of your system, you will understand the weak areas of your model in terms of subgroups of your dataset.

For example, imagine you are training a model to detect faults in a machine. By analyzing your metadata, you may discover that most of your data samples have come from machines of a specific production run. In this case, you may wish to collect data from other production runs to improve representation of your dataset.

In a different situation, you may be using a keyword dataset to evaluate a keyword-spotting model. By cross referencing the model's performance on different data samples with the samples' metadata, you may discover that the model performs better on samples taken from older speakers versus younger ones. In this case, you may be able to collect more training data from younger speakers in order to improve the performance.

In this way, metadata helps reduce risk. Without sample-level metadata, you are blind to the composition of your dataset and the way your model performs on different groups within it. When you're armed with detailed information about the provenance of your data, you're able to build better products.

Ensuring Data Quality

Earlier in this chapter we listed the properties that an ideal dataset should have:

- Relevant
- Representative
- Balanced
- Reliable
- Well formatted
- Well documented
- Appropriately sized

As we learned in "Data-Centric Machine Learning" on page 210, a high-quality dataset reduces both the amount of data that is required and the impact of algorithm choice on creating an effective system. It's a lot easier for machine learning systems to get useful results when they are trained and evaluated with good data.

But what is the best way to understand the quality of your dataset? The truth is that it comes down to domain expertise. If you have deep insight into the problem domain you are tackling, you'll be able to draw on that insight to help evaluate your data.

Ensuring Representative Datasets

The most important property of a dataset is that it is representative. The reason for this is that the goal of an AI algorithm is to model a real-world situation in order to make decisions. The only mechanism it has for learning about the real world is the dataset used to train or design it. This means that if a dataset is not representative, the resulting algorithms will fail to represent the real world.

For example, imagine you are building an AI system to help recognize different types of plant disease, using photographs of afflicted plants. If your dataset does not include photographs of the correct plants, or the appropriate symptoms, there is no way the AI system you design can be effective, no matter how sophisticated its algorithms.

Even worse, since the dataset is also used to evaluate the system's performance, we'll have no idea that there is even a problem until we deploy the model to the field.[11]

This is where domain expertise comes in. If you are an expert in plant diseases, you can use your knowledge to help understand whether the dataset is representative of real-world conditions. For example, perhaps your dataset is missing photos of some species of plants that are affected by the disease you wish to identify.

---

11 In this case our field may be literal, not metaphorical!

Metadata is incredibly helpful for this process. If your dataset contains metadata that indicates the plant species in each photograph, a domain expert can simply review the list of species and immediately notice whether one is missing.

Another useful way to use metadata is to plot the distributions of specific metadata attributes throughout the data. For example, you might choose to plot the numbers of samples that belong to each species. If this distribution does not look sensible with regards to real-world conditions, you may need to collect more data. For example, you may have significantly more records from one species than another, as in Figure 7-4.

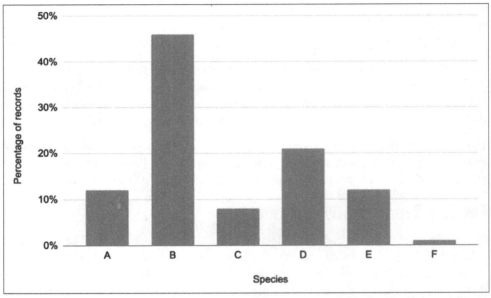

Figure 7-4. This dataset features many more records for some species than others. This may cause problems with fairness; for example, it's likely your algorithm will perform much better with species B than with species F.

In addition to the dataset at large, it's important that representation is maintained across labels. For example, you should ensure there is equally good representation of every affected species within each class of plant disease you are attempting to identify.

If your dataset represents individual entities, you should also check to ensure that your dataset is balanced with regards to those entities. For instance, perhaps all of the photos of one species were taken from a single plant, while the photos of another species were taken from multiple plants.

A domain expert should be able to help identify the axes of data that are important to explore in this way. But what if adequate metadata is not available? This is very common when using data that was not deliberately collected for a specific project. In this case, you'll have to embark on a systemic review of the dataset.

Representation and Time

One of the most important aspects of data quality is the idea that your dataset captures all of the variation present in the real-world context it is designed to represent. This is why we care so much about subgroup representation, like the species of plants in our plant disease dataset.

Plant species is an obvious subgroup in this example, but there is another major property that affects almost all datasets. That property is *time*. Our world is in a constant state of change, which means that data collected about a system at one moment in time does not necessarily represent the state of the system in the future.

For example, imagine we collect our photographs of plants during the springtime. Plant appearance naturally varies throughout the course of the year, as they grow and change with the seasons. If our dataset only includes photos of plants in the springtime, a model trained on it may not perform well during the autumn when the appearance of the plants has changed. This property of data is known as *seasonality*.

To combat this risk, we need to apply domain expertise. A domain expert will understand if there is likely to be seasonal variation in the data and can guide the data collection process accordingly—for example, to make sure that we collect images of plants throughout the year.

The idea of seasonality affects all datasets, not just those containing plants, and a *season* in this context can be any period of time. For example, a fitness wearable may need to account for natural changes in the human body that occur over the course of a day. If its dataset was collected only during the morning, it may be unreliable at night.

It's also worth checking for seasonality in your data even if your domain expert is not particularly concerned about it. There may be other variables at play, such as the effect of varying ambient temperatures on sensor noise. There are many algorithmic techniques you can use to identify seasonality in data, and you can also test your model on different time-based subgroups of your dataset to help identify any issues.

Reviewing Data by Sampling

The challenge of reviewing data quality, especially when there is limited accompanying metadata, is that it's often infeasible to look over every sample of data individually. Datasets can be gigantic, and the time of domain experts is precious (and expensive).

Fortunately, *sampling* gives us a way to review data without having to inspect every last item. For a given dataset, a sufficiently sized random sample of records will have approximately the same representation and balance as the larger dataset. This smaller sample can be inspected thoroughly by a domain expert in order to understand the quality of the dataset as a whole.

The tricky part is determining how large a sample needs to be. It needs to be large enough to have a reasonable probability of including the characteristics we care about but small enough to be reviewed in a reasonable time.

For example, imagine our domain expert is trying to understand whether the dataset contains enough instances of a certain species of plant. To do this, they can count the instances of that plant species in a sample of the data and calculate the ratio between instances of that species and any others. But how big a sample size is required in order for us to assume that the ratio between plant species is equivalent between the sample and the entire dataset?

There's actually a formula we can use to estimate the sample size. It looks like this:

$$Sample\ size = \frac{(Z\ score)^2 * standard\ deviation * (1 - standard\ deviation)}{(margin\ of\ error)^2}$$

In this formula, the *margin of error* represents the amount of difference we're willing to tolerate between the ratio in our sample and in our full dataset. It's common to set this to 5%, meaning we'll be OK with the ratio in our sample being either 2.5% higher or 2.5% lower than the ratio in the entire dataset.

The Z score expresses our confidence level, or how confident we need to be that the number we get will *actually* fall within the bounds of our margin of error. A reasonable confidence level is 95%, which would give us a Z score of 1.96,[12] assuming a dataset of typical size (anything more than tens of thousands of samples).

Finally, the standard deviation represents how much we expect the data to vary. Since there's no real way to know this ahead of time, we can just play it safe and set it to 0.5, which maximizes the sample size.

If we plug all of these together, we'll get the following:

$$Sample\ size = \frac{(1.96)^2 * 0.5 * (1 - 0.5)}{(0.05)^2} = \frac{0.9604}{0.0025} = 384.16$$

Since there's no such thing as a fraction of a sample, we can round the sample size up to 385. This tells us we'll need to randomly sample 385 items in order to have 95%

---

12 The Z score can be looked up in a table such as the one hosted by Wikipedia (*https://oreil.ly/3pKd5*).

confidence that the ratio of one species to another lies within 5% of the value we see in our random sample.

It turns out that this number doesn't vary too much with the size of the dataset, at least for datasets of sizes that are relevant for machine learning. It's most sensitive to changes in the margin of error: if you want a margin of error of only 1%, you'll need to review a sample with 9,604 items. Qualtrics provides a handy online calculator (*https://oreil.ly/wEjUk*) that makes it easy to experiment.

All this goes to say that it should generally suffice to randomly select a few hundred samples from your dataset.[13] This should be a manageable number to review and will also give you some reasonable insight into whether your dataset has acceptable quality.

Of course, this assumes that the subgroups you are looking for are large enough to fit within the error bounds. For example, if a plant species represents less than 5% of the data, then it's unlikely we will find it in a sample of 385 items. However, if you are hunting for underrepresented subgroups, then this will still be a helpful result: it will guide you to add more data, eventually allowing the group to be detectable with random sampling.

Label Noise

Beyond representativeness, another major source of dataset quality issues comes from something called *label noise*. Labels give us the values that we are trying to use AI to predict. For example, if we're training a plant disease classifier, a photo of an unhealthy plant might be labeled with the exact disease that is afflicting it. Labels don't have to be classes, though—for example, if we are solving a regression problem we would expect the data to be labeled with the number that we are trying to predict.

Unfortunately, the labels attached to data are not always correct. Since most data is labeled by human beings, it's common for errors to creep in. These errors can be quite significant. A research team from MIT found that an average of 3.4% of samples are incorrectly labeled across a set of commonly used public datasets[14]—they even built a website to showcase the errors (*https://oreil.ly/vrWZI*).

Label noise isn't a total catastrophe. Machine learning models are pretty good at learning to cope with noise. But it does have a significant impact,[15] and to squeeze the

---

13 To make sure the sample is truly random, it's a good idea to use sampling tools such as those provided by NumPy (*https://oreil.ly/fuBiY*).

14 Curtis G. Northcutt et al., "Pervasive Label Errors in Test Sets Destabilize Machine Learning Benchmarks," arXiv, 2021, *https://oreil.ly/Zrcu1*.

15 For a good exploration of the impact of label noise, check out Görkem Algan and Ilkay Ulusoy, "Label Noise Types and Their Effects on Deep Learning," arXiv, 2020, *https://oreil.ly/1LZKl*.

most performance out of your models it can be worth trying to clean up noisy labels. The constraints of edge AI already place a premium on model performance. Cleaning up noisy labels may deliver a good return on investment versus spending more time on algorithm design or model optimization.

The simplest way to identify label noise is by reviewing random samples of data, but with large datasets this can be like looking for needles in a haystack. Instead of sampling randomly, it's better to focus the search more intelligently.

A good method for doing this is by hunting for outliers within a class. If a sample is misclassified, it likely appears significantly different from the other members of the class it is mislabeled as. For simple data, this may be easy using standard data science tools. For high-dimensional data, like images or audio, it can be more challenging.

The end-to-end edge AI platform that Edge Impulse uses has an interesting solution to this problem. Edge Impulse's feature explorer uses an unsupervised dimensionality reduction algorithm to project complex data into a simplified 2D space, where proximity correlates with similarity. This approach makes it easy to spot outliers (*https:// oreil.ly/_9-Ny*), as in Figure 7-5.

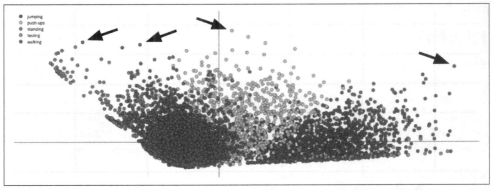

Figure 7-5. Each dot represents a sample of data, and the distance between dots represents their similarity. Outliers, such as those highlighted with arrows, are unusual samples. When samples appear close to those belonging to other classes, it's worth investigating to see if they have been mislabeled.

Another simple way to hunt for noisy class labels is to assume that a model trained on the data will be *less confident* at classifying noisy samples. If training samples are ranked in order of a trained model's confidence at assigning them a class, it's likely that mislabeled samples will appear toward the bottom of the list.

In datasets for problems other than classification, label noise looks a bit different. For example, label noise in a regression dataset consists of error in the target values, while label noise in an object detection or segmentation dataset means the bounding boxes or segmentation maps do not line up well with the objects they are supposed to enclose.

Label noise detection and mitigation is an ongoing area of study. If you have a particularly noisy dataset it may be worth digging into the scientific literature—a quick search for "label noise" in Google Scholar (*https://scholar.google.com*) will serve you well.

Avoiding label noise

Label noise typically occurs as a result of human error during the labeling of the data. Humans aren't great at producing reliable results for repetitive tasks like data labeling, even if they have the right knowledge. In addition, sometimes it's unclear from the data what the correct label should be. For example, even medical experts do not always agree whether or not a diagnostic image shows a disease.

In many cases, labeling errors are the result of a misunderstanding of the labeling task. In projects that require nontrivial amounts of labeling work, it's important to provide a "rater guide": a handbook for data labelers. The guide should include examples that clearly illustrate the guidelines. Over the course of a project, it can be updated with any interesting or unclear examples that are found.

To minimize the impact of human error, it may be useful to use multiple labelers. If the labelers disagree on a label, the sample can be flagged for closer inspection. If there's no clear answer for a given sample, a voting system can be used to come up with a definitive label—or the sample can be rejected. The correct course of action will vary depending on the project and will require the application of domain expertise.

Common Data Errors

Representation and balance problems are large, structural issues that reflect the way a dataset is designed, while label noise is a result of the collection process that impacts individual samples. Similar to label noise, there are a multitude of common errors that can affect your data on a per-sample level. Here are some of the common issues seen in edge AI projects:

Label noise
> As described in detail in "Label Noise" on page 229, it is common to find problems with the way that data is labeled, due to human or machine error.

Missing values
> For a variety of reasons, some records in your dataset may be missing values for certain features. For example, a bug in a data collection script might lead to a value not being written to the correct place. This is quite common, and one of

the most important data preparation tasks is figuring out the best way to address missing values.

Sensor problems

Technical issues with sensors can result in major data quality issues. Common problems affecting sensors include excessive amounts of noise, incorrect calibration, changes in ambient conditions that impact sensor readings, and degradation that leads to changes in values over time.

Incorrect values

Sometimes the values in a dataset do not reflect what was measured. For example, a reading may be corrupted while being transmitted from one place to another.

Outliers

An outlier is a value that is far outside of the expected range. Sometimes outliers can be natural, but often they are a symptom of things like sensor issues or unexpected variations in ambient conditions.

Inconsistent scaling

The same value can be represented in many different ways in a digital system. For example, a temperature reading could be in Celsius or Fahrenheit, and a sensor value may be normalized or not. If different scaling is used for values for the same feature, perhaps when data from two datasets are combined, problems will result.

Inconsistent representation

Beyond scaling, there are many other ways representation can vary. For example, a data point might be stored as either a 16-bit floating point value between 0 and 1 or an 8-bit integer between 0 and 255. The pixel order in a color image might be either red, green, blue, or blue, green, red. An audio file may be compressed as MP3 or exist as a raw buffer of samples. Inconsistent representation can lead to a lot of difficulties. It's important to document this stuff well—perhaps even in metadata attached to each sample.

Unexpected rates

A particularly nasty subtype of inconsistent representation is inconsistency in sampling rates. For example, a dataset may contain some samples collected at 8 kHz (8,000 times per second) and some collected at 16 kHZ. If they aren't processed differently, they'll seem to contain very different values. It's especially bad when variations in sample rate and bit depth combine—at a glance, it's very hard to tell an 8 kHz 16-bit sample from a 16 kHz 8-bit sample!

Insecure data

If you're collecting data from the field, it's imperative that you have secure mechanisms for collecting and transporting it. For example, you might cryptographically sign samples in a way that guarantees they have not been tampered with before being stored. If an attacker has the ability to tamper with your data, they can directly influence the resulting algorithms, distorting your system in their favor.

Nearly every AI project will involve work to fix some of these types of errors. In "Data Cleaning" on page 248, we'll encounter some of the methods used for addressing these issues.

Drift and Shift

> Everything changes and nothing stands still.
>
> —Heraclitus of Ephesus, 535–475 BC

A dataset is just a snapshot in time: it represents the state of a system during the period when it was collected. Since the real world tends to change over time, even the highest-quality dataset can start to get a bit stale. This process of change is known by a few terms, including *drift*, *concept drift*, and *shift*.

When drift occurs, a dataset is no longer representative of the current state of the real-world system. This means that any model or algorithm developed with the dataset will be based on a faulty understanding of the system, and it probably won't perform well once deployed.

Drift can happen in a few different ways. Let's explore them in the context of a dataset that captures the vibration of an industrial machine measured during normal use:

Sudden change

Sometimes there's an abrupt change in real-world conditions. For example, workers might move a vibration sensor to a different part of the machine, suddenly changing the nature of the motion it picks up.

Gradual change

Signals may change gradually over time. For example, the machine's moving parts may gradually wear down over time, slowly changing the nature of their vibration.

Cyclic change

It's common for changes to happen in cycles, or seasonally. For example, the machine's vibration may change with the ambient temperature of its location, which varies between summer and winter.

Because change is inevitable, drift is one of the most common problems faced by AI projects. It can happen in everything from physical configuration (like the placement of sensors) to cultural evolution (like the gradual shift in language and pronunciation over time).

Managing drift requires keeping your dataset updated over time, which we'll talk about more in "Building a Dataset over Time" on page 265. It also requires monitoring the performance of your model in the field, which we will cover in the following chapters.

Thanks to drift, an edge AI project is never really "finished"—it will almost always require ongoing effort in either monitoring or maintenance.

The Uneven Distribution of Errors

As we've seen, there are many different types of errors that can afflict a dataset. To achieve a high-quality dataset, you'll need to keep track of errors and make sure they stay within acceptable levels. However, it's important to not only measure the presence or absence of errors—but also how they affect different subsets of your data.

For example, imagine you are solving a classification problem with a balanced dataset of 10 classes. Across your dataset, you estimate via sampling that there is around 1% label noise: 1 in 100 data samples are incorrectly labeled. From an algorithmic point of view, this may feel acceptable. Perhaps you've trained a machine learning model on the data, and it appears to be effective based on its accuracy.

But what if the 1% of incorrect labels are not evenly (or *symmetrically*) distributed across the dataset but instead are concentrated *asymmetrically* in a single class? Instead of 1 in 100 samples being mislabeled, 1 in *10* of the data items in this class might be labeled incorrectly. This could be enough to seriously impact the performance of your model for this class. Even worse, it will impact your ability to measure the performance in the same way that you can for other classes.

Errors can also be asymmetric across subgroups that are not necessarily classes. For example, perhaps your dataset happens to include data that was collected from three different models of cars. If the sensors installed in one of the car models were faulty, the data for those models might contain errors. This is even more dangerous than when errors are asymmetric across classes because the impact is less easy to detect using standard performance metrics.

Asymmetric errors are likely to result in bias in your algorithms since they impact the performance of your system more for certain subgroups. When you're looking for error in your data, you should take extra care to consider error rates from subgroups of your data, even if the overall level of error seems acceptable. As usual, domain expertise will be extremely helpful in determining the subgroups and how to best inspect them.

Preparing Data

Going from raw data to a high-quality dataset is a long road with many steps. In this next section, we'll walk that road and begin to understand the process. These will be our stops along the way:

- Labeling
- Formatting
- Cleaning
- Feature engineering
- Splitting
- Data augmentation

One of these items, feature engineering, is really part of the algorithm development work we'll be covering in Chapter 9. However, it deserves a mention here because of the way its results are used in the process of refining your dataset.

Our journey's milestones assume you've already collected some initial raw data. You likely don't have a fully representative or balanced dataset yet, but you have made a solid start. The data preparation process will help guide you as you grow and improve your dataset.

Labeling

A typical edge AI dataset reflects a mapping between a set of raw inputs—for example, some time series sensor data—and a description of what those inputs *mean*. Our task is often to build or train a system of algorithms that can perform this mapping automatically: when presented with a set of raw inputs, it tells us what those inputs mean. Our application can then use that assumed meaning in order to make intelligent decisions.

In most datasets, that description of *meaning* comes in the form of labels. As we've seen, creating reliable algorithms requires high-quality labels. There are a few different ways that data can be labeled, and any given project may use a combination of them:

Labeling using features
> Some datasets are labeled using their own features. For example, imagine we're building a virtual sensor—a system that uses the signal from several cheap sensors to predict the output of one sensor that is higher quality but prohibitively expensive. In this case, our dataset would need to contain readings from both the cheap sensors and the expensive one. The readings from the expensive sensor would be used as labels.

Features may also be processed before they are used as labels. For example, imagine we wish to train an ML model to predict whether it is daytime or nighttime based on sensor data. We might use the timestamp of each row in our dataset, along with information about the local sunrise and sunset wherever the data was collected, to determine whether it was captured during daytime or nighttime.

Manual labeling

Most datasets are labeled deliberately, by human beings. For some datasets this is easy: if samples are collected during specific events, it may be obvious what their labels should be. For example, imagine you're collecting a dataset of vibration data from a vehicle, labeling it as either "moving" or "idle." In this case, if you're sitting in the vehicle at the time, you already know how each sample should be labeled.

In other cases, labeling may be a tedious manual process where a human being looks at each record in a previously unlabeled dataset and determines what the correct label should be. This process can be challenging: for example, it may require some training or skill to determine the correct label to apply. In some cases, even well-trained experts may find it hard to agree on the correct labels—medical imaging data often suffers from this problem.

Even if a task is easy, human beings will naturally make mistakes. Manual labeling is one of the most common causes of dataset quality issues. It's also the most expensive to detect and correct, so it's worth making sure you get it right.

Automated labeling

Depending on your dataset, it may be possible to apply labels automatically. For example, imagine you're planning to train a tiny, on-device ML model that can identify different species of animals from photographs. You may already have access to a large, highly accurate ML model that is able to perform this task but is much too big to fit on an embedded device. You could potentially use this large model to label your dataset automatically, avoiding the need for human effort.

This approach can save a lot of time, but it's not always possible. Even if it is possible, it's smart to assume that the automated system will make some mistakes and that you'll need some process for identifying and fixing them.

It's worth bearing in mind that there's often a difference between the labels of the large existing model and the model you are trying to train. For example, imagine you're building a system to recognize wildlife sounds. Your goal is to deploy a tiny model that can identify a sound as being made by either a bird or a mammal. If your large model is designed to identify individual species, you'll have to map each of these to either the "bird" or "mammal" label.

Assisted labeling

It's possible to design a hybrid approach between manual and automated labeling that provides the best of both worlds: direct human insight combined with the automation of tedious tasks. For example, imagine you are tasked with drawing bounding boxes around specific objects in a dataset of images. In an assisted labeling system, a computer vision model may highlight areas of interest in each image so you can inspect them and decide which require bounding boxes to be drawn.

Not all problems require labels

Depending on the problem you're trying to solve, you may not even need labels—although most of the time you will.

In "Classical machine learning" on page 103, we encountered the ideas of *supervised* and *unsupervised* learning. In supervised learning, a machine learning algorithm learns to predict a label given a set of input data. In unsupervised learning, the model learns a representation of the data that can be used in some other task.

Unsupervised algorithms do not require labels. For example, imagine we're training a clustering algorithm for anomaly detection.[16] The algorithm does not need labeled data; it just attempts to learn the innate properties of an unlabeled dataset. In this case, it could be argued that the labels are *implicit*: since the clustering algorithm must be trained on data representing normal (nonanomalous) values, it follows that your training dataset must have been carefully curated to ensure that it only contains nonanomalous values.

If you suspect you may be able to solve your problem with an unsupervised algorithm, you should try it out as an experiment early on in your process. You might find that you can get away without labeling much data, which would be a big savings in cost, time, and risk. However, it's likely that the majority of problems will turn out to require supervised learning.

Even if you're using an unsupervised algorithm, it is typically important to have some labeled data to use for testing. For example, if you're solving an anomaly detection problem, you'll need to obtain some examples of both normal values and anomalous values. These examples will need to be labeled so that you can use them in evaluating the performance of your model.

Semi-supervised and active learning algorithms

Labeling is one of the most expensive and time-consuming aspects of dataset collection. This means it's common to have access to a large pool of unlabeled data and a

---

16 See "Anomaly detection" on page 99.

smaller amount that has labels. Many organizations interested in edge AI may have stores of IoT data that they have been collecting over long periods of time. It is plentiful—but unlabeled.

Semi-supervised learning and *active learning* are two techniques designed to help make use of this type of data. The concept underlying both is that a model partially trained on a small, labeled dataset can be used to help label more data.

Semi-supervised learning, shown in Figure 7-6, begins with a large, unlabeled dataset. First, a small subset of this dataset is labeled, and a model is trained on the labeled records. This model is then used to make predictions on a batch of unlabeled records. These predictions are used to label the data. Some of them will likely be incorrect, but that's OK.

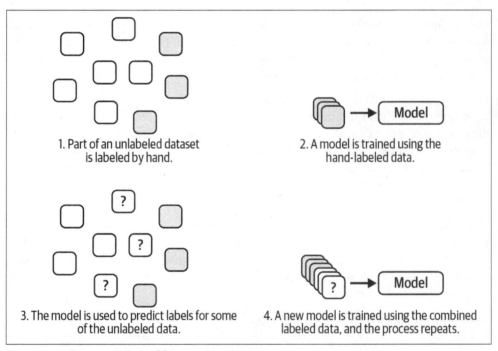

1. Part of an unlabeled dataset is labeled by hand.

2. A model is trained using the hand-labeled data.

3. The model is used to predict labels for some of the unlabeled data.

4. A new model is trained using the combined labeled data, and the process repeats.

Figure 7-6. Semi-supervised learning.

These newly labeled records are then combined with the original labeled data and a new model is trained using all of it.[17] The new model should be at least a bit better than the old one, even though it was trained on data that the old one helped to label. The process is then repeated, with progressively more data being labeled until the model is good enough for production use.

---

17 We might also use some mechanism that gives the manually labeled items more weight during training.

The second technique, active learning, is a little different. The process, shown in Figure 7-7, begins in the same way, with an initial model being trained on the small amount of labeled data that is available. However, the next step is different. Instead of automatically labeling a random sample of data, the model is used to help *select* a set of records from the dataset that look like they would be the most useful ones to label. A domain expert is then asked to label these samples, and a new model is trained that makes use of them.

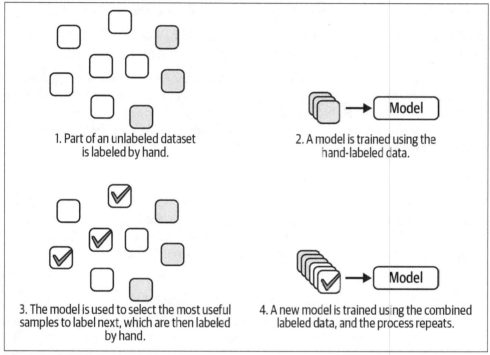

1. Part of an unlabeled dataset is labeled by hand.

2. A model is trained using the hand-labeled data.

3. The model is used to select the most useful samples to label next, which are then labeled by hand.

4. A new model is trained using the combined labeled data, and the process repeats.

Figure 7-7. Active learning.

The selection process is designed to maximize *information gain* by identifying which of the unlabeled samples contain the most information that will help the model learn. The two most common selection strategies are known as *uncertainty sampling* and *diversity sampling*, and they can be used either individually or in combination.

Uncertainty sampling is based on *confidence*. If the initial model appears confident at classifying a record then it can be assumed that there isn't much more information to be gained from using that record in training. If a model *isn't* confident about a particular record, that gives us a signal that the model has not seen many samples similar to it and does not know what to make of it. It's these samples that it's most impactful for us to label and add to the dataset.

Diversity sampling involves using statistical techniques to understand which of the samples best represent the underlying distribution of the data. For example, we might attempt to find a way to quantify the similarity between any two samples. To select new samples to label, we'd look for those that seem the most different to those in our existing labeled dataset.

This overall process—selecting a few samples to label, incorporating the new samples into the training data alongside the existing labeled samples, and retraining the model—happens as many times as necessary to get a model that performs well.

While these techniques are relatively new, they work very well. The section on "Labeling tools" on page 241 gives some examples that can help you use them.

That said, active learning tools are a potential source of bias in the labeling process. To evaluate them, it's a good idea to compare their results to the results of labeling randomly selected samples (instead of those selected by your active learning work-flow). This will allow you to better understand the type of model that your active learning process is creating.

Bias in labeling

In "Label Noise" on page 229, we discussed how label noise is a significant problem in datasets. One major source of label noise is bias in the labeling process. When this occurs, the dataset ends up reflecting the biases of the people and tools who are doing the labeling—rather than reflecting the underlying situation you are trying to model.

Bias in a Quality Control System

Imagine that you wish to create a system to detect defects in industrial products for a manufacturing company. You have collected a dataset of images of products and wish to label them as either "defective" or "normal." You work with a domain expert to walk through the dataset and apply the relevant labels.

This sounds great, in theory. However, your domain expert is new to the company and has only worked on the company's most recent industrial product. They are able to competently label defective items for this product. Unfortunately, your dataset also includes examples of older products. With these items, your domain expert is less confident, and their labels have a higher chance of being incorrect.

Through the labeling process, your dataset has taken on the bias of your domain expert, who is new to the job and unfamiliar with some of the company's products. This means that the system you are creating will also be less competent at recognizing defective instances of these products. When your system is used in production it may fail to identify defective items, or it may flag normal items as being defective. Both of these cases will cost the company money.

This is just one way that bias during labeling can impact the quality of your dataset. Unfortunately, these types of problems are common to the point of being almost inevitable. In addition, since your dataset is your most powerful tool for evaluating your system, any resulting bias in your system may be hard to detect.

The best way to avoid labeling quality issues is to have a rigorous procedure for evaluating the correctness of your labels. This might include:

- Using legitimate domain experts who have deep experience with the subject matter
- Following a documented labeling protocol established by domain experts
- Relying on multiple labelers who can check each other's work
- Evaluating samples of your labeled data for quality

This will increase the cost and complexity of your labeling process. If the cost of producing a high-quality dataset is beyond what you can afford, your project may not be feasible at the current budget. It's better to abort a project than release a harmful system to production.

Labeling bias is not only a feature of data that has been labeled by hand. If you use an automatic system to help label your data, any biases present in this system will also be reflected in your dataset. For example, imagine you are using the output of a large pretrained model to help label records in a new dataset that will be used to train an edge AI model. If the performance of the large model is not uniform across all of the subgroups in your dataset, your labels will reflect these same biases.

Labeling tools

There are several different categories of tools that can help with labeling data. The best choice will vary depending on the project:

- Annotation tools
- Crowdsourced labeling
- Assisted and automated labeling
- Semi-supervised and active learning

Let's explore each one in turn.

Annotation tools. If your data needs to be labeled or evaluated by a human being, they'll need to use some kind of tool. For example, imagine you're building a dataset of photographs labeled with any animals they contain. You'll likely need some form of user interface that can display each photograph and allow a domain expert to specify the animals that they see.

The complexity of these tools will vary depending on the data. A labeling interface for a dataset used for image classification will be relatively simple; it just needs to show photographs and allow the user to specify labels. An interface for an object detection dataset will need to be more complex: the user will have to draw bounding boxes around the objects they care about.

More exotic types of data, such as time series sensor data, may require more sophisticated tools that can help visualize the data in a way that a domain expert can understand.

Annotation tools are pretty much a requirement for interacting with a dataset of sensor data in any meaningful way. They're needed not only for labeling but also for visualizing and editing existing labels, since the evaluation of labels is an important part of the process.

Annotation tools are available as both open source and commercial software. Some things to look out for are:

- Support for the data type you are working with
- Support for the problem you are trying to solve (e.g., classification versus regression)
- Collaborative features, so multiple people can work on labeling
- Automation, and other features explained later in this section

Crowdsourced labeling. It's common for a team to have more data to label than they can handle internally. In this case, it may be useful to use crowdsourced labeling tools. These tools allow you to define a labeling task and then recruit members of the public to help complete it. The people helping to label your data may be compensated financially, receiving a small amount of money for each sample they label, or they might be volunteers.

The big advantage of crowdsourced labeling is that it can help you quickly label large datasets that would otherwise take prohibitively long. However, since the labeling process depends on minimally trained members of the public, you can't rely on any domain expertise.

This may put some tasks out of reach: for example, anything that requires sophisticated technical knowledge. Even for simpler tasks, you are likely to end up with far more quality issues than you would if your data was labeled by a domain expert. In addition, there'll be some significant overhead involved with defining the task clearly enough that members of the public can understand it. To get a good result, you'll have to educate your labelers on how to accurately complete the task.

Beyond quality issues, there are also confidentiality concerns: crowdsourcing may not be an option if your dataset contains sensitive, private, or proprietary information. In addition, crowdsourced datasets are potentially subject to manipulation by malicious actors.

Assisted and automated labeling. Assisted and automated labeling tools use some kind of automation to help humans (whether domain experts or crowdsourced labelers) rapidly label large amounts of data. On the simple end, this might involve using basic signal processing algorithms to help highlight areas of interest or suggest labels. More sophisticated tools may use machine learning models to help. The following examples of assisted labeling tools are taken from Edge Impulse.

First, this object detection labeling tool (*https://oreil.ly/IkzTs*) makes it easier to draw bounding boxes around objects in a sequence of images. It uses an object tracking algorithm to identify previously labeled items in subsequent frames, as shown in Figure 7-8.

Figure 7-8. Object tracking for labeling in Edge Impulse; cars that are labeled are tracked between successive frames.

In a more complex example of labeling tools, the data explorer in Edge Impulse Studio (*https://oreil.ly/Qxs5j*) uses a clustering algorithm to help visualize data, with similar samples appearing closer together, allowing users to quickly label samples based on those they are adjacent to. This is shown in Figure 7-9.

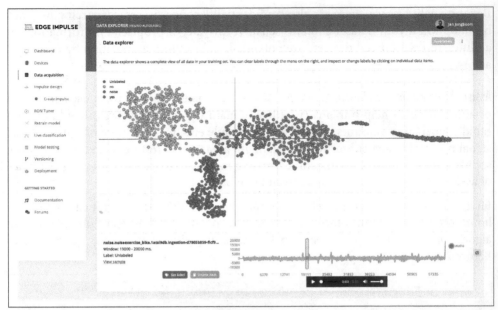

Figure 7-9. The data explorer in Edge Impulse being used to label a keyword-spotting dataset.

Finally, entire pretrained models can be used to help automatically label data. For example, Figure 7-10 shows the use of an object detection model pretrained on a public dataset (*https://oreil.ly/IZMoT*) in order to label instances of 80 known classes of objects.

Assisted labeling can save time and effort by shifting work from the human labeler to an automated system. However, since the automated system is unlikely to be perfect, it shouldn't be used alone—there needs to be a human "in the loop" to ensure good quality.

Figure 7-10. Data can be labeled automatically using pretrained models, as shown in this screenshot from Edge Impulse.

Semi-supervised and active learning. As discussed in "Semi-supervised and active learning algorithms" on page 237, various techniques exist that can help reduce the burden of labeling a dataset by using a partially trained model to assist. These methods are similar to assisted labeling, but they're especially exciting because they can intelligently reduce the amount of labeling that needs to be done. For example, an active learning tool may suggest a small subset of the data that needs to be labeled by hand in order to accurately provide automatic labels for the rest of the data.

Both techniques involve an iterative process of labeling a subset of data, training a model, and then determining labels for the next set of data. Over multiple iterations you will end up with an effective dataset.

An interesting variant of active learning can be found in Edge Impulse Studio's data explorer (*https://oreil.ly/sDAif*). The data explorer can use a partially trained model to help visualize an unlabeled dataset as clusters.[18] These clusters can be used to guide the labeling process, with the goal of ensuring clusters are distinct and that each

---

18 Activations are taken from a layer toward the end of the model, acting as embeddings.

contains at least some labeled samples. Figure 7-11 shows a dataset being clustered based on a partially trained model.

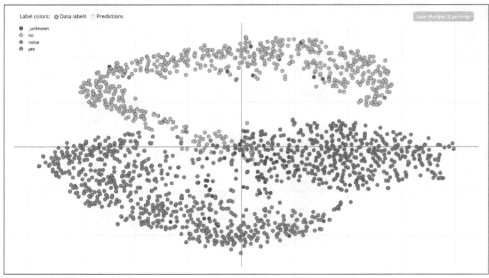

Figure 7-11. Data is clustered according to the output of a partially trained model; the visualization can be used to improve data quality by guiding labeling or identifying ambiguous samples.

As we've seen, data labeling has a major impact on the quality of AI systems. While there are sophisticated tools available that can reduce the required work, labeling will typically represent a large portion of the hours spent on an AI project.

Formatting

There's an almost infinite variety of formats that can be used to store data on disk. These range from simple binary representations to special formats designed specifically for training machine learning models.

Part of the data preparation process is bringing data together from disparate sources and making sure it is formatted in a convenient way. For example, you may need to pull sensor data from an IoT platform and write it into a binary format in preparation for training a model.

Each data format has different benefits and drawbacks. Here are some of the common varieties:

Text formats

Formats like CSV (comma-separated values) and JSON (JavaScript Object Notation) store data as text. For example, the CSV format stores data as text separated by delimiters, commonly either commas (hence the name) or tabs. It is very simple to work with since you can read and edit the values with any text editor. However, text-based formats are very inefficient—the files take up more space than binary formats, and they require more computational overhead to access and process.

CSV and JSON files are fine for small datasets that can be read entirely into memory, but with larger datasets that must be read from disk, it is better to translate the data into a binary format first.

Image and audio files

Images and audio are common data types and have their own typical formats (think JPEG images and WAV audio files). It's pretty common to store image and audio datasets as separate files on disk. While this isn't the fastest possible solution, it's good enough in many cases. Datasets stored in this way have the benefit of being easy to read and modify without any special tools. They are typically used along with manifest files (see the tip "Manifest Files" on page 248).

Some specialized types of data, such as medical imagery, have their own special formats that encode metadata, such as position and orientation.

Direct access binary formats

A binary data format is one that stores data in its native form (sequences of binary bits) as opposed to encoded in a secondary format (as in text-based formats). For example, in a binary format the number 1337 would be stored directly in memory as the binary values `10100111001`. In a text-based format the same number might be represented in a much larger value due to the overhead of text encoding. For example, in the text encoding known as UTF-8 the number 1337 would be represented in the bits `00110001001100110011001100110111`.

In a direct access binary format, many data records are stored in a single binary file. The file also contains metadata that allows the program reading it to understand the meaning of each field within a record. The format is designed so that any record in the dataset can be accessed in constant time.

Some common direct access binary formats include NPY (used by the Python mathematical computing library NumPy) and Apache Parquet. Different formats have different performance trade-offs, so it's useful to select the appropriate one for your specific situation.

Sequential binary formats

Sequential binary formats, such as TFRecord, are designed to maximize efficiency for certain tasks, such as training machine learning models. They provide fast access in a specific, preset order.

Sequential formats can be very compact and are fast to read. However, they are not as easy to explore as other data formats. Typically, transforming a dataset into a sequential format would be done as a last step before training a machine learning model. They are only really used for large datasets, where efficiency savings result in significant reductions in cost.

Manifest Files

A manifest file is a special file that acts as an index to the rest of your dataset. For example, a manifest file for an image dataset may list the names of all of the image files that are intended to be used during training. A common format for manifest files is CSV.

Since a text-based manifest file is simple and easy to work with, it's a convenient way to keep track of your data. Creating a sample of your dataset is as simple as selecting some of the rows of your manifest file at random.

Your dataset will typically occupy several different formats along its journey. For example, you may start with data from several different sources, perhaps in a mixture of text-based and binary formats. You may then choose to aggregate the data together and store it in a direct access binary format before cleaning and processing it. Finally, in some cases you might choose to translate that same dataset into a sequential binary format for training.

Data Cleaning

As you start to pull your dataset together into a common format, you'll need to make sure that all of the values it contains meet a consistent standard for quality. In "Common Data Errors" on page 231, we encountered the main types of problems that you will see in datasets.

Errors can creep in during any step of the process of collecting and curating a dataset. Here are some examples of errors occurring at different stages:

- Outliers in raw sensor data caused by faulty hardware
- Inconsistencies in data formats when aggregating data from different devices
- Missing values due to issues joining data from multiple sources
- Incorrect values due to bugs in feature engineering

Cleaning a dataset is a process that involves several steps:

1. Auditing the data using sampling to identify types of error (you can use the same approach to sampling discussed in "Reviewing Data by Sampling" on page 227)

2. Writing code to fix or obviate the types of errors you have noticed

3. Evaluating the results to prove the issues have been fixed

4. Automating step 2 so that you can fix the entire dataset and apply the same fixes to any new samples that are added in the future

Unless your dataset is quite small (for example, it is less than a gigabyte) it will typically make sense to operate on samples of data rather than the entire dataset. Since large datasets take a lot of time to process, working with samples will reduce the feedback loop between identifying issues, fixing them, and evaluating the fixes.

Once you have a fix that you are happy with on a sample of data you can confidently apply the fix to the entire dataset. That said, it's still a good idea to evaluate the entire dataset as a final step to make sure there are not issues that were missed during sampling.

Auditing your dataset

The problems listed in "Common Data Errors" on page 231 are typical of the types of problems you will run into. But how do you figure out which errors are present in your dataset?

The most powerful tools for identifying data cleanliness issues are those that allow you to view your dataset (or a representative sample of it) as a summary. This could mean creating a table that shows descriptive statistics and types that are present for a particular field. It may also mean plotting the distribution of values in a chart, allowing a domain expert to assess whether the distribution is in line with expectations.

The Python library pandas (*https://pandas.pydata.org*) is a fantastic tool for exploring and summarizing datasets. Once loaded into a pandas data structure, a DataFrame (*https://oreil.ly/69vWh*), the values of a dataset can be summarized. For example, the following command prints a statistical summary for the values in a time series:

```
>>> frame.describe()
            value
count   365.000000
mean      0.508583
std       0.135374
min       0.211555
25%       0.435804
50%       0.503813
75%       0.570967
max       1.500000
```

By looking at the statistics, we can see that the values for this time series are centered around 0.5, with a standard deviation of 0.13. We can use domain expertise to understand whether these values seem reasonable.

Even better, the Python library Matplotlib (*https://matplotlib.org*) allows us to visualize our data. For example, we can easily print a histogram (*https://oreil.ly/nfCXD*) for our data frame:

```
plt.hist(frame['value'])
plt.show()
```

The resulting plot is shown in Figure 7-12. The sensor readings clearly form a normal distribution.

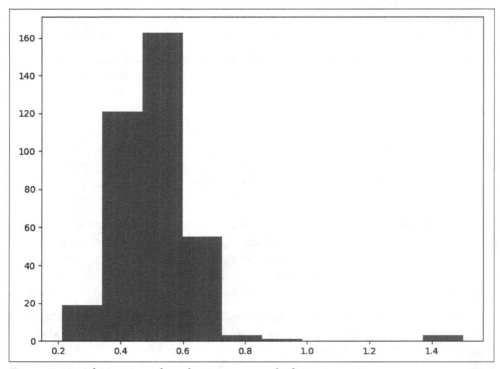

Figure 7-12. A histogram of a value in an example dataset.

From the histogram, we can see that the data is mostly centered around 0.5—but a few points have a value around 1.5. A domain expert can interpret this to understand whether the distribution seems appropriate. For example, perhaps a sensor issue has resulted in some outliers that do not reflect accurate readings. Once we've identified an issue we can dig deeper to determine the appropriate fix.

There are limitless ways to summarize data using common data science tools such as those in the Python and R ecosystems. An engineer or data scientist working on an edge AI project must be able to collaborate with domain experts to help explore the data and identify errors.

Fixing issues

Once you've discovered an error in your dataset, you will need to take some action. The type of action you will be able to take depends on the kind of error you have found and the overall context within which you are collecting data.

These are the main methods at your disposal when addressing errors:

- Amending values
- Substituting values
- Excluding records

In addition, once you have addressed any issues in the dataset you may need to address whatever upstream problem was the cause.

Amending values. In some cases, it may be possible to fix errors entirely. Here are some examples:

- Inconsistencies in data formats might be addressed by converting to the correct format.
- Missing values may be found and filled in if the data is available from another source.
- Faulty values due to bugs in feature engineering code can be fixed.

Typically, you can only fix errors entirely if the original raw data is available somewhere. In some cases, you may still not be able to find the correct value. For example, if some of your data was mistakenly captured at too low a frequency then it will not be possible to recover the original signal—just an approximation.

Substituting values. If you can't fix an error, you may still be able to substitute a reasonable value. Here are some examples of this happening:

- Missing values might be replaced with the mean of that field across the entire dataset.
- Outliers might be clipped or moderated to a reasonable value.
- Low-frequency or low-resolution data can be interpolated to approximate higher detail.

Substitution allows you to make use of a record even if some of the information it contains is missing. However, in exchange, it will introduce some noise to your dataset. Some machine learning algorithms are good at tolerating noise, but whether the information preserved is worth the added noise is a judgment call that will have to be made based on the application.

Excluding records. In some cases, errors may be unsalvageable, requiring you to discard affected records from your dataset. Here are some examples:

- A missing value may render a record unusable.
- Data from a faulty sensor may be beyond repair.
- Some records may be from sources that do not meet data security standards.

Rather than just deleting records that have problems, it's a good idea to mark them as problematic but store them somewhere. This will help you keep track of the kinds of issues that are occurring, and which types of records are being affected.

The correct way to address an error depends entirely on the context of your dataset and application. To obtain good results it's important that both domain expertise and data science experience are applied.

Writing Code to Fix Errors

The code that you are writing to fix errors needs to be high quality, well documented, and placed under source control—along with some record of its dependencies. This transformation code is both a record of the changes you have made to your dataset and a way to automate any future fixes.

Without a well-kept record, people working with the dataset in the future will not know how it was created, what its quirks are, or how it may have been reshaped in the pursuit of quality.

This code forms part of your data pipeline, which we'll be discussing in "Data Pipelines" on page 263.

Evaluation and automation

Once you've fixed the errors in a sample or subset of your data, you should perform another audit. This will help catch any problems that your efforts may have inadvertently introduced—along with any issues that may have been masked by the issues you have fixed. For example, you may remove the most egregious outliers from your dataset only to discover that there were other, less extreme outliers that are still a concern.

Once you've validated your fixes for a subset you can apply the fixes to your entire dataset. For large datasets, you'll need to automate this as part of a data pipeline (see "Data Pipelines" on page 263). Perform the same sort of sampling-driven audit with more of your dataset until you are confident that the issues have been adequately resolved.

 Keep a copy of your original, unimproved dataset so that you can roll back to it if you need. This will help you experiment without feeling afraid of making mistakes and losing data.

It's important that you keep track of the types of records that have been affected by errors. It may be the case that errors are disproportionately impacting certain subgroups of your data. For example, imagine you are training a classification model on sensor data. You may have a serious problem with some of your sensor readings that requires the associated records to be discarded. If these problems affect one of your classes more than the others, it may impact the performance of your classifier.

With this in mind, you should make sure your dataset still has a good standard of quality (as we explored in "Ensuring Data Quality" on page 225) *after* any fixes have been applied.

Keep track of how common various types of errors are in your dataset. If the proportion of bad records is high, it may be worth trying to fix any upstream cause before spending too much time on trying to repair the damage.

As your dataset grows, it will change—and it's possible for new issues to be introduced. To help identify any problems, it's a great idea to create automated assertions based on your initial evaluation. For example, if you've worked hard to improve your dataset by removing extreme outliers, you should create an automated test that proves that the dataset has the expected amount of variance. You can run this test every time you add new records, ensuring you catch any new problems.

Fixing balance issues

So far we've discussed how to fix errors in the values of a dataset. However, one of the most common problems with datasets is that they are unbalanced: they contain uneven numbers of records for their various subgroups. In "Ensuring Representative Datasets" on page 225, we used the example of a dataset of images showing plant diseases. In this context, if a dataset had a higher number of images showing one plant species than another it may be considered unbalanced.

The best way to fix balance issues in a dataset is to collect more data for the underrepresented subgroups. For example, we could go back into the field and collect more images for the underrepresented plant species. However, this isn't always feasible.

If you have to make do, you can potentially address balance issues by *oversampling* the underrepresented groups. To do this, you might duplicate some of the records for these groups until all subgroups have the same number of records. You could also *undersample* the overrepresented groups by throwing some of their records away.

This technique can be useful when you're building a dataset to use to train a machine learning model. Since models' learning is typically guided by aggregated loss values for an entire dataset if a subgroup is underrepresented it won't have much impact on the model's learning. Balancing out the numbers through sampling can help.

However, oversampling will not help if you simply do not have enough data to represent the true variance of the affected subgroup in the real world. For example, if one species in our plant dataset is only represented by images from a single plant, oversampling them may not lead to a well-performing model—since in the real world, there is a lot of variation between individual plants.

You should also be careful about using oversampled data to evaluate a system. The results of your evaluation will be less reliable for the subgroups that you have over-sampled.

An equivalent technique to oversampling is the *weighting* of subgroups during training. In this technique, each subgroup is assigned a weight—a factor that controls its contribution to either the training or evaluation process. Subgroups can be given weights that correct for any balance issues. For example, a subgroup that is underrepresented might be given a higher weight than a subgroup that is overrepresented.

Some datasets are naturally unbalanced. For example, in object recognition datasets the areas in images that contain objects are commonly smaller than the areas that do not.

In these cases, where resampling may not work, weighting is often used to increase the contribution of the underrepresented data to the training of the model.

Anomaly Detection and Balance

In anomaly detection, the goal is to identify unusual inputs. In some cases, the anticipated inputs are so unusual that no examples of them have occurred. For example, an industrial plant might want to use anomaly detection to provide warning in advance of a catastrophic failure. If a failure of this nature has never occurred before, it may not be possible to obtain example data.

In this situation, your dataset will consist of samples that represent nominal operation. Your task is to create a system that will identify when conditions become significantly different from that baseline. In terms of balance and representation, this means you should strive to capture a wide range of nominal conditions. For example, the work done in an industrial plant can vary day to day or seasonally. It's important that your dataset contains representative samples from all of the possible modes.

Testing anomaly detection systems can be challenging when no examples of true anomalies are available to build a test dataset. It may be necessary to simulate possible changes to determine whether they are picked up. In an industrial plant, this could potentially be done by deliberately running machines in an unusual way, or in a way that simulates a breakdown. You can also create synthetic data that introduces potential anomalies. For example, you could take a nominal input and modify it to simulate various changes. All of this will require input from domain experts.

Deploying a system that has not been tested on real-world data is never advisable. It should only be done within the tightly limited scope of a predictive maintenance scenario such as this one, and there should be a realistic understanding from stakeholders of the fact that the system's efficacy has not been proven. Postdeployment, there will need to be a period of intense scrutiny and evaluation to ensure the model is performing adequately.

Even then, it's worth trying to find a way to avoid a scenario such as this one. In many cases, breaking down the problem into smaller ones (for example, identifying known potential faults that may contribute to a catastrophic failure) may make it easier to obtain a balanced dataset.

Feature Engineering

The majority of edge AI projects will involve some feature engineering work (see "Feature Engineering" on page 85). This could be as simple as scaling features (see the sidebar "Feature Scaling" on page 95)—or it might involve extremely complex DSP algorithms.

Since ML models and other decision-making algorithms are run on features, not raw data, feature engineering is an important part of dataset preparation. Feature engineering will be guided by the iterative application development workflow that we'll meet in Chapter 9 but establishing a baseline for features will be necessary at the dataset preparation stage.

Doing some initial feature engineering will allow you to explore and understand your dataset in terms of features, not just raw data. Beyond this, some other important reasons for feature engineering at this stage are:

- Scaling values so that they can be used as inputs to machine learning models
- Combining values (see "Combining Features and Sensors" on page 93), perhaps to perform sensor fusion

- Precomputing DSP algorithms so that training runs faster[19]

It's almost certain that you will want to iterate on feature engineering later in your development process—but the earlier you can begin this work, the better.

Splitting Your Data

As we've seen, the workflow for AI projects involves an iterative process of algorithm development and evaluation. For reasons we'll soon expand on, it's important for us to structure our dataset so that it suits this iterative workflow.

This is typically done by splitting a dataset into three parts: training, validation, and testing.[20] Here is what each split is used for:

Training
>The training split is used directly to develop an algorithm, typically by training a machine learning model.

Validation
>The validation split is used to evaluate the model during iterative development. Each time a new iteration is developed, performance is checked against the validation dataset.

Testing
>The testing split is "held out"—it's kept aside until the very end of a project. It is used in a final pass to ensure that the model is able to perform well on data that it has never been exposed to before.

We use separate splits in order to detect overfitting. As discussed in "Deep learning" on page 106, overfitting is when a model learns to get the correct answers on a specific dataset in a way that does not generalize to new data.

To identify overfitting, we can first train a model with the training split. We can then measure the model's performance on both the training data and the validation data. For example, we might calculate the accuracy of a classification model on each split:

```
Training accuracy:    95%
Validation accuracy:  94%
```

If those numbers are similar, we know that our model is able to take what it has learned from the training split and use it to make accurate predictions about unseen data. This is what we want—the ability to *generalize*. However, if the model performs

---

19 During training, a machine learning model will be exposed to the entire dataset multiple times. Precomputing and caching DSP results avoids the need to run the DSP algorithms repeatedly on the same data, which can take a lot of unnecessary time.

20 Some people may use slightly different terms for these, but the underlying best practice is universal.

less well on the validation split it's a sign that the model has overfit to the training split. It's able to perform well on data it has seen before, but not on new data:

```
Training accuracy:     95%
Validation accuracy:   76%
```

With significantly low accuracy on the validation split, it's clear that the model is not performing well on unseen data. This is a strong signal that the model should be changed.

But if the validation split allows us to detect overfitting, why do we also need the testing split? This is due to a very interesting quirk of iterative development in ML. As we know, our iterative workflow involves making a round of algorithm changes, testing them on the validation split, and then making more algorithm changes to try to improve performance.

As we iteratively tweak and change our model to try to get better performance on the validation split, we may end up fine-tuning the model to the point that it *happens* to work well for the training and validation data—but would not work well on unseen data.

In this case, the model has become overfit to the validation data *even though it was not directly trained on it*. Via our iterative process, information about the validation split has "leaked" into the model: we've repeatedly modified it in a way that was informed by the data in the validation split, resulting in overfitting.

This phenomenon means we can't necessarily trust the signal that our validation split is giving us. Fortunately, the testing split gives us a way around this problem. By keeping the testing split aside until the very end of our process, once all the iteration has been done, we can get a clear signal that tells us whether our model is *really* working on unseen data.

When to Use the Testing Split

The iterative workflow allows information about our evaluation split to "leak" into the model, since we use the results of evaluation to guide model development. This means it's dangerous to use the testing split in an iterative manner: given enough iterations, we may overfit to the testing split, too.

This makes it very important to be strict about using the testing split. If your results on the testing split indicate overfitting, you can't just go back and tweak the model to try to fix it.

If you discover overfitting using your testing split, the best thing to do is start development again with a radically different approach. For example, you may select a different type of ML model, or select a different set of features (or signal processing algorithms) to train on. Once you've tried a number of approaches, you can use their testing split performance to compare them.

This implies that you should be very careful with your testing split. Don't use it until you are sure that you are satisfied with your model's performance on the training and validation splits. Otherwise, you're wasting your most precious evaluation tool—and forcing yourself to start development from scratch.[21]

How is data split?

Data is typically split by random sampling, according to proportion. A common standard is to first split the data 80/20, with the 20% becoming the testing split. The 80% split is then itself split 80/20, with the 80% becoming the training split and the 20% becoming the validation. This is shown in Figure 7-13.

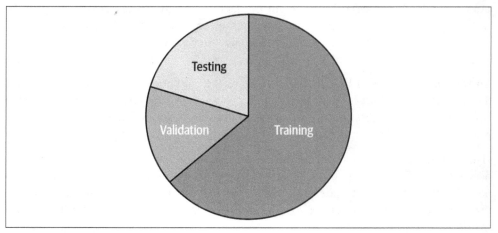

Figure 7-13. The dataset is split into chunks for training, testing, and validation.

Depending on your dataset it may be reasonable to use smaller amounts of data in your validation and testing splits, keeping more of it for use in training. The key thing is that each split is a representative sample of the dataset as a whole. If your data has low variance, this may be achievable with a relatively small sample.

Each split should also be representative in terms of the balance and diversity of the entire dataset. For example, the training, validation, and testing splits for a plant disease classification dataset should each contain the same approximate balance between different types of plant diseases.

---

21 Since your testing split should be a random sample of your entire dataset, it's hard to just go out and collect a new one. If your testing split was collected *after* the rest of your data, it may represent slightly different conditions, harming your ability to evaluate.

If the dataset is well balanced and has a low ratio of subgroups to total number of samples, this can be achieved simply through random sampling. However, if there are many different subgroups, or if some are underrepresented, it may be a good idea to perform stratified sampling. In this technique, the splits are performed individually for each subgroup and then combined. This means each split will have the same balance as the overall dataset. A simple example is shown in Figure 7-14.

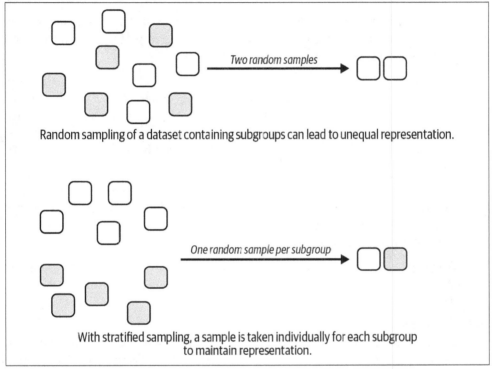

Figure 7-14. Stratified sampling can help preserve the distribution of subgroups when a dataset is split.

Cross-Validation

If you train on one split and evaluate on another, you will only ever know how your model performs on those specific splits. This makes your evaluation vulnerable to random quirks of the particular splits you have chosen. If this is a concern, a technique known as *k-fold cross-validation* may be of interest. When using k-fold cross-validation, a number (*k*) of different splits are performed, each resulting in a unique pair of training and validation splits. The model is trained and evaluated multiple times, once with each pair, and the results are averaged to obtain a fair representation of the overall performance.

Cross-validation provides a gold standard for measuring validation performance. It can be especially helpful when working with smaller datasets, where it may not be possible to do a great job of creating representative splits. The main drawback is that it can be time consuming: the model must be trained k times.

Pitfalls when splitting data

Splitting data incorrectly will deny you the ability to measure how your application performs on unseen data, which is likely to result in bad performance in the real world. Here are some common mistakes to avoid:

Curating splits
> Validation and testing splits are supposed to be representative samples of the overall dataset. A big no-no is hand-selecting which records are included in each split. For example, imagine you decided to put the records you think are the most challenging in the training split—with the theory that it would help your model learn.
>
> If these records are not represented in the testing split, you won't have any insight into how your model is really performing on them. On the other hand, if you put all your most challenging records in the testing split, your model won't get the benefit of being trained on them.
>
> Choosing which records go into each split is a job for a random sampling algorithm, not something you should do by hand. The Python library scikit-learn has a good set of tools for performing dataset splits.

Balance and representation problems
> As discussed earlier, it's important that each split has the same balance, and that all splits are representative. This applies to both classes (for classification problems) and "unofficial" subgroups. For example, if your data is collected from several different types of sensors you should consider performing stratified sampling to ensure that an appropriate proportion of data from each sensor type is contained within each split.

Predicting the past
> For models that perform predictions on time series data, things get a little more complicated. In the real world, we're always trying to predict the *future* based on the *past*. This means that to accurately evaluate a time series model we need to make sure it is trained on earlier values and tested (and validated) on later ones. Otherwise, we may just be training a model that can predict *past* values based on current ones—which probably isn't what we intended. This "leakage" of data backwards along the timeline is worth considering any time you are working with time series.

Duplicate values

When working with large amounts of data, it's easy for records to get duplicated. There may be duplicates in your original data, or they may creep in during whatever process you use for splitting data. Any duplicates between splits will harm your ability to measure overfitting, so they should be avoided.

Changing splits

If you're trying to compare multiple approaches using testing dataset performance, it's important that you use the same testing split each time. If you use a different set of samples each time, you won't be able to tell which model is better—any variations may merely be a result of the difference in split.

Augmented testing data

If you're performing data augmentation (which we'll learn about in the next section), only your training data should be augmented. Augmenting your validation and testing splits will dilute the insight they give you into real-world performance: you want them to be composed of pure real-world data. If you evaluate your model on augmented data you will have no guarantee that it works on nonaugmented data.

Data Augmentation

Data augmentation is a technique designed to help make the most of limited data. It works by introducing random artificial variations into a dataset that simulate the types of variations that are naturally present in the real world.

For example, an image might be augmented by modifying its brightness and contrast, rotating it, zooming into a specific region, or any combination of the above—as shown in Figure 7-15.

Any type of data can be augmented. For example, background noise can be mixed into audio, and time series can be transformed in many different ways. Augmentation can be performed both before and after feature engineering. Common augmentations include:

Additive

Incorporating other signals, such as random noise, or background noise sampled from the real world

Subtractive

Removing or obscuring values, or removing chunks of time or frequency bands

Geometric

Rotating, shifting, squashing, stretching, or otherwise spatially manipulating a signal

Filter-based

Increasing and decreasing properties of individual values by random amounts

Figure 7-15. An image of the author's cat augmented in several different ways.

Augmentation increases the amount of variation in the training data. This can have the benefit of helping the model generalize. Since there is a lot of random variation, the model is forced to learn general underlying relationships rather than perfectly memorizing the entire dataset (which would result in overfitting).

It's important that data augmentation is only applied to the training split of a dataset. Augmented records should not be included in validation or testing data since the goal is to evaluate the model's performance on real data.

Data augmentation is typically accomplished through libraries—most machine learning frameworks provide some built-in data augmentation features, and many data augmentation protocols have been documented in scientific literature and made available as open source code.

Augmentation can either be performed *online* or *offline*. In online augmentation, random changes are applied to each record every time it is used during the training process. This is great, since it results in a huge amount of random variation. However, some augmentations can be computationally expensive, so it can potentially slow down training a lot.

In offline augmentation, each record is randomly changed a specific number of times, and the changed versions are saved to disk as a larger, augmented dataset. This augmented dataset is then used to train a model. Since augmentation is done ahead of time, the training process is a lot faster. However, less variation is introduced when using offline augmentation because there are a finite (and usually limited) number of variants created of each record.

The types of augmentations applied to a dataset can be varied, and different variations may result in models that perform better or worse. This means that the design of an augmentation scheme must be part of the overall iterative development workflow. This is one reason why it's a bad idea to augment your validation or test datasets. If you were to do so, then any change to your augmentation scheme would also change your validation or test data. This would prevent you from comparing the performance of different models against the same datasets.

Designing an appropriate set of augmentations is a task that requires domain expertise. For example, an expert should have insight into the best types of background noise to mix into an audio dataset based on the context of the application.

Data Pipelines

Over the course of this chapter, we've encountered a sequence of tasks and considerations that are applied to data:

- Capture
- Storage
- Evaluation
- Labeling
- Formatting
- Auditing
- Cleaning
- Sampling

- Feature engineering
- Splitting
- Augmentation

This sequence of tasks, in whatever order you perform them, can be thought of as a *data pipeline*. Your data pipeline begins out in the field, where data is generated by sensors and applications. It then brings data into your internal systems, where it is stored, joined together, labeled, examined and processed for quality, and made ready for use in training and evaluating AI applications. A simple data pipeline is shown in Figure 7-16.

Figure 7-16. A basic data pipeline for capturing and processing data; every project has a different data pipeline, and their complexity can vary greatly.

You should consider your data pipeline a critical piece of infrastructure. It should be implemented in clean, well-designed code that is well documented, versioned, and includes whatever information on dependencies is required to be able to run it repeatably.

Any changes to your data pipeline have the potential for major downstream effects on your dataset, so it's critical that you understand exactly what is being done—both during initial development and in the future.

The nightmare scenario is that the processes that led to the creation of a dataset are lost, since the data pipeline was not documented or can no longer be run. As we saw earlier, a dataset represents the distillation of domain expertise into an artifact that can be used to create algorithms.

If the processes used to create that dataset are not documented, then it will no longer be possible to understand the decisions or engineering that went into its construction. This will make it extremely difficult to debug problems with the resulting AI systems and will make it very difficult to meaningfully improve on the system—even if new data becomes available.

In edge AI, where highly complex sensor data is common, keeping good track of data pipelines is especially vital. Unfortunately, this nightmare scenario is very common! It's only recently, with the rise of MLOps practices, that practitioners have been taking data pipelines as seriously as they deserve.

MLOps, a contraction of *machine learning operations*, is a field of engineering related to the operational management of machine learning projects. We'll be digging into it fully across Chapters 9 and 10. One of the most important reasons to think about MLOps is to make it possible to improve ML applications over time, by adding new data and training better models. This is our most important tool for fighting against the big enemy of production ML projects: drift.

Building a Dataset over Time

As we saw in "Drift and Shift" on page 233, the real world changes over time—often quite rapidly. Since our dataset is just a snapshot of a moment in time, it will eventually stop being representative. Any algorithms developed with a stale, outdated dataset will be ineffective in the field.

The fight against drift is one strong reason why you should always be collecting more data. With a constant trickle of new data, you can make sure that you are training and deploying up-to-date models that perform well in the real world.

Edge AI algorithms are often deployed to devices that must tolerate poor connectivity. This means it's often very difficult to measure the performance of devices that are deployed in the field. This provides another key benefit of continuously collecting data.[22] With fresh data available, you can understand the performance of the same algorithms that have been deployed on devices operating in the real world. If performance starts to degrade, those devices may need to be replaced. Without fresh data, you'll have no way of knowing it.

Beyond drift, it's pretty much always helpful to have more data. More data means more natural variation in your dataset, which means superior models that are better able to generalize to real-world conditions.

From a data-centric ML perspective, data collection itself should be part of our iterative development feedback loop. If we recognize that our application or model is falling short in certain ways, we can identify different types of additional data that will help improve it. If we have a good system for continually improving our dataset we can close the feedback loop and build more effective applications.

---

22 This is presuming that data can be collected in some other way that gets around the connectivity issues that deployed devices struggle with.

Obstacles to Improvement

The reality is that real-world projects often face constraints that make it challenging to continually improve a dataset. For example:

- Data collection may require custom hardware that is only in the field temporarily.
- The process of collecting data may be inherently batch-based, not continuous.
- There may not be long-term funding available for continued data collection.

It's important to bear in mind that without additional data, your ability to guarantee an application's performance in the field will decrease over time. If you're in the design stages of a project, it may be worth attempting to mitigate some of these constraints in order to reduce that risk. For example, you may need to ensure the budget of a project will cover continued long-term monitoring.

In some situations, you may have no way to avoid the risk of undetectable deterioration due to drift. If that is true, you should make sure the risks are well documented and communicated to the end users of the application so that they can determine whether they can be worked around. These issues may not be obvious to nonexperts; as the person with the most knowledge, it's your responsibility to make sure they are highlighted.

Well-engineered data pipelines are a critical tool in enabling continuous dataset growth. If you have a repeatable pipeline that can be run on new data, it will massively reduce the amount of friction involved with adding new records to your dataset. Without a reliable pipeline, it may prove too risky to add new data—there's no guarantee it will consistently match your original dataset.

Summary

The creation of a dataset is a continuous process that starts at the very beginning of an edge AI project—and never really ends. In a modern, data-centric workflow, the dataset will evolve along with the design and requirements of your application. It will change with every iterative step in your project.

We'll learn more about the role datasets play in the application development process in Chapter 9. In Chapter 8, we'll focus on the way applications are designed.

Designing Edge AI Applications

The design and development of an application is where all the threads of edge AI are woven together. It requires an understanding of everything we've discussed so far, including problem framing, dataset collection, technology choice, and responsible AI. These are in addition to the skills and knowledge required to design a product in the relevant domain and to implement the design in both software and hardware.

In this chapter, we'll walk through the process of designing an edge AI application, and we'll learn some of the most important design patterns that are used in real-world applications that can be applied to your own work. By the end of the chapter, you'll be comfortable with the requirements of edge AI product design and ready to start creating your own products.

There are two main parts to the design of an edge AI application: the product or solution itself, and the technology architecture that makes it work. These two parts are interdependent. The product design will impact the required technology architecture, and the constraints of the technology will influence the design.

In addition, the entire design and implementation process is informed by the specifics of the real-world situation in which the product will be deployed. Your designs will need to evolve fluidly as you collect data, experiment with different approaches, and test your solution under real conditions.

This dynamic system requires an iterative design process, where the solution is incrementally tried, tweaked, and improved. The best way to plan for this involves developing a strong understanding of both the problem you are trying to solve and the space of potential solutions.

Hardware product design and embedded software architecture are major topics on their own. In this book we'll focus specifically on the design considerations associated with edge AI.

Product and Experience Design

The goal of an edge AI product is to solve a particular problem. Most real-world problems have several components, all of which must be addressed in order to consider the problem "solved":

The problem itself
> How well the product addresses the fundamental issue

The human element
> How well the product meets the expectations of its users

The broader context
> How well the product meets the realities of our world

To illustrate this, let's consider a hypothetical example.

Tracking Weightlifting Workouts

Many people find it convenient to track their exercise activities using wearables. For example, a smart watch designed for runners can record the distance, time, and biosignals associated with a particular run. This helps runners understand the amount of exercise they are doing and track their progression over time.

However, some activities are more difficult to track than others. The key metrics for running are distance and time, which are easy to passively measure. Weightlifting, however, is more complicated. A weightlifting athlete must keep track of:

- The specific movement they are doing (e.g., bench press, squat)
- The amount of weight they are using
- The number of repetitions (reps) they successfully performed (e.g., 10 lifts up and down)
- The number of sets of reps they performed (e.g., 3 sets of 10 reps)
- The amount of time they are waiting between each set

It would be convenient for an athlete to be able to walk into a gym, perform their exercises, and have an immediate record of what they have done—without having to remember to jot it down in a notebook.

Let's consider two different ways we might solve the problem of tracking weightlifting workouts. Remember, we need to solve for three things: the problem itself, the human element, and the broader context.

In our first solution, the athlete wears a smart watch that is equipped with an accelerometer. Before each set, they input the movement type on the watch using hardware buttons, along with the weight they are lifting. During a set, the watch keeps track of the number of reps that are performed, using an AI algorithm to understand when a rep has been completed based on data from the accelerometer. After the workout, this information is synced to a mobile application for viewing.

Does this solve the problem itself? Technically, yes—the system allows the athlete to track their weightlifting workout without a notebook. In a broader context, this solution also seems fine: fitness wearables are common, affordable, practically designed, and well accepted in society.

However, things look less appealing when we consider the human element. Our design requires the athlete to enter a weight number into their smart watch between each set. It's questionable whether this is a superior solution to using a paper notebook. In fact, many people find it frustrating to interact with smart device interfaces when they are in the middle of a workout.

Let's consider another solution. It would be great to be able to understand which movement an athlete is performing and the amount of weight they are using without requiring them to enter data by hand. To achieve this, we could use a small, battery-powered camera that can be placed on the floor in front of the athlete while they work out. It would use computer vision techniques to count the amount of weight being used and determine the movements that are being performed.

From the point of view of the underlying problem, this sounds great—it would remove the need for a notebook for activity tracking. From a human perspective, this is a genuine improvement in experience: the athlete can focus on their exercises without having to interact with a smart device or a notebook in the middle of their flow.

Unfortunately, in a broader context this solution may not be a good one. Many people work out at public gyms, where there is an expectation of privacy. Fellow gym users are unlikely to feel comfortable with being "filmed" by a smart camera during their workouts. While an edge AI camera could easily preserve privacy by not storing any of the video footage, it might be tough to explain this to other gym users. The social context of what is considered acceptable can make it difficult to deploy an otherwise effective design.

As we can see, it's critical that your design addresses every aspect of a problem. Edge AI can overcome a lot of challenges, but there are many cases where usability issues or the broader human context neutralize its benefits.

Design Principles

A good way to approach design is through a set of principles that provide structure to our critical thought. Ovetta Sampson, VP of Machine Learning Experience Design at Capital One, authored a fantastic set of principles that apply specifically to the use of AI in design. In her own words:

> In the age of AI, where speed, scale, and scary can simultaneously all be components of the products we design, we have to change design from a noun to become a very, deliberate verb. We're entering a Brave New World. And that world requires designers to take on a larger responsibility for the outcomes produced, behavior induced, and effect on humanity the intelligent products we design to have.
>
> —Ovetta Sampson

Sampson's ten principles, inspired by an earlier set (*https://oreil.ly/Ez0ym*) written by the German designer Dieter Rams, are as follows, including our own explanation of each point:

Good design solves hard problems
    With great power but limited resources, we should focus on solving the problems that matter.

Good design promotes healthy relationships
    Users exist within a network of relationships with other people and other products, and our design should account for this.

Good design requires malleability
    AI enables incredible customization, and we should make use of it to build better products that work reliably for the people we are designing for.

Good design makes companies that understand and products that serve me
    Design should be based on accurate understanding of the needs of individual users, not by the needs of a marketing department.

Good design acknowledges bias
    Bias is always present, and designers must work consciously to mitigate it, and be transparent about the limits of their products.

Good design prevents dishonesty
    Designers must be honest about the potential for negative impact from their products in order to avoid it.

Good design expects unintended consequences
    Unintended consequences in AI systems can systematically harm people, and good design must acknowledge and work around this fact.

Good design fosters equity
> AI can inadvertently amplify inequity and injustice, but carefully designed AI systems can counter this effect.

Good design considers its effect on a collective, connected ecosystem
> The human contexts where AI is deployed are incredibly complex and diverse, and good design must reflect this.

Good design purposefully brings order to chaos
> AI products should make our world easier to understand and cope with, not more chaotic than it already is.

Sampson's original article (*https://oreil.ly/-4WvU*) provides a deeper explanation of each principle.

These principles are based on the acknowledgment that AI derives its power through scale. Functions that would previously have required human oversight can now be entirely automated. The associated reduction in cost means that these functions will become far more widespread and will have a far greater impact than they otherwise would.

Simultaneously, the nature of AI systems mean that a single implementation—created by a single engineering team—may end up in widespread use by millions of very different people. This means that any flaw in a system will also be magnified to affect large portions of our population.

In practical terms: while a bad doctor might harm thousands of patients over the course of their career, a bad medical AI system can harm millions. The risk of scaling harmful systems is why we need to be so careful when designing edge AI products and is what makes principles like Sampson's so valuable.

Scoping a Solution

As anyone who works in software or hardware can attest, estimating the amount of work required to implement a product or feature can be very challenging. Similarly, AI and ML development are inherently unpredictable. The need for a high-quality dataset and the exploratory nature of the algorithm development process make it very difficult to know exactly how long a project is going to take.

Algorithm development naturally informs hardware and software requirements. For example, a machine learning practitioner may determine that a deep learning model needs to be a certain size in order to produce acceptable results. The size of the model will limit the types of devices that it can be deployed to. This means it may not be possible to begin the hardware development process until at least some of the algorithm development work has been done.

Things That Can—and Do—Go Wrong

There are many ways an AI project can fail before it really gets started. Here are some of the most common risks:

- It's too difficult or expensive to obtain an adequate dataset.
- There's not enough signal in the data to train a usable model.
- The available hardware isn't capable enough to run a working algorithm.
- The problem demands a level of precision that AI cannot deliver.

The additional variables of AI development mean that it's even harder to make the right assumptions about the development process as a whole. It can be very easy to underestimate the amount of work required, or to have to go back to the drawing board after a significant investment of time and money if it becomes apparent that the original plans will not suffice.

The nature of AI development makes a "waterfall" development model very risky. It's dangerous to assume that your initial assumptions will always hold true. It would be disastrously expensive to develop a beautiful piece of hardware and then discover at the last minute that it isn't capable enough to run the required model.

So how do you avoid this type of problem and make it easier to ship products that work? The key is to limit your scope. While AI is exciting, and the sky is the limit for novel applications, it's much easier to avoid mistakes if you avoid being too ambitious out of the gate.

A fantastic demonstration of this principle is the reality of the self-driving car. In the heady days of the mid-2010s, many technologists thought that fully automated self-driving cars were just around the corner. The deep learning revolution had unlocked massive progress, and the capabilities of vehicles had made leaps and bounds from the earliest prototypes. A self-driving world seemed imminent.

Unfortunately, while it's proven possible to build a self-driving car that can usually get things right, *usually* has not proven acceptable when we're talking about high-speed interactions with the general public. The last few percentage points of reliability have gotten exponentially harder to unlock. While it's likely we'll see self-driving cars at some point, they're still a few years away.

While self-driving cars have stalled, a related—but less ambitious—set of technologies have become so successful that they are now present in at least a third of all new vehicles (*https://oreil.ly/Hz0QK*). Advanced driver-assistance systems, or ADAS, is a category of technologies designed to help human drivers have an easier time on the road. They include features such as adaptive cruise control, lane centering, and collision avoidance.

ADAS features, a classic use case for edge AI, are designed to help with specific, individual tasks. They ease the mental and physical burden on drivers and help improve road safety. While they are not as ambitious as self-driving systems, their more limited scope allows them to be a lot more successful.

For example, many modern cars feature an adaptive cruise control system that can take over acceleration, braking, and lane centering while the car is on the freeway. Because the system only needs to work in this constrained environment, it's a lot easier to build it with 100% reliability. While it won't work at all on city streets, that's OK: freeway driving occupies the most time of any long trip, so from the driver's perspective it is nearly as good as a self-driving car.

By addressing a limited scope, ADAS systems are able to attain far more utility than self-driving systems in today's vehicles. What's more, the companies developing and deploying ADAS systems are able to incrementally build their expertise and insight under real-world conditions. They can keep improving their products while actively participating in the market, gradually getting closer to the dream of a self-driving car.

This approach is sensible for any edge AI product. Instead of pursuing grand ideas from the beginning, try to identify the small, useful stepping stones that still deliver real value. Determine the minimum viable product: a simple, achievable benefit that is genuinely helpful to your users. Build something out, see how it performs in the real world, and iterate from there.

Here's a specific example. Imagine you are building a quality control system for a production line. Today, all quality inspection is done by hand. Time and cost constraints make it impossible to inspect every item, so random samples are inspected—meaning some defects make it through.

Your long-term goal might be to inspect every item automatically using an edge AI vision system, ensuring all defective products are caught, and saving money on inspections. However, at the outset of the project it may not be clear that this is achievable. Your dataset may not have examples of every possible type of defect, making your system hard to test. There's no way to know if it would work without trying—but failure could be expensive.

Let's take a step back and think about the scope of the problem. While catching *every* defect may be a big challenge, being able to catch *some* of them would still be an improvement on the current situation, since we know some defects make it through.

It may be relatively simple to train a model to detect one specific type of defect (rather than every defect possible) at least some of the time. If combined with the current manual inspection process, a model trained to catch one defect type could still provide a tangible benefit to the factory. They wouldn't reduce inspection costs, but they would still catch more defects and increase the average quality of their products.

By limiting the scope to what you know is achievable, you're able to deliver immediate value with greatly diminished risk. On the back of this success, there's nothing to stop you from iterating on your solution and gradually attaining the grand vision you initially had in mind. Even better, you may find that your initial system delivers enough value that further development is not required.

Setting Design Goals

In "Planning an Edge AI Project" on page 197, we learned about the need to set specific goals for our application development process. There are three main types of goals: systemic goals, which reflect on the overall performance of the system, technical goals, which reflect on the inner functioning of elements of your algorithms, and values that you want the system to adhere to.

To be effective, goals must be designed with input from stakeholders and domain experts (see "Building a Team for AI at the Edge" on page 123). You will need to work to determine the minimum viable performance characteristics for a project. These are the criteria that will be used to evaluate the project's success at both systemic and technical levels. Wherever possible, they should be quantifiable using standard metrics for the domain, so you can use them to concretely measure your progress.

The best way to set systemic goals is with an evaluation-first approach.

Systemic goals

An edge AI system is rarely developed as the first and only solution to a problem. Most of the time there are solutions already in existence. When we're developing an AI application, it's important that we take the time to measure our solution against the existing ones, not just against itself. If we measure our system against itself, we're almost guaranteed to see improvement throughout the development process. But to know that we genuinely have a *better* solution than the alternatives, we need to measure against those, too.

That's why an *evaluation-first* approach to development can be so powerful. In this style of approach, the first step of the development process is to come up with a set of evaluation metrics that are general enough to measure the performance of any potential solution to the problem—AI or otherwise.

For example, imagine you are developing an edge AI application to help retail employees know when shelves are empty and need to be restocked. One way to approach this might be to focus on the technology involved. As a goal, you might decide that your system must be able to predict with 90% accuracy when a shelf needs to be restocked.

This sounds pretty good: 90% accuracy means the model will be correct in identifying that the shelves are empty 9 times out of 10, which seems reasonable. But this metric only tells us the raw performance of our algorithms; it doesn't give us any insight into whether our system is really helping. It's also no use for comparing against the current solution: it's likely that a given employee can already tell with 100% accuracy whether a shelf is empty or full without any help from AI!

Instead of focusing on technical metrics, try to take a step back and look at the bigger picture. The real goal of our system is to make it easy for retail staff to guarantee that the store's shelves are always stocked, so that customers have enough products to buy. With this in mind, we can choose a more meaningful metric. A better metric may be the proportion of time that a given shelf is stocked with product.[1] As a goal, we might say that, on average, a given shelf should be stocked 90% of the time.

We can then measure our current system—the employees' manual efforts—against our goal. While it's easy for employees to determine whether a given shelf is empty, they may be extremely busy most of the day and not have time to check every corner of the store to make sure every shelf is stocked. This might lead to an average stocking rate of 70%.

We now know the baseline performance of our current solution (70%), plus our goal (90%). This 20% shortfall is what our AI solution needs to help recover. Knowledge of the current solution and the improvement that needs to be made can guide our product design and development process. For example, since we know that the problem results from employees being too busy to check the whole store, we might focus our design around making sure they are notified of empty shelves in a way that fits neatly into their other duties. Since we have a convenient metric for measuring success, we can deploy an initial system on some shelves and easily understand whether it is effective.

There's always the possibility that the insight provided by metrics helps us revisit our assumptions and decide to solve the problem in a different way, perhaps not including AI at all. For instance, maybe it ends up being cheaper to modify staffing schedules to solve the problem rather than implement an edge AI system in every store. Even though this is a nontechnological solution, it's still a victory for the evaluation-first approach to development.

It's important to remember that "you are what you measure"—meaning that the metrics you use to quantify your goals will have a huge influence on the direction you end up taking. If you measure the wrong thing, you'll end up wasting time, money, and opportunity—and perhaps even make the situation worse. If you can identify the right thing to measure and improve, the power of iterative development means you can have an extraordinary impact.

---

1 An even higher-level metric might involve store revenue, assuming that higher revenue is better—but that metric is affected by more factors and so is a noisier way to measure the effectiveness of our system.

> ## Upgrading an Existing Edge Solution
>
> In some cases, you might wish to improve an existing edge deployment by incorporating more sophisticated artificial intelligence. For example, you may have a system based on a simple heuristic algorithm that works acceptably but still has room for improvement.
>
> This is actually an ideal situation. Since you already have a working system deployed, you presumably have a great understanding of the domain and the unique challenges of the problem you are trying to solve. You also likely have some effective metrics for measuring success: otherwise, you wouldn't know that you need to improve. There's also the potential benefit of already having devices out in the field with which to collect data.
>
> To upgrade an existing system, you should follow roughly the same design process as if you were starting any other brownfield project (i.e., one where you are making use of existing hardware). At certain points, however, you'll find that you can reuse your prior work.
>
> Throughout the development process, you should continually measure your new system against the original and make sure it is on track to beat the old approach by a comfortable margin. If a simpler solution works nearly as well, it may be better just to stick with that rather than commit to the additional complexity and long-term support required by an AI solution.

Technical goals

While systemic goals are vital in ensuring you are building the right thing, the technological aspects of your system need to have their own set of goals. Understanding the current and target performance of an AI algorithm, for example, will help you direct development efforts to the appropriate area.

For example, imagine you are developing a keyword-spotting model for a smart home device. For keyword-spotting models, performance is often expressed as a combination of *false accept rate* and *false reject rate*: two numbers that together describe how likely the model is to make a mistake. To ensure a quality product, you may decide with your stakeholders and interaction designers to aim for a false accept rate of less than 5% and a false reject rate of less than 1%. These numbers will become your target.

The next task is to determine a mechanism for testing your work. Having a solid target provides no benefit unless you are able to measure your progress toward it. Often, testing relies on a test dataset—but there are always differences between performance on a test dataset, typically collected under ideal conditions, and real-world operation.

The most reliable metrics come from systems that are deployed in production. At this stage, it's valuable to determine which metrics will be available to you in the field. It can often be challenging to measure real-world performance, since real-world data doesn't tend to come with labels. If you struggle to determine how your application's performance can be measured in the field, it might be worth reconsidering your project: without metrics, you'll have no way of knowing if it even works.

You may be using AI to improve an existing system, and in some cases you might already have some evaluation metrics that have been used to measure the current system. In either case, it's a great idea to use the same metrics to evaluate your current system along with the proposed AI-enabled replacement. It's always helpful to have a yardstick to measure against.

Given the iterative nature of AI development, you should also consider the amount of time you have available. Your goal should be to increase the system's performance until you meet the minimum viable performance level that you have decided on. If progress stalls, you'll need to decide whether to try a different approach—or to abort the project entirely. It might make sense to come up with performance milestones along the way to your target, so you can keep track of your progress and feel confident that the project is progressing.

Values-based design goals

To build a responsible application, you need to create design goals that represent the values you wish your solution to embody. For example, imagine you are building a medical diagnostics system. Medical experts may agree that it would be irresponsible to ship a solution with a diagnostic accuracy that falls below a certain threshold.

You should therefore aim to determine—in agreement with stakeholders and domain experts—the minimum performance that is required for a responsible product. You can use this minimum performance to come up with a set of firm go/no-go criteria that can be used to gate the project's release.

There's not always agreement on values, which is why it's so important to work with a diverse and representative group of stakeholders. Since different groups of people often share different values, the values you agree on may be relevant only in a particular context—for example, the culture that a majority of your stakeholders belong to. If you can't agree on the appropriate values, it may be a sign that your project carries ethical risk.

During the development workflow, it's crucial to measure and document the metrics that describe the system's performance. This data will help you make a go/no-go decision. There's often significant organizational and interpersonal pressure to push projects through to completion. Documenting metrics and having firm, written criteria for quality allow you to take the decision off your own shoulders and make it a part of the organization's processes.

These criteria should extend to deployment in the field. It's vital to be able to monitor performance and potentially terminate a deployment if the system is not performing adequately in the real world. Since the metrics available in the field are often more limited than those available during development, monitoring can be a challenge. There'll be more on this topic in Chapter 10.

Goals for Long-Term Support

Another key part of your design process is your plan for long-term support. Most AI deployments require observation and maintenance once deployed in the field. Drift is inevitable and will lead to a reduction in performance over time. The application and hardware you choose should ideally have the ability to report back some metrics that help you understand the rate at which drift is occurring.

This insight will help you tell when you need to collect more data and train a new model. Your design goals should include your goals for supporting the product in the long term. There's much more on this topic in Chapter 10.

Architectural Design

The architecture of an edge AI system is the way that its component parts fit together in order to create an effective solution. There are many possible ways to architect any given system. Each architecture will have its own unique trade-offs. The task of a systems architect is to analyze a situation and pick the architecture that will maximize the benefits of the technology.

The next section of this chapter will lay out the fundamentals of systems architecture for edge AI applications. Software and hardware architecture is a broad topic, so we'll focus specifically on the parts that are relevant to edge AI. We'll establish a solid foundation and provide a set of design patterns that can be applied in order to solve many different problems.

Hardware, Software, and Services

Edge AI applications are made from three main components: hardware, software, and services.

Hardware includes the edge devices themselves, with their processors, memory, and sensors—the great diversity of which we encountered back in Chapter 3. It also includes the way the devices are powered, and their means of communication with the wider world.

Software is the magic that brings a system to life. It begins with the low-level drivers that allow software to interface with the hardware itself, including sensors, peripherals, and networking devices. It encompasses all the signal processing and AI algorithms that may run on a device. Most importantly, it includes all of the application logic that interprets the signals output by AI algorithms and determines how to act upon them.

Services are the external systems that an edge AI system can interface. They might include communications networks, wireless systems, IoT management platforms, web APIs, and cloud applications: anything that lives externally to the edge system and communicates via some channel. This could be your own infrastructure, or it might be provided by a third party.

Effective edge AI architecture involves taking these three components and combining them in creative ways that provide the optimal balance of trade-offs for a given situation. It requires a solid understanding of the problem, the constraints, and the domain. This is why it's important to conduct a thorough exploration of the entire problem before embarking on this stage of the design process.

Your understanding of a situation will inform your use of hardware, software, and services. For example, a setting with minimal connectivity may force you to focus on highly capable hardware and do without some of the benefits of services. A tightly constrained brownfield (see "Greenfield and Brownfield Projects" on page 26) hardware platform might encourage you to be more creative with your use of software. The need for sophisticated software and large models might result in a significant role for cloud AI services in your particular application.

Some important concepts in edge AI architecture that we have already encountered include heterogeneous compute (see "Heterogeneous Compute" on page 75) and multi-device architectures (see "Multi-Device Architectures" on page 82). These are the key ingredients for some of the most common architectures we'll encounter.

Basic Application Architectures

Simplicity is always a good choice, and you should always start with the least complex architecture you can get away with. Figure 8-1 shows the structure of a typical edge AI application.

The core of the architecture is the *application loop*. This is a series of repeating steps that capture and process signals, run AI algorithms, interpret their output, and use the results to make decisions and trigger actions. It's a loop because the steps run over and over again as the device ingests a constant stream of sensor data.

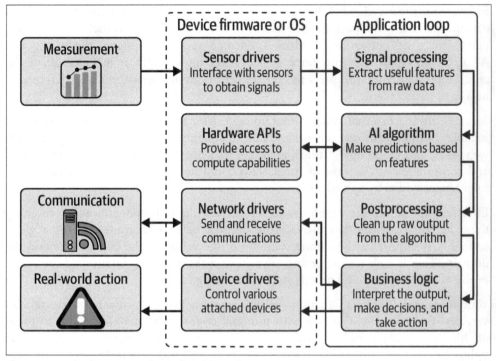

Figure 8-1. Architecture of an edge AI application

The application loop is supported by the *device firmware or OS* section.[2] These components provide a layer of abstraction between the hardware and the software. They typically provide convenient APIs that the application loop can use to control the hardware. Typical tasks involve reading data from sensors, sending and receiving communications, and controlling attached devices (such as lights, speakers, and actuators).

As we saw in "Heterogeneous Compute" on page 75, many devices have multiple processors. In our diagram, the *Hardware APIs* block represents the abstraction layer that allows computation to be performed in the processor of choice. For example, a deep learning model's operations may be computed on a separate neural network core for increased speed and efficiency.

---

2 Whether the system uses a firmware or an operating system depends on the hardware and the application, as discussed in "Processors for Edge AI" on page 68.

Before we move on, it may also be helpful to flip back to "Edge AI Hardware Architecture" on page 68 for a reminder of the way that edge AI hardware is structured.

Basic flow

In the most basic applications, there's a single pipeline of software, all running on one device, that takes sensor data, processes it, and makes decisions. This is shown in Figure 8-2.

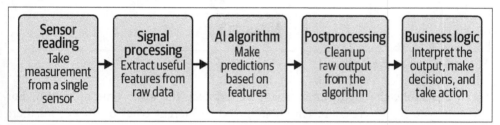

Figure 8-2. The basic edge AI application flow

Many successful applications use this flow, and it should be your starting point when developing a software architecture. Often, the AI algorithm in the flow is a single machine learning model. For example, a smart security camera might use this flow—with a vision model trained to detect people—as a trigger to send an alert. Figure 8-3 shows the same diagram with the real-world steps overlaid.

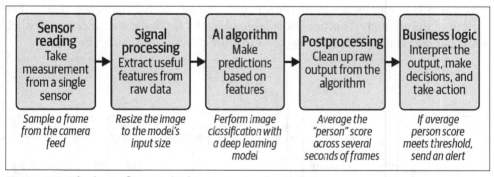

Figure 8-3. The basic flow applied to a smart camera design

Ensemble flow

Another common approach is to use an ensemble of algorithms or models, as described in "Combining algorithms" on page 113. In that case, the same sensor data is fed into multiple models that produce the same type of output, and their results are combined. It may look something like Figure 8-4.

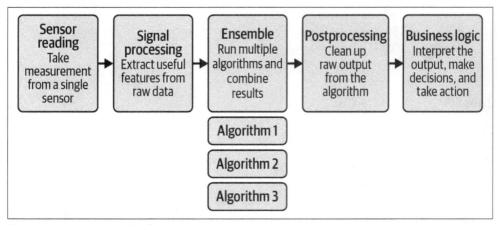

Figure 8-4. An ensemble flow

In an ensemble, the algorithms usually all produce the same type of output. For example, you might create an ensemble of three different types of image classifiers that are each trained to predict whether a person is present in an image. By combining the outputs of three different types of algorithms, you average the benefits and drawbacks of each, hopefully leading to an output that is less biased than any individual algorithm would be.

Parallel flow

It's also possible to combine algorithms that perform different functions. For example, you might combine a classification model with an anomaly detection model. The output of the anomaly detection model is used by the application to understand when the input data is out of distribution and therefore the classifier cannot be trusted.

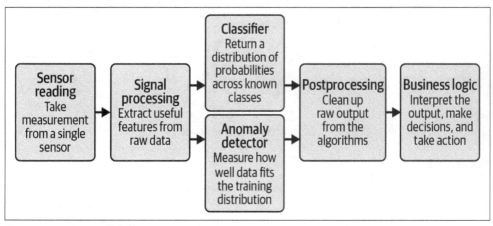

Figure 8-5. A parallel flow

In a parallel flow (Figure 8-5), the models' output may be combined either in the postprocessing step or in the business logic. For example, if the output of one model is used to moderate the output of another model (like in our classification and anomaly detection example) this moderation may be done in the postprocessing step. If the output of multiple models is used to drive a business logic decision, the models' outputs will be brought together there.

Parallel models doesn't necessarily mean parallel processing (as in multitasking). Many embedded processors are not capable of more than a single thread of computation, so you may increase the overall latency and energy use of your application with every model you add to the pipeline.

Series flow

It can also be useful to run models in series. In this flow, as shown in Figure 8-6, the output of one algorithm is fed into another, with or without postprocessing.

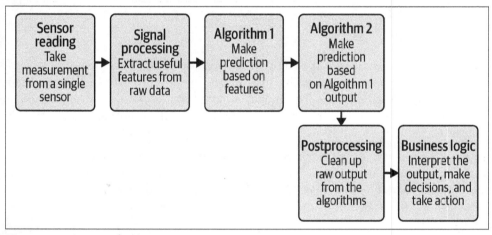

Figure 8-6. A series flow

Series flows are handy when you want to use one model to extract features from a raw input, then use another model to understand changes in the features. For example, you might use a pose estimation model to identify the position of a person's arms and legs from a photograph, then pass these positions into a classification model to determine which yoga pose they are doing.

Cascading flow

Another clever way to use algorithms in series is within a cascade. A cascading flow is shown in Figure 8-7.

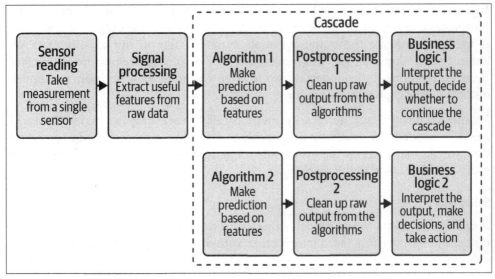

Figure 8-7. A cascading flow

Cascading flows are designed to minimize the cost of running inference in both latency and energy use. For example, imagine an always-on keyword-spotting system in a battery-powered device. The model required for keyword spotting might be relatively large and complex, meaning that running it all the time would quickly drain the battery.

Instead, we can run a smaller, simpler model designed merely to detect speech. This is the first layer of our cascade. When speech is detected, the input is passed to the second layer of the cascade, which is the full keyword-spotting model. Since the full keyword-spotting model ends up being run less often, energy is saved.

A cascade can have as many layers as necessary. Depending on the application, each layer in the cascade may also have its own independent signal processing algorithm. In some cases, reaching a certain stage of a cascade may even trigger the capture of data from another source—for example, a higher-quality microphone that provides better signal but uses more energy.

It often makes sense to tune the earlier models in the cascade for high recall (see "Precision and recall" on page 324), meaning it will err on the optimistic side when deciding whether something is a potential match. This configuration will still save energy versus a single large model, but it'll reduce the risk of the less accurate earlier models throwing away valid inputs.

Duty Cycle

The duty cycle is the percentage of time that a processor is actively working. When not actively working, it can be placed in a low-power state, saving energy. Cascades save energy because they allow for a reduced duty cycle.

This works because a smaller model takes less time to run than a larger one. Since the model only needs to be run periodically (for example, whenever the buffer of sensor data becomes full), the processor can be switched off for the rest of the time. In a cascade, the smallest model is the model run most frequently. This results in a lower duty cycle than if the larger model were being run at the same rate.

There's more about duty cycles in "Duty cycle" on page 333.

Sensor fusion flow

All of the architectures we've seen so far work with a single input. In a sensor fusion flow, as shown in Figure 8-8, inputs from multiple sensors are fed into the same AI algorithm.

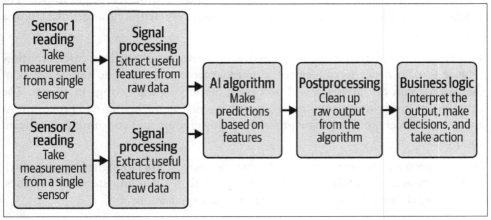

Figure 8-8. A sensor fusion flow

If different types of sensors are used, each sensor typically requires its own form of signal processing to create features for the AI algorithm to use. That said, there are also ways to perform sensor fusion with pure signal processing.

A classic example of sensor fusion is in sleep monitoring wearables, where signals from heart rate, temperature, and motion sensors are fused in order to accurately predict the user's sleep stage. Sensor fusion can also be combined with any of the other flows we've seen in this chapter.

Combining Rule-Based and ML Algorithms

All of these flows can be used to combine both rule-based and machine learning algorithms. For example, you might use a deterministic rule-based system designed by a domain expert to handle some percentage of decisions, with everything else being passed to a machine learning model. This combines the explainability benefits of rule-based systems with the ability of ML models to handle corner cases that aren't described by the rules.

Complex Application Architectures and Design Patterns

Basic application architectures can be combined with variations in hardware architecture in order to produce more complex systems that provide valuable benefits. These tried and true design patterns can be applied to many different projects.

Heterogeneous cascade

In a heterogeneous hardware architecture (see "Heterogeneous Compute" on page 75), multiple processors or coprocessors are available within a single device. For example, a single device may feature both an energy efficient midrange MCU, plus a more capable but higher-power high-end MCU.

This type of hardware can be combined with software written in a cascading flow (Figure 8-9) in order to implement a heterogeneous cascade. The earlier layers of the cascade run on the lower-end processor, amplifying the savings in energy. The latter layers, involving more complex algorithms, run on the higher-end processor. At any given moment, only a single processor is powered up and consuming significant energy.

Heterogeneous hardware increasingly includes accelerators designed to run deep learning models efficiently. These can be a great fit for running stages of cascades. This approach is used in a lot of keyword-spotting applications.

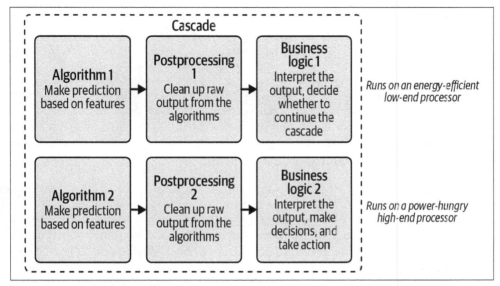

Figure 8-9. Heterogeneous cascade

Multi-device cascade

There's nothing to stop a cascade from spanning multiple devices, as shown in Figure 8-10. For example, a smart sensor may inspect data with a simple machine learning model. If a certain state is detected, it might wake up a more powerful gateway device that can analyze the data more thoroughly.

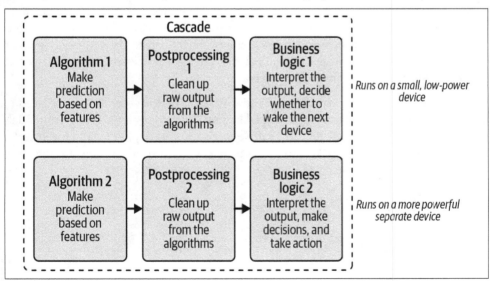

Figure 8-10. Multi-device cascade

The second-stage device can either use data transmitted by the first or capture new data with its own sensors. The devices might be physically distinct, like a smart sensor and a gateway device. They may also be combined as separate PCBs within the same physical product.

In some cases, entirely separate products may be arranged in a cascade. For example, a cheap off-the-shelf camera trap (which snaps a photo after detecting motion using an infrared sensor) can act as the first stage of a cascade, subsequently waking up a powerful SoC that is attached to the same storage device and can choose whether to keep or delete the photo depending on its contents.

Cascade to the cloud

Where bandwidth is less of an issue, cascades can span both a device and the cloud. This is a typical pattern in smart speakers that feature digital assistants, which use an always-on keyword-spotting model to detect keywords on-device with as low latency as possible. Once a keyword is detected, they stream the subsequent audio directly to the cloud, where a large and sophisticated model (too big to be deployed to the edge device) transcribes and interprets the user's speech.

In Figure 8-11, a sophisticated four-stage cascade is shown that makes use of multiple on-device models along with cloud compute. It may sound complicated, but this is similar to the flow used by modern mobile phones.

The first three stages occur on-device, across two different processors: a low-power always-on processor and a deep learning accelerator. When speech is detected by a model running on the low-power processor, a more powerful processor is woken up and used to look for the keyword. If the keyword is detected, an on-device transcription model attempts to turn the subsequent audio into text. Once transcribed, the text is sent to the cloud, where a large natural language processing model is used to determine what it means and how to respond.

The big trade-offs here are in energy, bandwidth, and privacy—as well as the need to provide long-term maintenance of a cloud system. In exchange, we get to use models that are too big to fit on-device, or that we don't want to deploy locally for security reasons. It's important to make sure these payoffs are worth it, since as a trade we're giving up most of the benefits of edge AI.

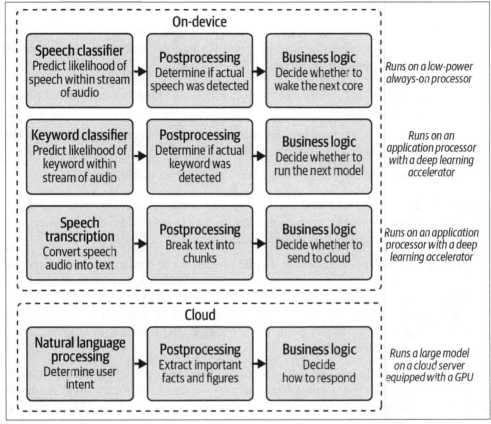

Figure 8-11. Cascade to the cloud for keyword spotting

Intelligent gateway

Sometimes it may make sense for the AI logic to live *near* the edge—but not at the actual leaf nodes of the network. For example, a network of IoT sensors may collect many different types of data about the operation of a factory. No single sensor has access to all the data—but they all send it back to a gateway device.

By running edge AI algorithms on the gateway device, all of the data can be analyzed together, which may result in more insight into the operation of the overall system. By doing the processing at the gateway, the sensors can remain small, cheap, and power efficient. All they need to do is capture and forward data; the gateway can take care of the intelligence.

Human-in-the-loop

In some contexts, it's not necessarily safe to allow AI algorithms to make decisions unchecked. This is typically where the risk of a bad decision could be extremely serious. Here are a few stark examples:

- Medical applications, where an incorrect diagnosis or badly administered procedure could endanger life
- Large machinery, such as self-driving cars or factory equipment, that has the potential to harm
- Security and defense applications, where deliberate harm may result

There are also many more subtle examples. For instance, if AI is used to enforce the rules of a sport—maybe analyzing video footage to detect foul actions—bias in a model might lead to unfair treatment of participants.

These types of challenges mean that it's often necessary to design a system to operate with human oversight. This can be implemented in different ways. In one model of human-in-the-loop architecture, a human is directly involved with every decision. For example, a medical diagnosis device might indicate that a patient has a certain condition, but a doctor is still required to interpret the information and make the final call using their own judgment.

In another model, the human acts as a passive observer unless they see fit to intervene. For example, while a self-driving car may be free to move by itself, its driver is still required to pay attention to the road and be ready to take over driving at a moment's notice. In this case, the self-driving car typically uses AI systems to detect when the driver is not paying attention to prevent them from forgoing their obligation. It's worth noting that there's significant debate around whether this model is effective. Humans tend to lose focus if they don't need to interact, which may compromise their ability to intervene.

In the third model, there is no direct human supervision—but samples of the algorithmic decisions are sent to human auditors for inspection. The overall process is monitored for reliability, but nobody is able to intervene live during a given activity. This approach is important in the long-term monitoring of applications and will be covered further in Chapter 10.

Graceful Degradation

Under production operation, there may be reasons why you wish to "turn off" any machine learning components of a system. For example, it may be discovered that an ML model is no longer performing effectively and can no longer be used (there'll be more on this topic in "Performance degradation" on page 353).

Whatever your architecture, it's important to build in some fallback that ensures the behavior of your entire system is still acceptable if you are forced to turn the ML component off.

In practical terms, this means including configurable conditional logic in your application that describes whether ML is used or bypassed for various scenarios with respect to the input. This could take the form of a "deny list," which indicates types of inputs that cause ML to be skipped. For example, each step in a cascade model might be guarded by an if statement like the following:

```
if matches_something_in_deny_list(input):
    return non_ml(input)
else:
    return ml(input)
```

Ideally, it's possible to update these deny lists on the fly—perhaps via a configuration update sent over the network. If the nature of your edge application doesn't allow for this type of remote update, you might at least be able to build in the ability to change configuration via hardware (for example, by switching a switch or connecting a jumper).

You will need to evaluate the performance of your product without the ML parts, so that you understand the impact that switching them off will have.

Working with Design Patterns

We've now encountered a wide range of design patterns that should provide some great starting points for your own projects. Of course, real-world situations do not always map neatly onto textbook patterns. Don't be afraid to adjust these ideas to fit the needs of your individual situation.

As we've learned, the edge AI workflow is innately an iterative one. It's helpful to take an iterative approach to using design patterns, too. Here's a step-by-step workflow you can follow:

1. Make sure you've spent some time exploring your dataset and understanding the types of algorithms you may need to use.

2. Begin with the simplest design pattern that you can: this will usually be Figure 8-2, especially if you are working on a single device.

3. Try to map your problem onto this pattern; write up some documents to describe it, including diagrams, and list the pros and cons.

4. Begin iterating through the development process, keeping the chosen design pattern in mind.

5. If it looks like you might need something more sophisticated, jump to the next simplest pattern that you can get away with.

6. Continue iterating and adjusting until you've reached something that works.

Don't be tempted to begin with a more complex design pattern than you know you need. The extra complexity will be a drag on your development process and will create additional constraints that force you down a certain path. All of this creates risk, and the number one way to be successful in AI projects is to keep risk to a minimum.

Accounting for Choices in Design

The designs we come up with in response to a particular problem are shaped by our individual perceptions, which means they may subtly encode our own (or our teams') biases. In addition, architectures themselves have innate bias. An architecture represents a set of compromises that direct the results of a solution one way or another. It's not necessarily intentional; it's what happens when we pick one particular option out of many.

There are three main categories of bias that have their roots in the design process (versus coming from the dataset). They are as follows:

Product bias

A product represents a particular solution to a problem. By its nature, it represents an opinion on the way a problem should be solved. It embodies the limitations and trade-offs that come with that opinion. All of this is unavoidable, but it's important we acknowledge that it results in bias.

For example, imagine we are building a smart home thermostat that can predict the perfect moment to adjust temperature levels based on user activity. We might need to choose between a basic architecture, with a single device that contains high-resolution sensors and a powerful processor, or an intelligent gateway architecture, where cheap, low-resolution remote sensors are installed in each room and communicate wirelessly with a central hub that performs the processing.

These trade-offs direct our product toward a preferred solution. With limited visibility but superior sensors, the system consisting of a single device is likely to work better in open-plan houses or small apartments. The system with remote sensors may work better in houses that have many different rooms.

Since every product design is created for a specific purpose, it's important to pick the design that best fits the problem you are trying to solve. If you're designing a smart home product, you may need to conduct some research to understand the styles of homes your target customers live in. This can inform your design process and help you select the appropriate architecture.

Algorithm bias

Algorithms themselves have innate bias. As with architectures, the design of every AI algorithm embodies a specific solution to a broad problem. Mathematicians and computer scientists try hard to find algorithms that work generally, across many different types of input, but in reality each type of algorithm has underlying assumptions that fit some problems better than others.

For example, we might be attempting to design an agricultural product that uses object detection to count animals on a farm. There are many different styles of object detection algorithm available to choose from. One such style is the single-shot detector (SSD),[3] which uses a deep learning model to predict precise bounding boxes around the items of interest. Another style is Faster Objects, More Objects (FOMO),[4] which uses a simpler, faster approach that identifies the centers of objects but does not draw a bounding box.

An effective product could be built with either algorithm. That said, different algorithms make different choices, and these will be noticeable in the product's performance. For example, due to the way their loss function is constructed, SSD models are better at identifying larger objects than smaller objects. In production, this might result in a product that works better when placed in smaller fields, where the animals are closer and take up more of the image frame. In contrast, FOMO is most effective when the centers of objects are not too close together. This means it may work best when animals are more spread out.

As with product bias, it's important that algorithms are chosen with the eventual deployment in mind. If the product will be marketed for counting sheep in large fields, FOMO may be the right choice. If it will be marketed for counting cows in a shed, SSD could be a better option. In either case, you should make sure your product is tested thoroughly before it goes on sale.

Your dataset will also inform your decisions here. As we've seen, it's very important to make sure your dataset is representative of real-world conditions. If your dataset adequately represents what your product will see "in the field," you won't

---

3 See Wei Lu et al., "SSD: Single Shot MultiBox Detector" (*https://oreil.ly/ZU6-S*), arXiv, 2016.

4 See Louis Moreau and Mat Kelcey, "Announcing FOMO (Faster Objects, More Objects)" (*https://oreil.ly/NdEG-*), Edge Impulse blog, March 28, 2022.

be surprised by algorithm bias. If your dataset is not representative, the bias will be undetectable and you may find that your system underperforms.

An interesting way to mitigate algorithm bias is through the use of ensembles, as described in "Combining algorithms" on page 113. Using an ensemble of different algorithms will smooth out the extremes, giving you the closest thing to an ideal approach. Ensembles often win machine learning contests, where high performance on an unseen dataset is the goal. That said, this doesn't mean ensembles are immune to bias. Plus, since they involve running multiple algorithms, they can be prohibitively costly on edge devices.

Deployment bias

This type of bias happens when a system is deployed in a way that it was not designed for. A product that is created to solve a particular problem has no guarantees of being effective when deployed in different contexts. It doesn't matter how carefully the developers have worked to mitigate bias; when applied to a different scenario from the one it was designed for, all bets are off.

For example, consider a medical device that is designed to monitor a patient's biosignals and predict the likelihood of a specific health condition occurring. The device has been carefully designed so that its inherent trade-offs match up well with the health condition it is designed to predict. The algorithms it uses have been evaluated and selected based on a high-quality, representative dataset collected from patients with the same condition.

This device may work very well on patients with the condition it is designed for. However, what if a doctor attempts to use it to predict a related condition that presents in a similar manner but differs in some subtle ways?

Since the product was designed around the original condition, there's no way of knowing how it will work on the new one without extensive testing with a lot of new data. Even if it appears to work for some patients, there may be others for whom it fails silently, putting their lives at risk. The bias of the doctor, in assuming that the conditions are similar enough for the product to continue to work, is reflected in the outcomes: the health of patients may be placed at risk.

To minimize deployment bias, it's important that the users of your product understand its design limitations and are responsible enough to avoid misusing it. In life-or-death situations, such as with medical devices, some of this may even be legislated: a device may be approved for legal use with a specific condition and no others, and only by licensed medical professionals.

There are huge benefits to publishing public information about the functioning of your product. For example, you may choose to share key facts about the dataset used to create the product, or statistics about the performance of your product in various scenarios. This way, your users can understand the exact nature and limitations of your product and will be less likely to mistakenly deploy it in the wrong setting.

There are some products that are so easy to deploy inappropriately that they are best left on the drawing board. For example, the Russian invasion of Ukraine in 2022 has led to some commentators calling for more development of autonomous weapons systems.[5] However, the unavoidable potential for misuse both on and off the battlefield—either by governments or by terrorist groups—has led many AI practitioners to pledge not to work on lethal AI. You can take this pledge yourself at *stopkillerrobots.org* (*https://oreil.ly/fMIPF*).

Design Deliverables

It's helpful to think of the design process in terms of the artifacts that result from it. The following three sidebars lay out the most common notes and documents that relate to the initial, exploratory part of the design process.

We begin the process by understanding our problem and coming up with some potential solutions.

Problem and Solutions

- Problem description (see "Describing a Problem" on page 172)
- BLERP analysis (see "Do I Need to Deploy to the Edge?" on page 173)
- Minimum viable product ideas (see "Scoping a Solution" on page 271)

Our next step is to determine the type of solution that is feasible.

Exploring Feasibility

- Moral feasibility study (see "Moral Feasibility" on page 187)
- Business feasibility study (see "Business Feasibility" on page 189)
- Dataset feasibility study (see "Dataset Feasibility" on page 191)
- Technological feasibility study (see "Technological Feasibility" on page 192)

Once we have a solution we think is feasible, we can start creating the design.

---

5 As covered in "Why Business Is Booming for Military AI Startups" (*https://oreil.ly/RekGr*), by Melissa Heikkilä, *MIT Technology Review*, July 7, 2022.

Design and Planning

- Design goals and standards (see "Setting Design Goals" on page 274)
- Description of time and resource constraints (see "Planning an Edge AI Project" on page 197)
- Proposed application flow (see "Architectural Design" on page 278)
- Proposed hardware architecture (see "Edge AI Hardware Architecture" on page 68)
- Proposed software architecture (see "Architectural Design" on page 278)
- Long-term support plan (see "Setting Design Goals" on page 274)
- Analysis of design choices (see "Accounting for Choices in Design" on page 292)

Summary

Since the design and development process is iterative throughout the course of a project, these should all be considered living documents—you can create new, updated versions of them as you proceed.

Once you have early versions of all these materials together, you can conduct a review and make sure the product still seems feasible and within acceptable thresholds for risk. If things look good, it's time to get started with active development.

## CHAPTER 9

Developing Edge AI Applications

Developing an edge AI application is a big task. In this chapter, we'll get familiar with the iterative development model that helps deliver successful edge AI deployments in real-world projects.

An Iterative Workflow for Edge AI Development

The process of developing a successful application is fundamentally simple: start small, make incremental changes, measure your progress, and quit when you meet your goals. The complexity comes when you introduce the vast number of moving parts that make up the technology of edge AI. This section of the book aims to provide a concrete process you can walk through to maximize your chances of success.

As we heard back in "The Edge AI Workflow" on page 169, the core idea behind this workflow is the power of feedback loops. Our goal is to create feedback loops between the various stages of the process, leading to an ever-improving understanding of the problem, our solution, and the best ways to fit them together (as shown in Figure 9-1).

While it's an iterative process, some parts are more iterative than others. The steps we tackle earliest—exploration, goal setting, and bootstrapping—are the parts where we're figuring what we want to do and how we may be able to go about doing it. They feature first in up-front planning and then during periodic reappraisal, as new information comes in: perhaps after an initial deployment, or when a significant amount of new data has come to light.

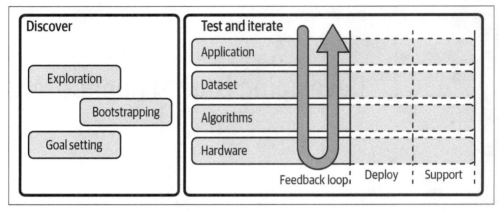

Figure 9-1. Feedback loops are central to the edge AI workflow, first introduced in "The Edge AI Workflow" on page 169

The middle parts of the workflow, in the *test and iterate* section, are more radically iterative. They're part of a tight spiral of development, testing, and improvement that is intended to home in toward whatever goals you have set. You can think of them more as four parallel tracks of development that inform one another as they evolve toward satisfying your requirements.

The deploy and support sections are also iterative, but again at a slower pace than the core section. This is part of their nature: once deployed and in the hands of users, the development of a system is destined to slow down. However, this is the stage at which the most vital feedback will start to arrive, and where your system will have to begin adapting to the evolving environment of the real world. The earlier you can deploy and tap into this vein of insight, the better.

The next section of the chapter will walk through each topic in the workflow and lay out some of the key activities and concepts.

Exploration

Exploration is the way we begin to understand what we are trying to do. It includes much of the type of work we learned about in Chapter 6 and consists of the following major tasks:

- Describing the problem you are trying to solve (see "Describing a Problem" on page 172)
- Determining whether you need edge AI (see "Do I Need to Deploy to the Edge?" on page 173 and "Do I Need Machine Learning?" on page 178)
- Figuring out whether the project is feasible (see "Determining Feasibility" on page 186)

- Framing a problem, by mapping it onto known methodologies (see "Framing problems" on page 195)

- Analyzing your proposed solution for potential risks, harms, and unintended consequences (see "Moral Feasibility" on page 187)

- Mapping out stakeholders and understanding what they want and need (see "Stakeholders" on page 128)

- Performing some initial data exploration

The final step depends a lot on whether you have the means to collect a dataset at this point, even if it's a small and limited one. It's strongly recommended that you have some data on hand while attempting to determine feasibility: data represents so much of the risk of an AI project that it's critical to start understanding it as soon as possible.

You should at the very least get a sense for how difficult it will be to collect an adequate dataset. It's likely to be one of your major challenges, and it's disastrous to invest a lot of work before discovering that data is impossible to obtain.

If you can't begin to conduct data exploration at this stage, you should do so at the earliest available opportunity.

Data Exploration

Data exploration, also known as exploratory data analysis (EDA), is the task of learning about a dataset. In our context, we're doing so with the goal of understanding whether the dataset is likely to be helpful in solving our problem, whether as a way to evaluate the performance of our algorithms or as a training dataset for use in machine learning.

Data exploration commonly involves the following:

Statistical analysis
 Using descriptive statistics to summarize the data's properties

Dimensionality reduction
 Transforming data so it is easier to analyze

Feature engineering
 Extracting useful signals, as seen in "Feature Engineering" on page 85

Visualization
 Generating graphics that represent the data's structure

Modeling
 Training machine learning models to explore relationships within data

---

Data exploration is a large and fascinating field, the natural domain of data scientists and machine learning practitioners. There are vast numbers of software tools available for use in data exploration—but due to the complex concepts and terminology, they can feel fairly inaccessible to users without some background in data science.

That said, it's possible to learn some reasonable beginner-level skills in a small amount of time from many resources available on the topic.[1]

One of the challenges of edge AI, however, is that much of the data we work with is sensor data in the form of high-frequency time series and high-resolution images: relative newcomers to the field of data science. Data exploration tools are often geared toward tabular data, low-frequency time series, and textual data, such as corporate financial data and social media posts. This means that it can be difficult to find tools and resources that can help.

You may find that engineers with expertise in fields outside of traditional data science have existing skills that can help with data exploration for edge AI. For example, digital signal processing engineers have many tools that are valuable for exploring sensor data, and natural scientists (such as biologists and physicists) often have strong practical skills in this area.

Goal Setting

Goal setting is where we attempt to describe what we're aiming for. We've seen various goal-setting activities throughout Chapters 6 and 8.

The process includes these key components:

- Determining the evaluation metrics you will use, before and after deployment (see "Setting Design Goals" on page 274)
- Setting the systemic goals for your design (see "Systemic goals" on page 274)
- Setting the technical goals for your implementation (see "Technical goals" on page 276)
- Agreeing on values with stakeholders (see "Stakeholders" on page 128)
- Creating a values-based framework for interpreting progress (see "Values-based design goals" on page 277)
- Setting up a review board to evaluate the ongoing project (see "Diversity" on page 126)
- Designing a scheme for testing your algorithms and your application

---

1 A highly rated book that covers the topic is *Data Science from Scratch: First Principles with Python* by Joel Grus (O'Reilly, 2019).

- Scoping out your long-term support goals
- Deciding how you will make the decision to abort a project

Goals must be measurable to be meaningful, so many of these items depend on having an effective process for testing and evaluating your system. This will be covered in depth in Chapter 10.

Calling it quits

Edge AI is a risky business, and a large proportion of projects do not make it into production. This is only natural, since a big part of the development process is devoted to understanding whether it's actually possible to solve the problem using the resources that are available.

However, when we're invested in a project—personally, financially, and organization-ally—it can be difficult to know when to quit. That's why it's so important to have a solid idea of your minimum viable performance characteristics right at the start of a project. You'll need to decide these minimum standards for every type of goal: systemic, technical, and ethical. For example, it's no good if you have a high-performing algorithm (according to your technical metrics) if your system, once deployed, does not have the business impact you were looking for.

Failure is a key part of the iterative process of discovery and innovation, especially where artificial intelligence is concerned. The important thing is to identify when a direction of development is not working out before too many resources have been burned in its pursuit: fail early, fail fast. If you can identify an unproductive effort early on, you can quickly change targets and avoid spending too much time.

For this reason, it's crucial to set milestones and go/no-go criteria for your project. At each stage during design and development, you should be prepared to measure your current status and make a call as to whether the current approach is working or whether it's time to try something else. Writing these milestones down during the early goal-setting phase is a good idea because it will force you to think critically about the project early on. You can always reappraise your goals as you make progress.

Some problems are simply intractable, especially when adequate data is hard to come by. In these cases, you may have to make the difficult call to abort a project entirely. To avoid being surprised by this, you should understand your budget in time and money before you begin and come up with limits in terms of what you are willing to spend to attain a certain amount of progress. If you don't seem to be close enough, you can make the decision to stop. It may be better to stop an unfruitful project midway and go back to the drawing board rather than spend your entire budget and end up with nothing.

Bootstrapping

Bootstrapping is how we get from an understanding of our problem to our first iteration of a solution. It involves getting our hands dirty with data and starting the process of building—topics we cover in Chapter 7 and in the chapter you are reading now. The key tasks are:

- Collecting a minimal dataset (see "Estimating Data Requirements" on page 211)
- Making an initial attempt at determining hardware requirements (see "Device capabilities and solution choice" on page 196)
- Developing the simplest possible initial algorithm
- Building the simplest possible end-to-end application (see Figure 8-1)
- Doing some initial real-world testing and evaluation (see Chapter 10)
- Performing a responsible AI review of your early prototype

We've encountered a couple of these concepts before, but this is the first time we're bringing together all of the components of an entire working application.

Why bootstrapping is helpful

The goal of bootstrapping is to quickly arrive at something that at least somewhat resembles a prototype—even if it's extremely limited, incomplete, and makes some faulty assumptions. But why waste time on a low-quality prototype if you can just develop the components separately and bring them together at the end?

There's a huge difference between reasoning about something on paper and experiencing a tangible piece of technology, especially when the technology is designed to interact with the physical world. By rapidly getting to an end-to-end prototype, you'll give yourself, your team, and your stakeholders the opportunity to try it out, understand the way it fits the problem you are trying to solve, and identify many potential issues far ahead of time.

Iterative development is all about testing your assumptions: trying to quickly determine whether a given decision is the right one so that you have time to course-correct if it is not. You can (and must) do this with the individual components of a system, but for something as complex as an edge AI product you really need to see it all working together. There are emergent phenomena and feedback loops within any complex system, and you can't truly understand how something works until you have seen it interact with the real world.

In addition to the massive benefits of early testing, there's a huge amount of power in being able to demo your product early on. Even before it's ready, an end-to-end demo can be highly convincing to stakeholders, potential customers, and to your own team. This might be essential to unlocking the support and resourcing that you need to complete the project. On the flip side, if you find that your early demos *aren't* convincing anybody, it's a good signal that you might need to revisit your design.

You can't always create an entire end-to-end flow at an early stage. That's OK: you can still benefit from integrating whichever components of the system that you can. That said, if a project is by nature difficult to integrate until the very end, it carries a much higher degree of risk.

Developing a baseline algorithm

In "Systemic goals" on page 274 we learned about the need to take an evaluation-first approach, where the performance of our system is continually measured and compared to a baseline. In many cases, there's an existing non-AI system whose performance we can measure and compare to. Either way, once we start developing our algorithm we should aim to immediately establish a baseline for algorithmic performance that we can try to beat.

To help illustrate this concept, let's imagine we are building a system to help reduce the time taken for quality inspections of chocolates being made on a production line. Our grand idea is that we could train a deep learning vision model to identify specific flaws in individual chocolates and provide real-time feedback to workers on the production line.

The first thing to do is establish our current baseline for performance. It may be that quality control is currently done manually by employees, and it takes 30 seconds per box of chocolates. With our stakeholders, we may decide that our goal is to reduce the time taken to at most 10 seconds.

Our first algorithm—and the hardware and software supporting it—should attempt to make progress toward this goal in the simplest manner possible. For example, rather than training a sophisticated deep learning model (which would require a large dataset, costing time and money to collect) to identify many different types of faults, perhaps we can use some simpler computer vision techniques (as in "Image feature detection" on page 92) to spot the characteristics of a single type of fault.

This simpler algorithm will be much easier to implement as a basic prototype. We can then try it out on the production line. For example, we might set up the system to alert the employee working on quality control when a box of chocolates has a very specific flaw. Although limited, this extra information might still make the employee's life easier and save a few seconds of time.

Now that we have an algorithmic baseline using a simple implementation, we know what we have to beat. In some cases, the simple baseline may prove effective enough that it changes our view on what is necessary. For example, if sufficient time is saved, it may make sense to forgo the expense of collecting the large dataset necessary to train a deep learning model: our stakeholders may be perfectly happy with the performance of the simple baseline, or at least a more polished version of it.

The approach of establishing a simple baseline algorithm helps protect us from overengineering, where we invest a lot of resources in developing a complex solution to a problem that is not proven to be necessary. It also provides a solid start to our evaluation-based approach, forcing us to set up the processes required to conduct realistic evaluation and allowing us to measure the rate of improvement over the existing system.

A baseline can also help inform the required architecture. For example, if the baseline can handle a large percentage of inputs, the best overall solution may be a simple algorithm that covers most inputs, combined with a cascade to a sophisticated ML model that can handle more challenging inputs.

Our first hardware

Being able to evaluate our baseline algorithm often implies that we have also arrived at an initial iteration of our hardware design. It should be the goal at this point to create something deployable so that we can test it in the field. However, this doesn't mean it has to meet the same requirements as our finished product.

Computer hardware runs the spectrum from general purpose to application specific. At one extreme, a modern personal computer is designed to be capable of running nearly any software and integrating with any hardware you can imagine. At the other end, a custom microcontroller-based board may be designed for a single function inside a specific product.

The more general purpose and capable a piece of hardware, the easier it is to develop for. This principle means that it's often much quicker to prototype something on a more powerful system, such as an SoC-based development board (see "System-on-Chip" on page 75) running Linux, than on a tiny, low-power, application-specific device that your team has designed in-house.

With this in mind, it's often a good idea to implement the first iteration of your product on a more general, capable piece of hardware—even if this compromises some of your design goals. For example, it could be quite easy to implement the first iteration of our chocolate quality control system on a Linux SoC board using some quick and dirty Python scripts.

The board may be far more expensive and power hungry than we can afford in our long-term solution, but for an initial prototype it still gets the job done—with a fraction of the development time. Once the concept is proven out on more general hardware, you'll have enough confidence to invest in the lengthy and expensive process of designing a smaller, more efficient device, and adapting your algorithms to fit.

Data Logging

If you don't already have a dataset (which is a majority of the time) you will have to get some hardware into the field in order to collect a dataset. As described in "The Unique Challenges of Capturing Data at the Edge" on page 217, this can be a challenge. Your data collection hardware typically needs to have the same sensors as your eventual final product, since substantial differences will make it hard to create effective algorithms. Often the shape, size, and materials of the hardware device can influence data collection, too.

If you're unsure of the exact sensors you'll be using, you can always use multiple types during data collection so that you know you won't have to throw away your dataset and start again from scratch if you are required to make a hardware change. For example, you could collect data using two types of microphone, giving you the flexibility to choose either one in your final design.

Aside from the sensors (and any physical considerations that might affect their readings), your data logging hardware can be a completely different type of device to what you intend for your actual product.

Responsible AI review

Deploying and testing the first end-to-end prototype of our application allows us to begin measuring performance, and also to better imagine how the finished version might work in the field. It also requires us to do some initial algorithm development, which often involves further understanding of our dataset and its limitations.

All this additional information that has come to light can help us test some of the assumptions we made while determining moral feasibility (as in "Moral Feasibility" on page 187) and stating our values-based design goals (see "Values-based design goals" on page 277). You should take a systematic approach to probing all of these assumptions using the results of your initial testing.

For example, in the case of our quality-control system for a chocolate factory, we may have assumed that our system would reduce the burden on employees by allowing them to get more done in the same amount of time. However, on exploring feedback on our prototype system we may discover that the system increases employees' stress by overloading them with information, leading to burnout. This discovery may inform the design of our product: we might decide to explore ways we can inform workers without creating an overwhelming experience.

With an evaluation-first approach, we're able to gather key metrics about the performance of the system and analyze them in terms of our goals and values. For instance, it's very important from a fairness perspective that our system works well for all employees. By evaluating metrics, we may find that the system performs better for some employees than others (for example, perhaps it provides visual feedback that is difficult for some people to see). In order to capture this type of insight, it's important to measure and collect relevant data from the beginning.

Test and Iterate

We're now in the core part of the workflow, where our initial implementation is incrementally improved over numerous iterations. There are four main areas of focus: application, dataset, algorithms, and hardware. These are shown in Figure 9-2.

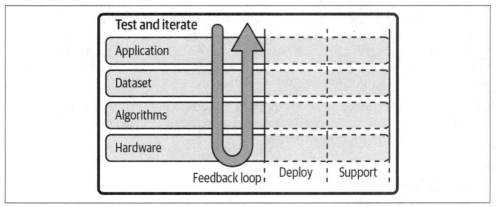

Figure 9-2. The test and iterate portion of the workflow consists of four focus areas: application, dataset, algorithms, and hardware

Each of these things is an essential component of the project. You can think of them as four siblings, growing up side by side, informing one another's development as they change in response to their environment. That environment is the evaluation-driven feedback loop that it's our job to deliberately create.

These four components advance together, each at their own pace, sometimes constrained by the practicalities of the situation—and sometimes by each other. For example, dataset collection can be a painstaking process and it might take a while before the dataset is big enough to train a machine learning model to an acceptable level of performance. During the waiting period, work on the physical hardware and the application code may continue unabated.

Interdependency

You'll notice early on that the dependencies between different components of the project can seem to cause gridlock. For example: your algorithm depends on having an adequate dataset, your hardware depends on the algorithm, and your application depends on the hardware.

If things get blocked, you should attempt to work around the situation through substitution. For example, you may choose to use a general-purpose hardware platform while you wait for your custom hardware to be ready (as we saw in "Our first hardware" on page 304). Similarly, you might try to make do with a less data-intensive algorithm if your dataset is causing a blockage.

From an engineering perspective, the riskiest components of a system are its algorithms. This is because it's hard to know ahead of time what type of algorithms will be required to solve a problem, and what their data and computational requirements might be. For this reason, it's always a good idea to design some flexibility into your hardware and application. For example, you may want to ensure there's additional RAM or ROM available in case you end up needing a larger-than-expected machine learning model to attain the accuracy you need.

There's obviously a cost associated with building excess capacity, so as with any engineering project, you'll sometimes just have to make a judgment call based on your best understanding of the situation.

The project's components do not exist in any particular order or hierarchy, and development is not a round-robin process where work is performed on one component and then the next. Instead, development occurs in parallel, typically with different engineers—or entire teams—working on each thread. Teams must synchronize regularly to share their current progress and anticipate whether there are any impending roadblocks that need to be worked around.

The key to successful development is to establish feedback loops between each of the four threads, and between the stages of the project (development, deployment, and support).

Feedback loops

The classic view of AI development, visualized in Figure 9-3, shows a simple, step-by-step feedback loop that starts with data collection and ends with deployment to device. This is a tempting idea since it provides an easily understandable view of the way that information flows through the system.

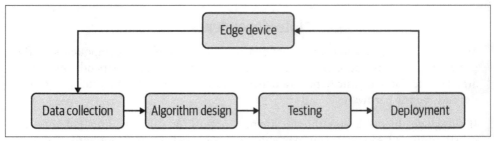

Figure 9-3. It's tempting to think of the AI development feedback loop as being a step-by-step process, the result of taking a linear workflow and making it iterative

However, as we learned in "The Edge AI Workflow" on page 169, the reality is that there is actually interplay between every single component of the system. Each of them relates to the others in a dynamic way that is not easily expressed in a basic diagram. Figure 9-4 shows the system expressed more realistically.

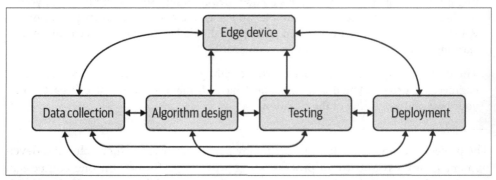

Figure 9-4. In reality, AI development involves a network of components that feed back into one another

When managing a project, it's critical to enable feedback to flow throughout the process unimpeded, from any one point to any other. For example, there will likely be aspects of the dataset (for example, the energy contained within specific frequency bands of the raw data) that inform the hardware design (since the hardware must be capable at sampling at a high enough rate to represent that frequency). The inverse is also true: if the hardware is constrained to include certain sensors, the dataset must reflect what those sensors can capture.

Some feedback loops are easier to establish than others. For example, a feedback loop between dataset and hardware can be created by having the responsible teams talk to each other regularly. On the other hand, depending on the application, it can be very expensive to deploy a device into the field and monitoring. For this reason, various tools exist to "close the loop" in a simulated or approximate way—as we will discuss in "Performance Calibration" on page 337.

Here are some of the most important feedback loops in the development process:

Algorithm and dataset
> Algorithms have varying data requirements. If plentiful data is available, many different algorithms may be used. If little data is available, fewer algorithms will work well. If a certain algorithm is desired for its specific properties, a suitable dataset will have to be collected.

Algorithm and hardware design
> In a greenfield project, the algorithm selected may determine the choice of hardware, since certain hardware might be required to run the algorithm efficiently. In a brownfield project, the constraints of existing hardware will limit the choice of algorithm.

Algorithm and performance in the field
> The selected algorithm will impact performance in the field—for example, a larger machine learning model may provide better results. Inversely, the required level of performance in the field may drive algorithm selection.

Dataset and hardware design
> The hardware design often informs the dataset since it may dictate which sensors are available for which to collect data. Alternatively, if a specific dataset is already available, the type or origin of the data it represents may influence the hardware design. For example, it may be helpful to ensure the exact same model of sensor is used.

Dataset and performance in the field
> If real-world performance is bad, it may be necessary to collect more data, guided by the areas in which the system is falling short. If only limited data is available, it may force you to settle for lower real-world performance than otherwise.
>
> Inversely, if performance in the field is limited or biased, this will influence the data you collect and the models you train over time. For example, if most people using your product belong to a certain group, you may begin to overfit performance to their needs.

Iterations in practice

The basic idea of an iteration is that you change something, measure its impact on your goals, and then decide what to do next. The canonical example of this technique in AI development is when training a machine learning model. A typical iterative process for training resembles the following:

1. Obtain some data and split it into training, validation, and test datasets.
2. Train a large model on the training split, aiming to overfit the data.[2]
3. Measure performance on the validation split.
4. Tweak the setup to improve validation performance: add more data, add regularization, or play with the type and size of the model.
5. Train and measure performance again.
6. Once the model performs well enough on the validation split, try it on the test split.
7. If it works well, great. If it doesn't work well, throw it out and start from scratch.

The flow for an edge AI project is similar, but it also includes the hardware and application pieces of the puzzle. For example, you might come up with an effective algorithm using something similar to the above flow, then attempt to deploy it to your hardware of choice and test it in a realistic way (such as with potential users). If it works, great. If it doesn't work, you'll have to make changes.

The key to all of this is making sure you test and iterate rapidly. If you spend a long time on each iteration, the penalty for making a regression (where improvement gets worse or something doesn't fit, as with a model that is too large for the available hardware) is much larger, since you may have wasted a lot of time going down an unproductive route.

If you iterate rapidly, so each change is small and is tested immediately, you'll never waste too much time going down a rabbit hole of development that ends up being incompatible with other parts of your system.

When you're lucky enough to have a large dataset, training a model can take quite a long time (think hours, days, or even weeks—although the small models of edge AI don't usually take that long). It's a nightmare to reach the end of a 48-hour training run and realize you made a mistake in your code and the resulting model is useless.

To cut down the time it takes for each iteration, it's a good idea to begin the process with a subset of your dataset. For example, you might begin with a 10% stratified sample (see Figure 7-14). Once you start to see promising results with this subset, you can gradually add more data in future iterations to improve the performance of your model.

---

2 By aiming to overfit the data, we can prove that the model has sufficient representative power to model the data, and that our training pipeline actually works.

Tools can help you avoid some of these problems altogether. For example, AutoML tools (see "Automated machine learning (AutoML)" on page 150) designed specifically for edge AI can factor in hardware constraints so that you never run the risk of exceeding your specifications.

Remember, you won't just be iterating on your model: you'll be changing and improving every part of your design, from hardware through to application code. To understand how your performance is changing, you'll need to use the right metrics and evaluation procedures—covered later in "Evaluating Edge AI Systems" on page 317.

The goals you set during the design process (see "Technical goals" on page 276) will help you understand when to stop iterating, either because you are no longer getting closer to your goal, or because you've surpassed it.

The iterative workflow naturally generates a lot of artifacts: datasets, models, training scripts, and all of the dependencies they bring with them. Keeping track of these is extremely important, since otherwise it can be difficult to understand your results and reproduce your work in the future. As we learned in "Machine learning operations (MLOps)" on page 151, MLOps provides a framework for doing this reliably.

Updating your plans.   During the course of a project, your understanding of the problem you are trying to solve, and the methods you are applying to it, is likely to evolve dramatically. It can sometimes become apparent that a goal is unrealistic, misguided, or not relevant to solving the core problem. If this seems to be the case, don't hesitate to bring your stakeholders together and reappraise your targets.

That said, goals shouldn't be expected to change frequently. Instead, if you need to make a course correction, the requirements and specifications of your project can be adjusted in line with your existing goals.

For example, imagine you are designing a smart lock that uses an image sensor and facial recognition to control entry to a building. Your goal for the project is to attain a false acceptance rate of close to 0%. During development you realize that this is unachievable using vision alone. You work with your stakeholders to update the scope of the project, allowing for an additional sensor to improve the reliability of the system.

You should consider this type of discovery a natural part of the iterative development process. If you realize you should be aiming slightly differently, don't panic—the purpose of the process is to allow you to course-correct so that you end up with a successful product at the end.

Of course, it's great if you can identify some of the possible risk factors during your design process and come up with ready-to-go contingency plans. For example, you may have predicted at the design stage that there might be a risk that vision alone is not adequate for ensuring a low false-acceptance rate and come up with some potential alternative solutions.

 Make sure that any changes in goals and direction are agreed upon by all stakeholders, communicated clearly to everyone involved with the project, and documented carefully for future reference. Differences in expectations can lead to major drama—but are easy to avoid.

Ethical AI review

As we've seen, projects can undergo serious changes in direction during iterative development. This means your iterative process needs to include regular ethical review of your work. Things you should investigate include:

- Is the project on track to meet its key performance metrics set out during the design process (see "Values-based design goals" on page 277)? If not, maybe a new approach is needed.

- Is your moral feasibility study (described in "Moral Feasibility" on page 187) still relevant, or has your project changed and it needs to be updated?

- Do you still have a sufficient dataset and domain expertise to embark on the project (see "Data, Ethics, and Responsible AI" on page 206)?

- Are your stakeholders in agreement that you are making progress, or are there any concerns?

It's a great idea to conduct some form of third-party ethical review at this stage in addition to the ethical analysis undertaken by your own team. It's much better to catch a potential ethical issue during iterative development, while it's still possible to change course, than once development is over or the product has been shipped.

Model Cards

As your algorithms take shape, it's important to document their characteristics for future users. This includes information such as how they are intended to be used, results of their evaluation against different benchmarks, and details of the processes used to evaluate them. Without this information, it's impossible to use a model safely. While you may have all of these details during the development phase of your project, it's important to document them for later reference.

One standard for this documentation comes in the form of model cards. Model cards provide a format for describing a model through textual information that can be shared along with the model itself. More information about model cards, along with a template for creating one, can be found in this repository on GitHub (*https://oreil.ly/gXkLF*).

Deployment

There are no distinct lines between iterative development, deployment, and support. Instead, a project evolves gradually toward satisfying its goals until at a certain point—hopefully, fairly early in the process—the software side of the project is deployed onto hardware, and the hardware is placed in the field. This gradual process is shown in Figure 9-5 (as in Figures 6-1 and 9-2).

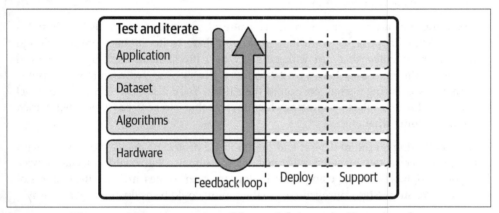

Figure 9-5. The test and iterate portion of the workflow gradually evolves from pure development to a mixture of development, deployment, and support; the feedback loop is maintained at all times

In the context of edge AI, deployment can mean one of two things:

- Deploying a piece of software onto a hardware device
- Deploying a set of hardware devices into the real world

In either instance, deploying early and often is the way to go. In the first case, it ensures you're always building hardware and software that work well together. In the second case, it guarantees that you will establish a feedback loop between your project's development process and its real-world performance. Deployment should never be considered a "last mile" operation that happens just before launch. Instead, it's a critical part of your development process.

The distributed nature of edge systems lends itself well to this style of approach. It's often possible to perform a staged rollout of a few devices at a time, carefully controlling the exact places where they are deployed and who is going to be interacting with them. This means you can ship prototype devices running a prototype application and get data on real-world performance—but still keep the associated risk to a minimum.

Deployment of a Livestock Monitoring System

Imagine you are working on a system for monitoring the activity of livestock in an agricultural setting. You're developing a smart collar that fits around the neck of a sheep and can keep track of how long it spends eating, moving, and sleeping. Your first deployment will happen when you begin to collect a dataset, since you'll need to gather real data from live animals.

Assuming you are working with an agricultural producer (sheep rustling is not a recommended approach), you'd first work with them to iterate on a physical design for the smart collar that can withstand life in a literal field. Next up, you'd need to deploy the necessary hardware to collect a diverse and representative dataset—perhaps by collaring a small portion of their flock. You'd also need some way to label the data—for example, by capturing video footage that can be used to tell when which animal is doing what.

After collecting an initial dataset and developing a prototype device, you'd work with the producer to deploy it on a limited set of animals. You could correlate device output with labels created using video footage in order to measure the effectiveness of the system. Successive improvements to the system could be evaluated the same way.

Once you meet a certain threshold of performance, you might begin to scale up the system, gradually adding devices and monitoring metrics to understand whether everything is functioning consistently. By adding devices slowly, you limit the risk of any negative effects. You may also trial different iterations of your hardware and software at the same time, on different animals, in order to compare its performance.

At a certain point you may feel confident enough in the output of the system that you consider that it meets your goals. At this point, development is mostly complete and you can transition into long-term support—which we'll cover in Chapter 10.

The best way to approach deployment is with a well-thought-out deployment plan. The steps involved are documented in "Deploying Edge AI Applications" on page 338.

Support

An edge AI project is never really *finished*. Instead, it gradually enters a different phase of life where the focus is on monitoring and maintaining its performance.

This work is necessary due to drift, which we learned about in "Drift and Shift" on page 233. Because the world is constantly changing, it's almost inevitable that an AI-based product will begin to lose efficacy over time. This makes ongoing maintenance necessary: updating the software so that it keeps pace with the change that is happening in its environment.

The support of edge AI applications is covered in depth in Chapter 10. Support is tightly coupled with evaluation, since evaluative metrics are what allow you to understand whether performance—or the environment—are changing.

Summary

We now have a high-level view of the entire development workflow. While it's a great general road map, the specifics of the journey will differ from project to project.

However, one thing shared by every project is a need for careful deployment, evaluation, and support. These are the topics we'll cover in our next chapter.

## CHAPTER 10

Evaluating, Deploying, and Supporting Edge AI Applications

This is the final theory chapter of this book, and we'll be covering the processes of evaluating, deploying, and supporting edge AI applications. These three things are intimately connected—and in an iterative project they happen in parallel throughout the course of the development workflow.

Evaluating Edge AI Systems

Evaluation is the key to a successful project. In fact, without evaluation you have no real way of knowing whether your project is successful or not. While it happens to be featured at the end of this book, it's something that occurs all the way through the development process. It may even start before development, when you're quantifying the performance of an existing process you aim to improve with edge AI.

Remember that throughout the process, evaluation needs to be conducted with participation from stakeholders and end users. It's very possible that different stakeholders may have conflicting criteria for evaluation, depending on their individual perspectives. Figuring out how to resolve these conflicts is an important part of evaluation.

Here are some of the stages where evaluation needs to occur:

Examining an existing solution
> Much of the time, we're developing edge AI systems to replace legacy systems that we think could be better. This makes it very important to understand the actual performance of the existing system at the beginning of the process. The goal of our development process will be to beat it, and we can't beat something that we haven't measured.

Even if there's no existing solution, it's a great idea to come up with a simple baseline that we can aim to outperform (as we saw in "Developing a baseline algorithm" on page 303). This brings direction and perspective to our work—and sometimes, the simple baseline ends up being the best choice.

Exploring potential algorithms

Evaluation is vital during the exploration stages of a project, while we're getting to know the dataset and experimenting with different types of algorithms. It's how we start to home in on the approaches that look promising. During this stage, quick and convenient evaluation is helpful in being able to move fast.

During iterative development

The iterative development process is driven by evaluation: we create a solution, evaluate it, and use the results of evaluation to course-correct so that our next iteration is better. There are many different ways to evaluate a system under development, and we'll meet some of them in "Ways to Evaluate a System" on page 319.

Before and after optimization

When we're deploying to edge devices, we often have to apply lossy optimization techniques that allow us to fit algorithms within our memory or latency constraints (see "Compression and optimization" on page 117). It's important to evaluate performance before and after optimization to determine how much loss has occurred. You should always evaluate, even if you are applying an optimization technique that you think is not lossy—just in case a bug in the process causes some kind of degradation.

On real hardware

There are many reasons why your application might perform differently once deployed to real hardware. For example, there may be some difference between the production hardware's sensors and those that the original dataset was collected from. Alternately, there could be some difference in the way your program runs when built for real hardware versus on your development machine. It's important to evaluate before and after deployment so you can understand if there's any impact.

During limited deployment

It's always a great idea to do a staged deployment, where you roll out your system incrementally so you can catch any issues before you scale up. This is another key moment for evaluation, since you'll need some way to measure whether your system is performing as expected.

Ongoing postdeployment

Performance should be monitored continually after you have deployed, which naturally requires evaluation. There'll be more detail on this stage in "Postdeployment Monitoring" on page 343.

Evaluation and Responsible Design

Ethical AI depends heavily on evaluation. For example, to detect bias, it's vital to understand how your system is performing on different types of input. By evaluating at every stage, you're giving your team visibility into the places where ethical concerns might creep in.

Ways to Evaluate a System

There are many ways to evaluate an edge AI system, and different mechanisms will be important during different stages of the development process. They all require varying amounts of time and investment—which may make them appropriate for either short, tight feedback loops or longer, broader ones.

Following are some of the key approaches.

Evaluating individual components

A system is made up of many smaller components, and there are different ways to evaluate each. For example, your algorithmic pipeline may include the following:

- Windowing
- Downsampling
- Digital signal processing
- Machine learning
- Postprocessing
- Rule-based algorithms

Each of these moving parts will have its own tools for evaluation, and experts in the relevant fields will understand how to use them. This type of evaluation is essential when building a pipeline of steps that work together to deliver a result. If you set up mechanisms for evaluating the individual components of your system, you will more easily be able to identify the cause of any systemic issues. It will also help you iterate individually on specific components in isolation, since they may be owned by different teams.

Evaluating integrated systems

It's not enough to know that all the individual pieces of a system work together: you also need to understand that they function correctly as a whole. Otherwise, emergent systemic problems may prevent your application from performing well.

For example, you may have a machine learning model and postprocessing algorithm that seem to function well when tested individually. However, on linking them together you may find that they do not perform adequately.

A combination of component-level tests and systemic tests is required to really understand the performance of a system. Testing an integrated system will tell you whether a system is underperforming, but it won't provide much explanation on its own.

Simulated real-world testing

In many cases, the datasets available for training are not realistic: they might represent an ideal set of conditions, having been collected in a lab or carefully cleaned up in order to present the best possible dataset for training. Evaluation on a dataset such as this may provide misleading results. To really understand performance, it's necessary to test things out in the real world.

It would be great if we could test all of our work in production at the click of a button, but the realities of embedded development make this impossible. Compared to software engineering on the web, it's a lot more time consuming, expensive, and risky to push an embedded application live. This means that in this respect, embedded development has a less effective feedback loop between development and real-world performance.

One solution to this problem is to simulate real-world conditions as closely as possible during development, so that changes to an algorithm or an application can be tested in close to real time. This might involve collecting a dataset that reflects the type of real-world conditions you expect to see, then running it through a fully integrated build of your application.

For example, imagine you are building a fitness tracking wearable. It could be tested using streams of data that have been captured from genuine users wearing dummy devices containing only sensors. The data would need to be labeled by an expert so that it can be used for evaluation.

If real-world data is too difficult to obtain, it's also possible to use synthetic data. Realistic streams of data can be constructed by layering samples from conventional training datasets on top of samples of background noise, applying augmentation to increase the variance of the data. This is an option available in Edge Impulse's performance calibration feature, described in "Performance Calibration" on page 337.

A prominent example of the use of simulated real-world testing is in Amazon's Alexa certification process (*https://oreil.ly/Pvi5L*). Hardware products that integrate Alexa must meet minimum standards for the performance of their keyword-spotting systems. Performance is evaluated by playing a number of clips of audio from a speaker that is a certain distance from the device, under varying conditions. To pass, the device has to successfully identify when a clip contains a keyword—and avoid activating when it does not.

Real-world testing

It's best to start testing your system in the real world as early as possible: as soon as you have hardware, if not before.[1] There are two main types of real-world testing:

- Quality assurance testing, where you deliberately put a product through its paces to try to identify any problems
- Usability testing, where you allow users to interact naturally with a product in order to understand how well it works

Real-world testing is slower and more expensive than some types of evaluation, but it's essential to product development. It's also a lot cheaper than bringing your product to market and then realizing it doesn't work.

Quality assurance testing. Quality assurance (QA) is a systematic way of exploring a product and understanding whether it meets the appropriate level of quality—typically based on the product's design goals (see "Setting Design Goals" on page 274). During development, QA engineers design and implement strategies for exercising the features of a product and trying to understand its effectiveness and overall fit for purpose.

QA is a major field with its own domain experts, and it's absolutely critical to the process of building a good product. It's too big an area to explore within the confines of this book, but here are some of the ways that QA professionals can be important in edge AI projects:

- Getting hands-on with a prototype and trying to find problems
- Testing individual components during development (for example, a keyword-spotting algorithm)
- Designing systems and procedures for testing products throughout the workflow
- Certifying whether a product meets its design goals

---

1 If you can get away with deploying to a development board before your official hardware is ready, you should go with it.

The QA process begins as soon as you have design goals, since the person in a QA role will have to come up with a system for testing them. Ideally, QA will happen throughout the development process as part of the procedure of evaluating each iteration's work.

Usability testing.   While QA testing is focused on deliberately trying to find problems, usability testing is about observing natural usage of your product and using your observations to guide improvements.

Usability testing happens with real users. They could be members of the public, potential customers, or people from inside your own team or organization. The key is that they are interacting with your product in a realistic way.

Some usability testing is done in studies, where people are brought in to a controlled environment and encouraged to interact with the product in certain ways. Other types of testing are more natural: for example, beta testing involves providing users with early versions of a product that they can take away, use for a while, and provide feedback on.

The best plan will vary depending on your situation, but typically usability studies are done earlier in the development process, where focused input is required to help steer the project, and beta testing is done later, when the product is nearing completion and a more general overview is needed.

An interesting variety of usability testing is known as *dogfooding* (from the concept of "eating your own dogfood" (*https://oreil.ly/tVnyZ*)). This is when members of an organization use their own prerelease hardware in order to understand its usability and generate feedback.

Usability testing is also an area with its own domain experts. It's the most expensive type of testing, but it's also the most valuable: you get to see how your system is performing in something close to reality.

Monitoring a deployed system

It's critical to understand the performance of a system once it's been deployed. As we'll see in "Postdeployment Monitoring" on page 343, this can be extremely challenging.

Useful Metrics

Any kind of quantitative evaluation will result in metrics: key numbers that represent some aspect of the performance of a product or component. Collecting the right metrics is extremely important: as the saying goes, "you are what you measure," and if you choose the wrong values to focus on, your iterative process will go in the wrong direction.

Fortunately there are lots of standard metrics that are relevant to edge AI systems; they'll likely be familiar to anyone who works in a connected field. Following are some of the most important ones.

Algorithmic performance

These metrics are useful in understanding the performance of AI algorithms. They typically vary depending on the algorithm type (as described in "Algorithm Types by Functionality" on page 96).

Loss. Loss is a way of measuring the correctness of a model's predictions. The higher the loss score, the more inaccurate the predictions are. The exact meaning of a loss metric is determined by a *loss function*. Standard loss functions exist for different types of problems, or you can come up with your own. Loss is calculated and used in the training process for some types of machine learning models, such as deep learning.

Loss can be computed for a single prediction, but it is common to calculate the mean loss for a whole dataset. For example, you might compute the mean loss over your validation dataset.

Loss doesn't have units, so it only means anything relative to itself. This makes it a good measure of how a model's performance changes over time during training, but not a particularly helpful metric if you're trying to understand how the model will work in the real world.

Where loss functions are used in the process of optimizing machine learning models, it's important that an improvement to the optimization loss corresponds to an improvement in other metrics. The loss function should be selected based on the problem you are trying to solve (most common problems have standard loss functions), and your metrics should be selected based on the same problem. Without agreement between the two, you'll end up with a model that does not solve the right problem.

Accuracy. Classification is a common task, and there are a few different metrics used to express how well a classifier is performing. Accuracy is the simplest and best known of these: it's just the percentage of classifications that were correct across a given dataset.

Accuracy is a reasonable way to understand the performance of a model at a glance, but as a single value it obscures a lot of context. For example, a single accuracy number can't tell us anything about how the individual classes in a dataset performed. A 90% accuracy metric on a balanced dataset might sound impressive, but on an unbalanced dataset (perhaps consisting 90% of one class and 10% of another) it could mean the model is terrible.

Because of this limitation, it's best to use accuracy in conjunction with other metrics that capture more nuance—or at least calculate it for each class individually.

Confusion matrix. A confusion matrix is a powerful tool for understanding how a model is performing. It's a simple table that shows the ways that individual samples were classified. An example is shown in Figure 10-1, a screenshot from Edge Impulse.

	NO	NOISE	YES
NO	96.3%	0%	3.7%
NOISE	2.7%	95.9%	1.4%
YES	4.7%	0.9%	94.4%

Figure 10-1. A confusion matrix showing results for a keyword-spotting model

In Figure 10-1, the row headers NO, NOISE, and YES represent three classes of samples in a dataset. They correspond with the similarly named column headers, which represent three classes identified by a classifier. The percentage in each cell indicates the proportion of samples from the dataset class (indicated by the row header) that were identified by the classifier as fitting into a particular class (indicated by the column header).

For example, we can see that 96.3% of the instances of NO were correctly classified as NO, while 3.7% of them were incorrectly classified as YES. This breakdown allows us to understand how our classifier is performing between classes. This is much more interesting than a single accuracy metric, since it helps us begin to understand exactly where our model is struggling.

Precision and recall. From the point of view of a single class in the confusion matrix, there are two different types of mistakes a classifier can make. Both of them are cases of mistaken identity.

In the first case, a genuine member of the class is misidentified as belonging to a different one. For example, a smart camera for bird spotting might mistake a bird for leaf, missing the bird entirely.

In the second case, a member of a *different* class is misidentified as belonging to the one we care about. For example, we might mistake a leaf for a bird.

Precision and recall provide ways to describe how often these mistakes occur. Precision tells us how frequently our model mistakes a boring old leaf for a lovely bird, while recall describes how often our model misses a bird it should have spotted:

$$\text{Precision} = \frac{\text{number of birds we got right}}{\text{number of inputs we thought were birds}}$$

$$\text{Recall} = \frac{\text{number of birds we got right}}{\text{actual number of birds in the dataset}}$$

Each of a dataset's classes will have its own precision and recall, but they can also be expressed as a mean over all of the classes. It's a great metric because it lets us characterize the types of mistakes made by a model.[2]

Precision and recall are both expressed as numbers between 0 and 1, with 1 being perfect and 0 being completely wrong. There's typically a trade-off between them: you can reduce one by increasing the other. This makes them important metrics for tuning.

Confidence Thresholds

Whether precision or recall is more important depends on your application. For example, if you're designing a voice-activated smart speaker, it would be pretty annoying to have it keep activating for random sounds. In that case, it's better to aim for a high *precision*—which may come at the cost of a lower recall.

Alternatively, if you're designing a system for detecting health issues, it may be better to have high *recall*, so you are unlikely to miss any health problems that could put somebody's life at risk. The trade-off might be a lower precision, meaning you are more likely to have a false alarm.

A common way to trade off between precision and recall is by adjusting the *confidence threshold* of your application. When it makes a prediction, a classifier usually outputs a *probability distribution*: a list of numbers, one for each class. These numbers sum to 1, and they represent the probability of the input belonging to each class.

For example, a model for detecting health issues may have an output that looks like this:

```
Healthy:    0.35
Sick:       0.65
```

If we wanted, we could say that whichever class has the highest score is the one we assume is true. For example, in the preceding case we would consider the patient to be sick because the probability of them being sick is higher than the probability of them being healthy.

---

2 Google's Machine Learning Crash Course has a great explanation of precision and recall (*https://oreil.ly/LLXBl*).

Since there are two classes, by taking whichever is the highest we are effectively assigning a confidence threshold of 0.5. If a class has a score of over 0.5, we are confident that it represents the truth.

However, we may not consider 0.5 a high enough probability to consider someone sick. If it's a serious, scary illness we may need to be more confident in our prediction than slightly better than a coin toss. For example, we might choose 0.75 as our confidence threshold. In that case, we would not consider the preceding result positive for either class. Instead, it represents an ambiguous outcome.

As we change the confidence threshold, the precision and recall will change. A lower confidence threshold tends to result in higher recall but lower precision, since for a given class we'll catch more of the examples—but at the cost of having more false alarms. A higher confidence threshold may increase the precision but reduce the recall, since some examples might not meet the threshold.

Positive and negative rates. Another name for recall is the *true positive rate*, or TPR. It's the rate at which true positives—meaning correct positive identifications—are expected to occur. There are three other acronyms that cover the other possibilities of errors within a classifier's confusion matrix. *False positive rate* (FPR) represents how often negative examples (items outside of our class of concern) were falsely identified as being things we care about.

$$\text{True positive rate} = \frac{\text{true positives}}{\text{total positives in dataset}}$$

$$\text{False positive rate} = \frac{\text{false positives}}{\text{total negatives in dataset}}$$

Inversely, *true negative rate* (TNR) describes how often those negative examples were correctly ignored. Finally, *false negative rate* (FNR) describes how often a sample belonging to the class we care about is incorrectly ignored.[3]

$$\text{True negative rate} = \frac{\text{true negatives}}{\text{total negatives in dataset}}$$

$$\text{False negative rate} = \frac{\text{false negatives}}{\text{total positives in dataset}}$$

---

3 The word *positive* is often replaced with *acceptance*, and the word *negative* with *rejection*.

These rates are all different ways of expressing how well your system is able to distinguish between classes. They can be traded off to determine performance in the same way we described in "Confidence Thresholds" on page 325.

F1 score and MCC. It's sometimes useful to have a single statistic to describe the performance of a classifier: for example, when comparing similar models. One such statistic is the *F1 score*, a single number that is derived from the precision and recall scores (by taking their harmonic mean):

$$F_1 = 2\frac{\text{precision} \cdot \text{recall}}{\text{precision} + \text{recall}}$$

While convenient, the F1 score has some limitations. It doesn't include any information about true negatives—meaning it isn't suitable for use with unbalanced classes, since if there are different numbers of items in each class the F1 scores between classes will be incomparable.

For this reason, a different metric known as *Matthews correlation coefficient* (MCC) (*https://oreil.ly/dtn0y*) can be a better choice. It includes all of the squares in the confusion matrix, so it's a better overall indicator of model quality.

Although the MCC is better, it's still limited by nature. Rolling an entire confusion matrix into a single number removes our ability to consider each cell individually. As we saw in "Confidence Thresholds" on page 325, every application has a slightly different ideal balance between precision and recall. The F1 and MCC scores prevent us from considering them individually—so if we're comparing multiple models we will be blind to some of the differences between them.

ROC and AUC.   As we've learned, it's possible to change the performance of a classifier by varying the confidence threshold. The impact of doing this can be visualized using a chart known as the *receiver operating characteristic curve*, or *ROC curve*, as shown in Figure 10-2.

Since the confidence threshold can be used to trade off between the TPR and FPR, the ROC curve plots one of them on either axis. To compute the curve, the TPR and FPR are calculated for a range of different confidence thresholds.

This chart is extremely useful since it describes all of our options for tuning the classifier. We can pick a point on the curve that represents the trade-off we desire based on the needs of our application. We'd then use the corresponding confidence threshold to gate the output of our model.

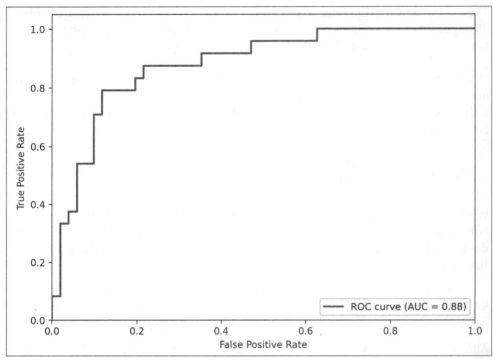

Figure 10-2. An ROC curve plotted using Matplotlib

We can also use the ROC curve to create a single metric that describes the performance of our model based on the probability that it gets a particular answer right. It's obtained by calculating the *area under the curve* (AUC, visible in Figure 10-2), and it has a value from 0 to 1. A model with an AUC of 1 gets every single prediction right, while a model with an AUC of 0.5 has a 50/50 chance of predicting the right class.[4]

The ROC is useful, but it's still a single statistic representing a complex set of behaviors. As such, it still isn't helpful if we're trying to understand how our model will perform in different circumstances. In that case, a combination of ROC curve and confusion matrix will give us a lot of helpful insight.

Error metrics. Classifiers are only one type of model. Another major category, regression models, have their own set of common metrics. Since a regression model is designed to predict a numeric value, the best way to understand its performance is with a metric that compares the difference between its output value and the value that a data sample is labeled with.

---

4 An AUC of 0 means the model is—weirdly—getting every single prediction wrong, which for a binary classifier means you could just flip the predictions to get perfect performance. If this happens, it's usually a sign that you have gotten your labels mixed up somewhere!

Here are some of the top error metrics used for regression models:

Mean absolute error (MAE)
This simple metric consists of the mean of the errors, where error is defined as the difference between a predicted and actual value. It's calculated for a dataset as follows:

$$\text{MAE} = \frac{\text{sum(error)}}{\text{number of samples}}$$

For example, imagine we've trained a regression model to predict the weights of apples from photographs. Let's assume the apples are weighed in grams. After testing the model, we calculate an MAE of 10. This means that, on average, the predicted weight is off the actual weight by 10 grams.

This simplicity makes the MAE very useful. However, there are some alternatives that can help shed light on different types of error.

Mean squared error (MSE)
The MSE is very similar to the MAE—except that the errors are squared before summation:

$$\text{MSE} = \frac{\text{sum(squared errors)}}{\text{number of samples}}$$

Since we square the errors, the MSE will always either be positive or zero—and large errors will make a bigger difference to its value. This can be helpful, since large errors are often worse than small ones but may be deceptively flattened out by the simple calculation of MAE.

Root mean squared error (RMSE)
The downside of MSE is that since it's based on squared values, it is harder to interpret than the MAE, which is provided in the original units. By calculating the square root of the MSE, known as the RMSE, we can express it in the same terms as the labels:

$$\text{RMSE} = \sqrt{\frac{\text{sum(squared errors)}}{\text{number of samples}}}$$

The RMSE has the same benefits as the MSE, but it's easier to interpret. The downside is that it's slightly more complicated to think about.

As with classification metrics, expressing the performance of a model as a single value can be risky. Your dataset may contain different subgroups that experience different performance. We'll cover some strategies for dealing with this issue in "Techniques for Evaluation" on page 334.

Mean average precision. *Mean average precision*, or mAP, is a fairly complex metric that is used to express the performance of an object-detection model. Object-detection models attempt to draw bounding boxes around any objects in the image; the mAP looks at how well the predicted bounding boxes overlap with the real boxes—either within a given image or across a dataset. It combines this with something like a confidence interval in order to come up with a score.[5]

The major downside of mAP is that while it's based on the area of the boxes, it doesn't take into account the number of boxes. This means a model can score well on mAP even if it predicts multiple boxes where a single box should be. That said, it's become the standard way of rating object detection models.

> The `sklearn.metrics` library (*https://oreil.ly/zq0CD*) contains implementations for most of the above metrics—along with many more. It's worth exploring the literature around metrics to determine the ideal ones to use for your task.

Computational and hardware performance

Edge AI almost always involves managing the balance between algorithmic and computational performance. While algorithmic performance metrics tell us how well an algorithm is doing its job, computational and hardware performance metrics tell us how quickly the algorithm is running, and what resources are being consumed in the process.

Informed by these metrics, we can make an educated trade-off between algorithmic complexity and computational resources. For example, the latency required for a particular application on given hardware may inform the size of the deep learning model that can be used.

The following metrics help us understand the size of the computational task and the burden that it places on our hardware.

Memory. Memory use includes both RAM and ROM, which have fairly different properties. ROM is where your algorithms are stored long term, including the parameters of any machine learning models. RAM is the working memory of your program while it is running. There are hard limits on RAM and ROM (or disk space) for any edge device, so it's important that your algorithms fit what is available.

---

5 There's a good explanation of mAP in the article "mAP (mean Average Precision) Might Confuse You!" (*https://oreil.ly/aJ3Dy*) by Shivy Yohanandan.

An algorithm can't run in isolation; it has to exist inside some kind of program. The rest of the program also takes up memory—so when you're thinking about RAM and ROM usage, you'll need to factor the rest of your application in, too. In most cases, you'll end up with a RAM and ROM budget that you need your algorithm to stick to in order to fit within the rest of your application.

For example, imagine you're adding edge AI to a brownfield system. You can analyze the memory being used by the existing application and decide what is left over for your new algorithms. Similarly, in a greenfield system you will have to decide how much of your ROM and RAM is budgeted for algorithms versus the other parts of your application.

Measuring the RAM and ROM usage of an application is nontrivial. ROM seems relatively easy: in theory, an embedded engineer can compile a simple program that contains your algorithms and then look at the output to determine how large it is. In practice, however, there may be some overlap between the dependencies required for your application and for your algorithms. This means that your algorithms could end up making less impact on your firmware's ROM usage than it might seem.

This means that the most reliable way of estimating your algorithms' ROM usage is to build your entire application both with and without them. The difference tells you how much ROM is being used.

Deep learning models tend to be big, so you may find yourself having to reduce the size of your model in order to fit within a ROM budget. It's always a good idea to try quantizing your model before spending a lot of time on optimizing the rest of your application—the resulting reduction in accuracy is usually very minor.

Measuring RAM usage is a bit more challenging. First, you typically have to run the algorithm in order to determine it. Second, if your program uses too much RAM it may not actually be able to run. Third, determining RAM usage on a running device will require some kind of test program or debugger.

A good approach to measuring RAM usage for a specific algorithm is to use a test program. The program should first fill the entire memory with a specific marker value. You can then run your algorithm. After running it, you should iterate through the device's memory and check how much of it is still filled with the marker value. This "high watermark" will give you an estimate of memory usage—although it won't tell you the worst-case memory usage, which may be higher.[6]

---

6 There are actually three uses of RAM: data (or global), stack, and heap. Data RAM usage is set at compile time, while stack and heap usage can change while a program runs. Some embedded programs intentionally only use data, to avoid any surprises. Stack and heap both require separate high watermark tests.

You can potentially use this technique with a simulator to estimate RAM use without having to deploy to an actual device. This can be convenient during development, and is the approach used within some end-to-end platforms (such as Edge Impulse).

Measuring RAM and ROM usage is much easier on devices with an operating system, since you can directly query the operating system for metrics.

Floating-point operations (FLOPs). A floating-point operation is a single computation involving two floating-point numbers, and FLOPS—or *floating-point operations per second*—is used as a measure of computing power.

The total number of FLOPs is sometimes used to describe the amount of work required to compute one inference of a deep learning model. This makes sense for server-side models, since computation is typically done in floating-point arithmetic.

Given the FLOPs of a model and the FLOPS of a processor (and looking past the confusing acronyms) it should, in theory, be possible to estimate the latency of a model. However, many edge models are quantized and therefore use integer math, making the FLOPs of the original model less relevant. In addition, the makers of embedded processors do not typically report FLOPS (or IOPS, the integer equivalent). Lastly, calculating FLOPs for a model is not always straightforward.

In combination, all of this makes FLOPs of limited use for determining edge AI performance. That said, it's worth mentioning in case you happen to encounter it.

Latency. In the context of edge AI, latency is the amount of time that it takes to run all of the parts of an algorithm, end to end. For example, it might take 100 milliseconds to capture a window of audio, downsample it, run it through a DSP algorithm, feed the result into a deep learning model, execute the model, and process the output. Latency is typically specified in milliseconds or as frames per second, the latter mostly for vision applications.

Latency depends on the algorithms used, the optimizations available, and the hardware itself. Faster hardware and better optimizations (for example, those provided in the libraries described in "Math and DSP libraries" on page 154) lead to lower latency—and generally, the smaller and simpler a machine learning model is, the lower latency it has.

Some applications require low latency. For example, if an application needs to respond in real time to user input, then it needs to operate with low latency. In other cases, latency is not as important: perhaps the application's response can be asynchronous and does not have to happen quickly.

In some situations, lower latency means better algorithmic performance. For instance, a keyword-spotting model running many times per second has more opportunity to detect a keyword than one running once per second.

Measuring latency usually requires access to a device, unless cycle-accurate simulation is available (see "Emulators and simulators" on page 160). However, there are some methods for estimating the performance of deep learning models based on benchmarking similar workloads on hardware.[7]

Duty cycle. Embedded applications are often required to limit energy usage in order to preserve battery life. They do so by performing computation periodically, as they receive new data, and then going into a low-power sleep mode while they wait for the next data to arrive.

The processor's wake/sleep pattern is known as its duty cycle. For example, a processor may wake up every 200 milliseconds to read some sensor data, taking 10 milliseconds to do so. It might then spend 50 milliseconds processing the data using an edge AI algorithm before going back to sleep.

In this case, the processor wakes up for 60 milliseconds every 200 milliseconds. Out of every second, it would spend 350 milliseconds awake and processing data. This would give it a duty cycle, expressed as a percentage, of 35%.

Duty cycle is important for determining the power consumption of an embedded system, since it determines how much energy the processor consumes.

Energy. Battery life is a common concern in embedded applications, so determining the energy consumption of a device is very important. It is measured in terms of current, and typically expressed in milliamperes (abbreviated mA, and also known as milliamps).

Each component in an embedded system has a different current draw, and it depends heavily on how it is being used. For example, a processor uses more or less current depending on which of its features are currently enabled, and a sensor may use more current while it is actively making measurements.

For this reason, it's important to measure energy consumption during typical usage. It may make sense to monitor a device for an extended period of time to determine its actual energy usage. This can be done with a special tool such as a current monitor or data logger.

Battery capacity is measured in milliamp hours (mAh), which indicates the number of hours the battery can sustain a 1 mA current. For example, a 2,000 mAh battery will power a 100 mA device for 20 hours.

---

7 This is used by Edge Impulse to provide latency estimates during model development.

For a processor, energy consumption is intimately connected with duty cycle, which is a function of latency. This means low latency algorithms save energy, so it's important to factor in energy usage when designing your algorithms and application.

Thermal. Electronic components produce heat as waste, and this can be relevant in some applications: processors can become hot during computation, and if there's nowhere for the heat to go they may have problems. In addition, some components have minimum operating temperatures.

Thermal energy is measured in degrees Celsius. Most components' datasheets will provide their operating ranges. Some processors, mostly SOCs, have built-in temperature sensors and can throttle their own performance if they start to get hot. MCUs don't typically have this functionality, so if you want to monitor their temperatures it is up to you to install a sensor.

The lower the duty cycle of a processor, the less waste thermal energy it will produce. This means that latency is a tool for limiting thermal emissions.

Techniques for Evaluation

Evaluation makes use of a toolbox of techniques, some of which we've seen before and others that are new. Here are the most important items:

Training, validation, and testing splits
> As we learned in "Splitting Your Data" on page 256, it's absolutely critical to divide your dataset into parts in order to prove that your model can perform on previously unseen data. The bulk of your evaluation should be done on your validation dataset.
>
> To preserve its value, you should only use your testing dataset when you think that you are done. If you test on your testing dataset and determine that your model doesn't work, you'll have to throw it out and start from scratch: otherwise, you'll risk overfitting your model by adjusting it until it works great on your testing dataset but doesn't work well on real data.
>
> Of course, you can potentially capture more data at any point during the development process. You should try to do this wherever possible, continually augmenting your entire dataset with new samples to improve your ability to train and evaluate models.

Cross-validation
> One of the downsides of splitting data for evaluation is that the model will only be as good as whatever data was in its training dataset. Cross-validation, which we previously encountered in "Cross-Validation" on page 259, attempts to work around this, allowing a practitioner to train multiple models on the same dataset and compare their performance.

To begin, a training dataset is split into training and validation parts. A model is trained using the training part and tested on the validation part. The metrics are logged, and then the data is recombined and split again at random. A second model is trained on the new training split, then evaluated on the new validation split. This process is continued any number of times—potentially dozens.

The result of the process is a series of models, each trained and validated on different subsets of the data. The metrics for the models can be analyzed to understand whether the model's quality is heavily dependent on the data's composition. The hope is that each of the models has similar performance. If so, the best-performing model can be selected and scrutinized in a final test against the testing dataset.

The most common type of cross-validation is known as k-fold cross-validation. Information on the process is provided in the scikit-learn documentation (*https://oreil.ly/5uy5t*).

Analyzing subgroups

The metrics we learned about in "Algorithmic performance" on page 323 can be calculated for an entire dataset, or a split—or they can be calculated for any arbitrary subgroup of your data. This can be an extremely powerful tool, especially useful for understanding the fairness of your algorithms.

Imagine you are building a computer vision application to identify different classes of vehicles: cars, trucks, and SUVs. You can calculate algorithmic performance metrics for each class, which will tell you how good the algorithm is at identifying each type of vehicle.

However, with a little extra information you can go beyond this. For example, if your dataset includes metadata about the make of a vehicle in each photograph, you can calculate the metrics for each of those subgroups. You can then conduct an analysis to make sure that your model performs equally well for each subgroup: for example, you might find that your model underperforms on a specific make of car, in which case you could try to collect more photographs of it for your training dataset.

The model itself doesn't care about the make of the vehicle, only the high-level type (car, truck, or SUV). Regardless, you can still use information about the make in order to better evaluate your system. You can imagine how useful this type of technique is when investigating ML fairness using almost any dataset.

Metrics and distribution

It's common for subgroups in datasets to be unevenly distributed. For example, imagine you are training a classifier to distinguish between classes A, B, and C. Your dataset may have 60% of samples in class A, 20% in class B, and 20% in class C.

The metrics you use for evaluation should be sensitive to problems in all of these classes. For example, the accuracy metric might be 60% across all classes. However, this single number won't tell you if the model is getting all of class A correct, but none of B or C.

One way to understand whether your metrics are adequate is by "evaluating" a fake model that returns deliberately bad results that fit the underlying distribution of the data. For example, you could create a random classifier that classifies a random 60% of examples as A, 20% as B, and 20% as C. By evaluating the output of this random classifier, you can understand how well your chosen metrics communicate the model's lack of performance.

Using multiple metrics

Many different metrics can be measured for a single project. For example, you may determine numbers that represent accuracy on a testing dataset, computational latency, and memory usage. Building an effective solution often means balancing constraints between multiple metrics. For example, we might choose to reduce latency by using a simpler model—but this could result in a drop in accuracy.

These individual metrics may all be important, but they don't always matter *equally*. For example, for a project that needs to work at high speed, you may place a higher priority on latency than accuracy. In a dataset with multiple subsets, you may care about performance on one subset more than another.

The overall weighting of different metrics—how much you care about them individually—is something you'll need to determine along with your stakeholders.

Synthetic testing data

Data is often hard to come by, especially if you're looking to test your system on rare and unusual inputs. For example, an anomaly detection system may be designed to catch catastrophic failures that have never actually been recorded in the real world.

One way to get around this problem is to generate synthetic data. Synthetic data is any kind of data that is created artificially. This could mean taking a real dataset and distorting its samples to create new ones, or it may mean generating entirely new inputs using some kind of algorithmic process. For instance, we could generate a set of inputs designed to simulate catastrophic failures in order to test our anomaly detection system.

Synthetic data can be a helpful concept. It potentially gives you access to an unlimited amount of labeled data that can be used for testing—or even for training models. However, not all data can be faked, and it's risky to depend entirely on synthetic data, especially for evaluation.

Performance Calibration

Most algorithms that operate on streaming data involve a postprocessing stage, where the raw result of running an AI algorithm over the data stream is filtered, cleaned up, and used to make decisions. For example, in a keyword-spotting application the raw output of an audio classification model is a stream of class probabilities, typically one set of probabilities every few milliseconds.

To identify specific utterances of a keyword, this stream needs to be filtered (to remove any brief, spurious misclassifications), thresholded (to identify when there is a strong positive signal), and debounced (so that a single utterance is not picked up multiple times). The postprocessing algorithm used to do this has various parameters that affect how it works: for example, a specific threshold must be chosen that provides the preferred balance of false positives versus false negatives (see "Algorithmic performance" on page 323).

In theory, this threshold could be chosen after deployment, with usage data collected and the number of false positives and false negatives determined. However, the cost and complexity of deployment and observation, and the potential disruption involved with deploying a version of the application that does not work well, make this an unappealing option. Even if feasible, the feedback loop for trying out new thresholds would not be very tight: it would take a long time to test out each new value.

To create a tighter and more convenient feedback loop, it's possible to simulate real-world conditions in the lab. For example, you might record and label a long sample of real-world audio that features different words being spoken. The keyword-spotting algorithm would then be run across this sample, creating a raw output. You could then experiment freely with various postprocessing configurations in order to clean up the output, measuring it against the sample's labels to understand performance.

The resulting procedure is far easier to run than one involving a full real-world deployment, and it can be automated during model development as a way of testing out different approaches. Tightening the feedback loop creates a powerful tool for evaluating performance in order to guide algorithm development. Edge Impulse Studio, an end-to-end platform for developing edge AI applications, provides an implementation of automated performance calibration.

Evaluation and Responsible AI

Proper evaluation is one of our core tools for developing AI applications responsibly. If you evaluate your applications well, you'll understand how they are likely to perform in the field—and across different subpopulations represented in your dataset. The better your evaluation, the less risk that you'll run into an issue in production.

Responsible design involves evaluating the problem-solution fit within its environmental context. Any evaluation is only as good as your understanding of the problem and the operating environment. This is what makes it so important to involve domain experts and stakeholders in the evaluation process.

Evaluation is also at the core of the iterative development workflow. This pretty much guarantees that if you don't do a good job of evaluation, you won't have a good product. You should make sure that you put a good deal of weight on evaluation, and it's worth having your stakeholders, domain experts, and advisory board give the process a lot of attention to make sure it will capture every detail possible.

You may have noticed that many evaluation techniques depend entirely on your dataset. This makes the construction of your dataset essential to ethical AI development (see "Data, Ethics, and Responsible AI" on page 206). Evaluation in the field is slow and costly, so datasets are a vital tool.

That said, there is no way to avoid the need for evaluation in a real-world environment, with real users. Quantifying the performance of your algorithms using test data is not enough. It's critical to understand the way your entire system works in context, and with the people who are going to be using it. You will need to find opportunities to weave this into the workflow as early as possible.

We've now covered the predeployment parts of evaluating a model. We'll look at tools for postdeployment evaluation in "Postdeployment Monitoring" on page 343.

Deploying Edge AI Applications

As we mentioned in "Deployment" on page 313, deployment is best considered an ongoing process rather than a single event at the end of a project. However, each time a new iteration of your system is put in contact with the real world there is the potential for major risk—along with valuable new learning. It's important to have a process set up to account for this.

For example, imagine you are deploying a new version of your sheep activity classification model. There's a chance it might produce incorrect predictions, which could have a negative impact on the agricultural operation if they are not quickly identified as such. It may also reveal new insights that can be applied to the next iteration of the design—but only if they are captured.

To make sure deployment goes smoothly, minimizes risk, and maximizes benefits, you should develop and document a deliberate process that you can follow each time. Ownership for these tasks is important; they should be tracked by members of your team, typically those who are responsible for product development and operations.

Next, we will look at some of the key tasks you might include.

Predeployment Tasks

These are tasks you should consider performing before a deployment happens. They should be guided by technical expertise, insight from stakeholders, and domain expertise from a subject matter expert:

Decide on the objectives

Each deployment should have clear, written objectives. For example, you might be deploying more devices in order to scale a system up, or you might be deploying the latest iteration of software to a set of hardware that is already in the field.

To better manage risk and improve your ability to measure performance, you should try to limit the number of objectives for a given deployment. Like any experiment, the more input variables you adjust, the more difficult it is to understand what caused changes in the output.

Identify key metrics

To understand the impact of a deployment, you'll need to keep track of metrics that describe what your system is doing. These should include performance metrics, if available, in addition to general numbers that will highlight any changes—such as the distribution of inputs and outputs.

You'll use these metrics to understand both the changes made by whatever you have deployed, and whether your objectives have been met.

Performance analysis

Before deploying a new iteration of your software or hardware, you need to have a good understanding of how it is likely to perform—and whether this performance is acceptable for a system that will be running in production. There are various methods of estimating performance in the lab (one such method is discussed in "Performance Calibration" on page 337)—you should make use of them wherever possible before deploying to the field.

If an iteration doesn't perform well in the lab, it's definitely not likely to perform well in the field. What's more, measuring performance can be *much* harder in a real-world context, since labeled data is rare, so you should take advantage of every mechanism for predeployment testing.

Document possible risks

Each time you take a new iteration into production, you're introducing some risk. Before you deploy, it's important to try to identify any possible risks, understand their impact, and think about how you might mitigate or recover from them.

If things go badly enough, you may need to halt the deployment or shut down the project to avoid causing harm. Based on the risks, you should put together a set of termination criteria (see "Termination Criteria" on page 354) that will help you know when to make the call.

Determine recovery plan

If something bad does happen as a result of deployment, you'll need a plan for recovering from it. This might mean rolling back to an earlier version of the system, or it could mean repairing some harm that has been caused to the processes you are interacting with.

Being prepared ahead of time will allow you to take more calculated risks without fear of disaster. You should have a plan for dealing with the consequences of all of the possible risks you have identified.

This may involve making use of the strategies for graceful degradation that you have designed into your application (see "Graceful Degradation" on page 291).

Deployment design

Based on your objectives, you'll need to design a strategy for deploying your work. For example, you may have to decide what version of your software and hardware to deploy, how many devices to deploy to, and to which specific places to deploy. You'll also need to figure out any automation that is necessary to reduce the time taken for deployment and to ensure consistency across devices. IoT device management platforms may help here.

For example, if you have devices located in multiple factories around the world, you might decide to deploy your latest software to a single factory for testing in order to isolate any risk. Alternatively, you could deploy to a few devices in each factory in order to get a cross-section view of how it performs across a diverse set of contexts. The best strategy depends on your particular situation, and figuring it out will require business and domain expertise.

If planning a widespread deployment, it's always a good idea to perform a staged rollout: start with a small subset of devices, see how it goes, and then deploy the remainder in waves. This will keep risk to a minimum and allow you to more easily recover if something goes wrong.

Review alignment with values

Any software or hardware that you ship must go through a detailed review for potential ethical issues. It's important to analyze any changes that have been made since the last deployment, in case they introduce novel concerns. In addition, your deployment plan itself should be subject to ethical analysis that incorporates domain expertise.

For example, if planning a staged rollout, it is worth considering whether the rollout is being done over a representative population of users. You may miss issues affecting some groups of users if they are not represented in the initial stages of the rollout.

Communication plan

It's critical to communicate any changes to a production system before, during, and after the deployment. By creating a plan for communication, you can ensure that this happens effectively. Your goal should be to make sure that anyone who might be affected by the deployment, including by any potential unintended issues captured in your risk documentation, is aware of the planned action, its risks, and any role they may have to play. This includes stakeholders and members of your development team.

Communication should go in both directions, since there may be factors you are unaware of that might affect your deployment plan. For example, you may find out about scheduled activities that might overlap with your planned deployment and influence the metrics you are trying to measure.

Go/no-go decision

Once all of the appropriate documentation has been assembled, the final step is to review it and make a go/no-go decision. You may determine that the level of risk is too high, or that some confounding factor means that the deployment should be delayed. Otherwise, you may make the call to go ahead.

It's important that the go/no-go decision involves input from stakeholders, domain experts, and your technical team, since all of them have insight into potential issues that are important not to overlook.

Mid-Deployment Tasks

These are tasks you should consider while the deployment happens, in addition to the mechanics of the deployment itself:

Two-way communication

You should communicate clearly with anyone who might be affected by the deployment, according to the plan created in your predeployment tasks. This includes listening out for any potential issues that might happen during the deployment and be noticed by people working adjacent to it.

Staged rollout

To keep risk to a minimum, deployment should be conducted in stages rather than all at once. Coordinating this staged rollout is a major task. The most important aspects are keeping track of what has been deployed where, and monitoring how each stage might be impacting the metrics you are tracking.

In some cases, you may already have devices in the field that can't be updated. For example, they might not be capable of firmware updates. If this is the case, you need to be very careful about keeping track of which devices have which version of the firmware and your algorithms.

Monitor metrics

You'll need to keep track of all your key metrics during deployment—and be prepared to halt or roll back the process if things are not going well. Based on your predeployment work, you should have an understanding of your expectations regarding how the metrics you are monitoring will change. If you observe something different, it's a good idea to pause the deployment and investigate what is happening. If it looks like something harmful has occurred, you should roll back to an earlier state and fix the issue.

 One of the core goals of a responsible AI workflow is to prevent any harm from being caused. One of your jobs is to anticipate the potential for harm in advance and create a design that prevents it from happening. While unexpected things may happen, an unanticipated instance of harm means that your ethical review process is broken.

Postdeployment Tasks

The work doesn't end immediately after completing a staged deployment. Here are some tasks that you may need to attend to afterward:

Communicate status

In line with your communication plan, you should make sure that everyone affected is updated with the status of the deployment after it has happened. They should also have a clear, continuously open channel via which to alert you of any unexpected changes they observe in the system.

Postdeployment monitoring

It's wise to keep monitoring a system for some time after deployment has concluded. There may be effects that show up with some delay. Ideally, these types of risks will have been identified during your risk documentation process with the help of a domain expert. There'll be more information about monitoring in "Postdeployment Monitoring" on page 343.

Deployment report

After deployment, you should create a written summary report that includes your original plans, what actually happened, and any actions that were taken. This report will help guide future deployments, and can be shared with your stakeholders.

This may all sound like a lot of activity—but by being systematic about deployments and documenting everything you do, you are less likely to suffer from unexpected issues. Over multiple deployments of the same project, you will begin to develop an efficient system that requires minimal work and is described by a solid set of documentation. This system will be an important part of the ongoing support of the project.

Supporting Edge AI Applications

Deployment marks the beginning of the support phase of your project. All technology projects require long-term support. From an edge AI perspective, support involves keeping track of the performance of the system over time. If you see performance change, you can take action—ranging from updating your algorithms to terminating the deployment.

It's important from an ethical perspective that projects are well supported. If a project is abandoned, or left to limp along without proper monitoring, it may end up causing harm. Drift (as seen in "Drift and Shift" on page 233) can transform a convenient gadget into a dangerous trap. If you aren't able to commit to proper long-term support of your project, you shouldn't launch it in the first place.

Since edge AI hasn't existed for very long, support is the least developed component of the workflow in terms of tools and best practices. Some of the best practices from server-side AI can be applied to edge problems, but many of them can't. The remainder of this chapter will explore the challenges and opportunities in this space.

Postdeployment Monitoring

The first part of long-term support is monitoring. As soon as the first prototypes of your hardware are deployed, you'll need to begin collecting data on how they are operating. This can be a big challenge, since sometimes you won't even have connectivity with devices.

Here are some possible scenarios:

- There's good internet connectivity with deployed devices, so it's possible to gather statistics and data samples from the field. For example, a connected appliance may be able to use home WiFi to send back large amounts of data.
- There is enough limited connectivity to obtain basic statistics and metrics, but not enough to sample data. For example, a smart sensor deployed on a remote oil well may be able to send a few bytes of data via LoRaWAN, a technology for long range, low power wireless communication.

- There's no connectivity, but user feedback is available. For example, the user of a smart wildlife camera can provide feedback on whether it photographs the correct animals.

- There is no connectivity and user feedback is not available.

As you can see, connectivity and the ability to obtain feedback can vary a lot between applications. Ideally, there's at least some connectivity: you should think twice about deploying in a context where there is no way to gather feedback whatsoever, since it means you'll have literally no idea how your system is performing.

Assuming you have some mechanism for feedback, the goal should be to collect as much information as possible about what is going on.

Types of feedback from deployed systems

Server-side ML applications have it easy. Since all of their input data is available on the server, it can be logged and stored for later analysis. For example, imagine a server-side application that uses computer vision to identify specific products from photographs.

Since it is on a server, it has effectively unlimited storage to keep records of the photographs people upload. This means that the developers can go through and analyze the model's predictions, determine whether they are effective, and even label the data and use it for training.

Some applications have it even easier: there's a built-in measure of success. For example, if you build an algorithm to recommend products that users might like, you can measure its effectiveness by counting how often a recommended product was bought.

These tight feedback loops allow for iteration and rapid improvement on algorithm and application design. But things are not so easy on the edge. We typically lack direct insight into outcomes—although not always. We also have less ability to keep a record of the model's inputs. Due to this lack of immediate feedback, we have to come up with some clever ways to understand what is going on.

Data samples.   In an ideal situation, we can collect samples of raw inputs and send them back to a server for storage. This is only possible when the stars align: we need a perfect combination of energy availability, connectivity and bandwidth, and a use case where privacy is not important.

For example, imagine we've built a low-power sensor that is designed to monitor how packages are treated during shipment. To save energy and cost, it may lack the ability to store or transmit data during transit. This means it has no way to send samples of raw inputs back for analysis.

As another example, imagine we've built a home security camera that uses a deep learning model for person detection. If the product is marketed as using edge AI to preserve privacy, it won't be feasible for us to capture samples of its input.

However, there are certainly situations where enough energy and connectivity are available for sending samples of data. And even if resources are scarce, there are still ways you can make it work.

Some applications are able to create a feedback loop by sampling limited amounts of data. Rather than try to send every input to a server, they pick specific instances. This could be at random (e.g., every one in a thousand), it could be periodic (e.g., once per day), or it could be based on some intelligent criteria. An interesting way to approach this is to identify when your algorithm is uncertain about an input—for example, when none of a classifier's classes meet the confidence threshold—and send those inputs. Since they're the ones the model appears to be struggling with, they may be the most useful to analyze.

What Do You Do with Sampled Data?

Samples of data sent back from the edge can be used for a few different things. First, they can be used to better understand real-world performance. Being able to see samples of data directly from the field gives us insight into whether our dataset is truly representative, and it helps us detect data-related problems such as drift.

A second reason this data is valuable is for debugging algorithms. For example, if our algorithm is uncertain about a data sample, it can be useful to try to figure out why, and to fix the problem. It may be that our training dataset doesn't have enough examples of similar images—so seeing the image can help guide more data collection. Or it may be that the algorithm inherently doesn't perform well on certain types of inputs, in which case we may need to think of ways to improve it.

A third reason to sample data is to add it to our dataset. This can be especially effective if we're collecting samples that the algorithm is not confident about, because those "hard examples" are especially helpful in both evaluating our algorithm's performance and in training effective machine learning models.

Another way to record some data while limiting energy and bandwidth usage is to downsample it first. For example, a raw image could be reduced in resolution before sending, or a time series could be reduced to a lower sample rate. Downsampling does throw away some information, but often the remaining information is still enough to allow for debugging (if not full training).

For example, a successful edge AI–powered trail camera sends thumbnail images of animals back to a server via a satellite connection. It would be too expensive to send full images, but thumbnails can still give valuable insight into what is going on in the field.

If downsampled data is still too heavy, you might choose to send only parts of the data. For example, you could send grayscale images instead of color. It can also be interesting to send aggregate statistics about inputs: for example, you might send a periodic moving average of a time series rather than the entire thing. This can help with detecting drift.

Often, your algorithm will use a fixed pipeline of signal processing algorithms before feeding the data into a model. In this case, since you know how the signal processing algorithms will behave, it's likely to be perfectly fine to send the processed data rather than the raw input. The processed data is typically smaller and therefore easier to transmit.

You may not be able to transmit much data once you're fully in production, but you shouldn't let this stop you from accessing real-world data during the initial stages of your deployment. For example, you might decide that it's worthwhile to pay for some expensive connectivity (via cellular or satellite modem, for instance) for the first couple of months of deployment so that you can gather feedback and use it to improve your system.

Another alternative way to obtain data is via sneakernet (*https://oreil.ly/BbyOS*)—have devices log data to local storage, then walk out and pick them up every so often. Like paying for expensive connectivity, this might not be scalable across an entire deployment—but it's certainly doable for some devices, or during a specific period of time.

Distribution changes. As we learned in "Drift and Shift" on page 233, the real world changes over time—but our dataset only represents a snapshot. If it turns out our dataset is no longer representative, we have a problem and we need to know about it.

The best way to do this is to collect a new dataset that represents current conditions, then compare it to our existing one. Unfortunately, collecting and labeling a dataset is extremely labor intensive, and—as we've seen—it's not often feasible to send actual data samples back from the field.

Instead, we need some mechanism for understanding whether the real-world data still resembles our dataset: whether its *distribution* has changed. If we see the distribution change more than a little, chances are that there has been some drift and we will need to account for it.

The simplest way of identifying drift is to calculate summary statistics (*https://oreil.ly/SbIKi*) for our dataset, compute the same statistics on-device, and compare them. *Summary statistics* are numbers that represent a group of measurements in aggregate. For example, you might calculate the mean, median, standard deviation, kurtosis, or skew of readings for a particular sensor.[8] You can even look at the amount of correlation between readings from multiple sensors. If the values are different between your dataset and what the device collects in the field, you may have a problem.

Summary statistics can only identify the simplest of changes in distribution. There are also some more sophisticated statistical tests that can analyze samples from two populations and determine how much they differ. Examples of some of these algorithms can be found in the documentation for Alibi Detect (*https://oreil.ly/bSlZu*), which is an open source library for drift detection (among other things). Unfortunately, many of these methods struggle with high-dimensional data such as images and audio spectrograms.

At the time of writing, there is still a great deal of work that needs to be done to understand the best drift detection approaches for use on edge devices. Today, drift detection is most commonly achieved by the use of anomaly detection algorithms (as seen in "Anomaly detection" on page 99). An anomaly detection model is trained on the training dataset, then run on-device on every new input. If a high proportion of inputs are classified as anomalous, there may be drift occurring. End-to-end platforms typically have some features that can help with this.

It can be interesting to monitor distribution changes in both the input data—for example, images, time series, or audio collected from sensors—and the output of algorithms, such as the probability distributions produced by a classifier. Distribution changes in the output can be a downstream sign of drift. For example, maybe the balance of classes is different in real-world data. This may be a sign that you should improve your dataset.

In addition, output distribution changes can notify you of bugs and errors in your algorithms or application code. For example, if you notice after an update that your model is always predicting the same class, perhaps a bug was introduced. Issues are usually more subtle than this, but it's always good to track the distribution of both inputs and outputs.

There are two ways you can use information about potential distribution changes. If you have access to some connectivity, you may be able to transmit distribution data to a central server for monitoring and analysis. It will allow you to have at least somewhat of a feedback loop with what is going on in production.

If you don't have any connectivity at all, you can still potentially use measures of distribution change to control application logic. For example, you might choose to reject any inputs that fall outside of the expected distribution. This can help prevent your application from making decisions based on input that its algorithms were not designed or trained for.

---

8 These are just a few summary statistics; there are many more choose from.

If you are noticing distribution changes, the best course of action is typically to collect more training data and use it to improve your algorithms. We'll learn more about this workflow in "Improving a Live Application" on page 350.

Application metrics.   Beyond the raw inputs and outputs of your model, it's a great idea to keep track of what your application is doing by storing or transmitting some logs. This might include things like:

System logs
> For example, when the device was started, how long it has been running, power consumption, and battery life

User activity
> Includes actions taken by a user, buttons pressed, or data entered

Device actions
> Things the device has done on its own, such as producing output as a result of an algorithmic decision

Back in "Artificial Intelligence" on page 6 we decided that the definition of intelligence is "knowing the right thing to do at the right time." Application metrics help us understand if this statement applies to our system once it is deployed in the field. By examining the relationships between different types of events, we can try to determine if the device is being used in the ways we anticipated. If it is not, there may be a problem.

For example, imagine we have built an edge AI microwave that can determine the best cooking time for a dish using computer vision. Our analysis of application logs might show that users are consistently running the microwave slightly longer than the estimated cooking time. This is a sign that our application may not be doing a good job and should be investigated further.

If you're able to access logs from multiple devices on a central server, you can do high-level analysis that looks across all of the devices. But depending on your level of connectivity, you may not be able to transmit full sets of logs—or even any logs at all. However, you may be able to send some form of summary statistics that describe what is occurring in your logs.

For instance, you might decide ahead of time that it is worth knowing whether the user is running the microwave longer than recommended. You could then send that specific information back for analysis without needing to upload an entire set of logs.

If you can't upload any data, you can always log it on-device anyway: you may be able to obtain it by collecting the device and physically downloading it. It may be helpful to compress logs for storage on-device, or to make transmission easier.

Outcomes. Most edge AI systems have goals that go beyond what happens on the device itself. For instance, a product may be designed to reduce the cost of an industrial process, encourage a user to stay fit, or improve the quality of an agricultural product.

With this in mind, it's essential to track the outcomes of whatever processes your system interacts with. This will help you understand whether your project is having a beneficial effect.

Measuring and interpreting the impact on outcomes requires deep domain expertise. The process needs to start before the system has been deployed: you'll need to measure the current outcomes of the system so that you have something to compare it to. This should already be part of the initial stages of your project.

You can also monitor outcomes as part of a staged deployment. If you deploy in some places and not others, you'll hopefully be able to measure the difference in results: the places where deployment has yet to happen will act as a control. That said, you should make sure that you account for any other factors that may cause differences between different locations.

The nice thing about outcomes is that you can measure them without needing any access to devices once they have been deployed. The downside is that there's typically a delay between deployment and results, which can make for a less effective feedback loop. It's also harder to account for the impact of external factors.

User reports. If users interact with your product, or the systems it impacts, you can potentially survey them for feedback. This can be a great source of feedback, since users are the first people who will notice any benefits or issues.

It's important to collect user feedback in a structured way, and to acknowledge that there are many factors that can lead individuals to come to different conclusions about the same situation. As such, aggregate feedback from many individuals is likely to be more reliable and actionable than feedback from just a few. If you don't have experience collecting user feedback, it's a good idea to work with a domain expert who does.

It's worth noting that users are not always honest. Employees may feel uncomfortable providing negative feedback on a major project, or they may find themselves in a position where they have an incentive to resist the deployment: for example, if they feel like the project is impacting their job in an undesirable way. These are completely valid and understandable reasons, and it's important to be sensitive to them.

Improving a Live Application

The iterative development process doesn't stop when you deploy, but it certainly changes. Once you have devices running in production, you lose some flexibility in making modifications. Depending on your project, there may be technical constraints that prevent you from updating your application once it has been deployed. And even with the ability to make changes, you may need to be conservative to avoid disrupting the user experience.

Solving problems using feedback

The types of feedback collected during monitoring (see "Postdeployment Monitoring" on page 343) can be put to good use in identifying and solving problems. There are multiple types of feedback, and they each focus on different aspects of the solution:

- Data samples give us insight into the evolving state of real-world data.
- Distribution changes also provide insight into real-world data, and they can also help us identify issues within our algorithmic pipeline (via monitoring output distribution).
- Application metrics give us a way to understand the high-level operation of our system at a technical level.
- Outcomes help us understand how the system is behaving holistically—and whether it is solving the problems it is intended to.
- User reports provide further evidence of the overall health and utility of our product.

By collecting feedback across all of these axes, you should be able to home in on the cause of any issues. For example, your outcomes data may indicate that the system is not making a positive impact on the problem it is trying to solve. To investigate, you might take a look at the change in input and output distributions. If the input distribution is the same as in your dataset but the output distribution is different from what you observed during development, there may be a problem with your algorithm's implementation on the device.

It's important to observe changes in the aspects you are monitoring over time. You might find that there are cyclic changes in input distribution, due to seasonality (see "Representation and Time" on page 227), which need to be factored into your application.

Refining an algorithm over time

All environments experience drift, and you'll almost certainly have to improve your system over time in order to keep up. In addition, since the field of edge AI is still rapidly evolving, it's very likely that new algorithmic approaches may become available over the course of your deployment.

The task of improving your algorithms is just an extension of the workflow you're familiar with from development. It's an iterative process, driven by data. Hopefully, by deploying to the field you've developed a better understanding of the conditions that exist in the real world. For example, monitoring differences in model output distribution may have alerted you to the fact that a different class balance exists in the field than in your dataset.

Even if you've gained no such information, your predeployment evaluation has hopefully informed you of the weak spots in your system's performance. For example, perhaps your application is underperforming for some subgroups of the overall population.

You can use this information to improve your dataset. If you're lucky, you may be able to obtain data directly from the field—although this may be restricted by technical or legal obstacles.[9] At the very least, you hopefully have some awareness into the parts that need improving: maybe you could benefit from better diversity, or by increasing the number of examples of a particular class.

The same applies to algorithms. If you think another algorithm might work better, you can explore its potential in much the same way you would in the initial development process. The difference is that you now have a live production system to compare against. You might even choose to deploy two different versions of algorithms on different devices in order to collect data on which seems to perform better.

Active Learning in Production

We encountered the concept of active learning in "Semi-supervised and active learning algorithms" on page 237 as a way to guide the curation and labeling of datasets. It's reasonable to think of the interaction between a deployed system and the algorithm development process as an *active learning loop*. Feedback from production is used to determine which types of samples are prioritized for collection as the dataset is extended, and new samples can potentially even be sourced from production devices (for example, samples that are not classified confidently could be uploaded to a server).

---

9 If you anticipate wanting to collect data from the field, it needs to be part of the terms of service of your product, and you must verify that a customer has agreed to it.

This guided evolution of dataset and algorithm can be powerful. However, it does come with some risks. The active learning process may inadvertently reinforce bias in the system by guiding dataset collection in a direction that results in a model that works better for some types of inputs than others. It's very important to make sure outcome-related feedback is also considered, so that the performance of the system as a whole is used to gate potential improvements.

Once you have an improved algorithm or application, you'll need to deploy it. As with most things in edge AI, this isn't always as simple as it sounds.

Supporting multiple deployed algorithms

Deploying server-side code can be as simple as pressing a button, with the latest version being immediately available to all users. Edge deployments are—unfortunately—a lot more complicated.

AI is often deployed to the edge as a way to work around challenges with connectivity and bandwidth. These challenges can make deployment tricky. In a multi-device deployment, it's not necessarily possible to push the latest version of your application down to every edge device at the same time. Even if you have enough bandwidth, some devices may be unavailable: powered down or offline. And in some cases, by design or by accident, there's simply no way to update a device once it has been placed in the field.

The situation is amplified by the way that edge AI applications are developed and deployed. A staged deployment within an iterative workflow will naturally result in many different combinations of hardware and software out in the field, and even after the initial rollout, new devices being placed in the field will likely feature newer versions of hardware and software than what is already there.

This means that at some point you are likely to end up with a range of application versions in production at the same time. In fact, there are several entities that may have different versions:

- The device hardware itself
- The application firmware running on a device
- The algorithm implementations or models within the firmware
- The datasets used to train any machine learning models
- Any backend web services that the device connects to

Since it's unlikely you can update all of these at the same time, there's a huge number of potential different combinations of artifacts that may be deployed in the field at any given moment. Keeping track of them is extremely important. If you don't have a good record of what is deployed where, you'll lose the ability to debug your system. If every device has a different mixture of components and you aren't sure what they are, it's very hard to figure out the root cause of a performance problem.

To permit debugging and traceability, you'll need a system for tracking which versions of each component are deployed in a given place. For example, you might maintain a database that is kept up to date every time you update firmware or create a new hardware iteration. This functionality can be provided by IoT device management software.

When monitoring metrics, you'll need to associate them with the records in your device management platform so that you can understand which components might be in need of attention.

Managing many different versions concurrently can be a nightmare, so it's in your interest to try to limit the combinations currently in use. If your devices connect to a backend, one way to enforce relative uniformity is to require a minimum firmware version. The drawback is that this may impact the robustness and usability of your system.

Ethics and Long-Term Support

The world and our applications are continually evolving, so it's important to continue to analyze our systems from an ethical perspective as long as they are still in use.

Here are some of the ethical issues that can affect a deployment in the long term.

Performance degradation

This chapter has introduced some techniques for monitoring and improving performance over time, which will naturally degrade as drift occurs. Unfortunately, the reality is that most deployments will have a finite useful life. At some point, either the drift will be too much to overcome, or the budget will not allow for the necessary maintenance.

For example, imagine a system designed to identify manufacturing defects. Over time, changes to the manufacturing process may produce different types of defects. If the system is not updated, the new defects won't be caught—potentially resulting in safety hazards.

A machine learning model doesn't necessarily know when it is being fed inputs that it wasn't trained to handle. Instead, it'll continue to produce an output—which may be completely wrong. If someone is depending on your application to do the right thing, this can be disastrous. If you are no longer supporting the hardware, there may be no way for anybody to know that there is a problem—beyond the fact that some harm is being caused.

This raises the question: what happens to projects that have exceeded their useful lifespan? The truth is that it isn't ethically acceptable to just abandon a project. Instead, you need to plan for what will happen in the event that it becomes unworkable. A responsible design covers the entire life cycle of your project, from cradle to grave.

For edge AI projects, this includes the hardware component. For example, you may need to have a plan to deal with harmful materials contained within hardware devices, such as lithium batteries. Is your hardware sustainable, or will it create problems of its own?

Termination Criteria

Every project that is deployed in production should be subject to termination criteria: a list of potential issues that would result in the deployment being halted, at least until the issues can be resolved.

A set of termination criteria might include the following:

- A maximum amount of drift in distribution versus the project's dataset
- Predicted impact on any associated systems, along with tolerance thresholds for deviation
- Minimum standards for successful business metrics

By coming up with this list ahead of time, you'll be prepared to act quickly if things do not go well. These termination criteria should be reviewed on an ongoing basis and updated if new information comes to light.

If termination needs to happen, you can hopefully rely on the graceful degradation capabilities of your product that were planned out during the design phase (see "Graceful Degradation" on page 291).

New information

After deployment, new facts may come to light that may result in an ethical re-evaluation of a project. Here are some examples:

- The discovery of algorithmic limitations that could be detrimental to fairness
- The discovery of security vulnerabilities that could be exploited
- Improvements in the understanding of the problem that expose flaws in an application
- Improvements in edge AI techniques that make the current application obsolete
- Changes in the problem domain that make the current application obsolete

Artificial intelligence is a rapidly moving field, and it's common for issues to be discovered with existing algorithms and techniques. For example, adversarial attacks (*https://oreil.ly/U4rq5*) make it possible for attackers to manipulate machine learning models by feeding them carefully constructed inputs in order to obtain the output they desire. New adversarial attacks are often discovered, and there's a minor arms race as defenses are invented and defeated.

It's also common to discover flaws in AI techniques that may lead to compromised performance. For example, "What Do Compressed Deep Neural Networks Forget?" (*https://oreil.ly/QlZng*) (Hooker et al., 2021) showed how popular model compression techniques can lead to a loss of performance for minority classes. As we learn more about the limitations of our techniques, we may find that our currently deployed systems have flaws that make them unsuitable for continued use.

Sometimes, a new discovery will make an existing technique obsolete. In some contexts, continuing to use the old technique might be considered unethical. For example, imagine you have a medical diagnosis product that is able to detect a fatal illness with a false negative rate of 20%. If a competing team creates a system with a false negative rate of 10%, anyone using your system instead of theirs may have an increased risk of death since their illness is less likely to be caught. You may have to consider whether it is ethical to continue marketing your product.

In some cases, new domain expertise may come to light that shows a system is not fit for purpose. For example, an improved understanding of human physiology might show that a previously adequate fitness wearable is in fact delivering bad advice to athletes.

Evolving cultural norms

Society changes quickly, and you may find that a previously deployed application gradually moves outside of the standards of acceptability. For example, the expectations of consumers around privacy is changing over time. Today, consumers are accepting of smart speakers that send recorded conversational audio into the cloud for processing—since historically there's been no other way to perform accurate speech recognition.

However, as on-device transcription becomes more widespread, it's likely that consumers will come to expect it, and will consider the use of server-side transcription an outmoded concept that violates their expectation of privacy.

It's worth noting that this phenomenon may also happen the other way around: previously unacceptable concepts, like smart cameras in private areas of the home, may become tolerated as we move toward systems where the image data never leaves the device.

As the custodian of a project, you should work with domain experts to keep track of cultural norms and make sure that your application does not violate them.

Changing legal standards

Legal standards tend to follow in step with cultural norms. For example, as privacy expectations have evolved on the web, laws like the European Union's General Data Protection Regulation (*https://oreil.ly/EBy2O*) have been drawn up to regulate the way that companies handle private information.

Whatever area you are operating in, you should work with domain experts to understand your legal obligations and ensure that you are handling them ethically.

 Bear in mind that law and ethics are not necessarily the same thing. In some situations, you may be legally required to do things that are not compatible with your ethical standards. For example, some companies have been pressured by governments (*https://oreil.ly/dIEyE*) to hand over the keys to encrypted user data. Bear this in mind when designing your application.

What Comes Next

Our discussion of long-term support concludes the final theory section of this book. Congratulations on making it this far!

In the next three chapters, we'll see everything we've learned in action. Each chapter provides an end-to-end application of the edge AI workflow to a practical use case, starting with an idea and ending with a product.

We hope these chapters are both informative and inspirational. By the end of the book, you'll be ready to apply these principles on your own.

## CHAPTER 11

Use Case: Wildlife Monitoring

Now that we understand the basics of developing machine learning models for edge applications, the first realm of use cases we will cover is related to wildlife conservation and monitoring. We will explore possible problems and their associated solutions for each use case chapter in this book via the development workflow outlined in Chapter 9.

There is a rapid decline of threatened species worldwide due to various human civilization impacts and environmental reasons or disasters. The primary drivers of this decline are habitat loss, degradation, and fragmentation.[1] The causes of these drivers are human activity, such as urbanization, agriculture, and resource extraction. As a result of this decline, many species are at risk of extinction.

A growing number of AI and edge AI applications are being developed with the aim of helping to protect wildlife. These applications range from early detection of illegal wildlife trade to monitoring of endangered species to automated identification of poachers. As previously discussed in this book, edge AI is used to process data locally on the device instead of in the cloud. This is important for wildlife conservation purposes because it can be used to process data in remote locations without the need for an internet connection. This means that data can be processed quickly and without the need for expensive infrastructure, helping prevent future poaching and thus protecting our planet's most vulnerable species.

When used responsibly, edge AI can and will have an extremely positive impact on society and our planet. However, technology and AI are what their developers make of them. They can thus be used for good, or sometimes be used for harmful and unethical purposes. It is therefore important to be thoughtful about how they are

---

1 See National Wildlife Federation article "Habitat Loss" (*https://oreil.ly/kpOVl*).

developed and used to ensure that their benefits outweigh their risks. The United Nations[2] and various major technology companies like Google,[3] Microsoft,[4] etc., are creating initiatives to utilize their resources for AI for social and environmental good.

One such usage of AI for good is in a well-known and well-researched method of protecting, identifying, monitoring and tracking endangered species, the *camera trap*. Camera trapping is a powerful tool that can be used for a variety of wildlife conservation research and monitoring purposes. It can be used to monitor endangered species, study animal behavior, and assess the impact of human activity on wildlife. This method can also be used to detect and track poachers, as well as to monitor the health and behavior of endangered species. Camera traps are often used in conjunction with other methods, such as DNA analysis, to create a more complete picture of what is happening in an area.

What Exactly is a Camera Trap?

A camera trap is a remotely activated camera that is used to take photographs of animals in their natural habitat. The camera is usually triggered by an infrared (IR) sensor that is triggered by the animal's movement.

A camera trap is usually confined to a singular location on the ground; camera trapping is especially useful for large, ground-dwelling animals. So, this method is most appropriate for only a small portion of the Earth's species, as camera traps are not useful for underwater applications, birds in flight, rapidly moving small insects, etc.

Problem Exploration

The term *wildlife conservation* is too broad of a concept to tackle in this one chapter and too large of a problem to be solved with just one machine learning model, so for the purposes of this book we will focus on wildlife conservation in terms of protecting specific animal species that are on the IUCN Red List of Threatened Species (*https://www.iucnredlist.org*).

We also need to explore the difficulty of the problem we are trying to solve: what are the costs, travel, implementation, and infrastructure or government restrictions that will inhibit the creation of machine learning models for a nonprofit purpose?

---

2 See the website, "United Nations AI for Good" (*https://aiforgood.itu.int*).

3 See Google's site, "AI for Social Good" (*https://oreil.ly/8L3BY*).

4 See Microsoft's site, "AI for Good" (*https://oreil.ly/8ZLQI*).

Solution Exploration

Since endangered species roam freely, they are difficult to spot by the human eye in broad daylight or at night. Camera traps are especially useful tools because they allow humans to track, count, and identify both the endangered animal and/or the animal's threats without interference in their natural habitat. Camera traps ultimately allow animals to be monitored so that they can be protected remotely without drastically affecting their behavior, movements, environment, food sources, etc.

An important step of protecting these endangered wildlife species is to provide their human custodians with actionable information. This can come in many different forms. Goal-wise, we can both generate a machine learning model that can identify threats to these specific species and alert humans of the threat's location, or we can identify, count, and/or track the animal's location. Both of these approaches accomplish the same goal, giving people the necessary information to protect a threatened species. However, they require a different combination of machine learning classes and sensor inputs to be solved.

Goal Setting

Poaching is the illegal hunting, killing, or trapping of animals. Poachers often target rare or endangered animals for their meat, horns, tusks, or fur. Poaching is a serious problem that threatens the survival of many wildlife species. Camera traps can be used to reduce poaching by helping to track the movements of poachers and by providing evidence that can be used to prosecute them. Camera traps can also be used to deter poachers by making them aware that they are being watched:

> Camera trapping in remote areas can potentially help protected area managers to increase rates of detection of IHA (illegal human activity) in their conservation landscapes and increase rates of arrests and prosecutions by providing appropriate supporting evidence.[5]
>
> —*Biological Conservation* article

Camera traps are also an important tool for studying, conserving, and monitoring endangered species. They allow researchers to collect data on the ecology and behavior of animals without disturbing them. This information can then be used to design conservation plans that protect endangered species and their habitats. Camera trapping also represents a unique opportunity for broadscale collaborative species monitoring due to its largely nondiscriminatory nature due to the amount of camera

---

5 Abu Naser Mohsin Hossain et al., "Assessing the Efficacy of Camera Trapping as a Tool for Increasing Detection Rates of Wildlife Crime in Tropical Protected Areas" (*https://doi.org/10.1016/j.biocon.2015.07.023*), *Biological Conservation* 201 (2016): 314–19.

data that is ingested by the device with no other trigger than IR movement; these trigger movements could be from a wide range of species.[6]

Solution Design

In order to avoid many ethical dilemmas by creating a machine learning model that will be used in a camera trap system to monitor endangered species, instead we can promote the conservation and welfare of endangered species by tracking as well as monitoring their environment's other invasive species. Monitoring the location and abundance of invasive animals in the device's environment with a camera trap and relaying this information to the environment's human custodians promotes the conservation of endangered animals: the local resources and unnatural species intrusions or unnatural predators will be reduced, allowing the endangered animal's population to recover and thrive.

In this book, we are choosing to design and implement a low-cost, efficient, and easy-to-train camera trap to monitor an invasive animal species of your choice. However, a conservation and monitoring trap does not always need to be a camera-based solution, and by using the principles and design workflow presented in this chapter and throughout the book, many other types of machine learning models and applications can be implemented for conservation and monitoring purposes, including using audio data to classify animal calls or birdcalls, underwater audio/radar to listen to ocean sounds and track and identify whales, and more.

What Solutions Already Exist?

Camera traps are already being used for commercial and conservation/monitoring purposes and have been extensively used since the 1990s. By integrating a movement sensor onto a camera setup, an outdoor wildlife camera is triggered when any movement is detected by the integrated movement sensor, resulting in thousands of images from the viewpoint of the camera's fixed location over many days or months.

As on-device networking capabilities used to be too power intensive to integrate into a remote field device, researchers would need to go into the environment where the device is located to manually retrieve the images from the camera, a sometimes labor-intensive task depending on where the camera was placed in the wild and how remote the location was. Once the images were retrieved, it would take weeks or months for researchers with trained eyes to comb through the images by hand to find their target species in the photographs.

---

6 From an article by Abu Naser Mohsin Hossain et al., "Pangolins in Global Camera Trap Data: Implications for Ecological Monitoring" (*https://doi.org/10.1016/j.gecco.2019.e00769*), *Conservation* 201 (2016): 314–19.

By integrating AI into the camera device itself, researchers are now able to dramatically reduce the time needed to locate their target animal/species since the device now has a probability reading of animals present for each and every image that is captured after the movement sensor is triggered. Only the highest probability images are sent over a network to the researcher's lab, eliminating the need for a human to physically go into the field to retrieve the camera's images manually (a potentially dangerous task as well, considering the environment) and reducing the man-hours required to sift through the captured images.

There are specific AI tools that already exist for the purpose of camera trapping, from automatic specific detection in your unlabeled images or video feeds to data ingestion tools for the purpose of postprocessing, tracking, and counting species in the cloud. These tools are very valuable for researchers, and as camera trapping is a well-researched and widely adapted method there is an abundance of these solutions available; a simple web search (*https://oreil.ly/RSnfF*) can help you find all of these prebuilt solutions. These prebuilt devices each have their own positives and negatives, considering that it is not yet possible to have a singular model that can identify and track all living animal species on our planet in all environments. We will not go into too much depth on these preexisting solutions in this chapter, and instead go through the process of designing and deploying a camera trap on our own for our own local habitats.

Solution Design Approaches

We can take our problem statement and design a solution many different ways, with the following pros and cons for each approach:

Identify an endangered animal.
> If there is a sufficiently big enough dataset available, or enough publicly available labeled images of the animal, the training/testing datasets will be easy to collate and the subsequent model will have high enough accuracy for the device's environment. However, framing the problem this way will potentially allow poachers and other human threats to easily create a device that is essentially an amazingly accurate hunting tool, especially depending on the quality of the data used for the environment the device is in.

Identify an endangered animal's invasive predators.
> In a well-researched environment, there is usually quite a bit of publicly available data for various regions around the world for invasive species, including invasive predators, plants, and other wildlife; this type of problem and its solution will generally be quite beneficial to people trying to increase the chances of success for endangered animals to replenish their numbers as humans can use the trap's data to find and remove invasive threats.

However, it could be hard to determine exactly which invasive species will likely be in the environment of the endangered animal at any given time, and invasive species that are detrimental to the animal could be any number of threats, from humans to other animals or invasive poisonous plant life. So, the problem statement here could be a bit too broad to protect the endangered animal from all sides.

Another con of this approach is that it requires the model creator to be aware that an invasive species model is only useful and ethical if used in an environment where the species being identified is indeed actually a verified invasive species. This requires a good faith effort on the ML model developer's side to ensure the creation of their model is indeed of an invasive species in their target area and requires the developer to try and limit model distribution to zones where the invasive species is actually not invasive.

This solution will also require the end user to ensure the model is not being used to overhunt the identified threat, and that it complies with a region's hunting rules and seasonal regulations as well as plant foraging/gathering/removal rules, if applicable.

Identify poachers and their associated threats.
A human/person image identification approach or even a person/object detection model is already a widely established area of machine learning model development. Many datasets already exist for the purpose of identifying humans in view of a camera's lens for both low-power and high compute–power computers. However, there are many ethical and security obligations related to the solution of this problem. The model developer must ensure that the data used in the training and testing sets represents the usage context and is permitted to be used under copyright/fair use law.

The resulting model must also only be used for binary classification: yes (there is a person present in the frame of the camera lens) or no (there is no person present in the image). This is similar to object detection of human bodies. It requires a good deal of good faith on the development side to ensure that facial data, biometric data, and other identifying information is not used or collected. The developer also needs to ensure that the model adheres to the many privacy and data laws that apply to the region where the model is to be deployed.

Identify other invasive species.
This approach provides a lot of options in terms of determining which other species could be a threat to endangered species in your selected environment. From plants, insects, and other animals, the variations for this type of model are endless and all go toward the benefit of protecting and ensuring survival of your designated endangered species. However, there are cons similar to those encountered when trying to identify an endangered animal's predators.

There are many pros and cons to each type of approach and their resulting solutions; you need to use your own exploratory methods to develop a pros/cons list for your chosen solution! A good first step is to brainstorm with a variety of stakeholders and people that have firsthand experience with your problem and solution. In addition to these pros/cons there are also many considerations we will need to take into account to ensure responsible design, which we will discuss later in this chapter.

Design Considerations

To achieve the overarching goal of supporting researchers who study our selected wildlife species, and/or identifying and tracking invasive species that are a threat to endangered species in our selected areas, from a technological standpoint, we can use a wide variety of data sources, including different types of sensors and cameras (Table 11-1).

Table 11-1. Sensors to accomplish various wildlife conservation goals

Goal	Sensor(s)
Counting elephants in the wild	Camera
Identify a bird based on its call	Microphone
Listen for whale calls in the ocean	Microphone, HARPs (high-frequency acoustic recording packages)[a]
Listen for threats in an environment (poachers, gunshots, etc.)	Microphone
Tracking and identifying poachers	Camera, microphone
General nonnative / invasive species control & tracking	Camera, microphone, accelerometer, Doppler radar

[a] See the NOAA Fisheries article, "Passive Acoustics in the Pacific Islands" (*https://oreil.ly/d-yVo*).

In all the preceding use cases, a typical machine learning approach, *classification*, is used; or by uploading a machine learning–training dataset containing the information you would like to spot in a new, unseen sensor data input stream on the device. To refresh your memory on various machine learning algorithms, see "Algorithm Types by Functionality" on page 96.

When choosing your wildlife monitoring goal and use case, you will also need to take into consideration how easy it will be to collect a large, robust, and high-quality dataset for training your machine learning model. As we found in previous chapters (especially in Chapter 7), your model is only as good as the quality of your input data. If you wish to create a model to identify the birdcall of a rare and endangered bird, for example, you may not be able to procure a sufficiently large enough dataset to successfully train a highly accurate classification model.

Refer to "Dataset Gathering" on page 367. Thankfully, in the age of the internet and widely available research datasets and collaboration projects, model developers are able to use and acquire many preexisting databases of images to identify a specific animal species or download freely available research, including various sensor or audio datasets of the animal's call, vocalizations, environment chemical footprint, etc. "Getting Your Hands on Data" on page 215 discusses some of the pros and cons to this approach of dataset gathering.

Also, consider where the device will be located and what sensors will be required for the desired environment:

- Device location during initial data collection phase
- Device location postdeployment
- Average weather conditions of the device's location
- Battery-powered versus USB-powered versus permanent powerline
- Environmental requirements (i.e., water, fog, dirt, and other environmental factors) that could inhibit nominal usage of the sensor or destroy the device

The device could be located in a very remote field; depending on the use case it may need more or less processing power, and thus more battery. The device could also be affixed to a permanent energy line or could be super low power and thus run on batteries that only need to be replaced once a year or every few years. A permanent powerline may not be feasible for the use case or target environment.

Consider also communicating the model's inferencing results back to some cloud platform. This communication could be energy and power limiting depending on the type of networking protocol chosen and will affect how long the device can be in the field without human intervention, battery replacement, etc. If the device is moving all the time, how will the model need to adapt in order to work well in all of these environments and situations?

Environmental Impact

Please reread "Building Applications Responsibly" on page 41, and then return to this section. We will discuss the specific considerations for the solution's environmental impact.

Model developers also need to consider how their device will directly impact the environment it will be placed in. For example, if you were to put a large device in the rainforest just to track human activity, that device is likely to be inherently invasive regardless of the measures and attachments used on the physical device; however we need to consider how many animals or endangered species will be potentially saved from this device and resulting inferencing data, and then weigh the pros and cons.

Other notes and questions to take into consideration include:

- Is the target creature itself invasive to the installation environment?
- Will the device be invasive in the environment? Device anchoring could inadvertently negatively impact other species, bugs, bacteria, etc.
- How many humans will be required to physically install the device in the environment? What travel and installation footprint will result after installation? (human litter, tracks, destroying other animal's habitats, etc.)
- How will the device alert the user or cloud system when it has identified the target species?
- Where is the device placed, and how often will humans need to physically traverse to the device?

We also need to ensure that the device is not emitting lights, sounds, noises, and chemicals that are not natural or native to the environment that it is placed in. These factors could cause the animal that you are trying to track to behave abnormally, thus skewing your data and inferencing results.

 Warning! Camera Traps Can be Heard and Seen by Animals[7]

The developer of the camera trap needs to consider the following ways the device can be intrusive in the animal's environment:

- Auditory intrusions
- Olfactory intrusions
- Learned association
- Visual (day)
- Visual (night)

In another vein of environmental impact, the camera trap may also cause an ethical dilemma if used for detecting poaching activity, and could cause direct, negative impacts to the local people of the lands we are trying to protect. There are reports that antipoaching initiatives have been used by governments to exclude local minorities from areas they've traditionally lived and gathered food in.

Any AI that's designed to highlight people for punishment has a high risk of abuse, because it can be used in ways the model developers didn't intend, for example, a tribe being evicted from their village, and the government placing "antipoacher" cameras

---

7 See the article by Paul D. Meek et al., "Camera Traps Can Be Heard and Seen by Animals" (*https://doi.org/10.1371/journal.pone.0110832*).

to make sure they don't come back, or an authoritarian regime using them against rebels. This capability being provided by Western organizations also echoes a lot of harmful technology transfers that have happened over the years.[8]

Bootstrapping

For this chapter, we will implement a solution that is geared toward "identifying an endangered animal's invasive predators" (see "Solution Design Approaches" on page 361) and design a model that will detect and classify the animal *Callosciurus finlaysonii* (Finlayson's squirrel) (*https://oreil.ly/JRz_2*), also known colloquially as the "Thai squirrel," which is a certified invasive species in the Netherlands according to the European Union list as of August 2, 2022 (*https://oreil.ly/fSbmw*). The author of this chapter is a resident of the Netherlands; thus, a certified Netherlands invasive species has been chosen as an example for this use case. Once we have collected our dataset with our target trap animal, we will also add another class of data for general environmental images that do not include *Callosciurus finlaysonii*. These two classes will allow our image classification machine learning model to identify when the camera is triggered by movement in the environment: the camera takes an image and the trained machine learning model inferences and determines where the *Callosciurus finlaysonii* is present in the environment. The resulting image, if it includes our invasive species, will be sent over our selected network connection for further processing by a human or in the cloud.

According to the Dutch government and the European Union (*https://oreil.ly/v1XZh*):

> In Italy, the Thai squirrel (*Callosciurus finlaysonii*) strips the bark of trees, increasing the chance of infestation by fungi and invertebrates. In its native range, the Thai squirrel is considered a frequent predator of bird eggs, but there is no information known about such an effect in areas where this squirrel has been introduced. Stripping bark from trees is mentioned as a negative effect on ecosystem services. This can be significant for both individual trees and entire production forests. Stripping the bark can also lead to secondary contamination with, for example, fungi. A result of this is felled trees in Italy.[9]

---

8 See this article in *The Guardian*: "Report Clears WWF of Complicity in Violent Abuses by Conservation Rangers" (*https://oreil.ly/JQ2tE*).

9 "Thai Squirrel," Dutch Food Safety Authority, 2022.

Define Your Machine Learning Classes

Table 11-2 shows potential combinations of use cases, sensor and data input types, and machine learning classes one would use to collect and label their training and testing datasets. The use cases and their associated class labels are important for the type of machine learning algorithm we're employing in this chapter, specifically "classification." You can learn more about this in "Classification" on page 96.

Table 11-2. Machine learning classes for various use cases

Use case	Training data	Class labels
Camera trap	Images	Target animal, background environment (with or without other animals)
Audio trap	Microphone data	Target animal call, ambient environment noise, "other" animal calls that are NOT the target animal's call
Animal object detection	Images (with bounding boxes)	Target animal
Motion trap	Accelerometer, radar, or other spatial signals	Movement of desired animal
Chemical trap	Gas signals	Ambient environment, target species chemical signature

In this chapter, we will select and build upon the traditional camera trap use case for machine learning image classification using transfer learning techniques, answering the question, "Is my target animal present in the field of view of the camera?" Our project's machine learning classes will be "target animal" and "background environment (with or without other animals)," or more simply, "unknown."

Dataset Gathering

For technical and specific information about how to gather a clean, robust, and useful dataset, see "Getting Your Hands on Data" on page 215. You can also utilize various strategies on how to collect data from multiple sources to create your own unique dataset for your use case:

- Combining public research datasets
- Combining no-animal-present environment images from multiple public datasets with a dataset of labeled images of the target trap animal
- Using existing massive image datasets like COCO (common objects in context)

Sourcing Publicly Available Image Datasets

You can always use a dataset from a seemingly nonrelevant source; for example, if your target invasive species lives in Portugal but there is not an abundance of labeled image datasets for your target species in that environment, you can find research datasets for other Portugal species and use their data as "nontarget invasive species" in your training/testing dataset. Your target invasive species could possibly even be present in those images, which your model can identify after training, without the original dataset developer's knowledge!

Edge Impulse

The Edge Impulse Studio is a freely available cloud-based platform containing all the tools and code required for the entire end-to-end machine learning pipeline, including collecting and labeling high-quality training/testing datasets, extracting your data's most important features using various digital signal processing techniques, designing and training your machine learning model, testing and validating your model for real-world performance/accuracy, and deploying your model in various library formats with the easy-to-use Edge Impulse SDK. For this chapter, and the subsequent use case chapters in this book, we will use the Edge Impulse Studio to reduce our model development time and the amount of code we will need to write in order to achieve a full edge machine learning model development pipeline process and subsequent deployment.

For further justification for using Edge Impulse for edge machine learning model development, review "End-to-End Platforms for Edge AI" on page 162.

To follow along with the rest of the instructions in this chapter, you will need to create a free Edge Impulse account (*https://edgeimpulse.com*).

Public project

Each use case chapter of this book contains a written tutorial to demonstrate and achieve a complete end-to-end machine learning model for the described use case. However, if you would like to just get straight to the point and see the exact data and model that the authors have developed for the chapter in its final state, you may do so by navigating to the public Edge Impulse project (*https://oreil.ly/DP1gJ*) for this chapter.

You may also directly clone this project, including all of the original training and testing data, intermediate model information, resulting trained model results, and all deployment options by selecting the Clone button at the top right side of the Edge Impulse page (see Figure 11-1).

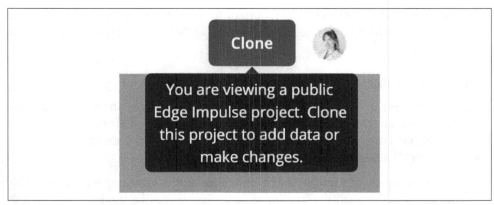

Figure 11-1. Clone Edge Impulse public project

Choose Your Hardware and Sensors

In this book, we try to remain as device agnostic as possible, but we also need to discuss how one can use an off-the-shelf, easy-to-use development kit to create this use case's solution, since we are under the assumption that the tutorial outlined in this chapter will most likely be used for an ethical, nonprofit purpose, meaning that the reader's potential access to embedded engineering funds, resources, developers, etc., will be limited. Thus, this book aims to make this hardware selection as easy, affordable, and accessible as possible.

For a quick and easy data ingestion and deployment option, without having to write any code, we will both ingest new data and deploy the resulting trained model to a mobile phone with the Edge Impulse WebAssembly library and mobile client. For other equally easy deployment devices, Edge Impulse provides a large array of officially supported platforms (*https://oreil.ly/stMSR*), from MCUs to GPUs, of which all include an open source prewritten firmware available for you to use. If you have a device that is not listed as an officially supported platform by Edge Impulse, you can still use the device, but you will need to integrate the deployed C++ library and your device's driver code into your application code, just as you would normally during a typical embedded firmware development workflow.

Platform selection is not as important to this book because we are trying to make sure that every use case chapter can be realistically solved with almost any physical device platform (barring any memory or latency constraints). You could solve all of the use case chapters with a Raspberry Pi and various sensor configurations and still achieve the same goal discussed here.

However, depending on the use case goal, choosing a Raspberry Pi will force you to consider the costly power requirements necessary for the Pi to function, but in contrast, this device selection will potentially be lower in cost and have dramatically reduced total software development time (for a single field unit; of course, if a large number of the same device is required, then a Raspberry Pi + sensor/camera configuration will likely be more expensive than an MCU/integrated sensor/camera solution, for example).

Hardware configuration

There are endless combinations to choose from for your main edge device and add-on camera attachment. For this chapter, we will remain device agnostic, but assume that our target device is similar to that of an OpenMV Cam H7 Plus (*https://oreil.ly/hZddx*) (with RGB-integrated camera).

This generic setup already implies a few limitations: our camera trap will only reliably work in daylight; the quality of the input frame image may be too low to accurately spot all instances of our target animal if the animal is too far away from the lens; your device may be too battery intensive to live unattended in the field for long periods of time; and if you are trying to trap an animal with a specific coloring using grayscale, the input image may yield inaccurate predictions.[10]

Following is a list of some other camera attachment options and requirements to ponder in order to improve the accuracy of your wildlife monitoring model for your specific environment, use case, project budget, and more:

- High-quality cameras
- Low-quality cameras
- Infrared, thermal cameras
- Grayscale versus color (RGB) input
- Lens focal length
- Input image pixel density

Data Collection

Using Edge Impulse, there are many options available to upload and label data in your project:

Edge Impulse Studio uploader (https://oreil.ly/b3url)
The web uploader allows you to directly upload files from your computer to your Edge Impulse project in a variety of file formats. You can also have the studio automatically label your samples based on the filename.

---

10 This article gives some more information: Fischer et al., "The Potential Value of Camera-Trap Studies for Identifying, Ageing, Sexing and Studying the Phenology of Bornean Lophura Pheasants" (*https://oreil.ly/id-Bc*).

CLI uploader (https://oreil.ly/cxdp4)
> The CLI uploader allows you to directly upload files locally from your computer's command-line terminal to your Edge Impulse project with a variety of file formats and input options. You can also have the studio automatically label your samples based on the filename.

Ingestion API (https://oreil.ly/myL7K)
> Write a data collection script connecting your platform over a networking protocol to your Edge Impulse project by simply calling the ingestion API. Using the scripting language of your choice, you can set timers and triggers to automatically upload images to your project using your Edge Impulse project API key (*https://oreil.ly/623ly*).

Data sources (cloud bucket integration) (https://oreil.ly/1QweQ)
> Directly pull data from your cloud data bucket and automatically trigger responses in your Edge Impulse project (this feature is especially useful for improving your model over time with active learning strategies).

Further details regarding the Edge Impulse data acquisition format can be viewed in the Edge Impulse API reference documentation (*https://oreil.ly/Z5IzD*).

Connecting your device directly to Edge Impulse for data collection

There are many ways to upload data directly from your desired platform to your Edge Impulse project.

If your chosen device platform is *officially supported*, you can follow the firmware update guide found for your target within the Edge Impulse development boards documentation (*https://oreil.ly/ULIdQ*).

If your chosen device platform is *not officially supported*, follow the development platform porting guide (*https://oreil.ly/iOo23*) to fully integrate the Edge Impulse ingestion API (*https://oreil.ly/FsCTx*) into your embedded device firmware (note that porting is usually time consuming and not necessary for most projects, unless you want your target to be featured on the Edge Impulse community boards page (*https://oreil.ly/xxTwr*)), or use the Edge Impulse CLI serial data forwarder (*https://oreil.ly/c9qb0*) to quickly and easily ingest data over the serial port or with WebUSB into your Edge Impulse project.

You can also use a mobile phone or your computer to directly upload new images from the camera on your device; check out all of the device connection options via your project's Devices tab (see Figure 11-2).

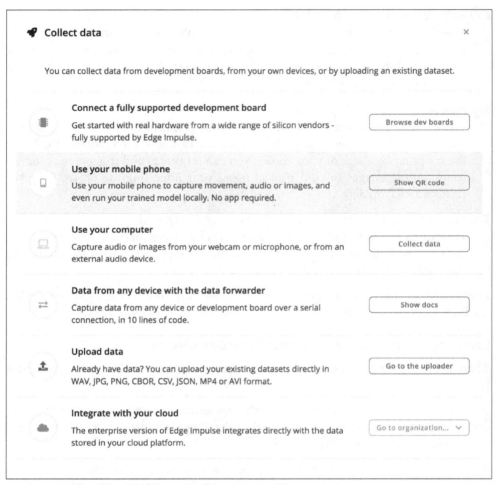

Figure 11-2. "Collect data" view in the Devices tab

iNaturalist

Since most people likely do not have a large dataset of invasive species images available at their disposal, a secondary form of data collection is required in order to start our dataset of images of our invasive animal. For this tutorial, rather than setting up a device in the field to collect new, unlabeled raw images of animals, we will instead use images acquired from the community in our desired location that have already been (somewhat) reliably labeled with the name of our target species. Using iNaturalist (*https://www.inaturalist.org*), we will query their database for images with our identified species, query on this species name, and download a dataset of images with the iNatural image ID and photographer's username attributed to each file download.

You will need an iNaturalist account to log into the iNaturalist export website (*https://oreil.ly/u4m7i*) and process the following queries.

First we will query on our desired trap animal species name and retrieve a CSV file with the following columns in iNaturalist: id, user_login, quality_grade, license, url, image_url (see Example 11-1 and Figure 11-3).

Example 11-1. Query for Callosciurus finlaysonii

```
q=Callosciurus+finlaysonii&search_on=names&has%5B%5D=photos
   &quality_grade=any&identifications=any
```

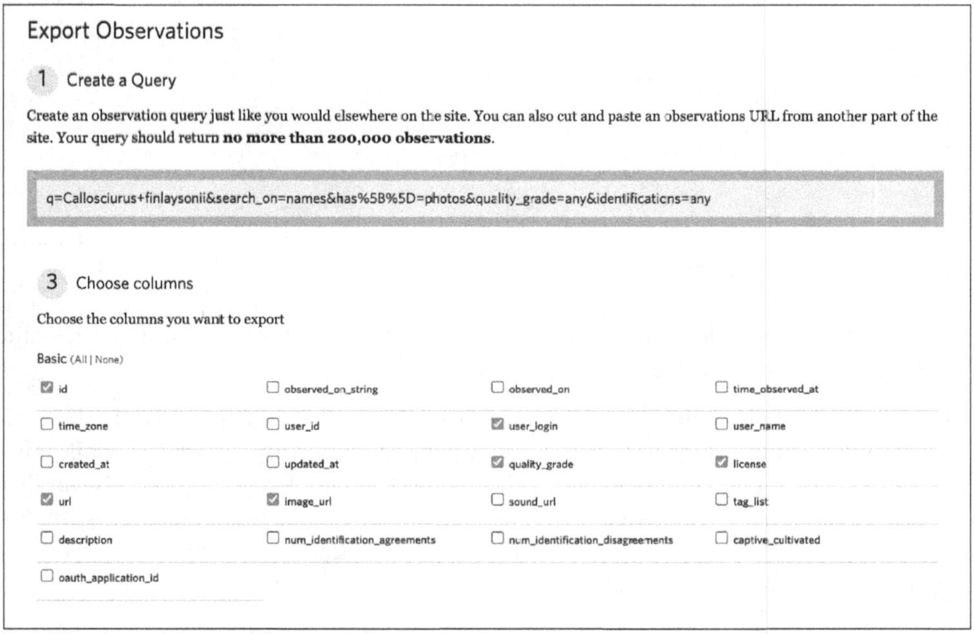

Figure 11-3. Select the columns for the CSV file

We will also need a dataset of images that include "unknown" species or images of the environment in the Netherlands that do not include the *Callosciurus finlaysonii* (or any animals at all). This "unknown" data will allow us to train our model to more accurately predict when our trap animal has been photographed/captured by our device. Query for this data with the following columns in iNaturalist: id, user_login, quality_grade, license, url, image_url (see Example 11-2 and Figure 11-4).

Example 11-2. Query for unlabeled images in place ID 7506 (Netherlands)

```
search_on=place&has[]=photos&quality_grade=any&identifications=any
   &iconic_taxa[]=unknown&place_id=7506
```

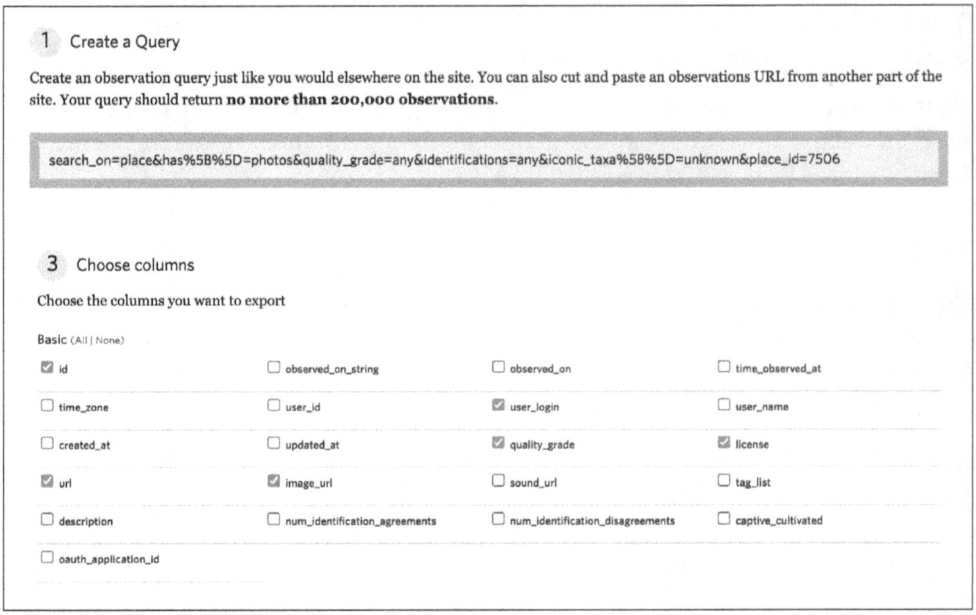

Create a Query

Create an observation query just like you would elsewhere on the site. You can also cut and paste an observations URL from another part of the site. Your query should return **no more than 200,000 observations**.

```
search_on=place&has%5B%5D=photos&quality_grade=any&identifications=any&iconic_taxa%5B%5D=unknown&place_id=7506
```

3 Choose columns

Choose the columns you want to export

Basic (All | None)

☑ id	☐ observed_on_string	☐ observed_on	☐ time_observed_at
☐ time_zone	☐ user_id	☑ user_login	☐ user_name
☐ created_at	☐ updated_at	☑ quality_grade	☑ license
☑ url	☑ image_url	☐ sound_url	☐ tag_list
☐ description	☐ num_identification_agreements	☐ num_identification_disagreements	☐ captive_cultivated
☐ oauth_application_id			

Figure 11-4. Select the columns for the CSV file

Download the CSV files generated from iNaturalist from the preceding queries and save the files to your computer.

Now, using the CSV files we generated, use the Python code in Example 11-3 to download and save the iNaturalist query images to your computer, while also attributing the files we download with the username of the original iNaturalist uploader. Run the script twice, once for your trap animal images, and again for your "unknown" images. Save these files in two different directories, for example */unknown/* and */animal/* (see Example 11-3).

You may also need to install the `requests` package via `pip` if you don't already have it: `python -m pip install requests`.

Example 11-3. Python code to download images from iNaturalist

```
import csv
from pathlib import Path
import requests

directory = Path("unknown")  # Replace directory name, "unknown" or "animal"
directory.mkdir(parents=True, exist_ok=True)

with open("observations-xxx.csv") as f:  # Replace csv filename
    reader = csv.reader(f)
    next(reader, None)  # skip header row
```

```
for data in reader:
    # filename is constructed as id.user_login.extension
    id_, user_login, url = data[0], data[1], data[5]
    extension = Path(url).suffix
    path = directory / f"{id_}.{user_login}{extension}"
    img = requests.get(url).content
    path.write_bytes(img)
```

If you'd like to drop query params in image URLs (as explained above), replace
Path(url).suffix with Path(url.split("?")[0]).suffix.

This script may take a while to run depending on how big your CSV file is and how
many entries resulted from your iNaturalist query. For this use case, I recommend
keeping your iNaturalist query to under 4,000 results. You can reduce the output
of your iNaturalist query by changing the query settings to include only research
quality–grade images, images from a specified place ID, etc. You can find a specific
place ID by going to the iNaturalist website (*https://oreil.ly/SGCIr*) and typing in a
location in the Place textbox of the Identify search bar, then the place ID value will
populate in the URL after pressing Go. For example, New York City has place ID 674:
https://www.inaturalist.org/observations/identify?place_id=674.

Dataset Limitations

Even with a robust dataset acquired from iNaturalist, there are still many limitations
that arise. When a camera records multiple detections of an unmarked animal, one
cannot determine whether the images represent multiple mobile individuals or a
single individual repeatedly entering the camera viewshed.[11]

iNaturalist also tends to prefer images of animals that are close-up/large within the
image frame. This bias of animal images could reduce the accuracy of the resulting
machine learning model in the real world as the close-up images tend to not include
a large background of the surrounding environment, resulting in a model that expects
every animal to be close to the camera lens.

In order to counteract this bias, an "active learning" approach may be necessary in
order to improve the model over time—i.e., initially deploy a subpar model to camera
trap new images of the target creature, store these new images directly on the device
or upload them to a cloud bucket, then confirm the animal is located in these images,
label and upload them to our project's original training dataset, and finally retrain the
model and redeploy to the device.

---

11 See the article by Neil A. Gilbert et al., "Abundance Estimation of Unmarked Animals Based on Camera-Trap
Data" (*https://doi.org/10.1111/cobi.13517*).

Dataset Licensing and Legal Obligations

Upon Edge Impulse account creation, every Edge Impulse user must abide by the following terms of use, licenses, and policies:

- Edge Impulse Privacy Policy (*https://oreil.ly/Ud6ja*)
- Edge Impulse Terms of Service (*https://oreil.ly/0y-PK*)
- Edge Impulse Responsible AI License (*https://oreil.ly/rmeaN*)
- Edge Impulse DMCA (Digital Millennium Copyright Act) Policy (*https://oreil.ly/a6SwO*)

Assuming you are abiding by the above rules and conditions, once you create and deploy your model to your device, you have no subscription or fees; as of writing this book (2022) all free Edge Impulse users are allowed to distribute and deploy their model to an endless amount of devices in production, for free. If your data was originally your own, you maintain your IP throughout the entire life cycle of your edge AI model.

If you are using a dataset downloaded from a third-party site such as iNaturalist, you will need to ensure that the data you have acquired is eligible to be redistributed or used for commercial use. More details about iNaturalist's Terms of Use can be viewed on their website (*https://oreil.ly/Thjyc*).

For any other datasets, please ensure you are acquiring, distributing, and using the data legally, fairly, and ethically. Many dataset collection sites will use licenses such as Creative Commons (*https://oreil.ly/AyCfy*), Apache, etc. You will need to use your best judgment when using these datasets for the purposes of edge machine learning model training and testing. If you have any doubts, email the dataset owner or data collection site support team for more information on data usage requirements or attribution obligations and legal clarification.

Cleaning Your Dataset

Because we have downloaded our image dataset from iNaturalist and thus have already labeled our images with their associated machine learning class, we do not need to do much further dataset cleaning before we upload our images into our Edge Impulse project.

However, if you have a small dataset of *labeled* images and also a larger dataset of associated but *unlabeled* images, Edge Impulse provides a tool called the "data explorer" (*https://oreil.ly/uhD9P*) to allow you to use a pretrained model (see Figure 11-5), a previously trained impulse, or your preprocessing block to bulk label unlabeled images in your training or testing datasets. Of course, this tool will not work if you have not already trained a model on a smaller subset of your data, as unique species names are not pretrained on existing ImageNets like MobileNetV2, for example. You can also select between two different types of dimensionality reductions, t-SNE (works well with smaller datasets) and PCA (works with any dataset size).

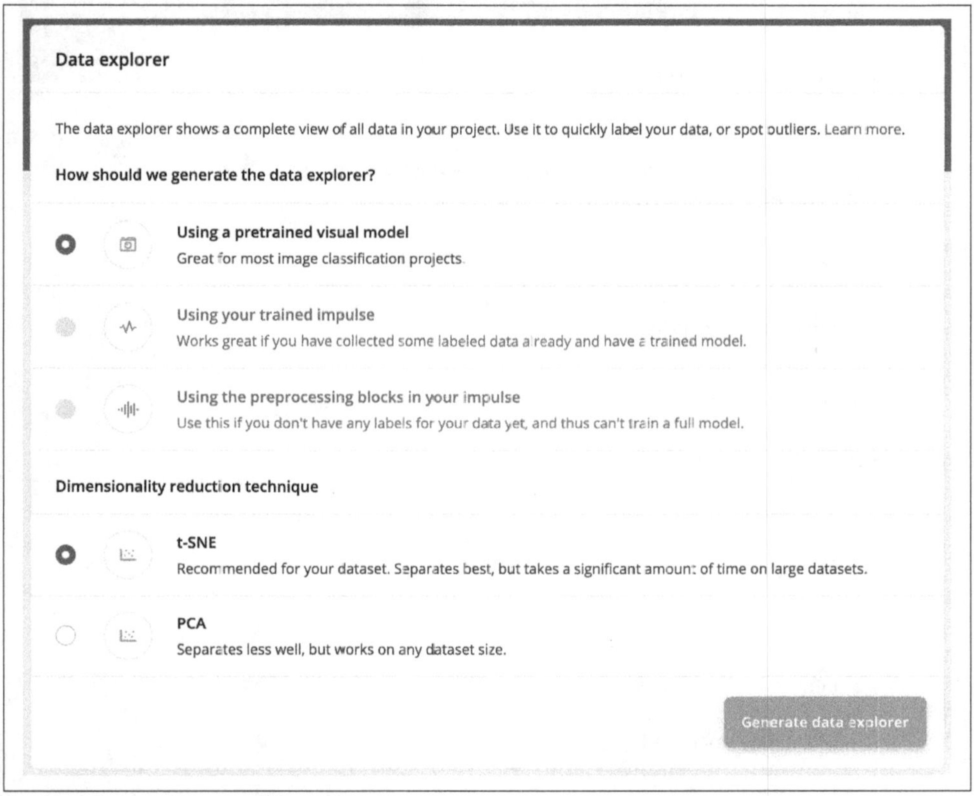

Figure 11-5. Edge Impulse Studio data explorer

Uploading Data to Edge Impulse

Following the iNaturalist Python data downloading script, upload your images to your Edge Impulse project (see Figure 11-6) using the Edge Impulse project web GUI, or with the following Edge Impulse CLI uploader (*https://oreil.ly/l_OQo*) command, and make sure to replace [your-api-key] with the API key of your Edge Impulse project, [label] with "unknown" or the name of your trap animal, and [directory] with the file directory you specified in the iNaturalist Python script:

```
$ edge-impulse-uploader --api-key [your-api-key] --label [label] \
    --category split .[directory]/*
```

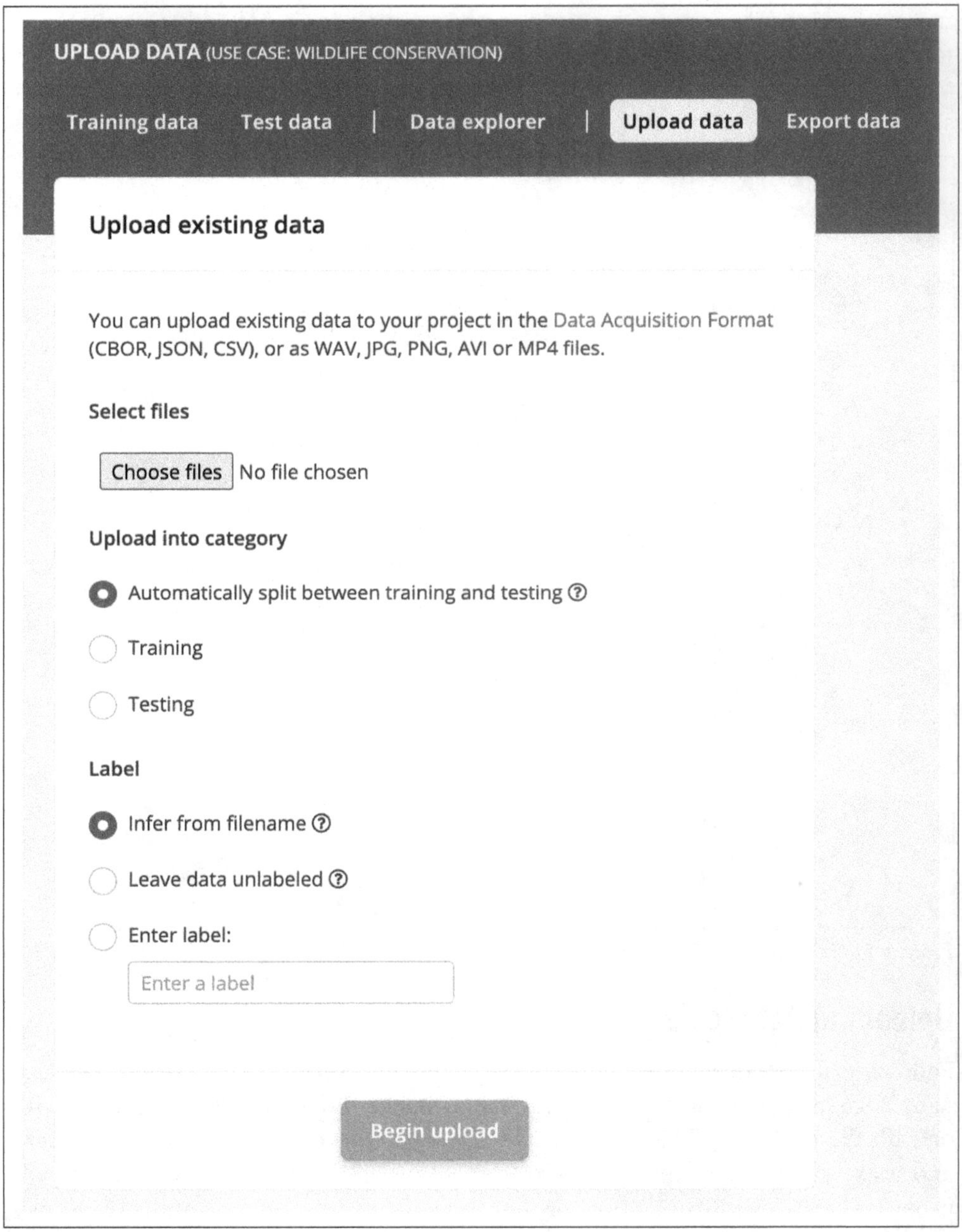

Figure 11-6. Uploading existing dataset into the Edge Impulse web uploader

Both the web GUI and the uploader CLI allow you to automatically split the uploaded images into both the `training` and `testing` datasets at an 80/20 split (a good ratio for most machine learning projects).

DSP and Machine Learning Workflow

Now that we have uploaded all of our images into our training and testing datasets, we need to extract the most important features of our raw data using a digital signal processing (DSP) approach, and then train our machine learning model to identify patterns in our image's extracted features. Edge Impulse calls the DSP and ML training workflow the "Impulse design."

The "Impulse design" tab of your Edge Impulse project allows you to view and create a graphical, simple overview of your full end-to-end machine learning pipeline. On the far left is the raw data block where the Edge Impulse Studio will ingest and preprocess your data; in our case for images it will normalize all our images so they have the same dimensions, and if the dimensions are not square, it will crop the image via your method of choice.

Next is the DSP block, where we will extract the most important features of our images via an open source digital signal processing script. Once we have generated our data's features, the learning block will train our neural network based on our desired architecture and configuration settings.

Finally, we can see the deployment output information, including the desired classes we would like our trained machine learning model to classify.

In your Edge Impulse project, set up your "Impulse design" tab the same as in Figure 11-7, or as listed by selecting from the various block pop-up windows, then click Save Impulse:

Image data
- Image width: 160
- Image height: 160
- Resize mode: Fit shortest axis

Processing block
- Image

Learning block
- Transfer Learning (Images)

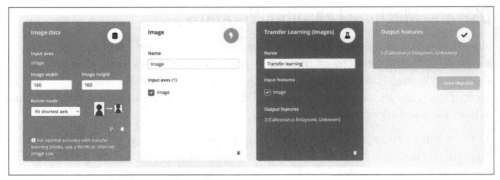

Figure 11-7. Impulse design tab configuration

Digital Signal Processing Block

For the project presented in this chapter, we will be using the Image DSP algorithm that is included by default in the Edge Impulse Studio. This image processing block we selected on the "Impulse design" tab is prewritten and available for free use and free deployment from the platform. The code used in the Image block is available in the Edge Impulse GitHub repository "processing-blocks" (*https://oreil.ly/jjL2E*). You can also learn more about the specifics of the Spectral Analysis algorithm in "Image feature detection" on page 92.

If you would like to write your own custom DSP block for use in the Edge Impulse Studio, it's easy to do so in your language of choice by following the Edge Impulse custom processing blocks tutorial (*https://oreil.ly/Dx2KJ*).

However, if you do decide to write your own custom DSP processing block for your application, note that you will need to then write the corresponding C++ implementation of your custom DSP Python/MATLAB/etc. code in order for your model deployment to work as intended within the Edge Impulse SDK. This is a major advantage of using a readily available DSP block in the Edge Impulse Studio as it reduces the total development time from data collection to feature extraction and then deployment—you do not need to write any of your own custom C++ code on the application side; everything is already integrated within the deployed library and ready for compilation.

From the Image tab in the navigation sidebar, leave the color depth as RGB and click on "Save parameters." Now, select "Generate features" to create a view of the "Feature explorer" (see Figure 11-8).

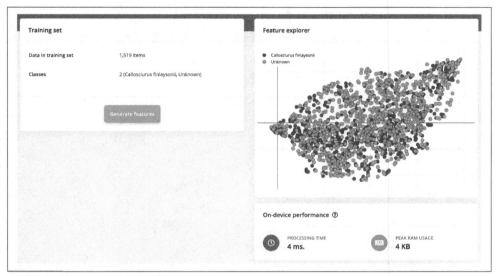

Figure 11-8. Image DSP block and feature explorer

Machine Learning Block

We are now ready to train our edge machine learning model! There are multiple ways to train your model in Edge Impulse, the easiest of which is the visual (or web GUI) editing mode. However, if you are a machine learning engineer, expert, or if you already have experiencing coding with TensorFlow/Keras, then you can also edit your transfer learning block locally or in expert mode within the Edge Impulse Studio.

We can set the neural network architecture and other training configuration settings of our project from the "Transfer learning" tab.

Visual mode

The easiest way to configure and set our machine learning training settings and neural network architecture is through the Edge Impulse Visual mode, or the default view when you select the "Transfer learning" tab under "Impulse design" in the navigation bar. The following settings are automatically applied by default when you save an impulse with the transfer learning block (see Figure 11-9); if these settings differ in your project, go ahead and copy these settings into your transfer learning block configuration:

- Number of training cycles: 100
- Learning rate: 0.0005
- Validation set size: 20%
- Auto-balance dataset: unchecked

- Data augmentation: unchecked
- Neural network architecture: MobileNetV2 96x96 0.35 (final layer: 16 neurons, 0.1 dropout)

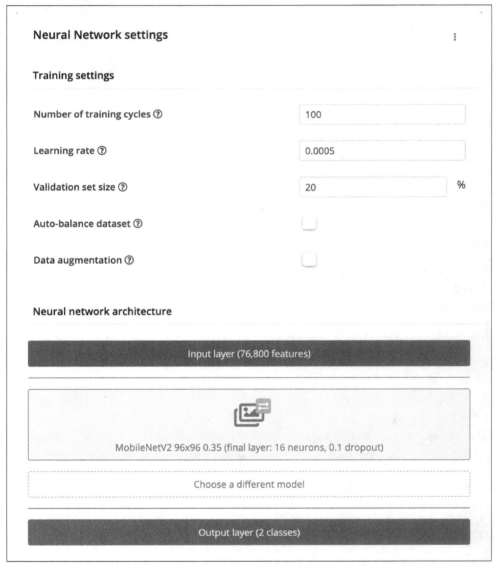

Figure 11-9. Default transfer learning Neural Network settings

Once you have entered the settings, all you need to do is click "Start training" below the neural network architecture configuration to spawn your training job on the Edge Impulse servers. The job that is spawned is training your model exactly how you would normally train your model if you were running a TensorFlow/Keras script locally on your own computer. By using Edge Impulse, we do not need to use up local resources on our own computer, and instead are leveraging the cloud compute time that Edge Impulse offers for free to all developers. Depending on the size of your dataset, this training step may take a while, in which case you can select the bell icon on the "Training output" view to get an email notification when your job has completed and you can see the output of the training results (see Figures 11-10 and 11-11).

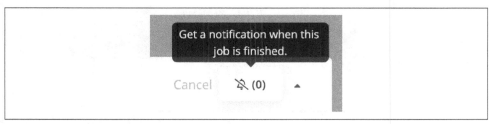

Figure 11-10. Training job notification bell icon

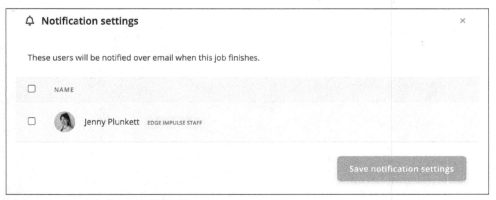

Figure 11-11. Configure job notification settings

Once your model training has completed, you can view the transfer learning results in the "Model > Last training performance" view (see Figure 11-12).

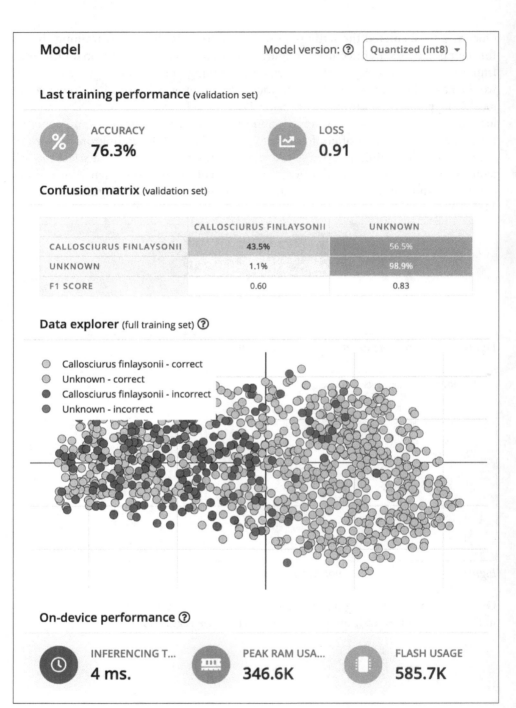

Figure 11-12. Transfer learning results from default block configuration (76.3% accuracy)

Considering that all we have done so far is upload our training and testing datasets, extracted the most important features with the image DSP block, and trained our model all with the default block configuration settings and without writing any code, these results are pretty decent! The result of 76.3% is a fairly good initial accuracy considering we haven't done any custom configuration to our neural network architecture, DSP block, etc., for our specific use case. However, we can further increase the accuracy of our model by using the other tools available in Edge Impulse, such as the EON Tuner, which we will describe in the next section.

Expert Mode

Are you a machine learning engineer, or do you already know how to write TensorFlow/Keras code in Python? Use the Expert mode option in Edge Impulse to upload your own code or edit the existing block code locally by clicking the three-dot drop-down button to the right of "Neural Network settings" and selecting "Switch to Expert (Keras) mode" (*https://oreil.ly/wpEzB*) or "Edit block locally" (*https://oreil.ly/sYSIP*) from the menu.

EON Tuner

Auto machine learning tools are valuable tools that can automatically select and apply the best machine learning algorithms for your data and automatically tune the parameters of your machine learning model, which can further improve its performance on the edge device. The Edge Impulse Studio provides an auto machine learning tool in your project, called the EON Tuner. The EON Tuner will evaluate many candidate model architectures and DSP blocks (selected based on your target device and latency requirements) concurrently to help you find the best performing architecture for your machine learning application.

From the EON Tuner tab of your Edge Impulse project, configure the settings shown in Figure 11-13.

Select the following options from the EON Tuner's configuration drop-down settings:

- Dataset category: Vision
- Target device: Cortex-M7 (or any other supported platform; if you are not using an officially supported platform, choose a platform with hardware internals most similar to that of your device)
- Time per inference (ms): 100

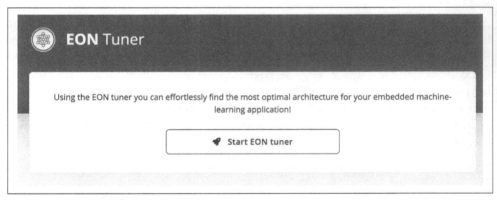

Figure 11-13. EON Tuner configuration settings

Then click "Start EON tuner," as shown in Figure 11-14.

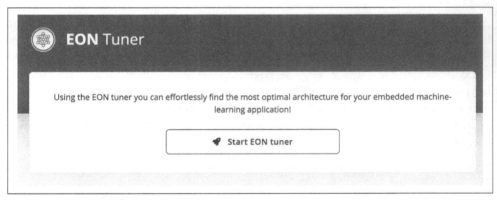

Figure 11-14. Start the EON Tuner

When comparing the results of the EON Tuner with the default image classification blocks included in a default Edge Impulse project, we can see a vast difference between them. With auto machine learning tools we can more quickly and efficiently determine better performing neural network architectures, DSP blocks, parameters, and more for our use case.

Figure 11-15 shows the default block results with the Image RGB DSP block and the original "Transfer learning" neural network block with MobileNetV2 96x96 0.35 (final layer: 16 neurons, 0.1 dropout), 100 training cycles, and 0.0005 learning rate.

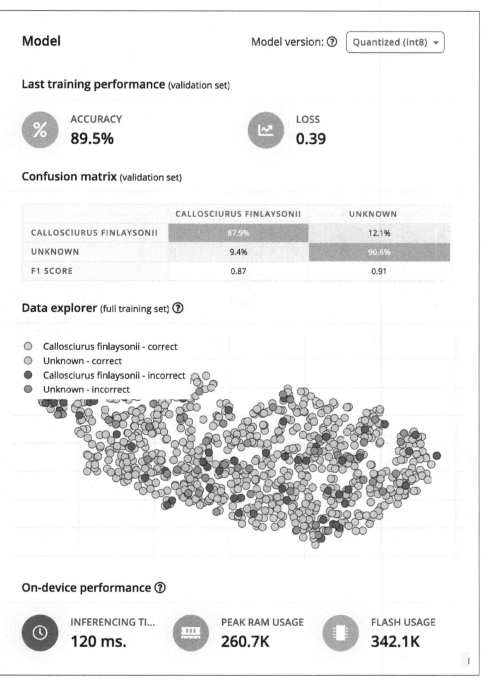

Model

Model version: ⑦ [Quantized (int8) ▾]

Last training performance (validation set)

% ACCURACY
89.5%

⌇ LOSS
0.39

Confusion matrix (validation set)

	CALLOSCIURUS FINLAYSONII	UNKNOWN
CALLOSCIURUS FINLAYSONII	87.9%	12.1%
UNKNOWN	9.4%	90.6%
F1 SCORE	0.87	0.91

Data explorer (full training set) ⑦

- ○ Callosciurus finlaysonii - correct
- ○ Unknown - correct
- ● Callosciurus finlaysonii - incorrect
- ● Unknown - incorrect

On-device performance ⑦

🕐 INFERENCING TI...
120 ms.

▥ PEAK RAM USAGE
260.7K

▯ FLASH USAGE
342.1K

Figure 11-15. Transfer learning results with EON Tuner block configuration (89.5% accuracy)

Once the EON Tuner auto machine learning job has completed, we can see the results. For the EON Tuner results shown in Figure 11-16, the first result achieves an accuracy of 90%; however, we will not select this model as the RAM and ROM both exceed our target's hardware specifications. So, the result we will select is the second best option, at 89% accuracy.

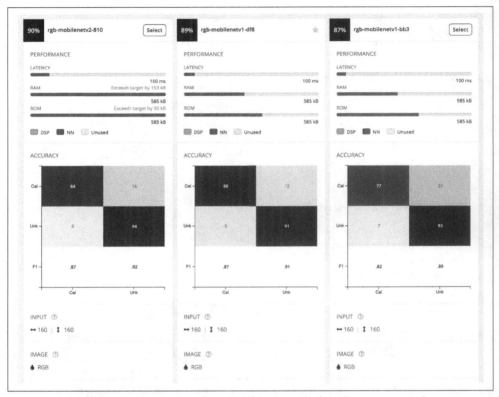

Figure 11-16. EON Tuner results matrix (the best result that does not exceed target RAM has 89% accuracy)

Based on these results, we definitely will want to update the primary block information with the blocks generated automatically for our use case with the EON Tuner. Next to the configuration with the best accuracy, click the Select button and update the primary model, as shown in Figure 11-17.

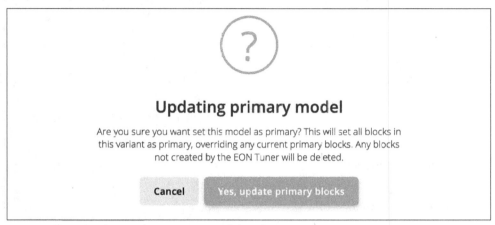

Updating primary model

Are you sure you want set this model as primary? This will set all blocks in this variant as primary, overriding any current primary blocks. Any blocks not created by the EON Tuner will be deleted.

Cancel   Yes, update primary blocks

Figure 11-17. Updating the primary model with EON Tuner

Wait for the Studio to update the "Impulse design" blocks in your project (see Figure 11-18), then click on "Transfer learning" and see your updated trained model results, accuracy, and latency calculations, as shown in Figure 11-19.

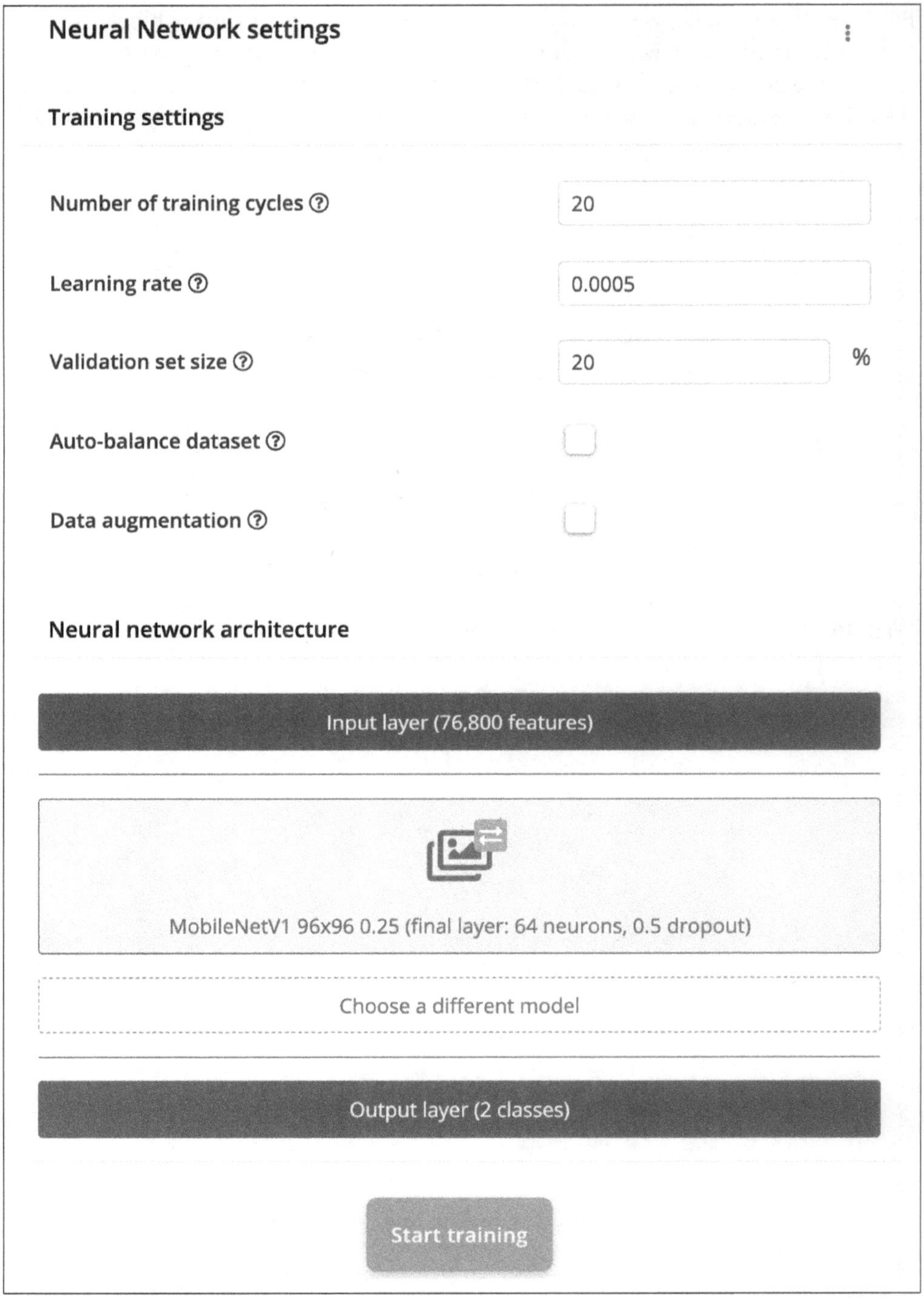

Neural Network settings

Training settings

Number of training cycles ⑦   20

Learning rate ⑦   0.0005

Validation set size ⑦   20   %

Auto-balance dataset ⑦

Data augmentation ⑦

Neural network architecture

Input layer (76,800 features)

MobileNetV1 96x96 0.25 (final layer: 64 neurons, 0.5 dropout)

Choose a different model

Output layer (2 classes)

Start training

Figure 11-18. EON Tuner Neural Network settings

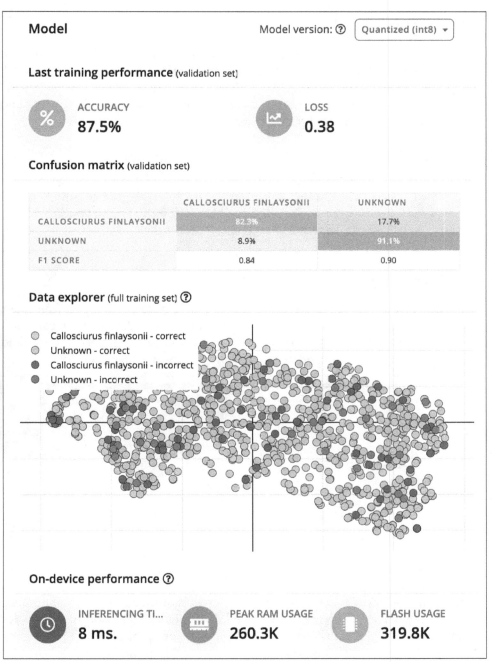

Figure 11-19. Primary transfer learning model updated with EON Tuner

Testing the Model

Edge Impulse provides multiple types of testing and verification tools to increase your confidence in the real-world accuracy of your trained machine learning model, or impulse. After you have finished training your impulse, on the navigation bar of your project, you can access the "Live classification" (*https://oreil.ly/lBG87*) and "Model testing" (*https://oreil.ly/gO2EL*) tabs.

Testing Your Audio Models with Performance Calibration

If you developed an audio trap, as described in "Deep Dive: Bird Sound Classification Demo with Lacuna Space" on page 402, then you can also use Performance Calibration (*https://oreil.ly/B3eQh*) model testing and real-world performance tuner in your Edge Impulse project.

Live Classification

From the "Live classification" tab, you can test individual test samples from your testing dataset against your trained model or connect your device and record new images and test samples in real time, then view the image's extracted features and resulting classification result and inferencing predictions (see Figure 11-20).

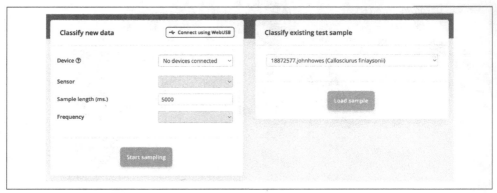

Figure 11-20. Live classification

Connect an officially supported device to the "Live classification" tab via the installed Edge Impulse device firmware, or via the Edge Impulse CLI data forwarder; for example, connect an Arduino Nano 33 BLE Sense to your project to take new testing images in the device's environment via the following CLI command: `edge-impulse-daemon`. Follow the CLI prompts to connect your device to your project and record new samples.

Or load an existing testing dataset image in "Classify existing test sample" to view this sample's extracted features and your trained model's prediction results (as shown in Figure 11-21).

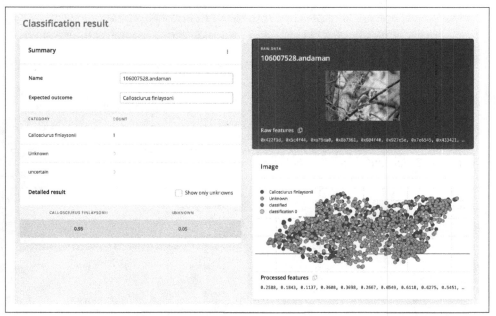

Figure 11-21. Live classification result

Model Testing

You can also bulk classify your testing dataset against your trained model by navigating to the "Model testing" (*https://oreil.ly/gPhj3*) tab of your project (see Figure 11-23). From here, you can select the "Classify all" button to automatically collect your testing data's inferencing results and model predictions in one long table. You can also set the confidence threshold (shown in Figure 11-22) for your model's inferencing results here by clicking on the three-dot drop-down button "Set confidence thresholds." The threshold score determines how to trust the trained neural network. If the confidence rating is below the value you set, the sample will be tagged as "uncertain." You can use inferencing results with "uncertain" to increase the accuracy of your model even further with an "active learning" model development strategy; upload these uncertain images, label them, retrain your model, and redeploy to your edge device! See Figure 11-23 for the model testing results.

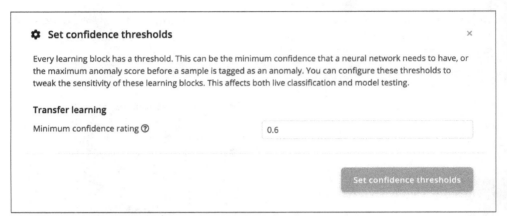

Figure 11-22. Set confidence thresholds

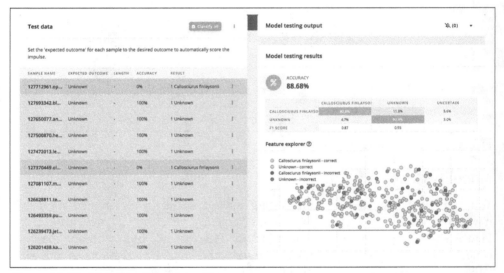

Figure 11-23. Model testing tab results

Test Your Model Locally

You can also download all of the intermediate block results and trained model information to test your model locally through any method you desire—i.e., with a Python script to test your model as you normally would for a TensorFlow/Keras workflow. Navigate to the Dashboard of your Edge Impulse project to view all of the block output files available, as shown in Figure 11-24.

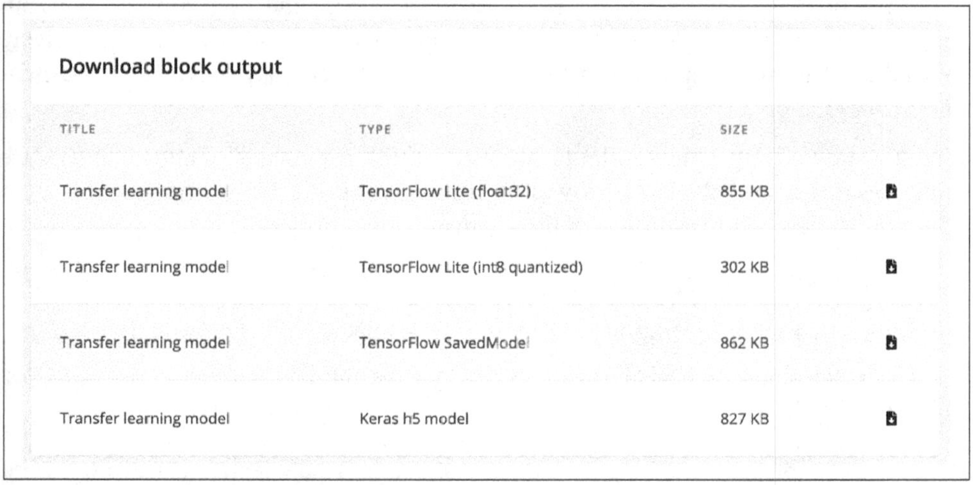

Download block output			
TITLE	TYPE	SIZE	
Transfer learning model	TensorFlow Lite (float32)	855 KB	
Transfer learning model	TensorFlow Lite (int8 quantized)	302 KB	
Transfer learning model	TensorFlow SavedModel	862 KB	
Transfer learning model	Keras h5 model	827 KB	

Figure 11-24. Download block output

Deployment

Congratulations! You have just finished collecting and labeling your training and testing datasets, extracting your data's features with the DSP block, designing and training your machine learning model, and testing your model with your testing dataset. Now that we have all of the code and model information needed for inferencing on our edge device, we need to flash the prebuilt binary to the device or integrate the C++ library into our embedded application code.

Select the Deployment tab of your Edge Impulse project and follow the steps for one of the many deployment options in the next sections to run your trained machine learning model on your edge device.

Create Library

For a simple development experience, Edge Impulse provides many prewritten code examples for integrating your deployed model into your embedded application firmware. Using an officially supported development board will allow for the quickest deployment and least amount of development time, as you will be able to drag-and-drop the resulting prebuilt firmware application onto your development board, or clone the board's open source firmware repository from the Edge Impulse GitHub organization (*https://oreil.ly/rH9iO*), which contains all device firmware and drivers needed in order to get started quickly with your embedded application development and debugging process.

If you are deploying your model to an "unofficially supported" platform, there are many resources available to help you with integrating the Edge Impulse SDK into your application code, regardless of library deployment option:

- Prebuilt Edge Impulse firmwares (*https://oreil.ly/V3eRI*)
- Integrating the Edge Impulse SDK into your application (*https://oreil.ly/yAlgD*)
- Understanding the C++ library code and getting model inference results (*https://oreil.ly/-gPy_*)

A majority of projects utilizing an "unofficially supported" device will deploy using the C++ library option available under the "Create library" view of your project's Deployment tab (see Figure 11-25). The C++ library is portable, with no external dependencies, and can be compiled with any modern C++ compiler.

Custom Processing Blocks

If you decided to use your own custom DSP block in your Edge Impulse Studio project, you will need to write the DSP block's equivalent C++ implementation and integrate this into the Edge Impulse SDK code. More information can be found in the Edge Impulse documentation (*https://oreil.ly/t1K1_*).

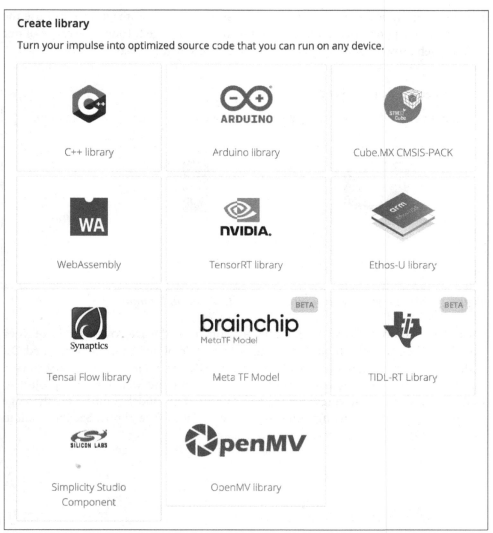

Create library

Turn your impulse into optimized source code that you can run on any device.

C++ library	Arduino library	Cube.MX CMSIS-PACK
WebAssembly	TensorRT library	Ethos-U library
Tensai Flow library	Meta TF Model	TIDL-RT Library
Simplicity Studio Component	OpenMV library	

Figure 11-25. Create an open source library

Mobile Phone and Computer

Quickly deploy your model to the edge with your computer or mobile phone by clicking the Edge Impulse "Computer" and "Mobile phone" deployment options. These deployment options utilize an open source mobile client firmware (*https:// oreil.ly/4-S9S*) that builds a WebAssembly library for your trained impulse to classify brand-new data directly from the camera on your phone or computer. This option is great for quick model prototyping and testing, since you do not need to write any code for this deployment option if you are using a default/integrated sensor type in your training/testing datasets.

For this project, because our training and testing data is just images, we can use the camera on our phone to test our model directly on the edge through the cache of our phone's web browser and integrated camera data (see Figure 11-26).

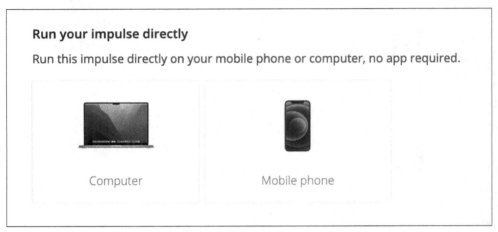

Run your impulse directly

Run this impulse directly on your mobile phone or computer, no app required.

Computer   Mobile phone

Figure 11-26. Run your impulse directly (mobile phone and computer)

Select the "Computer" or "Mobile phone" icon from the Deployment tab of your project, and click Build. If you are using your mobile phone, scan the generated QR code with your phone's camera and open the URL in your phone's web browser. Give the mobile client access to your phone's camera and wait for your project to build. Now you are viewing your trained camera trap model running on the edge and printing your inferencing results directly on your mobile phone! See the result in Figure 11-27.

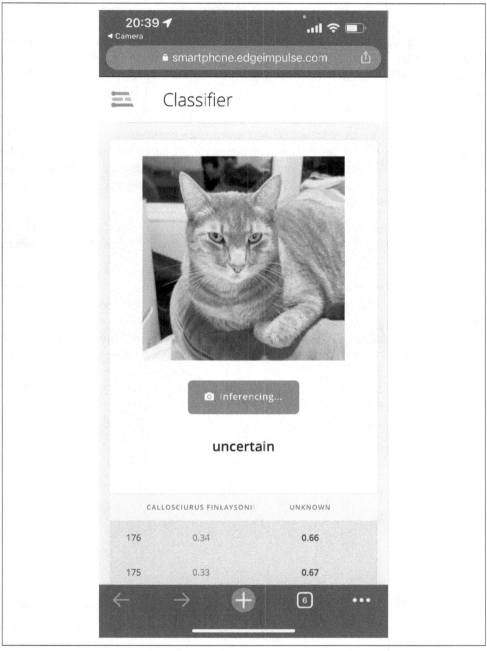

Figure 11-27. Camera trap model running on mobile phone deployment

Prebuilt Binary Flashing

From the Deployment tab, select your officially supported Edge Impulse development platform under "Build firmware" and then select Build. You also have the option to utilize the EON Compiler, which lets you run neural networks using 25–55% less RAM, and up to 35% less flash, while retaining the same accuracy, compared to TensorFlow Lite for Microcontrollers.[12]

Then, drag-and-drop or flash the resulting firmware application onto your officially supported platform by following the instructions shown after clicking Build from the Deployment tab. More in-depth instructions for flashing your prebuilt binary can be found in the Edge Impulse documentation for your chosen development platform (*https://oreil.ly/llg9B*).

For this project, we will select the "OpenMV Library" deployment option to run our trained model on the OpenMV Cam H7 Plus (*https://oreil.ly/EfJwe*), shown earlier in Figure 11-25.

Follow the instructions in the OpenMV deployment documentation on the Edge Impulse website (*https://oreil.ly/82tKN*) to download and install software prerequisites. Then extract the downloaded ZIP file of your model firmware and drag-and-drop or copy the *labels.txt* and *trained.tflite* files into the filesystem of your plugged-in OpenMV Cam H7 Plus. Open the *ei_image_classification.py* script in the OpenMV IDE. Connect to your OpenMV Cam board via the USB icon and run the Python script to see your model's inferencing results running on the edge in the serial terminal view, as shown in Figure 11-28.

---

12 See Jan Jongboom's blog post, "Introducing EON: Neural Networks in Up to 55% Less RAM and 35% Less ROM" (*https://oreil.ly/3-kTN*) (Edge Impulse, 2020).

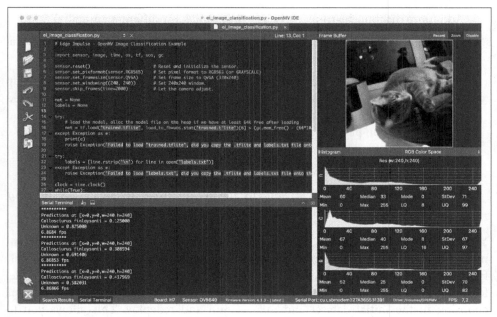

Figure 11-28. OpenMV IDE model deployment to OpenMV Cam H7 Plus

Impulse Runner

You can also use the Edge Impulse CLI (*https://oreil.ly/KVUJf*) to download, deploy, and run your models continuously through a USB serial connection to an officially supported platform of your choosing. Or use the Edge Impulse Linux runner (*https://oreil.ly/SJZex*) to download, deploy, and run the Edge Impulse model on a Raspberry Pi 4 or other Linux device.

GitHub Source Code

The application source code used in this chapter, including the deployed library from the public Edge Impulse project (*https://oreil.ly/I_EIA*) and completed application code, is available to view and download from the GitHub repository (*https://oreil.ly/rmE7-*).

Iterate and Feedback Loops

Now that you have deployed the first iteration of your wildlife monitoring model to the edge, you may be satisfied with the results and discontinue development here. However, if you wish to further iterate over your model and further improve the accuracy over time or with newly acquired equipment upgrades, for example, there are many adaptations and variations to consider and improve upon for this project:

- Add more machine learning classes to your model for different animal(s).

- Create a camera trap for invasive plant species instead of animals: for local gardening/foraging purposes, etc.

- Use different sensors to achieve the same goal—i.e., a wildlife conservation trap using a gas sensor or switching your camera training data input from labeled images to bounding boxes for species object detection (see "Object detection and segmentation" on page 97).

- Use the same model to achieve a *different* goal or place it in a different environment, refining the "unknown" class.

- Utilize a combination of sensors to further improve the accuracy of your model—i.e., camera + audio input, audio + gas input, etc.

You can also create multiple projects in Edge Impulse, to create many different machine learning models for multiple device locations, multiple datasets, and classifying other trap animals. For example, you can use the same Sahara desert model for multiple animal species, and just swap out the main species for another of your choosing in the initial dataset and then retrain and redeploy. This allows you to utilize the same model configuration as you used for one environment on another.

Deep Dive: Bird Sound Classification Demo with Lacuna Space

Following is an interesting demo of using bird sounds to classify and track specific species of birds throughout the world using space satellites and LoRaWAN, created by Edge Impulse and Lacuna Space (*https://lacuna.space*) (see Figure 11-29).[13]

Using a web tracker, you can determine the next good time a Lacuna Space satellite will be flying in your device's location, then you can receive the signal through The Things Network (*https://www.thethingsnetwork.org*) application and view the model's inferencing results for bird call classification in your device's environment:

```
{
    "housesparrow": "0.91406",
    "redringedparakeet": "0.05078",
    "noise": "0.03125",
    "satellite": true,
}
```

---

13 See Aurelien Lequertier et al. blog post: "Bird Classification in Remote Areas with Lacuna Space and The Things Network" (*https://oreil.ly/4Rneh*), Edge Impulse, 2021.

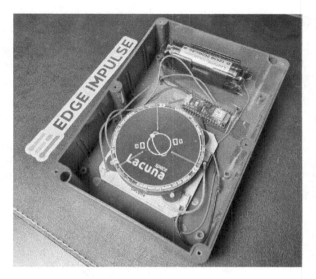

Figure 11-29. Lacuna Space demo

You can check out the training/testing data, digital signal processing code, and machine learning code used for this project by navigating to the Edge Impulse "Bird sound classifier" project page (*https://oreil.ly/Vf4Q0*).

A downside to this solution is that, although you are able to identify and monitor the classified birdcalls in your device's environment, you are only able to receive the general classification data using this approach and not any accurate location or tracking/counting data of specific singular birds. Therefore, this method is likely more effective in tracking whole species, migration patterns, and seasonal identification data rather than as a method for preventing overhunting, analyzing the impact of the species' invasive threats, etc.

AI for Good

Throughout this book, we have discussed the importance of using the machine learning tools and knowledge described here in an ethical fashion. Many companies have already put the idea of "technology for good" to use—from Edge Impulse to Google, many environmental/wildlife conservation efforts and pledges have been established:

- 1% for the Planet (*https://oreil.ly/_xwYK*)
- Edge Impulse's commitment (*https://oreil.ly/CRH0m*) to 1% for the Planet
- Google, "Tale of a Whale Song" (*https://oreil.ly/wtIpX*)
- Microsoft, AI for Good (*https://oreil.ly/o0TGV*)

Related Works

As stated throughout this chapter, camera traps and conservation traps are an established, known, and widely adopted device in research efforts and in ethical hunting practices. The next sections describe various devices, datasets, research articles, and books on the topic of ethical camera trapping for the problem of decreasing populations of various endangered species and the resulting protection of existing populations.

This book also notes the sources for various applications, methods, devices, and quotes from various research and commercial adoption of camera traps throughout the chapter in the footnotes on each page.

Datasets

There are many existing datasets and dataset collection platforms available for this type of use case on the internet. A simple Google search can yield many results; however, a few more data collection platforms and research datasets for our use case have been listed below:

- Kaggle Invasive Species Monitoring Competition (*https://oreil.ly/H4Y3N*)
- Invasive Alien Plant dataset (*https://oreil.ly/xfBKr*)
- iWildcam 2021 (*https://oreil.ly/76OW4*)
- Labeled Information Library of Alexandria: Biology and Conservation; list of other conservation datasets (*https://oreil.ly/-IUvi*)
- Caltech-UCSD Birds-200-2011, classification of birds by camera (*https://oreil.ly/lLU00*)
- Caltech Camera Traps (*https://oreil.ly/boZ8q*)

Again, be mindful that you are using each dataset for ethical purposes and ensure that your model's target species is not considered endangered or threatened in your device's installed location/region.

Research

- Ahumada, Jorge A. et al. *Wildlife Insights: A Platform to Maximize the Potential of Camera Trap and Other Passive Sensor Wildlife Data for the Planet* (*https://doi.org/10.1017/S0376892919000298*). Cambridge University Press, 2019.
- Apps, Peter, and John Weldon McNutt. "Are Camera Traps Fit for Purpose? A Rigorous, Reproducible and Realistic Test of Camera Trap Performance" (*https://doi.org/10.1111/aje.12573*). Wiley Online Library, 2018.

- Fischer, Johannes H. et al. "The Potential Value of Camera-Trap Studies for Identifying, Ageing, Sexing and Studying the Phenology of Bornean Lophura Pheasants" (*https://oreil.ly/udikH*). ResearchGate, 2017.

- Jang, Woohyuk, and Eui Chul Lee. "Multi-Class Parrot Image Classification Including Subspecies with Similar Appearance" (*https://doi.org/10.3390/biology10111140*). MDPI, November 5, 2021.

- O'Brien, Timothy G., and Margaret F. Kinnaird. *A Picture Is Worth a Thousand Words: The Application of Camera Trapping to the Study of Birds* (*https://doi.org/10.1017/S0959270908000348*). Cambridge University Press, 2008.

- O'Connell, Allan F. et al., eds. *Camera Traps in Animal Ecology: Methods and Analyses* (*https://doi.org/10.1007/978-4-431-99495-4*). Springer Tokyo, 2011.

- Rovero, Francesco et al. "Which Camera Trap Type and How Many Do I Need?" (*https://doi.org/10.4404/hystrix-24.2-8789*) *Hystrix* 24 (2013).

- Shepley, Andrew et al. "Automated Location Invariant Animal Detection in Camera Trap Images Using Publicly Available Data Sources" (*https://oreil.ly/FUEJN*). ResearchGate, 2021.

## CHAPTER 12

Use Case: Food Quality Assurance

Industrial edge AI is used in food quality assurance to automatically detect and correct food defects and prevent food spoilage. This is done by training a machine learning model to recognize patterns in food images or from various industrial sensors that indicate a defect. The model is then deployed on an edge device, such as a camera, to automatically detect and correct defects in real time. This helps to ensure that food is of the highest quality and minimizes waste.

By using edge AI, food waste can be prevented by monitoring and managing food production and distribution more effectively. For example, if there is a problem with food spoilage, edge AI can be used to track the problem and take corrective action. In this chapter, we will brainstorm various approaches to using edge AI for food quality assurance purposes, their associated sensor and device configurations, and a deep dive tutorial into our selected approach and use case solution.

Problem Exploration

The term "food quality assurance" is too broad of a concept to tackle in this one chapter and too large of a problem to be solved with just one machine learning model; so for the purposes of this book, we will focus on food quality assurance in terms of preventing and minimizing food waste in a home kitchen environment, on a food product manufacturing line, or in cold storage/pantry shelving at a grocery store.

Preventing food waste can come in many different forms. Goal-wise we can both generate a machine learning model that can identify when a food item is about to spoil or has already spoiled, or we can create a model that identifies factors in the food manufacturing environment or product mishandling that will tend to the creation of foodborne illnesses. Both of these approaches accomplish the same goal, preventing and minimizing food waste, but could require a different combination of machine learning classes and sensor inputs in order to solve.

Deploying edge AI devices in smart factories can also lead to higher productivity and improved quality. Introducing AI into the manufacturing process can help to reduce errors and save time and money. By using a smartphone connected to the cloud, quality-control personnel can monitor the manufacturing process from anywhere. By applying machine learning algorithms, manufacturers can detect errors immediately.[1]

Solution Exploration

Industry 4.0, or the colloquial term for the "Fourth Industrial Revolution," conceptualizes a rapid change to technology, industries, and societal patterns and processes in the 21st century due to increasing interconnectivity and smart automation.[2]

Major Trends of Industry 4.0

- Smart factory
- Predictive maintenance
- 3D printing
- Smart sensors (agriculture and food industries)

Edge AI is being used more and more for food quality assurance as AI can help to inspect food for contaminants, test food for quality, and even predict food safety issues before they happen. Food quality assurance is a process that helps to ensure that the food we consume is safe and of high quality. This process includes a variety of steps, such as inspecting food for contaminants, testing food for quality, and maintaining clean and safe food-handling practices. By following these steps, we can help to ensure that the food we eat is safe and of good quality.

We can begin to intuitively think about how to apply edge AI and machine learning to the problem of food quality assurance by thinking about and researching the existing issues and factors that contribute to food spoilage, allergens, cross-contamination manufacturing processes, and more. By diving into these existing areas of research and industries, many problems will arise that have associated sensors and machinery. By simply tapping into existing sensors or adding a small, minimally invasive microcontroller onto an existing machinery structure we can identify new patterns in established datasets and sensor configurations, or even create a brand new sensor (a

---

1 See the IBM article, "What Is Industry 4.0?: How Industry 4.0 Technologies Are Changing Manufacturing" (*https://oreil.ly/ZMhe7*).

2 See the Wikipedia entry "Fourth Industrial Revolution" (*https://oreil.ly/39viN*).

"virtual sensor") through a concept called "sensor fusion" (see "Combining Features and Sensors" on page 93).

Goal Setting

Food safety is important because it helps to ensure that the food we consume is free of harmful contaminants. These contaminants can come from a variety of sources, including bacteria, viruses, and chemicals. By following food safety guidelines, we can help to reduce our risk of becoming sick from eating contaminated food through foodborne illnesses.

Factors of Food Spoilage

There are many factors that can contribute to food spoilage, including bacteria, viruses, fungi, chemicals, and other various environmental factors, including:

- External heat/cold
- Internal temperature
- Oxygen
- Salt
- Humidity
- Waste exposure
- Moisture
- Light
- Protozoa

AI tools for food quality assurance are important in order to ensure the health of workers on food production lines and the consumer that purchases the food product, and to reduce overall food waste and minimize climate change and negative effects on the environment. Food quality assurance edge AI also represents an opportunity to explore other meaningful social impact areas, such as assisting those with food allergies to determine which foods are safe to eat or not depending on their own personalized allergy matrix.

Solution Design

In this book, we are choosing to design and implement a low-cost, efficient, and easy-to-train food quality assurance edge AI model to reduce food waste with a microcontroller with a gas sensor attachment. However, an edge AI model for detecting food spoilage does not only need to be created with a gas sensor. By using the principles and design workflow presented in this chapter and throughout the book, many other types of machine learning models and applications can be implemented for food quality assurance purposes, including using camera image input to monitor food safety regulations and equipment, identifying various foodborne diseases or allergens with various environmental sensors, and more.

What Solutions Already Exist?

Food quality assurance has been and will continue to be a top priority for many companies; for a grocery store that relies on a volatile food product to be sold before it hits its sell-by date or before it spoils or gets stale, any technology or solution that can help improve profits and reduce food waste is a high value investment. Uber has taken AI advances in stride as well to circumvent food delivery losses with Michelangelo, Uber's machine learning platform (*https://oreil.ly/dtgfZ*). This model predicts the meal estimated time of delivery and assists both the delivery drivers and the restaurant with real-time feedback and estimation calculations on each part of the process to get the Uber Eats user's order from the restaurant's kitchen to their home.

Local governments also have a large stake in preventing and reducing the amount of food that is wasted every day. The Food and Agriculture Organization of the United Nations (*https://oreil.ly/RFgSO*) estimates that 1.3 billion tons of food is wasted every year, nearly one-third of all food produced.[3] This is enough food to feed 815 million people, four times over.[4]

Food quality assurance concepts and AI solutions are also being applied to products that help people who suffer from various food-related allergies. The world's smallest and fastest consumer food allergen sensor, Allergy Amulet (*https://oreil.ly/ECfGo*), allows the end user to collect a sample of their food, and within seconds, receive a report if a food allergen is present.

Solution Design Approaches

We can take our problem statement and design a solution via many different approaches, a few of which we describe here:

Detecting food spoilage, for consumer or industrial use
> A gas sensor is a device that can detect the presence of various gases in the air. It is often used in industrial settings to monitor for hazardous gases. However, it can also be used to detect when meat or fish, or other particularly smelly/gaseous food products are about to spoil. Combined with edge AI, a food spoilage device

---

3 Pini Mandel, "Putting the AI in Grocery Aisles" (*https://oreil.ly/WrkjE*), *Food Logistics*, 2021.

4 Food Loss and Waste Database (*https://oreil.ly/xe0z6*).

is a great tool for both industrial and home contexts in order to minimize food waste and prevent foodborne illness.

Installing a gas sensor inside of a fridge or on a food production line allows the user of the AI device to gain insight as quickly as possible about their food's spoilage status. The sensor could work by detecting the levels of carbon dioxide, ammonia, or other gases in the air that are produced when meat or fish starts to spoil. By detecting these gases early on, the sensor can alert the user or factory worker to dispose of the food before it has a chance to contaminate other products.

Monitoring food safety compliance

In the food industry, safety and compliance is a top priority and is commonly regulated by local governments. One way to protect the end consumer is to ensure that all humans on food packaging lines are wearing adequate food safety apparel, such as white coats, hairnets, goggles, and gloves. A computer vision model can be used to track this information and identify any anomalies. Additionally, audio data can be used to listen for any unusual sounds that may indicate a problem with the food preparation process.

In addition to monitoring adequate production line apparel, a model can also be developed to track handwashing to ensure that all workers are following proper safety and health protocol. This can be done with audio or other sensor data. By tracking these data points, we can help to ensure a safe and efficient food manufacturing process.

Monitoring quality control of food production

Food adulteration and consumer deception is an unfortunate reality in the modern world. Adulteration with cheaper or lower-quality oils, for example, has a huge impact on the quality of oil in the product; with olive oils, the most frequent adulterations are sunflower oil, maize oil, coconut oil, and hazelnut oil. In order to combat this, the use of e-noses in this part of processing is a game changer in terms of quality checks.[5]

We can also monitor the temperature of food throughout the production pipeline, from production time to packaging to eventual store shelving, or from delivery car to customer, etc. It is also important to monitor freezer and refrigerator temperature over time and how it affects product quality (number of ice crystals, freezer burn, etc.), as well as the spoilable status of foods, whether they are past sell-by date or if the food is identified to be rotten. By implementing these various quality-control measures, we can help ensure that the food we consume is of the highest possible quality.

---

5 Ilker Koksal, "Using AI to Increase Food Quality" (*https://oreil.ly/kvHri*), *Forbes*, 2021.

Detecting cross-contamination and food allergens

Allergens like nuts and gluten can cause serious reactions in some people, and even death. Factory machines can sometimes break, and pieces of metal can end up in the food. Human handling of food can also introduce contaminants like bacteria. There are a few ways to detect if allergens have come into contact with food items. The first is to check for any signs of contamination. This can be done by looking for any changes in color, texture, or smell. If the food item looks or smells different than it did when it was first packaged, it may be contaminated.[6]

So how can we detect these potential problems? There are several ways. First, we can look for signs of allergens in the food. If we see nuts or gluten listed as ingredients, for example, we know that they may be present in the food. We can also look for signs of metal contamination, like small pieces of metal in the food. Finally, we can look for signs of human contamination, like the lack of gloves or other protective gear.

Any one of the previously described use case solution approaches can help to ensure that the food we eat is safe and free of contaminants, promoting this chapter's use case goal of reducing food waste, ensuring overall food quality, and increasing the welfare of the consumer and production line worker.

Design Considerations

To achieve the overarching goal of preventing and minimizing food waste and improving food production/storage quality control and safety concerns, from a technological standpoint, we can use a wide variety of data sources, including many different types of sensors and cameras (see Table 12-1) to accomplish a similar goal (reducing food waste and improving food safety).

Table 12-1. Sensors to accomplish various food quality assurance goals

Goal	Sensor(s)
Identifying food packaging leaks	Gas, moisture, water level, camera
Inspecting food for contaminants or foreign objects	Camera
Food doneness and quality control	Camera, temperature, gas
Detecting food spoilage	Environmental, chemical, camera
Identifying food allergens	Environmental, chemical, gas
Human food safety equipment/apparel identification	Camera, audio
Detecting packaging expiration dates	Camera
Packaging line cross-contamination	Camera, chemical, thermal camera, X-ray, infrared, gas

---

6 Nicholas J. Watson et al., "Intelligent Sensors for Sustainable Food and Drink Manufacturing" (*https://oreil.ly/weN5Q*), *Frontiers in Sustainable Food Systems*.

When choosing your food quality assurance goal and use case, you will also need to take into consideration how easy it will be to collect a large, robust, and high-quality dataset for training your machine learning model. As we found in previous chapters (especially in Chapter 7), your model is only as good as the quality of your input data. If you wish to create a model to identify food safety apparel and equipment in a specific factory, you may not be able to procure a sufficiently large enough dataset to successfully train a highly accurate classification model on the first try. Of course, with techniques like "active learning," a subpar accuracy model can be deployed to your factory, and over time the model can be improved upon with new ingested data, and other environmental background information of the device's location.

Also, consider where the device will be located and various sensor and device requirements:

- Device location during initial data collection phase.
- Device location postdeployment.
- Battery-powered versus USB-powered versus permanent powerline.
- Environmental requirements (i.e., water, fog, dirt, and other environmental factors) that could inhibit nominal usage of the sensor or destroy the device.
- How often the sensor will need to be replaced: does it have a degradation life cycle?
- Does the sensor need to be always on in order to achieve nominal operation parameters (i.e., gas sensor burn-in specifications)?
- How long the sensor will need to achieve nominal recording state, temperature heat-up time, etc.

Environmental and Social Impact

As the world population continues to grow, so does the amount of food waste we produce. It is estimated that over one-third of the food produced globally is wasted. That's 1.3 billion tons of food each year! Not only is this a huge waste of resources, but it also has a significant impact on the environment.[7]

Food waste is a major source of greenhouse gas emissions. When food rots in landfills, it releases methane, a gas that is more potent than carbon dioxide. Reducing food waste is one of the simplest and most effective ways to reduce our impact on the planet and reduce the development of global climate change.[8]

---

7 See the Food and Agriculture Organization of the United Nations website (*https://oreil.ly/ie2sk*).

8 See the US Department of Agriculture article, "Food Waste and Its Links to Greenhouse Gases and Climate Change" (*https://oreil.ly/AMnGh*).

In addition to the environmental benefits, reducing food waste can also have a positive impact on our health. Spotting food spoilage or diseases early on could eliminate outbreaks of food poisoning, salmonella, and other foodborne illnesses. And reducing food allergens and cross-contamination will improve the lives of people with deadly food allergies.

Increasing food safety and quality on food production lines benefits the physical safety of the workers and the overall health of the end consumer. Quality control inspectors play a vital role in ensuring that the food we eat is safe and of the highest quality. By reducing waste of all resources in general, when food quality issues are identified ASAP, we can save lives when food allergens are identified and removed.

Bootstrapping

Similarly to Benjamin Cabé's "Building an Artificial Nose" on page 180, this chapter is going to dive into an end-to-end solution for food quality assurance, particularly pertaining to the reduction of food waste through identifying and classifying when a fillet of salmon has been purchased (and is hopefully fresh) versus when it has spoiled. Once we have collected our dataset with our "spoiled" and "purchase date/fresh" gas sensor data samples, we will also collect a third class of data for our environment's "ambient" environment, to ensure that our trained machine learning model can distinguish the gas data that is produced when the freshness of the fish changes near the device.

These three classes will allow our classification machine learning model to identify what type of fish is present in the range of the gas sensor onboard our target edge platform. The edge device takes continuous raw samples from the gas sensor, and the trained machine learning model infers and determines if the salmon fillet near the device is close to its original purchase date or has spoiled. The resulting prediction result and gas signal data, if it concludes that the salmon fillet is spoiled, will be sent over a network connection, or stored locally on the device for further processing by a human or in the cloud.

Define Your Machine Learning Classes

Table 12-2 shows potential combinations of use cases, sensor and data input types, and the machine learning classes one would use to collect and label their training and testing datasets. The use cases and their associated class labels are important for the type of machine learning algorithm we're employing in this chapter, specifically "classification." You can learn more about this in "Classification" on page 96.

Table 12-2. Machine learning classes for food quality use cases

Use case	Training data	Class labels
Food spoilage detection	Gas	Spoiled, fresh, ambient environment
Food safety apparel detection	Images (with bounding boxes)	Safety apparel or PPE (personal protective equipment)
Detect package expiration date	Images (with bounding boxes)	Expiration date
Detect food packaging leaks	Water level, humidity, moisture	Nominal, leak
Food doneness/quality control	Temperature, gas	Done, undercooked, overcooked, ambient environment

In this chapter, we will select and build upon a food spoilage detection use case using machine learning sensor data classification, and our project's machine learning classes will be "spoiled," "purchase date," and "ambient."

Dataset Gathering

For technical and specific information about how to gather a clean, robust, and useful dataset, see "Getting Your Hands on Data" on page 215. You can also utilize various strategies on how to collect data from multiple sources to create your own unique dataset for your use case:

- Combining public research datasets
- Using existing sensor datasets from community-driven data collection sites like Kaggle
- Enlisting the help of your colleagues to collect samples for your collaborative Edge Impulse project

Edge Impulse

As described in "Edge Impulse" on page 368, you will need to create a free Edge Impulse account (*https://edgeimpulse.com*) to follow the instructions described in this chapter.

For further justification for using Edge Impulse for edge machine learning model development, review "End-to-End Platforms for Edge AI" on page 162.

Edge Impulse public project

The public Edge Impulse project (*https://oreil.ly/W3_vb*) for this chapter is available.

Choose Your Hardware and Sensors

In this book, we try to remain as device agnostic as possible, but we also need to discuss how one can use an off-the-shelf, easy-to-use development kit in order to create this use case's solution. Thus, this book aims to make this hardware selection as easy, affordable, and accessible as possible.

Because Edge Impulse already provides a large array of officially supported development platforms with various integrated sensor drivers and open source firmware, for the simplicity of this project and the collection of our food quality assurance gas sensor data, we will use an Arduino Nicla Sense ME (*https://oreil.ly/tepYH*) with its onboard Bosch BME688 (*https://oreil.ly/z1BzE*) gas sensor.

Hardware configuration

The Arduino Nicla Sense ME's (*https://oreil.ly/QrdR1*) onboard BME688 gas sensor can detect volatile organic compounds (VOCs), volatile sulfur compounds (VSCs), and other gases such as carbon monoxide and hydrogen in the part per billion (ppb) range.[9]

Following is a list of some other sensor types to ponder to improve the accuracy of your food quality assurance model for your specific environment, use case, project budget, and more:

- Other gases: ammonia, methane, oxygen, CO_2, etc.
- Temperature
- Pressure
- Humidity
- Radar
- Air quality

Sensor Fusion

Sensor fusion is a popular technique in embedded systems where you combine data from different sensors to get a more encompassing or accurate view of the world around your device. Read more about combining multiple sensors in "Combining Features and Sensors" on page 93.

---

9 See the Bosch article on the BME688 sensor (*https://oreil.ly/z1BzE*).

Data Collection

Using Edge Impulse, there are many options available to upload and label data to your project; many of the most common data ingestion tools have previously been described in "Data Collection" on page 370. The next sections will discuss the specific data collection tools we will use for this chapter on food quality assurance.

Data Ingestion Firmware

In order to ingest data from our Arduino Nicla Sense ME, we will need to flash a data ingestion sketch from the Arduino CLI (*https://oreil.ly/YyOZ6*) onto our device.

Then, using the Edge Impulse CLI (*https://oreil.ly/rPI3S*) we will connect our device to our project and start recording new data samples from the gas sensor onboard the Nicla Sense.

First, create a new directory on your computer, *food*, and a new file, *food.ino*, with the code shown in Example 12-1.

Example 12-1. Arduino sketch to write Nicla Sense gas data to the serial terminal

```
/**
 * Configure the sample frequency. This is the frequency used to send the data
 * to the studio regardless of the frequency used to sample the data from the
 * sensor. This differs per sensors, and can be modified in the API of the sensor
 */
#define FREQUENCY_HZ        10

/* Include ------------------------------------------------------------------- */
#include "Arduino_BHY2.h"

/* Constants ----------------------------------------------------------------- */
#define INTERVAL_MS         (1000 / FREQUENCY_HZ)
#define CONVERT_G_TO_MS2    9.80665f

/* Forward declarations ------------------------------------------------------ */
void ei_printf(const char *format, ...);

/* Private variables --------------------------------------------------------- */
static unsigned long last_interval_ms = 0;

Sensor gas(SENSOR_ID_GAS);

void setup() {
    /* Init serial */
    Serial.begin(115200);
    Serial.println("Edge Impulse sensor data ingestion\r\n");

    /* Init & start gas sensor */
    BHY2.begin(NICLA_I2C);
```

```
    gas.begin();
}

void loop() {

    BHY2.update();
    delay(INTERVAL_MS);

    ei_printf("%.2f", gas.value());
    ei_printf("\r\n");
}

/**
 * @brief       Printf function uses vsnprintf and output using Arduino Serial
 *
 * @param[in]  format      Variable argument list
 */
void ei_printf(const char *format, ...)
{
    static char print_buf[1024] = { 0 };

    va_list args;
    va_start(args, format);
    int r = vsnprintf(print_buf, sizeof(print_buf), format, args);
    va_end(args);

    if (r > 0) {
        Serial.write(print_buf);
    }
}
```

Using the Arduino CLI (*https://oreil.ly/YyOZ6*), compile and upload your sketch to the Arduino Nicla Sense ME board, as shown in Example 12-2.

Example 12-2. Arduino CLI commands

```
$ cd food
$ arduino-cli core install arduino:mbed_nicla
$ arduino-cli lib install Arduino_BHY2
$ arduino-cli lib install ArduinoBLE
$ arduino-cli compile --fqbn arduino:mbed_nicla:nicla_sense --output-dir . --verbose
$ arduino-cli upload --fqbn arduino:mbed_nicla:nicla_sense --input-dir . --verbose
```

Uploading Data to Edge Impulse

Now that we have flashed our data ingestion sketch to the Nicla Sense board, using the Edge Impulse CLI (edge-impulse-data-forwarder), log in to your project and connect your device to ingest your data from the serial port of your computer into your Edge Impulse project (see Example 12-3).

Example 12-3. Connect the Nicla Sense to your Edge Impulse project

```
$ edge-impulse-data-forwarder

Edge Impulse data forwarder v1.16.0
Endpoints:
    Websocket: wss://remote-mgmt.edgeimpulse.com
    API:       https://studio.edgeimpulse.com
    Ingestion: https://ingestion.edgeimpulse.com


? Which device do you want to connect to? /dev/tty.usbmodemE53378312 (Arduino)
[SER] Connecting to /dev/tty.usbmodemE53378312
[SER] Serial is connected (E5:33:78:31)
[WS ] Connecting to wss://remote-mgmt.edgeimpulse.com
[WS ] Connected to wss://remote-mgmt.edgeimpulse.com


? To which project do you want to connect this device?
  AI at the Edge / Use Case: Food Quality Assuran [SER] Detecting data frequency...
[SER] Detected data frequency: 10Hz
? 1 sensor axes detected (example values: [9513]). What do you want to call them?
  Separate the names with ',': gas
? What name do you want to give this device? Nicla Sense
[WS ] Device "Nicla Sense" is now connected to project "Use Case: Food Quality
Assurance"
[WS ] Go to https://studio.edgeimpulse.com/studio/115652/acquisition/training
  to build your machine learning model!
```

Now, place your Nicla Sense ME close to your spoiled or fresh (date of purchase) food (in this case, salmon) or somewhere in your room's ambient environment.

From your project's "Data acquisition" tab, set the following settings under "Record new data," then click "Start sampling." This will tell your Nicla Sense board over the serial connection to start recording 20 minutes (1,200,000 ms) of data from the onboard BME688 gas sensor (see Figure 12-1). Make sure to enter the corresponding sample label for your device's current recording configuration:

Label
    spoiled, purchase_date, or ambient

Sample length (ms.)
    1200000

Sensor
    Sensor with 1 axes (gas)

Frequency
    10Hz

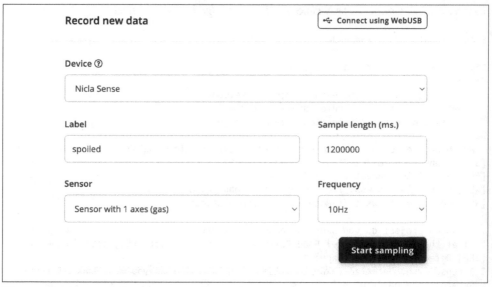

Figure 12-1. Data acquisition: record new data

Repeat this process until you have at least 20–60 minutes of data per machine learning class between your training dataset and testing dataset (total).

Autosampling with Browser Automation

You can easily create an automation in your web browser's developer console with a JavaScript call to automatically reclick on the "Start sampling" button in your Edge Impulse project every 22 minutes (or 1,320,000 ms):

```
const delay = ms => new Promise(res => setTimeout(res, ms));
while(1) {
    document.getElementById("input-start-sampling").click();
    await delay(1320000);
};
```

Cleaning Your Dataset

Review the tips provided in "Cleaning Your Dataset" on page 376, and then return to this chapter.

Because we have recorded the gas sensor samples in 20-minute lengths, in order to get a clearer view of the contents of each sample, we will split the samples into multiple subsamples of 30,000 ms (or 29,880 ms in this case). From the "Data acquisition" tab, select a sample's three-dot drop-down and then click "Split sample" (see Figure 12-2).

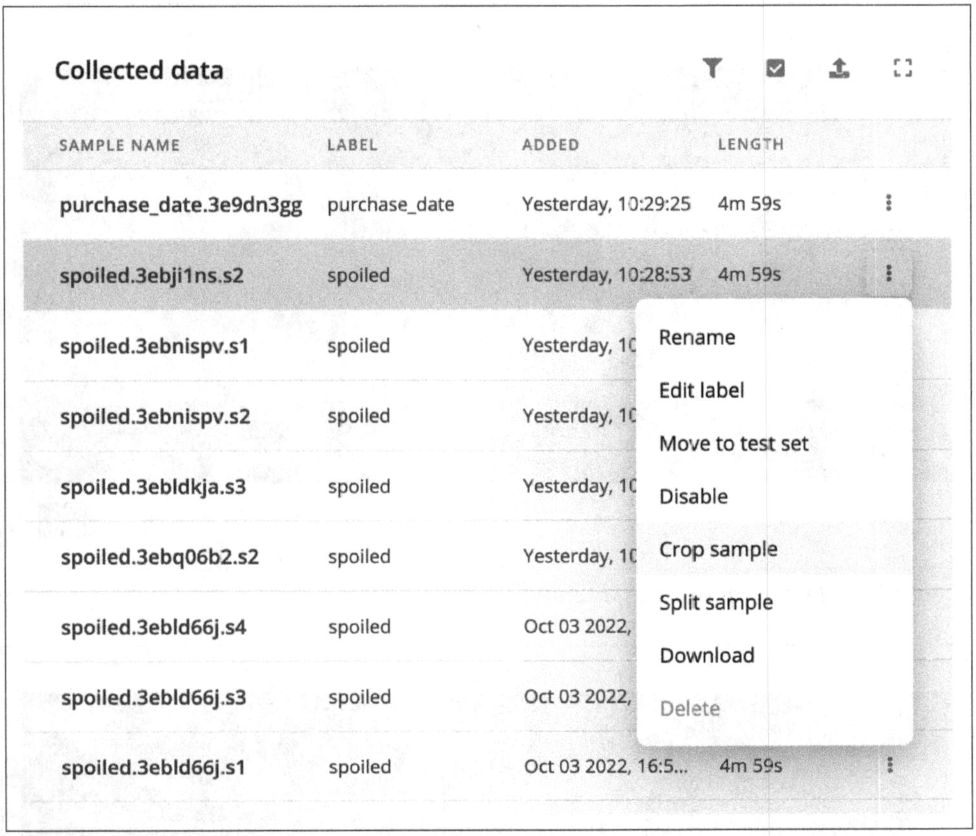

Figure 12-2. Data acquisition: sample drop-down menu

You can likely fit four subsamples of around 30,000 ms in length from the "Split sample" view; click "+ Add sample" to add more split segmentations, then click "Split" (see Figure 12-3).

You can also crop your samples by selecting the "Crop sample" option from the drop-down menu next to a sample name as shown in Figure 12-4.

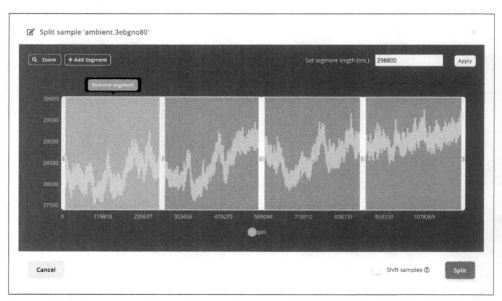

Figure 12-3. Data acquisition: split sample

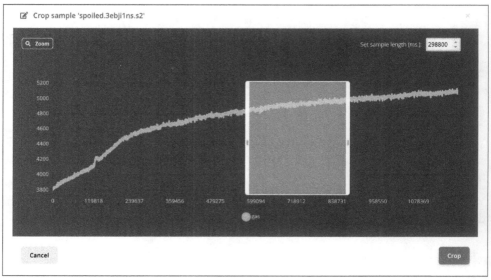

Figure 12-4. Data acquisition: crop sample

Dataset Licensing and Legal Obligations

Please review "Dataset Licensing and Legal Obligations" on page 376 for determining your dataset's licensing and legal obligations. Since we are directly uploading and using data that we have collected from our home and personal Nicla Sense device over the serial port of our computer, we will not have any dataset licensing or legal concerns to review.

However, if you are using gas data or other sensor data from a public source in addition to your own gas data from a device like the Arduino Nicla Sense ME, use due diligence to determine data usage rules and attribution requirements before uploading the data to your training/testing datasets and using a resulting trained model from that data.

DSP and Machine Learning Workflow

Now that we have uploaded all of our images into our training and testing datasets, we need to extract the most important features of our raw data using a digital signal processing (DSP) approach, and then train our machine learning model to identify patterns in our sensor data's extracted features. Edge Impulse calls the DSP and ML training workflow the "Impulse design."

The "Impulse design" tab of your Edge Impulse project allows you to view and create a graphical, simple overview of your full end-to-end machine learning pipeline. On the far left is the raw data block where the Edge Impulse Studio will ingest and pre-process your data, and set your window increase and size. You can also downsample or upsample your time series data from this view, if you have uploaded sample data from devices that recorded at varying frequencies.

Next is the DSP block, where we will extract the most important features of our gas data via an open source digital signal processing script, Flatten. Once we have generated our data's features, the learning block will train our neural network based on our desired architecture and configuration settings. Finally, we can see the deployment output information, including the desired classes we would like our trained machine learning model to classify, "purchase_date," "spoiled," and "ambient."

In your Edge Impulse project, set up your "Impulse design" tab the same as in Figure 12-5, or as listed by selecting from the various block pop-up windows, then click "Save Impulse":

Time series data
- Window size: 10000 ms.
- Window increase: 500 ms.
- Frequency (Hz): 10
- Zero-pad data: Checked [x]

Processing block
- Flatten

Learning block
- Classification (Keras)

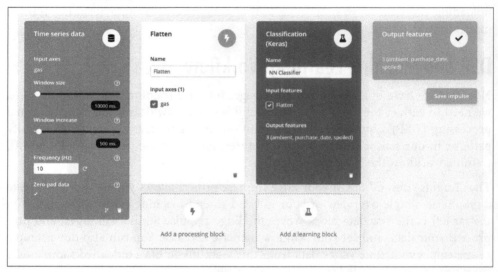

Figure 12-5. Impulse design configuration

Digital Signal Processing Block

For the project presented in this chapter, we will be using a digital signal processing algorithm that is included by default in the Edge Impulse Studio; this Flatten processing block is prewritten and available for free use and free deployment from the platform. The code used in the Flatten block is available in the Edge Impulse GitHub repository "processing-blocks" (*https://oreil.ly/_dSjf*). You can also learn more about the specifics of various digital signal processing algorithms in "Digital Signal Processing Algorithms" on page 88.

If you are familiar with writing your own digital signal processing code or would like to use your own custom DSP blocks, please review the details provided in "Digital Signal Processing Block" on page 380.

Set up your Flatten block by selecting the Flatten tab from the navigation bar and select the same parameters as shown in Figure 12-6, or as listed by editing the various checkboxes and text inputs. Then click "Save parameters."

Scaling
- Scale axes: 0.001

Method

- Average: checked [x]
- Minimum: checked [x]
- Maximum: checked [x]
- Root-mean square: checked [x]
- Standard deviation: checked [x]
- Skewness: unchecked [ ]
- Kurtosis: unchecked [ ]

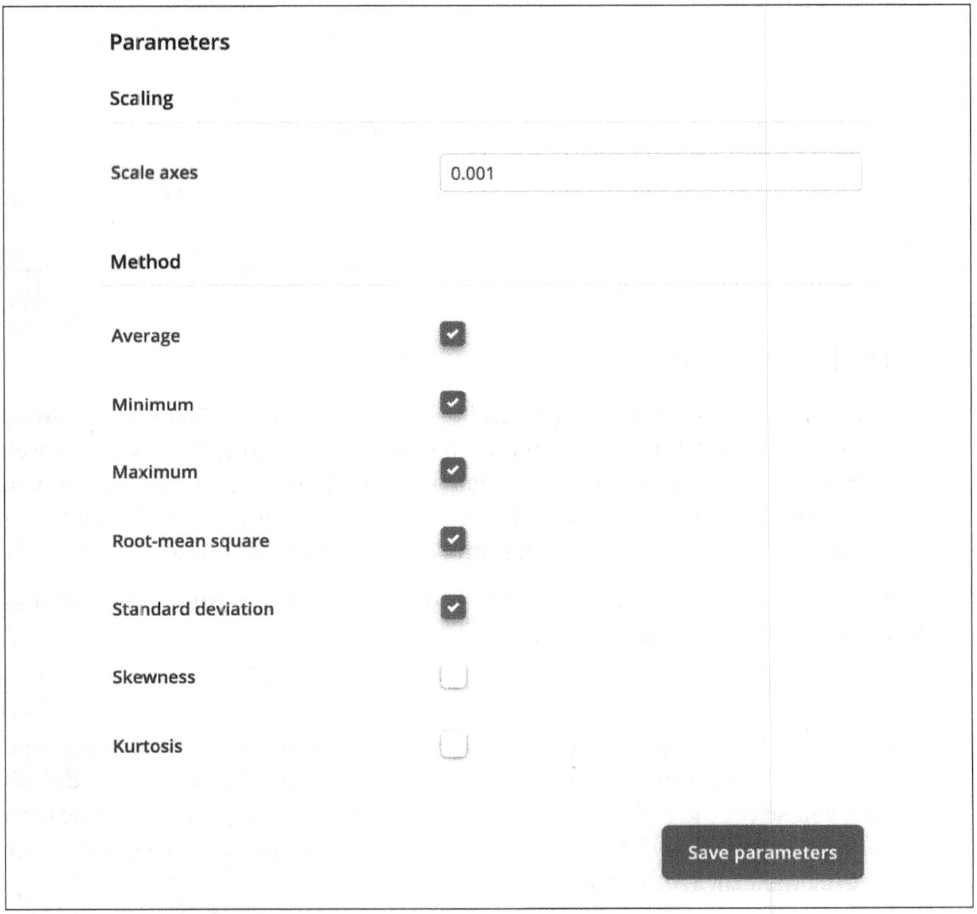

Figure 12-6. Flatten block parameters configuration

Now, click "Generate features" to view your data's feature explorer (see Figure 12-7).

Figure 12-7. Flatten block feature explorer

Machine Learning Block

We are now ready to train our edge machine learning model! There are multiple ways to train your model in Edge Impulse, the easiest of which is the visual (or web GUI) editing mode. However, if you are a machine learning engineer, expert, or if you already have experiencing coding with TensorFlow/Keras, then you can also edit your transfer learning block locally or in expert mode within the Edge Impulse Studio.

We can set the neural network architecture and other training configuration settings of our project from the NN Classifier tab.

Visual mode

The easiest way to configure and set our machine learning training settings and neural network architecture is through the Edge Impulse Visual mode, or the default view when you select the NN Classifier tab under "Impulse design" in the navigation bar (see Figure 12-8). Copy these settings into your neural network classifier's block configuration, then click "Start training":

- Number of training cycles: 50
- Learning rate: 0.0005
- Validation set size: 20%
- Auto-balance dataset: unchecked [ ]

- Neural network architecture:
  - Dense layer (8 neurons)
  - Dense layer (4 neurons)
  - Flatten layer

Neural Network settings

Training settings

Number of training cycles ⑦   50

Learning rate ⑦   0.0005

Validation set size ⑦   20   %

Auto-balance dataset ⑦

Neural network architecture

Input layer (5 features)

Dense layer (8 neurons)

Dense layer (4 neurons)

Flatten layer

Add an extra ayer

Output layer (3 classes)

Start training

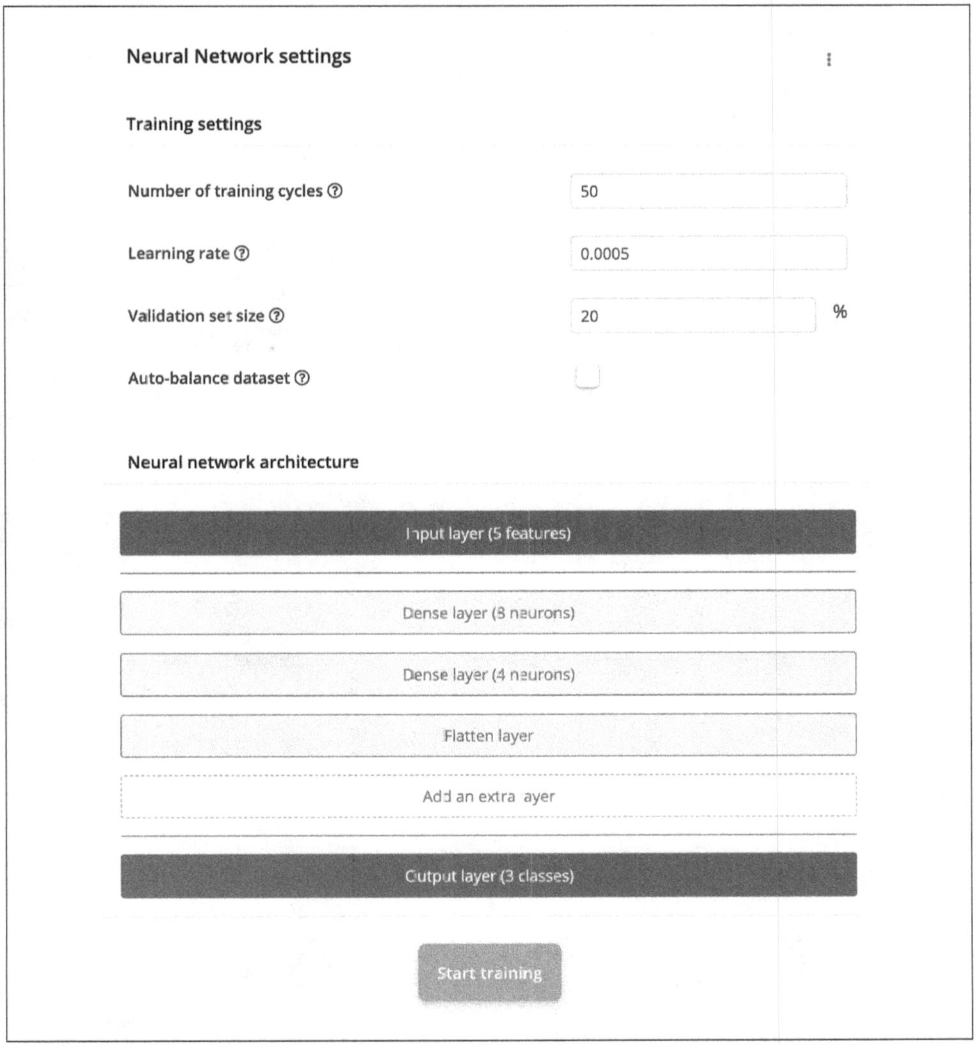

Figure 12-8. Neural Network settings

The dense layers are fully connected layers, the simplest form of a neural network layer. We use this for processed data, from the output of the Flatten DSP block. The flatten layer transforms multidimensional data into a single dimension. You need to flatten data from a convolutional layer before returning. You can learn more about the neural architecture configuration in the Edge Impulse documentation (*https://oreil.ly/J57H-*). Once your model training has completed, you can view the transfer learning results in the "Model: Last training performance" view (see Figure 12-9).

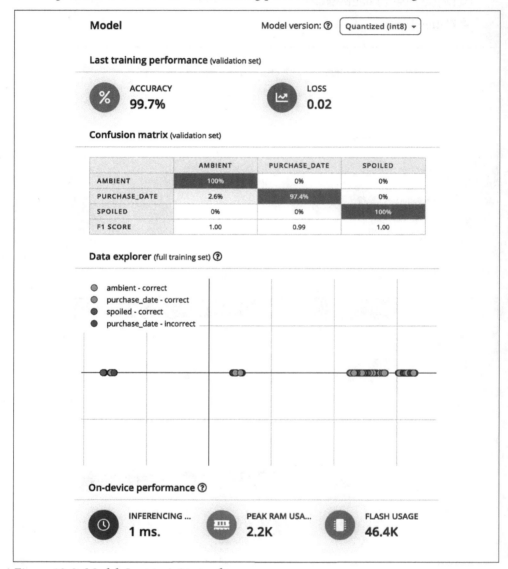

Figure 12-9. Model: Last training performance

Do you already know how to write TensorFlow/Keras code in Python? Use the Expert mode option in Edge Impulse to upload your own code or edit the existing block code locally by selecting the three-dot drop-down button to the right of the "Neural Network settings" block heading (see Figure 12-10).

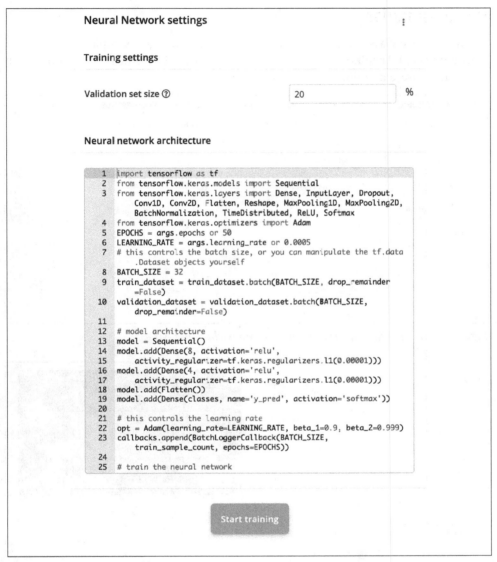

Neural Network settings

Training settings

Validation set size ⑦   20   %

Neural network architecture

```
1   import tensorflow as tf
2   from tensorflow.keras.models import Sequential
3   from tensorflow.keras.layers import Dense, InputLayer, Dropout,
        Conv1D, Conv2D, Flatten, Reshape, MaxPooling1D, MaxPooling2D,
        BatchNormalization, TimeDistributed, ReLU, Softmax
4   from tensorflow.keras.optimizers import Adam
5   EPOCHS = args.epochs or 50
6   LEARNING_RATE = args.learning_rate or 0.0005
7   # this controls the batch size, or you can manipulate the tf.data
        .Dataset objects yourself
8   BATCH_SIZE = 32
9   train_dataset = train_dataset.batch(BATCH_SIZE, drop_remainder
        =False)
10  validation_dataset = validation_dataset.batch(BATCH_SIZE,
        drop_remainder=False)
11
12  # model architecture
13  model = Sequential()
14  model.add(Dense(8, activation='relu',
15      activity_regularizer=tf.keras.regularizers.l1(0.00001)))
16  model.add(Dense(4, activation='relu',
17      activity_regularizer=tf.keras.regularizers.l1(0.00001)))
18  model.add(Flatten())
19  model.add(Dense(classes, name='y_pred', activation='softmax'))
20
21  # this controls the learning rate
22  opt = Adam(learning_rate=LEARNING_RATE, beta_1=0.9, beta_2=0.999)
23  callbacks.append(BatchLoggerCallback(BATCH_SIZE,
        train_sample_count, epochs=EPOCHS))
24
25  # train the neural network
```

Start training

Figure 12-10. Expert mode editor

Testing the Model

In-depth details and descriptions of all model testing features available in Edge Impulse are described in "Testing the Model" on page 392.

Live Classification

From the "Live classification" tab, you can test individual test samples directly from your connected Arduino Nicla Sense ME (see Figures 12-11 and 12-12). Connection instructions were described in Example 12-3.

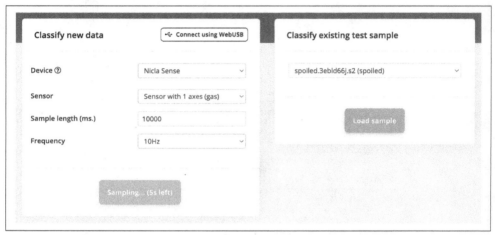

Figure 12-11. Live classification with Arduino Nicla Sense ME

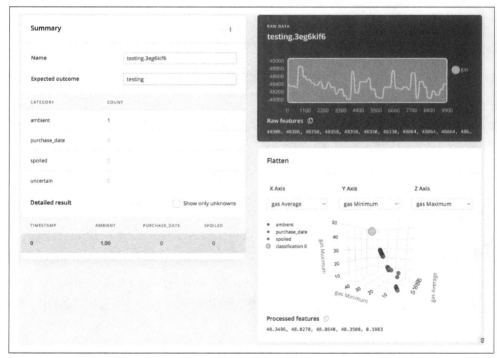

Figure 12-12. Live classification with unlabeled testing result

Or load an existing testing dataset image in "Classify existing test sample" to view this sample's extracted features and your trained model's prediction results, as shown in Figure 12-13.

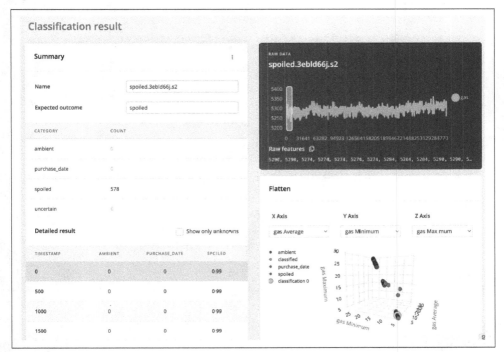

Figure 12-13. Live classification with preexisting labeled testing result

Model Testing

You can also bulk classify your testing dataset against your trained model by navigating to the "Model testing" tab (*https://oreil.ly/1Xc63*) of your project. Learn more about this tab in "Model Testing" on page 393.

Select "Classify all" to get a matrix of the inferencing results from your trained model on your test dataset samples (see Figure 12-14).

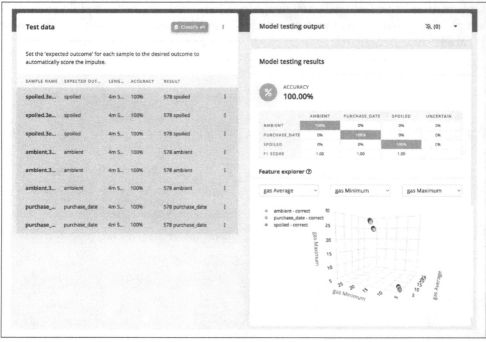

Figure 12-14. Model testing results

Deployment

Congratulations! You have just finished collecting and labeling your training and testing datasets, extracting your data's features with the DSP block, designing and training your machine learning model, and testing your model with your testing dataset. Now that we have all of the code and model information needed for inferencing on our edge device, we need to flash the prebuilt binary to the device or integrate the C++ library into our embedded application code.

Select the Deployment tab of your Edge Impulse project and follow the steps for one of the many deployment options in the next sections to run your trained machine learning model on your edge device. Many other deployment options are also available, some of which have already been described in "Deployment" on page 395.

Prebuilt Binary Flashing

From the Deployment tab, select your officially supported Edge Impulse development platform under "Build firmware" and then select Build. You also have the option to turn on/off the EON Compiler.[10]

Then, drag-and-drop or flash the resulting firmware application onto your officially supported platform by following the instructions shown after clicking Build from the Deployment tab. More in-depth instructions for flashing your prebuilt binary can be found in the Edge Impulse documentation for your chosen development platform (*https://oreil.ly/O-ZFY*).

For this project, we will select the "Arduino library" deployment option to run our trained model on the Arduino Nicla Sense ME (*https://oreil.ly/9QfS6*) (as shown in Figure 12-15).

Follow the instructions in the Arduino deployment documentation on the Edge Impulse website (*https://oreil.ly/CmTyr*) to download and install software prerequisites.

First, import the downloaded Arduino library ZIP file into the Arduino IDE (see Figure 12-16).

---

10 See Jan Jongboom's blog post, "Introducing EON: Neural Networks in Up to 55% Less RAM and 35% Less ROM" (*https://oreil.ly/B6Df7*), Edge Impulse, 2020.

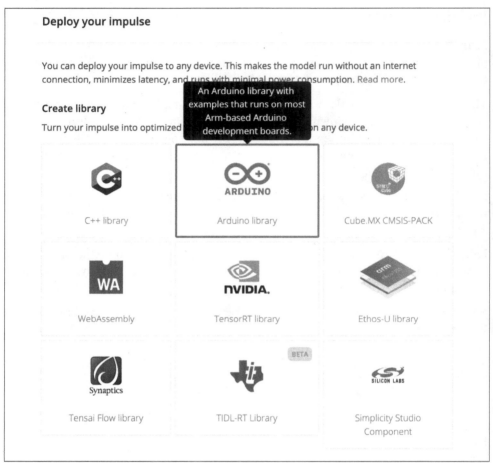

Figure 12-15. Arduino library deployment option

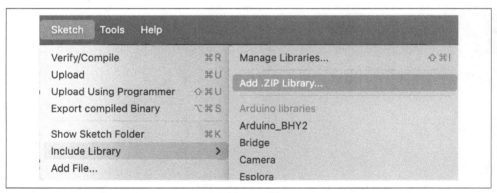

Figure 12-16. Arduino IDE: import ZIP library file

Then, open the Arduino library example from the deployed Edge Impulse Arduino library for the Nicla Sense within the Arduino IDE (see Figure 12-17).

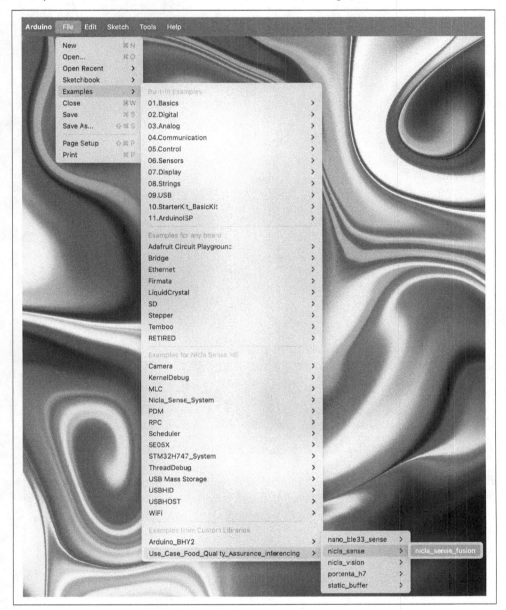

Figure 12-17. Arduino IDE: select Nicla Sense

Now save the *nicla_sense_fusion.ino* sketch file somewhere on your computer (see Figure 12-18).

Figure 12-18. Arduino IDE: save nicla_sense_fusion.ino sketch

Either compile and flash to the Nicla Sense directly from the Arduino IDE, or navigate to the directory where you stored the sketch on your computer in a command line terminal, and run the Arduino CLI commands shown in Example 12-4.

Example 12-4. Arduino CLI commands for flashing inferencing sketch

```
$ cd nicla_sense_fusion
$ arduino-cli compile --fqbn arduino:mbed_nicla:nicla_sense --output-dir . --verbose
$ arduino-cli upload --fqbn arduino:mbed_nicla:nicla_sense --input-dir . --verbose
```

View the inferencing results of your food quality assurance model running directly on the edge on the Arduino Nicla Sense ME in a serial terminal on baud rate 115,200 (see Figure 12-19).

```
●  ◉  ◉              Nicla Sense CMSIS_DAP — 80x24 — 115200.8.N.1

Predictions (DSP: 0 ms., Classification: 0 ms., Anomaly: 0 ms.):
ambient: 0.93750
purchase_date: 0.06250
spoiled: 0.00000

Starting inferencing in 2 seconds...
Sampling...
Predictions (DSP: 0 ms., Classification: 0 ms., Anomaly: 0 ms.):
ambient: 0.99609
purchase_date: 0.00000
spoiled: 0.00000

Starting inferencing in 2 seconds...
Sampling...
Predictions (DSP: 0 ms., Classification: 0 ms., Anomaly: 0 ms.):
ambient: 0.99609
purchase_date: 0.00000
spoiled: 0.00000

Starting inferencing in 2 seconds...
Sampling...
```

Figure 12-19. Arduino Nicla Sense ME trained model inferencing results

GitHub Source Code

The full application source code used in this chapter, including the deployed library from the public Edge Impulse project (*https://oreil.ly/wPTwd*) and completed application code, is available to view and download in GitHub (*https://oreil.ly/91usE*).

Iterate and Feedback Loops

Now that you have deployed the first iteration of your food quality assurance model, you may be satisfied with the results and discontinue development here. However, if you wish to further iterate over your model and further improve the accuracy over time or with newly acquired equipment upgrades, for example, there are many adaptations and variations to consider and improve upon for this project:

- Add more machine learning classes to your model for different types of food.

- Create an enclosure for the device that ensures no food contaminants will impact the readings of the gas sensor.

- Add machine learning classes to specifically identify how many days the food item is past the purchase date.

- Add other sensor axes like temperature or humidity to the input training/testing data samples using sensor fusion (see "Sensor Fusion" on page 416).

- Run multiple food quality assurance models in parallel or on devices nearby for unrelated but similar goals, i.e., food spoilage and allergens detection.

Deep Dive: Perfect Toast Machine

The AI-powered toaster shown in Figure 12-20 uses odor to produce perfect toast!

Figure 12-20. Shawn Hymel's toaster

Shawn Hymel used Edge Impulse and machine learning to build a device that makes the perfect toast every time, regardless of bread thickness, composition, or starting temperature. The model was trained on a variety of gas sensor data and uses regression to predict when the toast will burn.

Shawn hacked an inexpensive toaster so that the toasting process could be controlled by a microcontroller. The microcontroller continuously samples odor data from the gas sensors, performs inference with the machine learning model, and stops the toasting process 45 seconds before the toast would be burned.

This seemingly superfluous application of embedded machine learning has several important implications.

First, we may not need to rely on timers and intuition to cook food in the future. We might one day see kitchen appliances that have smart sensors built in to help us serve the perfect dish and prevent food waste due to discarded overcooked meals. Second, creating the perfect toast is a great demonstration of predictive maintenance. Replace *toast* with *machinery* in this example. Can we train machine learning models to predict when parts of our car will go bad before they actually do? Downtime in large-scale industrial equipment might cost thousands or millions of dollars, and predictive maintenance can help identify problems before they become worse.

Check out the Perfect Toast Machine's GitHub repository (*https://oreil.ly/DlRu4*).

Related Works

As stated throughout this chapter, edge AI is an up-and-coming technology being employed in a wide range of food quality assurance devices, from manufacturing lines to consumer allergen detectors. The next sections describe various devices, datasets, research articles, and books on the topic of edge AI for food quality assurance.

This book also notes the sources for various applications, methods, devices, and quotes from various research and commercial adoption of food quality assurance machine learning models and methods throughout the chapter in the footnotes on each page.

Research

- Banús, Núria et al. "Deep Learning for the Quality Control of Thermoforming Food Packages" (*https://oreil.ly/8Oaec*). *Scientific Reports*, 2021.
- Gerina, Federica et al. "Recognition of Cooking Activities Through Air Quality Sensor Data for Supporting Food Journaling" (*https://oreil.ly/2Dj7L*). Springer-Open, 2020.
- Hassoun, Abdo et al. "Food Quality 4.0: From Traditional Approaches to Digitalized Automated Analysis" (*https://doi.org/10.1016/j.jfoodeng.2022.111216*). *Journal of Food Engineering*, 2023.
- Hemamalini, V. et al. "Food Quality Inspection and Grading Using Efficient Image Segmentation and Machine Learning-Based System" (*https://oreil.ly/1z5z0*). *Journal of Food Quality*, 2022.
- Ishangulyyev, Rovshen et al. "Understanding Food Loss and Waste—Why Are We Losing and Wasting Food?" (*https://oreil.ly/Vmwyg*), National Library of Medicine, 2019.
- Iymen, Gokce et al. "Artificial Intelligence-Based Identification of Butter Variations as a Model Study for Detecting Food Adulteration" (*https://doi.org/10.1016/j.ifset.2020.102527*). *Journal of Food Engineeering*, 2020.
- Jathar, Jayant et al. "Food Quality Assurance Using Artificial Intelligence: A Review Paper" (*https://oreil.ly/9WUim*). ResearchGate, 2021.

- Kaya, Aydin, and Ali Seydi Keçeli. "Sensor Failure Tolerable Machine Learning-Based Food Quality Prediction Model" (*https://oreil.ly/eGnDv*). ResearchGate, 2020.

- Kumar, G. Arun, "An Arduino Sensor-Based Approach for Detecting the Food Spoilage" (*https://oreil.ly/ECgqq*). *International Journal of Engineering and Applied Sciences and Technology*, 2020.

- Nturambirwe, Jean et al. "Classification Learning of Latent Bruise Damage to Apples Using Shortwave Infrared Hyperspectral Imaging" (*https://oreil.ly/2zmhw*). MDPI, 2021.

- Rady, Ahmed et al. "The Effect of Light Intensity, Sensor Height, and Spectral Pre-Processing Methods When Using NIR Spectroscopy to Identify Different Allergen-Containing Powdered Foods" (*https://oreil.ly/vGyiR*). National Library of Medicine, 2019.

- Sonwani, Ekta et al. "An Artificial Intelligence Approach Toward Food Spoilage Detection and Analysis" (*https://oreil.ly/SImft*). National Library of Medicine, 2021.

- Watson, Nicholas J. et al. "Intelligent Sensors for Sustainable Food and Drink Manufacturing" (*https://oreil.ly/IaoqI*). Frontiers in Sustainable Systems, 2021.

News and Other Articles

- Machine Learning for Automated Food Quality Inspection (*https://oreil.ly/kIdsz*)

- NIRONE Sensors Show Promising Results on Detection on Food Allergen Identification (*https://oreil.ly/O-GVd*)

- Using AI to Increase Food Quality (*https://oreil.ly/OOj3H*)

- What Is Industry 4.0?: How Industry 4.0 Technologies Are Changing Manufacturing (*https://oreil.ly/0YzAK*)

- The Best Technologies Against Food Allergies (*https://oreil.ly/mKQyc*)

- Considering a Smart Toaster Oven? Get a Multi-Oven Instead (*https://oreil.ly/TuZ3P*)

## CHAPTER 13

Use Case: Consumer Products

Edge machine learning is used in consumer electronics and products to enable devices to make decisions based on data without sending that data to the cloud. This can save time and bandwidth and can also be used when data is sensitive and needs to be kept private. Edge machine learning can also be used for consumer-focused tasks like facial recognition, object detection, voice recognition, and sensor classification. By analyzing and recognizing patterns in the consumer data being ingested on the device before sending it to the cloud for further processing, products can quickly adapt to the user's needs: show the desired product usage, provide customized alerts to the user about the product, and more.

By using edge AI, consumer products can integrate with and leverage the data of onboard sensors for an almost unlimited amount of use cases. For example, a bike can analyze the rider's surrounding environment for traffic information and environmental data that can affect ride quality, and a smart fridge can automatically detect when a product has almost been used up and add the product to a purchase list. In this chapter, we will brainstorm various approaches to using edge AI for consumer products, their associated sensor and device configurations, and a deep-dive tutorial into our selected approach and use case solution.

Problem Exploration

Many consumer technology products are already constantly connected to the internet, such as smart home devices, security cameras, wearables, autonomous vehicles, and drones. These devices need to process large amounts of data or send these large amounts of data to be processed remotely in a cloud-based platform. Edge ML allows these consumer products to respond quickly to changes in their environment, from the massive amounts of sensor data that is already being ingested on the device, without needing to send it to the cloud for further processing, which usually requires a lot of time, battery usage, bandwidth consumption, etc.

Applying the techniques we have learned in this book, developing an edge machine learning model for the purposes of end consumer electronics is an extremely broad task. In order to narrow our focus, we will discuss a multitude of overarching, general goals and then deep-dive into an implementation of one of them. An example of this overarching consumer goal is a product that soothes a pet in some way. Goal-wise, we can both generate a machine learning model that analyzes the pet's water bowl and alerts the human when the water is almost depleted, or we could integrate a device into a pet's collar to detect a certain kind of distressed noise or sound and then provide soothing feedback. Both of these approaches accomplish the same goal, soothing a pet through an end product device, but each could require a different combination of machine learning classes and sensor inputs in order to solve.

Goal Setting

Creating useful and efficient consumer products with edge AI technology is useful as the world evolves. Consumers will begin to expect their technology to get smarter and smarter, but without infringing on their data privacy rights. There are almost an endless amount of options for consumer products to integrate their onboard sensor data with an edge machine learning model. By bringing the intelligence gained from these onboard sensors to edge AI, consumer products can achieve better overall performance, increased battery life (depending on the use case), and overall increased end user satisfaction and user-friendliness/accessibility.

Solution Design

In this chapter, we are choosing to design and implement a low-cost, efficient, and easy-to-train edge AI model for a consumer products use case pertaining to a bicyclist monitoring device with an onboard accelerometer sensor. However, an edge AI model for detecting hazards and monitoring a bicyclist's safety does not only need to be created with an accelerometer. By using the principles and design workflow presented in this chapter and throughout this book, many other types of machine learning models and applications can be implemented for a bicyclist monitoring device, including using camera image input to monitor surrounding environment information and potential collisions/traffic accidents, identifying crashes via incoming audio signal data, and more.

What Solutions Already Exist?

An abundance of smart, edge AI consumer products already exist on the market or have been recently released from prototyping stages. Smart kitchen appliances like the June Oven (*https://oreil.ly/W_aZa*) and the Haier Series 6 (*https://oreil.ly/yS58F*) come equipped with AI technology that can help you with everything from meal planning to cleaning up. Mobile phone users around the world are locked into their hardware vendor's ecosystem of choice with AI wearables like the Apple Watch, Samsung Smartwatch, or Fitbit.

Health devices are increasingly being developed for the end user in mind; the Oura Ring (*https://ouraring.com*) is equipped with sensors that track your sleep, activity, and overall health, allowing you to get a better understanding of your daily habits. The future of many consumer technological products will include the integration of onboard sensors and real-time edge AI inferencing, which improves both the performance of those products and their usefulness and attractiveness to the end consumer, while reducing their power consumption.

Solution Design Approaches

We can take our problem statement and design a solution via many different approaches, a few of which are described below:

Pet soother and monitor

As a pet owner, it's important to be aware of your pet's vital signs and overall health. By monitoring your pet's vital signs with edge AI devices, you can be alerted to any changes in their health or behaviors and take appropriate action. There are various sensor inputs available to help you monitor your pet's vital signs, including camera sensors and smart water bowls. You can also use an AI-powered collar to track your pet's location and activity levels. These smart pet products can help ease our anxiety about our pet's health and well-being and give us peace of mind.

Bicycling monitor

Many forms of transportation are being outfitted with edge AI integration, including bikes, with manufacturers offering a variety of features that make commuting safer and more enjoyable. The potential for data collection via sensor-equipped bikes or add-on consumer products is immense. With various sensor configurations, bikes could collect data on the terrain, weather, and traffic conditions in real time, allowing for a more comprehensive understanding of conditions on the ground and in the cyclist's surrounding environment.

Additionally, bikes could be equipped with sensors that detect when they are being ridden in an unsafe or illegal manner, such as weaving in and out of traffic or riding on the wrong side of the road. Other sensor combinations could also be integrated to enable automated theft detection and help to make biking a safer overall experience, inside and outside of a city center. Finally, bikes equipped with a rearview camera or radar sensor would also be able to detect traffic behind the rider, potentially avoiding accidents by alerting the user to move out of the way, speed up, or slow down depending on the incoming traffic movement/information or visual obstacles.[1]

Children's toys

There are three main categories of interactive children's toys incorporating edge AI technology: teaching, responding to emotions, or monitoring health and safety of the child and their environment. Teaching toys are designed to help children learn new skills or information. They often come in the form of educational games or puzzles that can help children practice things like counting, shapes, and colors. Emotional response toys are designed to interact with children and respond to their emotions. These toys can listen for audio cues like screaming or crying, and they may even recognize facial expressions or other visual cues that relate to a child's emotional state. Safety and health monitoring toys are designed to help keep children safe and healthy. These toys can detect when fingers are about to touch a hot stove, for example, or they may monitor a child's heart rate and breathing. Some of these toys even come equipped with GPS tracking in case a child gets lost, further increasing the parent's comfort level.

However, the advancements in edge AI technology requires the promotion of very reasonable and ethical guidelines for AI usage in any toy, device, or service that interacts with children. Unfortunately, the more sophisticated AI technology becomes, the harder it is to regulate, and the possibility of AI being used to exploit children, their emotions, and their personal data increases.[2] The regulation of AI technology is a complex issue, and one we won't discuss in detail in this chapter; however there are many government agencies and companies doing research and policy development into this exact field of study, as there is no easy solution.[3] Given the potentially harmful consequences for children using AI technology falling into the wrong hands, it is clear that some form using regulation is necessary.[4]

---

1 See the Edge Impulse article, "Bike Rearview Radar" (*https://oreil.ly/12O4I*).

2 See "Digital Child's Play: Protecting Children from the Impacts of AI" (*https://oreil.ly/2rc83*) from UN News.

3 See UNICEF's article, "Good Governance of Children's Data". (*https://oreil.ly/EzNvZ*)

4 See "Artificial Intelligence for Children" (*https://oreil.ly/aHH3E*) from the World Economic Forum.

Home appliances

Edge AI–enabled home appliances like a refrigerator can detect when food is running low and automatically order more, so you never have to worry about running out of milk again. They can also track your eating habits, so you can get insights into your nutritional intake, and even cook food for you perfectly.

But it's not just fridges that are getting smarter. There are all sorts of smart cooking devices that are using computer vision and other sensor inputs to perfectly cook food with visual size estimation[5] and automated temperature control. And coffee machines are using edge machine learning to personalize coffee according to the user's preferences. Even laundry machines are using machine learning to identify different types of clothes and adjust the wash and dry cycles according to the inference results.

Any one of the previously described use case solution approaches are consumer products that promote this chapter's use case goal of designing ethical and valuable consumer products for widespread use and ensuring that the data ingested regarding the end user is used ethically and responsibly.

Design Considerations

To achieve the overarching goal of designing a useful, ethical, and accessible consumer edge AI product, from a technological standpoint, we can use a wide variety of data sources, including many different types of sensors and cameras to accomplish a similar goal (see Table 13-1).

Table 13-1. What sensors can be used for each use case?

Goal	Sensor(s)
Bicyclist crash/theft detector	Accelerometer, audio, radar, camera
Pet soother	Camera, audio, radar
AI-powered oven	Infrared camera, temperature, gas
Health-monitoring wearable	PPG, heart rate, ECG, temperature, water/sweat level
Home security and automation	Camera, audio
Robotic children's toy	Camera, audio, accelerometer, gyroscope, radar
Automated laundry machine	Camera, chemical, gas, color, light intensity

"Getting Your Hands on Data" on page 215 discusses further approaches to sensor data gathering and dataset collection.

---

5 See the Edge Impulse blog, "Estimate Weight From a Photo Using Visual Regression in Edge Impulse" (*https://oreil.ly/qfZxT*).

Also, consider the following points during your design process and brainstorming sessions:

- Who are the end users of the product?
- Who are the primary stakeholders in the product?
- How could this product be used maliciously or unethically?
- Where is the data being stored? Are inference results being sent back to a cloud platform?
- How is the consumer/end user being made aware of how the incoming sensor data is being used on the device and in the cloud or over a networking connection?

Environmental and Social Impact

While edge AI advances in consumer technology can make our lives easier, it also comes with its own set of problems, including being inaccessible or limited in use by a large part of the population, leaving a portion of end users unable to take advantage of the advances in much of edge AI technology. One way that manufacturers are trying to alleviate these issues is by making devices that are more user friendly and accessible for everyone. One such example is that some companies are now making devices to reduce the burden of home chores. These devices can assist the elderly or disabled with tasks that they may find difficult, such as cleaning or cooking. This not only helps to make their lives easier, but it can also help to prevent accidents or injuries. Companies are also working to reduce technology or general waste by alerting customers beforehand of potential issues or repairs that their device may need. This not only helps to keep devices in good working condition, but it can also help to prevent harm to children that may interact with them.

Putting Children and Youth FIRST Checklist[6]

The following checklist (FIRST) is a great starter set of ideas and limits to put in place when you are brainstorming new edge AI product ideas for consumer consumption, even if the product's intended audience/users are not children:

Fair
  Ethics, bias, and liability

Inclusive
  Accessibility, neuro-differences, and feedback from kids/target age group

---

6 See "Artifical Intelligence for Children" (*https://oreil.ly/aHH3E*) from the World Economic Forum.

Responsible
> Age-appropriate and developmental stage-appropriate; reflects the latest learning science and is designed with target age in mind

Safe
> Does no harm; cybersecurity and addiction mitigation

Transparent
> Can explain how the AI works and what it is being used for to a novice or lay audience

Bootstrapping

This use case chapter is going to dive into an end-to-end solution for creating a consumer product edge AI model, particularly pertaining to a device that will monitor and protect a bicyclist through traffic and collision alerts. To create our initial bicyclist monitoring model, we will collect samples for the machine learning classes "idle," "sudden stop," and "nominal" from our edge device's accelerometer sensor.

These three classes will allow our classification machine learning model to identify what type of motion events are being experienced by the bicyclist in real time. The edge device takes continuous raw samples from the accelerometer, and the trained machine learning model infers and determines if the motion detected by the device is idle, performing a turn, experiencing a sudden stop (perhaps indicative of a crash), or traveling on uneven terrain. For the resulting prediction outcome, anomaly score, and accelerometer signal data, if the device concludes that the anomaly score is high, or a sudden stop was experienced, this information will be immediately alerted to the device end user through an audio output notification or LED warning, and the data will also be sent over a network connection or stored locally on the device for further processing by a human or in the cloud.

Define Your Machine Learning Classes

Table 13-2 shows potential combinations of use cases, sensor and data input types, and the machine learning classes one would use to collect and label their training and testing datasets. The use cases and their associated class labels are important for the types of machine learning algorithms we are employing in this chapter, specifically "classification" and "anomaly detection." You can learn more about these algorithms in "Classification" on page 96 and "Anomaly detection" on page 99.

Table 13-2. Machine learning classes for bicyclist safety use cases

Use case	Training data	Class labels
Detect bicycle crash	Accelerometer	Nominal, anomaly (or a specified "crash" label if the data already exists)
Monitor oncoming traffic	Camera (with bounding boxes)	Car, bicycle, motorcycle, other traffic objects
Monitor cyclist's blind spots	Radar	Nominal, object in close proximity to cyclist
Listen for car alarms, crashes, and other traffic sounds	Audio	Background, noise, car alarm, car crash, car honk, human voice/yelling

In this chapter, we will select and build upon a consumer bicyclist monitoring device use case for machine learning sensor data classification, and our project's initial machine learning classes will be "idle," "sudden stop," and "nominal," pertaining to the eventual use case of "detecting bicycle crashes." However, because you likely do not want to specifically get into a bicycle crash to record and upload these data samples, we will employ the use of the machine learning techniques classification and anomaly detection to achieve this use case goal.

Dataset Gathering

For technical and specific information about how to gather a clean, robust, and useful dataset, see "Getting Your Hands on Data" on page 215. You can also utilize various strategies on how to collect data from multiple sources to create your own unique dataset for your use case:

- Combining public research datasets
- Using existing sensor datasets from community-driven data collection sites like Kaggle
- Enlisting the help of your colleagues to collect samples for your collaborative Edge Impulse project

Edge Impulse

As described in "Edge Impulse" on page 368, you will need to create a free Edge Impulse account (*https://edgeimpulse.com*) to follow the instructions described in this chapter.

For further justification for using Edge Impulse for edge machine learning model development, review "End-to-End Platforms for Edge AI" on page 162.

Edge Impulse public project

Each use case chapter of this book contains a written tutorial to demonstrate and achieve a complete end-to-end machine learning model for the described use case. However, if you would like to just get straight to the point and see the exact data and model that the authors have developed for the chapter in its final state, you may do so by navigating to the public Edge Impulse project (*https://oreil.ly/iuJp9*) for this chapter.

You may also directly clone this project, including all of the original training and testing data, intermediate model information, resulting trained model results, and all deployment options by selecting the Clone button at the top right side of the Edge Impulse page (see Figure 13-1).

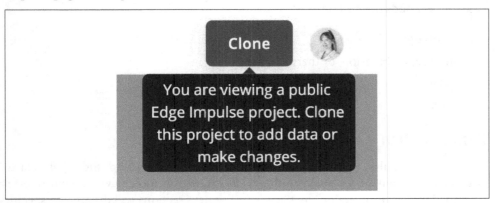

Figure 13-1. Clone Edge Impulse public project

Choose Your Hardware and Sensors

In this book, we try to remain as device agnostic as possible, but we also need to discuss how one can use an off-the-shelf, easy-to-use development kit in order to create this use case's solution. Thus, this book aims to make this hardware selection as easy, affordable, and accessible as possible.

Because Edge Impulse already provides a large array of officially supported development platforms with various integrated sensor drivers and open source firmware, for the simplicity of this project and the collection of our accelerometer data for a bicyclist consumer product use case, we will use a combination of our mobile phone with the Edge Impulse mobile client (*https://oreil.ly/RKAWb*) and a Nordic Semi Thingy:53 (*https://oreil.ly/WfU0M*) with the nRF Edge Impulse mobile phone application (*https://oreil.ly/OnTtw*) for data ingestion and model deployment.

However, if you do not have the exact hardware described in this chapter, you can consult the Edge Impulse documentation (*https://oreil.ly/zQryl*) for other suitable boards with various officially supported sensors for easy data ingestion and deployment. Or you can bring your own development platform in and your own sensor combinations, and continue following along with this chapter after you have created a running device firmware for initial sensor data ingestion (the easiest way being with the Edge Impulse data forwarder (*https://oreil.ly/MXDZM*)).

Hardware configuration

The Nordic Semi Thingy:53's onboard accelerometer inertial measurement unit (IMU) and/or your mobile phone's internal IMU will be used to detect motion events on the bike, affixed to your bike's front handlebars.

Following is a list of some other sensor types to ponder in order to improve the accuracy of your consumer bicyclist monitoring model for your specific environment, use case, project budget, and more:

- Gyroscope
- Infrared, night vision, or thermal camera
- Radar
- Audio

Data Collection

Using Edge Impulse, there are many options available to upload and label data to your project; many of the most common data ingestion tools have previously been described in "Data Collection" on page 370. The next sections will discuss the specific data collection tools we will use for this chapter on consumer products for a bicyclist monitoring use case.

Data Ingestion Firmware

In order to ingest data from our Thingy:53, we will need to flash the Edge Impulse firmware onto our device by following the instructions in the documentation (*https://oreil.ly/bHbVN*). Then, using the Edge Impulse CLI (*https://oreil.ly/DSrv7*) or the nRF Edge Impulse mobile phone application (see "nRF Edge Impulse mobile phone application" on page 451), we will connect our device to our project and start recording new accelerometer data samples from onboard the Thingy:53 or from our mobile phone.

Mobile phone

One of the easiest ways to upload new accelerometer data is to connect your mobile phone directly to your Edge Impulse project and record accelerometer data from your phone's integrated IMU. You can find instructions for connecting your mobile phone in the Edge Impulse documentation (*https://oreil.ly/UoiqJ*) (see Figure 13-2).

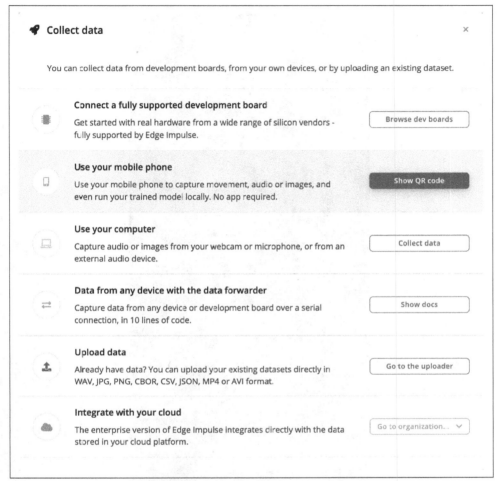

Figure 13-2. Connecting your mobile phone to your Edge Impulse project

nRF Edge Impulse mobile phone application

First, download and install the Nordic nRF Edge Impulse app for your iPhone (*https://oreil.!y/2w5nO*) or Android phone (*https://oreil.ly/Q_bVH*). Then, follow the instructions in the Edge Impulse documentation (*https://oreil.ly/orK3a*) to log in to the nRF Edge Impulse app with your Edge Impulse account and connect your Thingy:53 to your project.

To record and upload a new data sample into your project, click on the "+" button at the top right of the app. Select your sensor, type in the sample label, and choose a sample length and frequency, then select Start Sampling (see Figure 13-3).

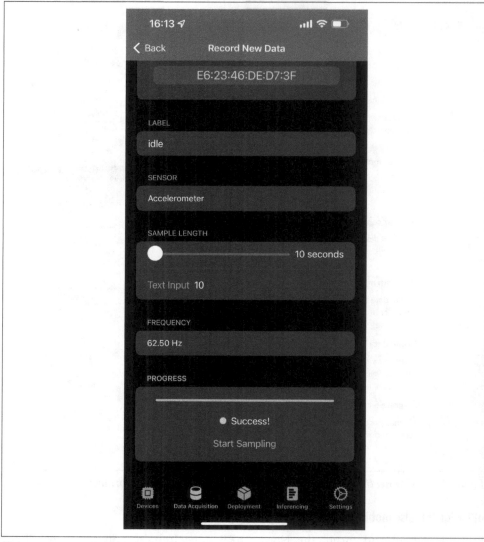

Figure 13-3. nRF Edge Impulse phone application data acquisition

Continue collecting data samples on your bike for all three of the machine learning classes, "idle," "sudden stop," and "nominal." Please be careful and pay attention to your surroundings while collecting your data!

Cleaning Your Dataset

Review the tips provided in "Cleaning Your Dataset" on page 376, and then return to this chapter.

Because we have recorded the gas sensor samples in 30-second (30,000 ms) lengths, we will split the samples into multiple subsamples of 10 seconds (10,000 ms) long. From the "Data acquisition" tab, select a sample's three-dot drop-down and then click "Split sample." You can likely fit three subsamples of around 10,000 ms in length from the Split sample view; click the "+ Add Segment" button to add more split segmentations, then click Split (see Figure 13-4).

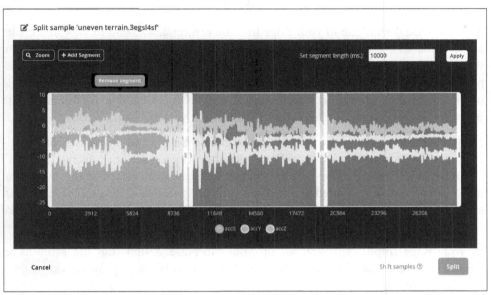

Figure 13-4. Data acquisition: split sample

You can also crop your samples by selecting the "Crop sample" option from the drop-down menu next to a sample name, as described in "Cleaning Your Dataset" on page 420.

Dataset Licensing and Legal Obligations

Please review "Dataset Licensing and Legal Obligations" on page 376 for determining your dataset's licensing and legal obligations. Since we are directly uploading and using data that we have collected from our home and personal mobile phone (*https://oreil.ly/RZxE0*) or Nordic Thingy:53 device (*https://oreil.ly/E91_-*) over the serial port of our computer or the Nordic nRF Edge Impulse mobile phone app (*https://oreil.ly/VxQKE*), we will not have any dataset licensing or legal concerns to review.

However, if you are using accelerometer data or other types of sensor data from a publicly sourced dataset in addition to your own data from your mobile phone or a device like the Nordic Thingy:53, use due diligence to determine data usage rules and attribution requirements before uploading the data to your training/testing datasets and using a resulting trained model from that data.

DSP and Machine Learning Workflow

Now that we have uploaded all of our accelerometer motion samples into our training and testing datasets, we need to extract the most important features of our raw data using a digital signal processing (DSP) approach, and then train our machine learning model to identify patterns in our sensor data's extracted features. Edge Impulse calls the DSP and ML training workflow the "Impulse design."

The "Impulse design" tab of your Edge Impulse project allows you to view and create a graphical, simple overview of your full end-to-end machine learning pipeline. On the far left is the raw data block where the Edge Impulse Studio will ingest and preprocess your data, and set your window increase and size. You can also downsample or upsample your time series data from this view, if you have uploaded sample data from devices that recorded the accelerometer data at varying frequencies.

Next is the DSP block, where we will extract the most important features of our accelerometer data via an open source digital signal processing script, "Spectral analysis." Once we have generated our data's features, the learning block will train our neural network based on our desired architecture and configuration settings. Finally, we can see the deployment output information, including the desired classes we would like our trained machine learning model to classify: idle, sudden stop, and nominal.

In your Edge Impulse project, set up your "Impulse design" tab the same as in Figure 13-5, or as listed by selecting from the various block pop-up windows, then click "Save Impulse":

Time series data
- Window size: 5000 ms.
- Window increase: 250 ms.
- Frequency (Hz): 62.5
- Zero-pad data: Checked [x]

Processing block
- Spectral Analysis

Learning block
- Classification (Keras)
- Anomaly detection (K-Means)

Figure 13-5. Impulse design configuration

Digital Signal Processing Block

For the project presented in this chapter, we will be using a digital signal processing algorithm that is included by default in the Edge Impulse Studio; this Spectral Analysis processing block is prewritten and available for free use and free deployment from the platform. The code used in the Spectral Analysis block is available in the Edge Impulse GitHub repository "processing-blocks" (*https://oreil.ly/oAvIn*). You can also learn more about the specifics of the spectral analysis algorithm in "Spectral analysis" on page 91.

If you are familiar with writing your own digital signal processing code or would like to use your own custom DSP blocks, please review the details provided in "Digital Signal Processing Block" on page 380.

Set up your Spectral Analysis block by selecting the "Spectral features" tab from the navigation bar and selecting the same parameters as shown in Figure 13-6, or as listed in the following by editing the various checkboxes and text inputs:

Filter
- Scale axes: 1
- Type: none

Spectral power
- FFT length: 16
- Take log of spectrum?: checked [x]
- Overlap FFT frames?: checked [x]

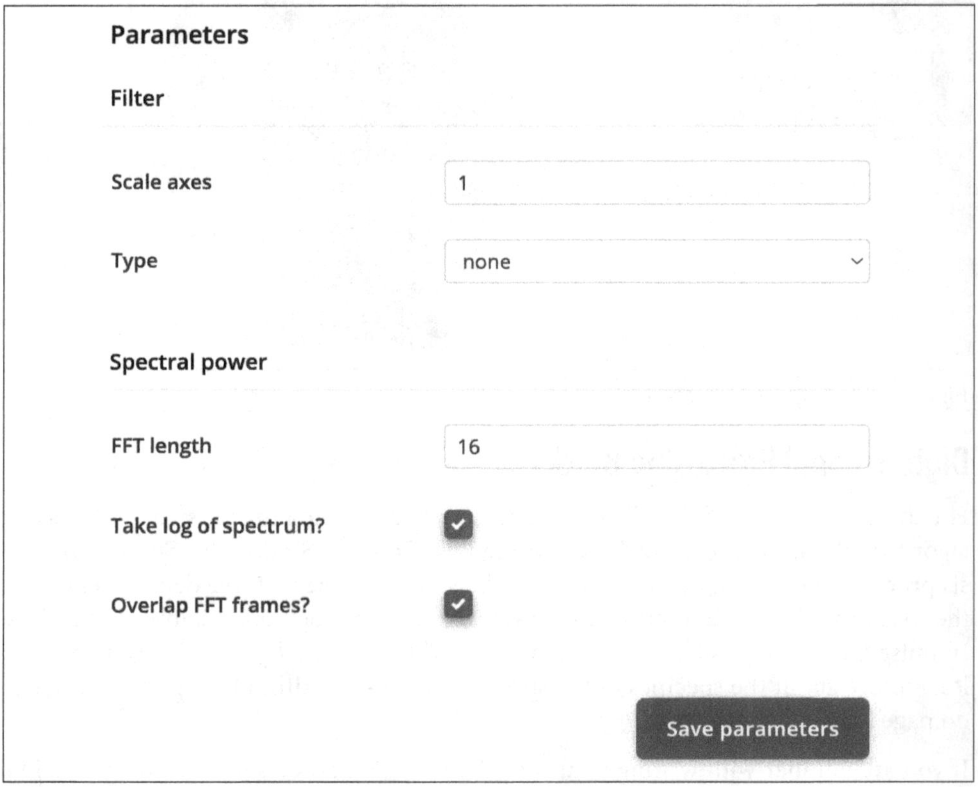

Parameters

Filter

Scale axes

1

Type

Spectral power

FFT length

16

Take log of spectrum?

Overlap FFT frames?

Save parameters

Figure 13-6. Spectral features block parameters

Now click "Save parameters." In order to use the advanced anomaly detection features available in Edge Impulse (*https://orei!.ly/bQUyh*), check the "Calculate feature importance" check box on the "Generate features" view (see Figure 13-7).

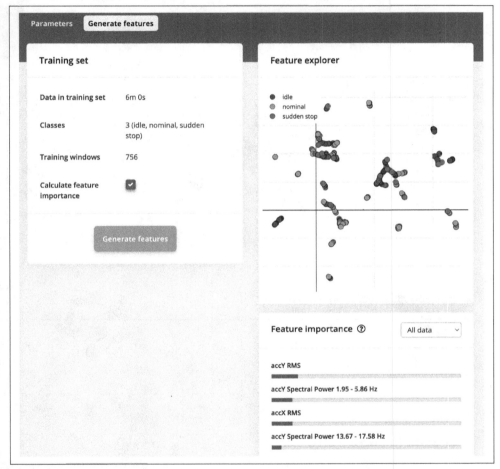

Figure 13-7. Generate features with feature importance

Now, click "Generate features" to view your data's feature explorer and feature importance list (see Figure 13-8).

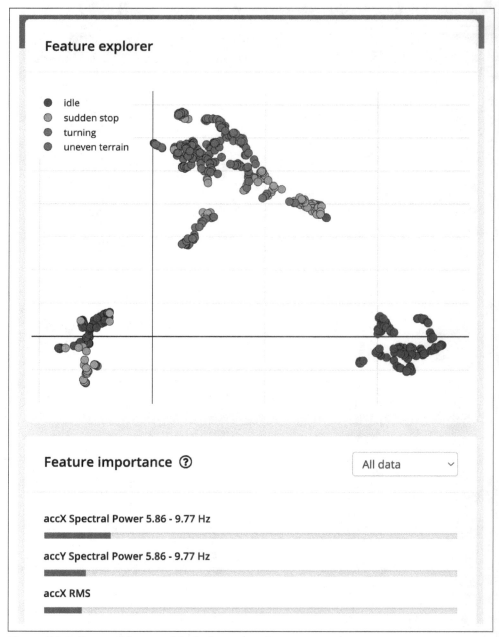

Figure 13-8. Spectral features block: feature explorer

Machine Learning Blocks

We are now ready to train our edge machine learning model! There are multiple ways to train your model in Edge Impulse, the easiest of which is the visual (or web GUI) editing mode. However, if you are a machine learning engineer, expert, or if you already have experiencing coding with TensorFlow/Keras, then you can also edit your transfer learning block locally or in expert mode within the Edge Impulse Studio.

We can set the neural network architecture and other training configuration settings of our project from the NN Classifier tab.

Visual mode

The easiest way to configure and set our machine learning training settings and neural network architecture is through the Edge Impulse Visual mode or the default view when you select the NN Classifier tab under "Impulse design" in the navigation bar (see Figure 13-9). Copy these settings into your neural network classifier's block configuration, then click "Start training":

- Number of training cycles: 30
- Learning rate: 0.0005
- Validation set size: 20%
- Auto-balance dataset: unchecked [ ]
- Neural network architecture:
  — Dense layer (20 neurons)
  — Dense layer (10 neurons)

You can learn more about the neural architecture configuration in the Edge Impulse documentation (*https://oreil.ly/oMVFa*). Once your model training has completed, you can view the transfer learning results in the "Model: Last training performance" view (see Figure 13-10).

See Chapters 11 and 12 for more information about editing your neural network block locally or in expert mode (especially "Machine Learning Block" on page 381).

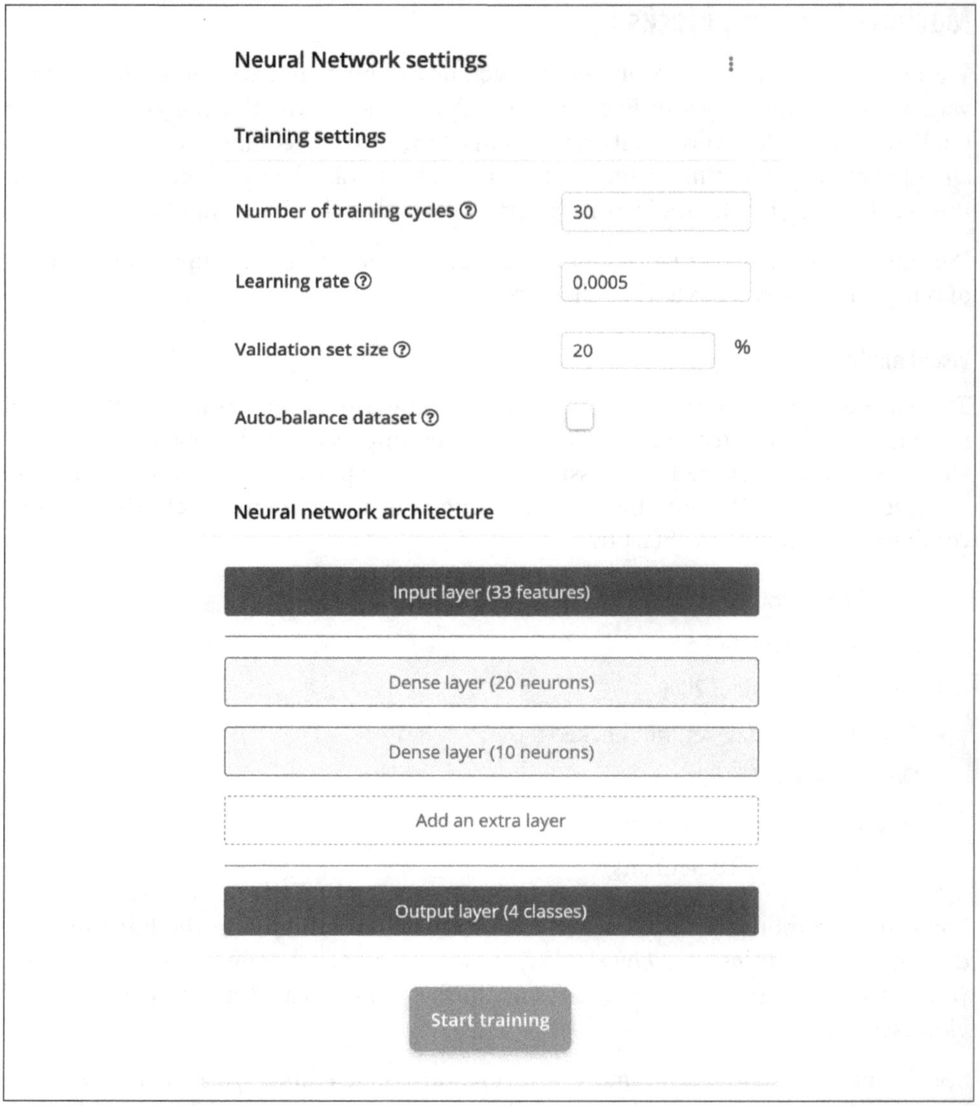

Figure 13-9. Neural Network settings

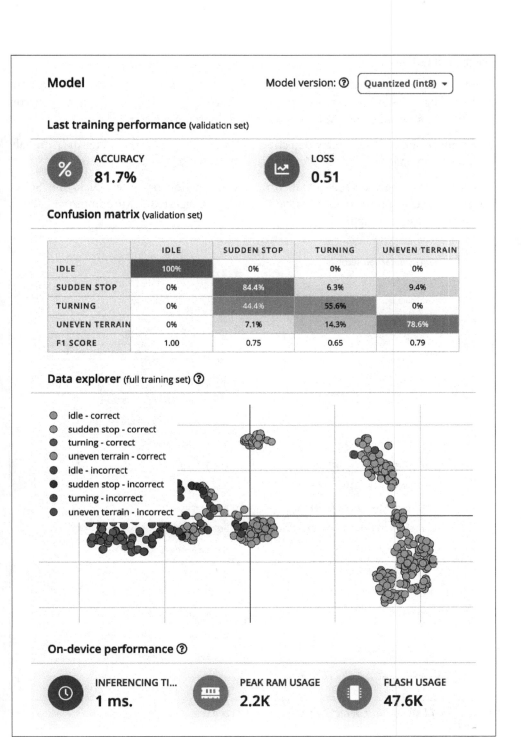

Figure 13-10. Model: Last training performance

Anomaly detection

Neural networks are great at pattern recognition, but they have difficulty with new, unseen data. This is because they are only trained on a specific set of data, so if you give them something new, they will not be able to properly classify it.[7]

Learn more about the anomaly detection technique used in this chapter in "Anomaly detection" on page 99.

Select the "Anomaly detection" tab from the navigation bar, then click the "Select suggested axes" button to automatically select the suggested feature importance axes for our use case (see Figure 13-11).

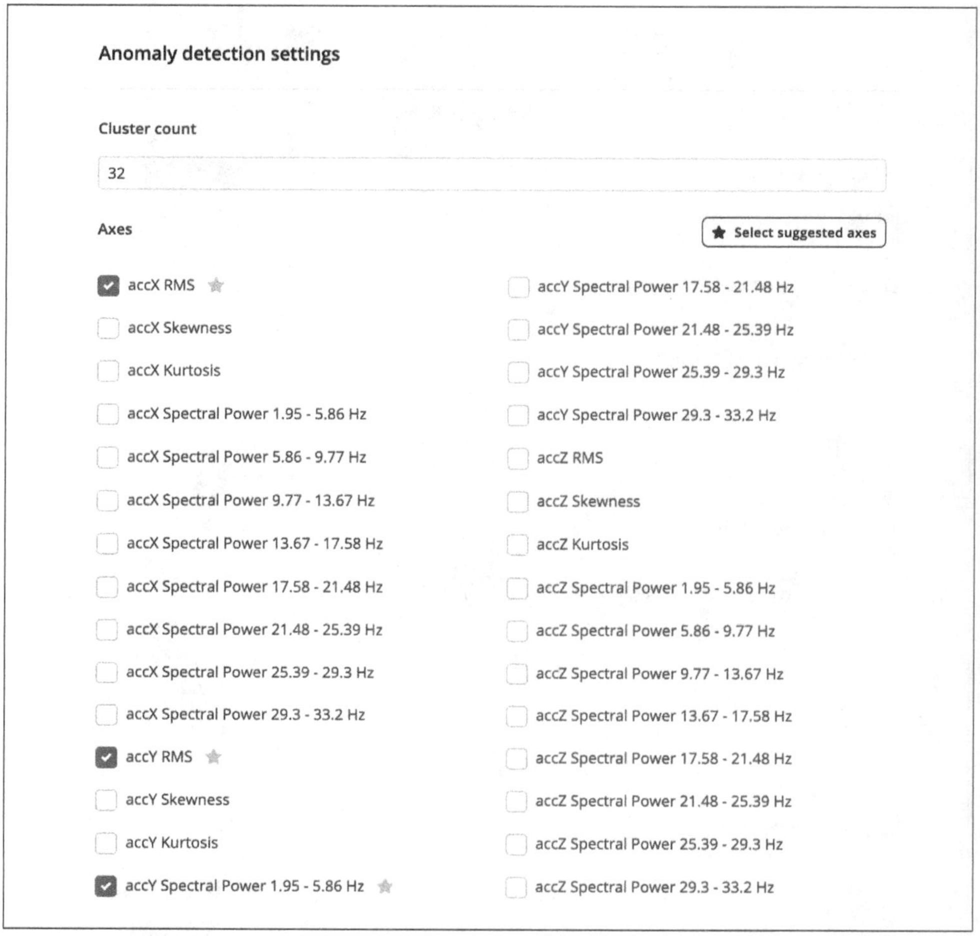

Figure 13-11. Anomaly detection: Select suggested axes

---

7 See the article "Anomaly Detection (K-Means)" (*https://oreil.ly/kGM6C*) from Edge Impulse.

Then click on "Start training" to view the resulting "Anomaly explorer" (as shown in Figure 13-12).

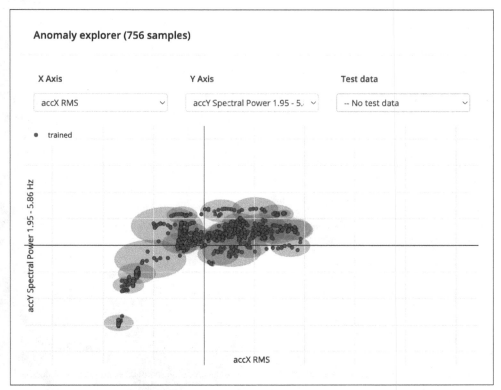

Figure 13-12. Anomaly detection: Anomaly explorer

Testing the Model

In-depth details and descriptions of all model testing features available in Edge Impulse are described in "Testing the Model" on page 392.

Live Classification

From the "Live classification" tab, you can test individual test samples directly from your connected Nordic Thingy:53 (see Figures 13-13 and 13-14). Connection instructions are described in "Data Ingestion Firmware" on page 450.

Figure 13-13. Live classification with Nordic Thingy:53

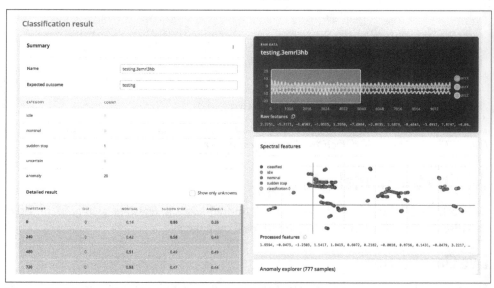

Figure 13-14. Live classification for unlabeled testing result

Or load an existing testing dataset image in "Classify existing test sample" to view this sample's extracted features and your trained model's prediction results, as shown in Figure 13-15.

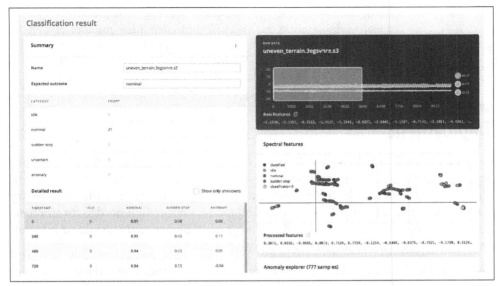

Figure 13-15. Live classification with preexisting, labeled testing result

Model Testing

You can also bulk classify your testing dataset against your trained model by navigating to the "Model testing" tab (*https://oreil.ly/Ngn8a*) of your project. Learn more about this tab in "Model Testing" on page 393.

Select "Classify all" to get a matrix of the inferencing results from your trained model on your test dataset samples (see Figure 13-16).

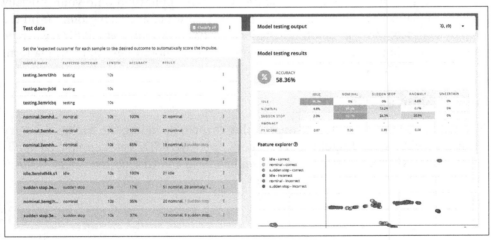

Figure 13-16. Model testing tab results

Although the model testing results tab here doesn't look promising for real-world usage, as we have only uploaded a few minutes of training data, the more data we uploaded the better the model would perform in the real world, and on our testing dataset. You can learn more about improving your model and achieving a production-ready model for a consumer product in Chapter 9.

Deployment

Congratulations! You have just finished collecting and labeling your training and testing datasets, extracting your data's features with the DSP block, designing and training your machine learning model, and testing your model with your testing dataset. Now that we have all of the code and model information needed for inferencing on our edge device, we need to flash the prebuilt binary to the device or integrate the C++ library into our embedded application code.

Select the Deployment tab of your Edge Impulse project and follow the steps for one of the many deployment options in the next sections to run your trained machine learning model on your edge device. Many other deployment options are also available, some of which have already been described in "Deployment" on page 395.

Prebuilt Binary Flashing

From the Deployment tab, select your officially supported Edge Impulse development platform under "Build firmware," and then select Build. You also have the option to turn on/off the EON Compiler.[8]

Then, drag-and-drop or flash the resulting firmware application onto your officially supported platform by following the instructions shown after clicking Build from the Deployment tab. More in-depth instructions for flashing your prebuilt binary can be found in the Edge Impulse documentation for your chosen development platform (*https://oreil.ly/socrt*).

GitHub Source Code

The full application source code used in this chapter, including the deployed library from the public Edge Impulse project (*https://oreil.ly/rKSDT*) and completed application code, is available to view and download from the GitHub repository (*https:// oreil.ly/bjJw1*).

---

8 See the Edge Impulse blog, "Introducing EON: Neural Networks in Up to 55% Less RAM and 35% Less ROM" (*https://oreil.ly/kXvlt*).

Iterate and Feedback Loops

Now that you have deployed the first iteration of your food quality assurance model, you may be satisfied with the results and discontinue development here. However, if you wish to further iterate over your model and further improve the accuracy over time or with newly acquired equipment upgrades, for example, there are many adaptation and variations to consider and improve upon for this project:

- Iterate on the design of the device to make it more sensitive to crashes (change the hardware used in this guide with a more sensitive sensor, or higher-end CPU).

- Utilize active learning strategies to improve the algorithms used in this model, the DSP, and the machine learning neural network. Further strategies are also described in Chapters 9 and 10.

- Upload more training and testing data for the existing model classes and also create new classes to train in your model.

- Evaluate the performance of the device regularly and make improvements accordingly over time; your model is only as good as the locations/environments the training data was recorded from.

- A camera instead of an accelerometer could be mounted on the handlebars of the bike.

- Move the location of the device mounted on the bike from the handlebars to the head and see how the device performs.

Related Works

As stated throughout this chapter, edge AI is an up-and-coming technology being employed in a wide range of consumer products, from toys that monitor your child's health and bikes that monitor incoming traffic and potential accidents, to home appliances that automatically cook your food to the perfect doneness. The next sections describe various news articles, products, research articles, and books on the topic of edge AI for consumer products.

This book also notes the sources for various applications, methods, devices, and quotes from various research and consumer products utilizing edge machine learning models throughout the chapter in the footnotes on each page.

Research

- Digital Child's Play: Protecting Children from the Impacts of AI (*https://oreil.ly/0RRNY*), UN News, 2021.
- WEF Artificial Intelligence for Children (*https://oreil.ly/aHH3E*), World Economic Forum, 2022.
- Good Governance of Children's Data (*https://oreil.ly/9Dy2B*), Unicef.
- FTC: Children's Privacy (*https://oreil.ly/6v-hh*)
- Children's Online Privacy Protection Rule ("COPPA") (*https://oreil.ly/RP-BI*)
- "Examining Artificial Intelligence Technologies Through the Lens of Children's Rights" (*https://oreil.ly/etUlC*). EU Science Hub, 2022.
- EU AI Act (*https://oreil.ly/ERfTX*)
- Fosch-Villaronga, E. et al. "Toy Story or Children Story? Putting Children and Their Rights at the Forefront of the Artificial Intelligence Revolution" (*https://oreil.ly/FlrVc*). SpringerLink, 2021.
- Morra, Lia et al. "Artificial Intelligence in Consumer Electronics" (*https://oreil.ly/58KzE*). IEEE, 2020.
- Sane, Tanmay U. et al. "Artificial Intelligence and Deep Learning Applications in Crop Harvesting Robots: A Survey" (*https://oreil.ly/tNhwh*). IEEE, 2021.
- Mohanty, Saraju P. "AI for Smart Consumer Electronics: At the Edge or in the Cloud?" (*https://oreil.ly/pZToK*) *IEEE Consumer Electronics Magazine*, 2019.
- Go, Hanyoung et al. "Machine Learning of Robots in Tourism and Hospitality: Interactive Technology Acceptance Model (iTAM)—Cutting Edge" (*https://oreil.ly/dxShS*). Emerald Insight, 2020.
- Xu, Tiantian et al. "A Hybrid Machine Learning Model for Demand Prediction of Edge-Computing-Based Bike-Sharing System Using Internet of Things" (*https://oreil.ly/UKtYx*). IEEE, 2020.
- Bike Rearview Radar (*https://oreil.ly/AI9cL*), Edge Impulse.
- Silva, Mateus C. et al. "Wearable Edge AI Applications for Ecological Environments" (*https://oreil.ly/MdkaY*). MDPI, 2021.
- Kakadiya, Rutvik et al. "AI Based Automatic Robbery/Theft Detection using Smart Surveillance in Banks" (*https://oreil.ly/SDPYG*). IEEE, 2019.
- Ogu, Reginald Ekene et al. "Leveraging Artificial Intelligence of Things for Anomaly Detection in Advanced Metering Infrastructures" (*https://oreil.ly/Iesae*). ResearchGate, 2021.

News and Other Articles

- "AI's Potential for Consumer Products Companies" (*https://oreil.ly/IOYQR*). Deloitte, 2022.

- "Consumer Goods: Increase Product Innovation and Revenue with Edge AI" (*https://oreil.ly/ZEn7F*). Gartner, 2021.

- "Innovate with Edge AI" (*https://oreil.ly/I-lhF*). Gartner, 2019.

- "Edge Machine Learning: From PoC to Real-World AI Applications" (*https://oreil.ly/x_0ja*). Strong, 2021.

- "Ducati and Lenovo Continue Partnership to Lead Innovation in MotoGP" (*https://oreil.ly/YcOrE*). BusinessWire, 2022.

Index

computational performance
  and optimization of algorithms for edge
    devices, 116-119
  duty cycle, 333
  energy consumption, 333
  floating-point operations, 332
  latency, 332
  memory, 330
  metrics, 330-334
  thermal energy, 334
computer vision algorithms, 92
conditional logic, 101
confidence thresholds, 325
confusion matrix, 324
connectivity issues, 217
constraints
  understanding, 198
  when developing AI applications, 190
consumer products, edge AI-enabled use case,
    441-469
  design considerations, 445
  environmental/social impact, 446
  existing solutions, 443
  goal setting, 442
  learning resources, 467
  problem exploration, 441
  solution design, 442-467
  solution design approaches, 443-445
containerization, 139
convolutional models, 109
COVID-19 pandemic, 209
cropping images, 89
cross-contamination, 412
cross-validation, 259, 334
crowdsourced labeling, 242
cultural norms, 355
curating splits, 260
current sensors, 65
cutoff frequency, 90

D

data augmentation, 261-263
data bias, 48
data capture, 141
data cleaning, 248-255
  amending values, 251
  auditing your dataset, 249-251
  bicyclist monitor dataset, 452
  evaluation/automation, 252

  excluding records, 252
  fixing balance issues, 253
  fixing value issues, 251-252
  food quality assurance use case, 420-421
  substituting values, 251
  wildlife monitoring use case, 376
  writing code to fix errors, 252
data collection
  connecting device directly to Edge Impulse
    for, 371
  wildlife monitoring use case, 370-371
data errors, 231-233
data exploration, 299
data explorer (Edge Impulse tool), 376
data formatting, 246-248
  manifest files, 248
  types of formats, 55-58, 246
data forms, 220
data loggers, 141
data logging, 305
data pipelines, 142, 263-265
data preparation, for dataset, 235-265
  data augmentation, 261-263
  data cleaning, 248-255
  data pipelines, 263-265
  feature engineering, 255
  formatting, 246-248
  labeling, 235-246
  splitting data, 256-261
data quality, 225-234
  common data errors, 231-233
  drift and shift, 233
  ensuring representative datasets, 225-227
  label noise, 229-231
  representation and time, 227
  reviewing data by sampling, 227-229
  uneven distribution of errors, 234
data requirements, estimating, 211-214
data retrieval, 220-224
data samples, 344-346
data scientists, 130
data sourcing
  capturing data at the edge, 217-219
  data forms, 220
  for dataset construction, 215-219
  overcoming data limitations, 217
  sourcing publicly available image datasets,
    368
  synthetic data, 219

force sensors, 63

forest fires, power line fault detection for preventing, 27-29

formatting of data, 246-248

Fourth Industrial Revolution, 408

FPGAs (field programmable gate arrays), 78

FPR (false positive rate), 326

FPU (floating-point unit), 69

frame rate, 86

framing problems, 195

frequency domain, 91

frequency response, 90

fully connected models, 108

G

gas sensors, 66, 180, 410, 416

generalization, defined, 10

Global Positioning System (GPS), 63

goal setting, 300-301

"good enough" performance, 22

Google Speech Commands dataset, 211

greenfield hardware, 218

greenfield projects, 26

greenhouse gases, food waste and, 413

gyroscopes, 63

H

hardware description language (HDL), 156

hardware engineers, 131

hardware, edge AI, 55-84

    architectural design and, 278

    architecture of, 68-70

    automated testing, 161

    bicyclist monitor use case, 449

    configuration, 370

    data logging and, 305

    diversity of device types, 22

    embedded hardware tools, 158

    initial iteration of hardware design, 304

    processors, 68-84

      (see also processors for edge AI)

    sensors/signals/data sources, 55-68

    sustainability issues, 354

    unique challenges of projects, 199

    unique design challenges of, 199

    wildlife monitoring use case, 370

harmful technology, 49-52

    costs of negligence, 50

    mitigating societal harms, 51

HDL (hardware description language), 156

Heraclitus of Ephesus, 233

Herzberg, Elaine, 207

heterogeneous cascade, 286

heuristics (rule-based algorithms)

    AI algorithms and, 102

    combining with ML, 286

    downsides, 103

    ML solutions versus, 178

    reasons to use, 179

    weaknesses, 179

high-pass filters, 90

Hikvision surveillance camera, 49

hiring, for edge AI, 132-134

histograms, 250

home appliances, 445

human bias, 48

human error, label noise and, 231

human role, ML augmentation of, 185

Hutiri, Wiebke (Toussaint), 43

hyperparameter optimization, 150

I

ideal solution, as focus when determining feasibility, 186

IDEs (integrated development environments), 159

if statements, 101

image feature detection, 92

image sensors, 60-62

images, 247

    as data, 57

    resizing/cropping, 89

    sourcing publicly available image datasets, 368

implicit association, 120

improving a live application, 350-353

    refining an algorithm over time, 351-352

    solving problems with feedback, 350

    supporting multiple deployed algorithms, 352

Impulse runner, 401

IMU (inertial measurement unit), 63

iNaturalist

    for dataset creation, 372-375

    limitations on datasets constructed from, 375

inductive proximity sensors, 65

industrial designers, 132

cloud providers, 140
containerization, 139
dependency management, 139
distributed computing, 140
operating systems, 137
programming/scripting languages, 138
software engineers, 132
software, architectural design and, 279
space exploration, 15
sparse model, 118
spectral analysis, 91
spectrogram, 91
spectroscopy sensors, 65
spiking neural networks (SNNs), 118
splitting data (see data splitting)
SSD (single-shot detector), 293
staged deployment, 349
staged rollout, 341
stakeholders, team building and, 128
standard deviation, 228
standards, for acceptable performance, 198
storage of data (see data storage)
strain gauges, 64
subgroups, analyzing, 335
subject matter experts (SMEs), 205
summary statistics, 346
supervised learning, 104, 237
support vector machine, 105
supporting edge AI applications, 315, 343-356
    changing legal standards, 356
    ethics and long-term support, 353-356
    evolving cultural norms, 355
    improving a live application, 350-353
    new information and ethical re-evaluation,
        354
    postdeployment monitoring, 342-349
    termination criteria, 354
switches, as sensors, 64
synthetic data, 219, 320, 336
system-on-chip (SoC) devices, 75-77
    embedded Linux and, 161
    microcontrollers versus, 111
systems
    predictive maintenance at an oil rig, 35
    understanding/controlling, 34-36

T

tactile sensors, 63
talent acquisition, for edge AI, 132-134

task performance, algorithm optimization and,
    116-119
teaching toys, 444
teams, 123-136
    algorithm development roles, 130
    building, 123-136
    diversity, 126-128
    domain expertise, 124-126
    hiring for edge AI, 132-134
    knowledge/understanding roles, 129
    learning edge AI skills, 134
    planning/execution roles, 130
    product engineering roles, 131
    psychological safety and ethical AI, 51
    roles and responsibilities, 129-132
    stakeholders, 128
    technical services roles, 132
technical services, as team role, 132
technological feasibility, 192-196
    brainstorming ideas for warehouse security
        application, 194-195
    device capabilities and solution choice, 196
    framing problems, 195
temperature sensors, 66
TensorBoard, 149
TensorFlow, 147-148
TensorFlow Federated, 157
TensorFlow Lite, 148, 161
TensorFlow Model Optimization Toolkit, 148
termination criteria, 354
testing and iteration
    automated hardware testing, 161
    developing edge AI applications, 306-313
    ethical AI review, 312
    feedback loops, 307-309
    iterations in practice, 309-312
    Live classification tab, 392, 430, 463
    local model testing, 395
    model cards, 312
    Model testing tab, 393, 431, 465
    real-world testing, 321-322
    simulated real-world testing, 320
    wildlife management model, 392-395
testing bias, 48
testing dataset, 334
testing split
    defined, 256
    when to use, 257
text data formats, 247

About the Authors

Daniel Situnayake is head of machine learning at Edge Impulse, where he leads embedded machine learning research and development. He is coauthor of the O'Reilly book *TinyML: Machine Learning with TensorFlow Lite on Arduino and Ultra-Low Power Microcontrollers*, the standard textbook on embedded machine learning, and has delivered guest lectures at Harvard, UC Berkeley, and UNIFEI. Dan previously worked on TensorFlow Lite at Google, and cofounded Tiny Farms, the first US company using automation to produce insect protein at industrial scale. He began his career lecturing in automatic identification and data capture at Birmingham City University.

Jenny Plunkett is a senior developer relations engineer at Edge Impulse, where she is a technical speaker, developer evangelist, and technical content creator. In addition to maintaining the Edge Impulse documentation, she has also created developer-facing resources for Arm Mbed OS and Pelion IoT. She has presented workshops and tech talks for major tech conferences such as the Grace Hopper Celebration, Edge AI Summit, Embedded Vision Summit, and more. Jenny previously worked as a software engineer and IoT consultant for Arm Mbed and Pelion. She graduated with a BS in electrical engineering from The University of Texas at Austin.

Colophon

The animal on the cover of *AI at the Edge* is a Siberian ibex (*Capra sibirica*). They can be found across Asia in places like China, Mongolia, Pakistan, and Kazakhstan. Siberian ibexes are essentially a large species of wild goat. The color of their fur ranges from dark brown to light tan with an occasional reddish tint. Males have large, black, ringed horns while females have smaller gray horns. Both sexes have beards. Their coat lightens in color during the winter and darkens during the summer. They tend to travel in single-sex herds of 5 to 30 animals.

The ideal habitat for Siberian ibexes is above the tree line on steep slopes and rocky scree. They can be found as low as 2,300 feet in semiarid deserts. Their diet consists mainly of grasses and herbs found in scrublands and grasslands.

Because Siberian ibexes are found in abundance in their natural habitat, they are considered a species of Least Concern even though their population is decreasing. Their biggest threat is hunting for food and poaching for sport. Many of the animals on O'Reilly covers are endangered; all of them are important to the world.

The cover illustration is by Karen Montgomery, based on a black-and-white engraving from *The Natural History of Animals*. The cover fonts are Gilroy Semibold and Guardian Sans. The text font is Adobe Minion Pro; the heading font is Adobe Myriad Condensed; and the code font is Dalton Maag's Ubuntu Mono.

O'REILLY®

Learn from experts.
Become one yourself.

Books | Live online courses
Instant Answers | Virtual events
Videos | Interactive learning

Get started at oreilly.com.

CPSIA information can be obtained
at www.ICGtesting.com
Printed in the USA
JSHW051538240423
40755JS00004BA/20

9 781098 120207